HOUSING ISSUES, LAWS AND PROGRAMS

HOUSING, HOUSING COSTS AND MORTGAGES: TRENDS, IMPACT AND PREDICTION

HOUSING ISSUES, LAWS AND PROGRAMS

Pluralism in Housing Provision in Developing Countries: Lessons from Brazil
Ramin Keivani, Alex Abiko and Edmundo Werna
2004 ISBN: 1-59033-857-X

Housing the Poor: An Overview
Morton J. Schussheim (Editor)
2003 ISBN: 1-59033-724-7

Fannie Mae and Freddie Mac: Scandal in U.S. Housing
James R. Cristie (Editor)
2006 ISBN: 1-60021-356-1

Re-Use of Construction and Demolition Waste in Housing Developments
V.W.Y. Tam and C.M. Tam
2008 ISBN: 978-1-60456-362-7

Department of Housing and Urban Development Appropriations
Maggie McCarty, Libby Perl, Bruce E. Foote, Eugene Boyd, Meredith Peterson , David Randall Peterman, and John Frittelli (Editors)
2008 ISBN: 978-1-60456-789-2

Improving Consumer Mortgage Disclosures
Jason C. Castleman (Editor)
2009 ISBN: 978-1-60692-923-0

Housing: Socioeconomic, Availability, and Development Issues
Edward P. Hammond and Alex D. Noyes (Editors)
2009 ISBN: 978-1-60692-371-9

Housing: Socioeconomic, Availability, and Development Issues
Edward P. Hammond and Alex D. Noyes (Editors)
ISBN: 978-1-60876-747-2 (E-book)

Green Affordable Housing
Gerald N. Burlinghouse (Editor)
2009 ISBN: 978-1-60692-831-8

HUD Housing Programs for Persons with Disabilities
Ervin C. Felker (Editor)
2009 ISBN: 978-1-60741-113 0

Homes in Peril: A Study of Foreclosure Issues
Timothy R. Allertone (Editor)
2009 ISBN: 978-1-60741-800-9

Homes in Peril: A Study of Foreclosure Issues
Timothy R. Allertone (Editor)
2009. ISBN: 978-1-60876-565-2 (E-book)

Housing, Housing Costs and Mortgages: Trends, Impact and Prediction
Szilárd Kis and Istvan Balogh (Editors)
2010. ISBN: 978-1-60741-813-9

HOUSING ISSUES, LAWS AND PROGRAMS

HOUSING, HOUSING COSTS AND MORTGAGES: TRENDS, IMPACT AND PREDICTION

SZILÁRD KIS
AND
ISTVAN BALOGH
EDITORS

Nova Science Publishers, Inc.
New York

LIBRARY OF CONGRESS CATALOGING-IN-PUBLICATION DATA

Housing, housing costs and mortgages : trends, impact and prediction / editors, Szilárd Kis and Istvan Balogh.
p. cm.
Includes index.
ISBN 978-1-60741-813-9 (hbk.)
1. Housing--Finance. 2. Mortgages. 3. Home ownership--Costs. I. Kis, Szilárd. II. Balogh, Istvan, 1954-
HD7287.55.H688 2009
333.33'823--dc22

2009039828

Published by Nova Science Publishers, Inc. ✢ New York

CONTENTS

PREFACE

The mortgage crisis in the US has resulted in lower housing costs, as well as greater future income uncertainty. This book examines the effects of financial regulation and deregulation on default risk exposure of mortgages and the past housing bubbles. The possible solutions to fix the loopholes in regulations are discussed. In this book, the authors also take the readers through a reasoning process on how economic estimates and geostatistical analyses can support the necessary decision making process started with new national policies on social housing. All the examples aim to demonstrate that only an integrate, multilevel approach, supported by appropriate analysis can succeed in improving policies for increase supply and quality of housing stock. Furthermore, it is well-known that innovations in housing add value to the buyer but increase the cost of production. This book examines several methods to test a buyer's willingness to pay for new features. Other chapters in this book analyze the effectiveness of the policies in the US and the UK towards the reduction of mortgage fraud in light of the 'credit crunch,' and discuss possible effects of transportation conditions and inflation policy on long-term economic growth and geography.

The aim of Chapter 1 is to critically consider the effectiveness of the policies adopted in the United States of America (US) and the United Kingdom (UK) towards the reduction of mortgage fraud in light of the ‘credit crunch’. The chapter begins by commenting upon how organised criminals have exploited the ‘subprime mortgage crisis’ which has contributed towards an increase in the amount and frequency of mortgage fraud. This contribution is divided into two parts. Part I critically considers the policies adopted by the US Treasury Department’s Financial Crimes Enforcement Network (FinCEN) and the recent legislative measures introduced by President Obama in light of the increase in mortgage fraud and the subprime mortgage crisis. This is subsequently divided into two parts. Firstly, it seeks to investigate the appropriateness and effectiveness of financial intelligence gathered from suspicious activity reports (SARs). The second part critically assesses the potential impact of the Fraud Enforcement and Recovery Act 2009. Part II of the chapter analyses the approaches adopted in the UK and thus concentrates upon the policies adopted by the Financial Services Authority (FSA) towards mortgage fraud as part of its statutory objective to reduce financial crime. The second part considers four issues. The first reviews the risk based approach adopted in the UK by the FSA towards financial regulation, the reduction of financial crime and thus mortgage fraud. The second part considers the rule making powers of the FSA under the Financial Services and Markets Act 2000 (FSMA 2000) and it’s Handbook. Thirdly, the effectiveness of the enforcement policies adopted by the FSA towards the reduction of mortgage fraud is considered. The final part of chapter discusses the usefulness of the FSA's Intermediary Fraud Initiative.

As explained in Chapter 2, the mortgage crisis in the US has resulted in lower housing costs, as well as greater future income uncertainty. Until the economy recovers from the recession, it is expected that the rate of new buildings will decrease, and the average size of the new houses will be smaller than we have seen during the housing boom, leaving the rural and suburban areas with more open spaces than initially expected, which may be put to beneficial use. At the same time, a reduction in available income and credit, and increased uncertainty regarding future income even among those who have not been affected by the current downturn, have led to reduced spending on everything from luxury goods to food products. Both housing and income uncertainty trends point in the direction of increased crop cultivation by individual households.

For many families in the low and middle-income range, food is a significant part of their total expenses, and a more flexible cost item than other major expenses such as housing and utility costs. This is an especially pronounced problem in fruit and vegetable consumption, as fresh produce tends to be relatively more expensive than "fast foods". As a result, more and more people, especially in rural areas, have begun cultivating crops for self-consumption, or increased their existing level of crop cultivation.

The trend towards increased food self-reliance affects the local sustainable development in many ways, including a variety of social, economic, and environmental impacts. Estimating the monetary value of these impacts is an important tool in regional planning and local policy-making. Economic methods for carrying out these estimates include social impact valuation methods such as the relative housing prices and surveys of willingness to pay to preserve local agricultural crops; and environmental impact valuation methods such as attaching a monetary value to the time lost due to illnesses caused by local environmental impacts. Existing studies show that the value of the social and environmental impacts of local production is much higher than that of the economic impacts; the highest-value social impact is the public benefit from the scenery provided by agricultural crops, which varies greatly by type of crop. As these trends are naturally driven by private economic interests, an economic valuation of the social and environmental impacts of different crops can help local decision-makers to determine how to react to these trends.

Hong Kong has long suffered from the problem of building dilapidation, particularly in the old districts. Other than stricter enforcement against irresponsible homeowners and intensive public education campaigns, the local government initiated to solve the problem via an incentive approach. In November 2000, the government announced publicly a list of poorly-performing buildings, hoping that the property owners would be motivated to undertake building repair or refurbishment by market forces. As the literature suggested, physical conditions of residential properties, particularly those concerning communal areas and services, might not be fully priced by the market due to information asymmetry. It is envisaged that additional information pumped into the housing market will alter the price gradient between high-quality and low-quality properties as the purchasers will undertake self-protection behaviours in view of the risks associated with the poorly-performing properties. Chapter 3 aims to empirically examine whether public knowledge of poor conditions of apartment buildings affected the sale prices of these properties based on an analysis of panel data in Hong Kong. Yet, the analysis results showed that properties in blacklisted buildings were not transacted at a discount, compared with those in non-blacklisted buildings before the blacklisting exercise, and the release of public information about the blacklist did not create a relative diminution of the property prices of the blacklisted buildings. Policy implications follow.

The purpose of Chapter 4 is to introduce transportation conditions and money into a growth model with economic geography. The study examines possible effects of transportation conditions and inflation policy on long-term economic growth and geography. The model describes dynamic interactions among capital accumulation, real model, travel time and cost, housing, residential distribution, amenity, and endogenous time distribution among work, travel, and leisure. Although transportation systems are simple in this paper in the light of contemporary literature in transportation research, the paper demonstrates a way to integrating some important models in the literature in transportation research, economic growth theory and urban economics so that the significance of transportation systems upon economies can be properly analyzed.

Chapter 5 shows a reasoning about how economic estimates and geostatistical analyses can support the necessary decision making process started with new national policies on social housing. The decision about priorities of housing policies, the dissemination of funding in the different parto of Italy can be helped by regional and local economic analyses.

In this light the role of evaluation is examined, in order to show which kind of approach can be referred to each dimension, context and level. After a general introduction explaining the main aspects of the National Housing Plan, an example of integrate assessment of rent market and difficulty in housing access is shown. The result is a scaling that profiles some Italian metropolitan reality, and identify the geographical general/local differentiation among cities/part of cities. All the examples are aiming to demonstrate that only an integrate, multilevel approach, supported by appropriate analysis can succeed in improving policies for increase supply and quality of housing stock.

Innovations in housing add value to the buyer but increase the cost of production. While innovations may increase the homes function or save money in the long run, it is an open question as to whether or not builders can recoup the additional cost. Chapter 6 examines several methods to test a buyer's willingness to pay for new features. The case of innovations designed to mitigate and protect residents from certain natural hazards is used to illustrate market acceptance of the added cost to construct safer homes.

Chapter 7 provides an example of the operation of free markets by applying a hedonic pricing model to explain housing price differentials *within* a historic landmark district. By considering home sales solely within such a district, in principle the market experiment transpires within an institutionally homogenous framework, i.e., all sales share a common characteristic in that they occur within a land area designed as "historic." This exercise demonstrating the operation of free markets involves in the Savannah Historic Landmark District, which is located in and adjacent to the downtown of Savannah, Georgia. Estimating the model in semi-log form reveals that the natural log of the *real* sales price of a house in this particular environment was positively affected by the number of bathrooms, fireplaces, rooms, stories in structure, garage car spaces, and square feet of finished living space, the presence of a custom kitchen, a deck, a private courtyard, an exterior construction of brick or stucco, an underground sprinkler system, and whether or not the house was new. The *real* sales price was negatively affected by the presence of a rental apartment on the premises and by an exterior of either vinyl or wood siding. Listing a house for sale during the peak selling season from May through July also acts to raise the *real* sales price of the house. Finally, the analysis also demonstrates that property taxes are capitalized into housing prices. Ultimately, the analysis demonstrates the efficiency of free markets within a model which systematically permits the evaluation of a host of housing characteristics within a somewhat homogeneous context.

Chapter 8 argues that hostage used in informal contracts normally only deal with two contractual parties. Build upon and enforced by the formal law, the device of mortgages can cope with multiparty conflict of interest. Section II of this essay explains this thesis. Section III uses evidence of increasing use of mortgages in China to show the role of mortgages in facilitating bank lending. Conclusions follow in Section IV.

The purpose of Chapter 9 is to examine effects of financial regulation and deregulation on default risk exposure of mortgages and the past housing bubbles. Our findings suggest that financial deregulation in the early 1980s, along with other macroeconomic factors, encouraged reckless mortgage lending and thus helped create the real estate bubble in the late 1980s. The crash of the real estate market prompted two regulation acts which raised capital requirements for financial institutions. As a result, mortgage lending became more prudent. However, policy loopholes opened a door for subprime mortgage lending in early 2001. The significantly weakened default risk exposure in mortgages triggered another round of housing market appreciation. This bubble burst in 2006. The possible solutions to fix the loopholes in regulations are discussed.

Income elasticity is a classical measurement in economics. For many years economists have earnestly studied the income elasticity of housing demand, even though little consensus has ever been reached. Part of the difficulty came from the fact that housing is both a consumption and investment at the same time. Many studies have been devoted to disentangling these two components, but no one has tried to measure the income elasticity of housing demand over time to observe any notable change. Because of the dual motives to purchase a home, most economists do agree that housing demand is best measured as home price rather than home size. The recent housing boom in the United States, however, dramatically inflated home price and widely increased housing costs. When home price is inflated flatly, one may have a reason to expect a suppressed income elasticity of housing demand, because a relatively smaller percentage change in home price can adequately reflect the same amount of difference in the absolute price of homes purchased. On the other hand, given the investment motive of owning homes, it is reasonable to expect that a higher income elasticity of housing demand should correspond to a higher home price appreciation. In fact, a study by Turner (2003) using selected metropolitan data from the 1985 to 1995 American Housing Surveys (AHS) did find that "families are less likely to own and housing demand is reduced during episodes of relatively high, anticipated house-price volatility," i.e. uncertainty in home price appreciation. So, which hypothesis is correct? Using the national data from the 1985 to 2007 AHS survey data, my study found evidence to support both hypotheses described above, though at different times. In addition, it discovered another powerful factor that has a strong impact on the income elasticity of housing demand. That is, cash inflows from the equity market to the real estate due to the market crash in 2000 depressed the income elasticity of housing demand drastically. This is not surprising though, because in theory, as Hoyer (1998) pointed out a long time ago, "in broad terms a declining immediate correlation between changes in income and consumption reflects more liberal capital markets." In short, Chapter 10 examines one important impact of changing home prices, which not only fits the theme of the entire book, *Housing, Housing Costs and Mortgages*, but adds some theoretical flavor to a perhaps highly practical-sounding title.

As discussed in Chapter 11, much government policy in recent years has been directed at increasing homeownership among low-income households. Many have argued for the unconditional acceptance of increasing low-income homeownership as an important policy goal. However, evidence from household expenditures in the Consumer Expenditure Survey suggests many difficulties of this conceptually appealing target. Low-income homeowners are more likely to purchase homes with proportionally higher "hidden" ownership costs such as maintenance and utilities. Further, tax policies direct homeownership benefits towards high-income households, often generating no tax deductions for low-income households. Because of these distinctions, currently available consumer information on "rent v. buy" calculations can be particularly misleading for low-income households. Government policies mandating increased lending to low-income households combined with the realities of housing costs differences for these households may have ultimately contributed to the current mortgage default crisis.

The objective of Chapter 12 is to design a building electric energy management system able to determine the best energy assignment plan, according to given criteria. A building energy management system can be seen from two points of view: load management and local energy production management. [House et Smith (1995)] and [Zhou et Krarti (2005)] have proposed optimal control strategies for an HVAC (Heating Ventilation and Air Conditioning) system taking into account the natural thermal storage capacity of buildings where the HVAC consumption is shifted from the peak period to the off-peak period. [Zhou et Krarti (2005)] have shown that this control strategy affords savings of up to 10% of the electricity cost of a building. However, these approaches do not take into account energy resource requirements, which generally depend on the autonomy needs of off-grid systems [Muselli *et al.* (2000)], or on the total power production limits of suppliers in grid-connected systems.

During the recent financial crisis default rates in the US mortgage business reached unprecedented levels. Apart from huge write–downs, losses and bankruptcies, this had serious implications, primarily on the assessment and quantification of risks. The authors consider the Swiss mortgage market with its financial behavior and develop a scenario regarding future default rates. Based on bankruptcy rates at hand, in Chapter 13 the authors investigate to what extent increasing default rates affect default correlation and thus, statistical measures of credit portfolio loss distributions. Empirical bankruptcy rate time series are analyzed, translated into default rates and compared to the results arising from our scenario. The impact is analyzed using a simple estimator for default correlation.

In: Housing, Housing Costs and Mortgages
Editors: Szilárd Kis and Istvan Balogh, pp. 1-22
ISBN: 978-1-60741-813-9

Chapter 1

'THE CREDIT CRUNCH AND MORTGAGE FRAUD – TOO LITTLE TOO LATE?' A COMPARATIVE ANALYSIS OF THE POLICIES ADOPTED IN THE UNITED STATES OF AMERICA AND THE UNITED KINGDOM

Nicholas Ryder **and** ***Clare Chambers***[+]
University of the West of England, Bristol, United Kingdom

Abstract

The aim of this chapter is to critically consider the effectiveness of the policies adopted in the United States of America (US) and the United Kingdom (UK) towards the reduction of mortgage fraud in light of the 'credit crunch'. The chapter begins by commenting upon how organised criminals have exploited the 'subprime mortgage crisis' which has contributed towards an increase in the amount and frequency of mortgage fraud. This contribution is divided into two parts. Part I critically considers the policies adopted by the US Treasury Department's Financial Crimes Enforcement Network (FinCEN) and the recent legislative measures introduced by President Obama in light of the increase in mortgage fraud and the subprime mortgage crisis. This is subsequently divided into two parts. Firstly, it seeks to investigate the appropriateness and effectiveness of financial intelligence gathered from suspicious activity reports (SARs). The second part critically assesses the potential impact of the Fraud Enforcement and Recovery Act 2009.[1] Part II of the chapter analyses the approaches adopted in the UK and thus concentrates upon the policies adopted by the Financial Services Authority (FSA) towards mortgage fraud as part of its statutory objective to reduce financial crime. The second part considers four issues. The first reviews the risk based approach adopted in the UK by the FSA towards financial regulation, the reduction of financial crime and thus mortgage fraud. The second part considers the rule making powers of the FSA under

---

* Reader in Financial Services Law, Head of Commercial Law Research Unit, Bristol Law School, University of the West of England, Bristol, United Kingdom,
+ Senior Lecturer in Law, Commercial Law Research Unit, Bristol Law School, University of the West of England, Bristol, United Kingdom

[1] Pub.L. 111-21.

the Financial Services and Markets Act 2000 (FSMA 2000) and it's Handbook. Thirdly, the effectiveness of the enforcement policies adopted by the FSA towards the reduction of mortgage fraud is considered. The final part of chapter discusses the usefulness of the FSA's Intermediary Fraud Initiative.

"The potential impact of mortgage fraud on financial institutions and the stock market is clear. If fraudulent practices become systemic within the mortgage industry and mortgage fraud is allowed to become unrestrained, it will ultimately place financial institutions at risk and have adverse effects on the stock market".[2]

Mortgage Fraud – An Introduction

In the last two decades we have witnessed significant instances of fraud involving multinational corporations resulting in the collapse of the Bank of Credit Commerce International, Barings Bank, Enron and Worldcom. The amount of money in these cases runs into to billions of dollars. The impact and scale of these scandals are about to be overshadowed by a new threat to the financial markets in the US and the UK – mortgage fraud.[3] Mortgage fraud has been defined by the Federal Bureau of Investigation (FBI) as "the intentional misstatement, misrepresentation, or omission by an applicant or other interested parties, relied on by a lender or underwriter to provide funding for, to purchase, or to insure a mortgage loan".[4] Vacco defined mortgage fraud as providing "false or inaccurate information in connection with the mortgage application [that] causes a lender or another in the chain of approving and funding that loan to make the loan on terms and conditions different than if the true facts were known".[5] There are two types of mortgage fraud – fraud for property and fraud for profit.[6] There is evidence to suggest that mortgage fraud is becoming increasingly popular with organised criminals, who will seek finance through a number of property transactions.[7] For example, a fictitious purchaser of the property, with an inflated value, will take out a mortgage equalling the inflated value.[8] In many instances, when the monthly

---

[2] Chris Swecker, former FBI Assistant Director, Criminal Investigative Division, Introductory Statement: House Financial Services Subcommittee on Housing and Community Opportunity, 7 October 2004, as cited in Federal Bureau of Investigation *2007 Mortgage Report* (Washington, Federal Bureau of Investigation, 2008).

[3] The mortgage sector in the USA constitutes approximately twenty percent of the countries gross domestic produced. J A Heroy 'Other people's money: how a time-gap in credit reporting may lead to fraud' (2008) North Carolina Banking Institute 12 321-351, at 322. For an excellent discussion about the relationship between fraud and financial crises see P Blanque 'Crisis and Fraud' (2003) Journal of Financial Regulation and Compliance 11(1) 60-70.

[4] Federal Bureau Investigation, above n 1.

[5] P Vacco 'RESPA and avoiding mortgage fraud: what goes on the HUD settlement statement?' (2008) Illinois Bar Journal May 96 248-249, at 249.

[6] M O'Donnell and K Planer 'It it sounds too good to be true: identifying and avoiding common mortgage fraud scams' (2008) New Jersey Lawyer October 254 54-57, at 54. For a more detailed commentary on the types of mortgage fraud scams see B Dilley and F Weller 'Mortgage fraud and the credit crunch' (2008) Fighting Fraud summer 35 1-31, at 11-13.

[7] For a more detailed discussion about the links between mortgage fraud and other types of financial crime see FinCEN *Mortgage loan fraud connections with other financial crime* (FinCEN: Washington, 2009). Mortgage fraud is not exclusive to organised criminals and in many instances it is committed by sole traders. See for example the recent case of Sofique Ullah who was banned by the Financial Services Authority in May 2009 for "knowingly submitting mortgage applications supported by inaccurate and misleading employment details". See Financial Services Authority 'FSA bans Bradford Mortgage Broker for mortgage fraud', FSA Press Release, 14th May 2009, available from www.fsa.gov.uk.

[8] BBC News 'Mortgage fraud is funding crime', 6 March 2008, available from www.bbc.co.uk. For a more detailed illustration of the different types of mortgage fraud see Financial Crimes Enforcement Network *Mortgage*

repayments are not met and when the financial institution seeks the monies due, the organised criminals raise another mortgage with another financial institution and sell the property back to them at an even greater valuation. Due to the fact that the second mortgage is inflated, the first mortgage is repaid together with the arrears, leaving the organised criminals with a significant profit.

The extent of mortgage fraud, like all types of financial crime, is difficult to determine. The FBI, citing research by the Prieston Group, estimated that the annual level of mortgage fraud in the US is between $4bn and $6bn.[9] The potential threat and suspected increase in mortgage fraud has resulted in 63,173 related SARs being filed with FinCEN in 2008, reporting over $1.5bn in losses.[10] In comparison, during the first quarter of April 2009, FinCEN has received over 40,000 such reports, approximately two thirds of reports filed in 2008. In response to the threat of mortgage fraud the FBI has established 65 task forces, and, at the time of writing, is undertaking over 2,000 investigations into suspected instances of mortgage fraud. Similarly, it is impossible to provide an exact figure for the extent of fraud in the UK.[11] Levi *et al* conservatively estimated that the extent of fraud was £13.9bn.[12] The study concluded that "it is likely that fraud represents a £20bn annual loss to the UK. To put this figure into perspective, such losses would pay for an additional 200,000 police officers or save every man, woman and child £330 per year".[13] Button *et al* took the view that the "cost of fraud to the [UK] economy is difficult to gauge, but one fact is clear, fraud amounts to at least £16bn in the public sector and £72bn in corporate fraud".[14] There is evidence to suggest that organised criminals are using mortgage fraud to fund their illegal activities. Patricia Scotland, the UK's Attorney General stated "fraud is a revenue stream for organised criminal networks that causes substantial harm to our communities, including some of our most vulnerable citizens, and damage public trust".[15] The UK's National Fraud Strategic Authority (NFSA) took the view that mortgage fraud can also lead to the collapse of companies and subsidise other illegal activities.[16] According to the Association of Chief Police Officers (ACPO), the annual level of mortgage fraud in the UK is approximately £700m.[17] However, it must be noted that the Council of Mortgage Lenders (CML) took the view that "we do not believe that the report [by ACPO] presented evidence of 'confirmed mortgage fraud' of

---

Loan Fraud – An update of trends based upon an analysis of suspicious activity reports (Washington, Financial Crimes Enforcement Network, 2008) at p.12-18.

9 Federal Bureau Investigation, above n 1.

10 *Ibid.*

11 The Attorney General's Office *The Fraud Review – Progress Report December 2007* (London, Attorney General's Office, HMSO) at p.21. For a more detailed examination of the problems associated with determining extent of fraud see M Levi and J Burrows 'Measuring the impact of fraud in the UK: a conceptual and empirical journey' (2008) British Journal of Criminology 48(3) 293-318, at 297-298.

12 M Levi, J Burrows, M Fleming, and M Hopkins, *The Nature, Extent and Economic Impact of Fraud in the UK* (London, ACPO, 2007) at p.iii.

13 *Ibid.*

14 M Button, L Johnston, K Frimpong and G Smith 'New directions in policing fraud: The emergence of the counter fraud specialist in the United Kingdom' (2007) *International Journal of Sociology Law* 35(4) 192-208, at 192-193.

15 National Fraud Strategic Authority *Fighting mortgage fraud together – a progress report* (National Fraud Strategic Authority: London, 2009) at p.9.

16 *Ibid.*

17 Association of Chief Police Officers 'Police Committed to Tackling Mortgage Fraud, Press Release, 5th March 2008, available from http://www.acpo.police.uk. The full report has not been made available to the general public.

around £700m".[18] Sandra Quinn, the Programme Director of the NFSA stated that "mortgage fraud is only a small fraction of the UK's mortgage market. But it is a serious criminal threat".[19] Conversely, Mike Brown, ACPO's lead officer on economic crime, argued that "organised mortgage fraud can take many forms and while difficult to measure accurately, it remains a significant element of the UK's annual fraud losses".[20] Therefore, mortgage fraud is a significant problem and it can be argued that the current economic conditions have been exploited by organised criminals to disguise their proceeds of crime and to maximise their illegal profits. The next part of the chapter now investigates the link between mortgage fraud and the subprime mortgage crisis.

Mortgage Fraud and the Subprime Mortgage Crisis

The current financial crisis originated in the US mortgage lending sector.[21] This position was exacerbated when the Federal Loan Mortgage Corporation, or Freddie Mac, announced that it did not wish to buy any more high-risk mortgages and when New Century Financial Corporation filed for bankruptcy.[22] These announcements had a domino effect, not only in the US, but around the world. In March 2008 Bear Stearns was purchased by Morgan Chase with the assistance of the government,[23] IndyMac also buckled under the financial crisis and its ownership transferred to the government,[24] in September 2008 Lehman Brothers also filed for bankruptcy[25] and the Federal Reserve Bank of New York agreed to lend $85bn to American International Group.[26] The unprecedented increase in mortgage fraud has been fuelled by the US subprime mortgage crisis. Subprime mortgage loans are designed for persons with blemished or limited credit histories. To compensate for the increased credit risk, subprime loans carry a higher rate of interest than prime loans.[27] The increase in the total amount of outstanding loans for the subprime mortgage market has increased at an alarming rate.[28] In

[18] Council of Mortgage Lenders '£700 million fraud claim not substantiated' (2008) *Council of Mortgage Lenders New and Views* 5(18) 5.

[19] Attorney General's Office Sandra Quinn 'The National Fraud Strategy' speech to Council of Mortgage Lenders, Wednesday 13 February 2008, available from www.attorneygeneral.gov.uk.

[20] *Ibid.*

[21] For an excellent summary of the events see A Ceresney, G Eng and S Nuttall 'Reguatory investigations and the credit crisis: the search for villans' (2009) American Criminal Law Review 46 225-273, at 229-235. Hereafter Ceresney *et al.*

[22] See CNN 'New Century files for Chapter 11 bankruptcy', April 2 2007, available from http://money.cnn.com/2007/04/02/news/companies/new_century_bankruptcy/.

[23] See A Sorkin and L Thomas Jr. 'JPMorgan Acts to Buy Ailing Bear Stearns at Huge Discount' March 16 2008, New York Times, available from http://www.nytimes.com/2008/03/16/business/16cnd-bear.html.

[24] Catherine Clifford and Chris Isidore 'The fall of IndyMac', July 13 2008, available from http://money.cnn.com/2008/07/12/news/companies/indymac_fdic/index.htm.

[25] See BBC News 'Lehman Bros files for bankruptcy', 16 September 2008, available from http://news.bbc.co.uk/1/hi/business/7615931.stm.

[26] E Andrews, M de la Merced and M Walsh 'Fed's $85 Billion Loan Rescues Insurer', New York Times, September 16 2008, available from http://www.nytimes.com/2008/09/17/business/17insure.html.

[27] A subprime mortgage loan is defined as "a mortgage loan to a borrower with sub-standard credit". See Chase Manhattan Mortgage Corp. v. Advanta Corp., No. Civ.A.01-507 KAJ, 2005 WL 2234608, at *1 (D. Del. Sept. 8, 2005) as cited in K Johnston, J Greer, J Biermacher and J Hummel 'The subprime morass: past, present, and future' (2008) *North Carolina Banking Institute* 5(12), 125-139, at 125.

[28] For an excellent commentary on the subprime mortgage market see C Linn 'They way we live now: the case for mandating fraud reporting by persons involved in real estate closings and settlements' (2009) Journal of Financial Crime 16(1) 7-27, at 7-9.

the UK, the impact of the credit crunch was clearly illustrated by the near collapse of Northern Rock. Northern Rock was established in the middle of the nineteenth century, demutualised in 1997 and by 2006 it was worth over £100bn.[29] In September 2007 the bank was incapable of acquiring loans from other financial institutions via the inter-bank lending market; also known as 'the Libor'.[30] The Bank of England agreed to lend Northern Rock £25bn, which it has promised to repay by 2010.[31] This led Tomasic to conclude "the rescue of Northern Rock Plc by the Bank of England in September 2007 has been a significant event in the history of British banking and in the wider application of corporate rescue ideas".[32] After the loan was made public, thousands of Northern Rock's customers queued in desperation to withdraw their live savings, despite their finances being protected by the Financial Services Compensation Scheme. HM Treasury announced that it would cover all the deposits of Northern Rock.[33] In February 2007, the share price of Northern Rock was 1,200 pence, by January 2008 the price had fallen below 200 pence and its shares were suspended in February 2008.[34] The bank was later nationalised after emergency legislation was rushed through the House of Commons.[35] As a result of this financial scandal, the FSA has been severely criticised and in March 2008 it published a review of its actions.[36] HM Treasury Select Committee took the view that "the FSA was asleep on the job ... A very clear signal of a bank running a big risk is rapid expansion. Northern Rock was giving that signal quite clearly; it is remarkable that [the FSA] missed it".[37] However, it must be noted that the Bank of England and the Securities and Investment Board also got it wrong during the collapse of several financial institutions in the 1980s and early 1990s. It is impossible for the FSA to implement a regulatory regime that will achieve a failure rate. The FSA must learn lessons from this incident and ensure that it does more to maintain market confidence and protect the consumers who have been adversely affected by Northern Rock.

According to accountancy firm KPMG, "the origins of the credit crunch lie with the sub-prime lending and the ensuing house price bubble in the US. Mortgage fraud – by borrowers, brokers and appraisers – was a key contributor".[38] Similarly, the FBI stated that during the subprime mortgage crisis "mortgage fraud perpetrators may take advantage of industry personnel attempting to generate loans to maintain current standards of living".[39] The FBI concluded that the "subprime mortgage issues remain a key factor in influencing mortgage fraud directly and indirectly".[40]The NFSA stated that in the UK "falling house prices and

---

[29] R Tomasic 'Corporate rescue, governance and risk taking in Northern Rock: part 2' (2008) The Company Lawyer 29(11), 330-337, at 330.

[30] See X Lok 'Libor and market disruption: the future of LIBOR' (2008) Butterworths Journal of International Banking and Financial Law 23(8) 421.

[31] BBC News, Rock pledges to repay tax payers, 31 March 2008, available from www.bbc.co.uk. For a more detailed discussion of the options available to the Bank of England when a bank collapses see C Bamford 'Northern Rock and the single market' (2008) The Company Lawyer 29(3) 65-66.

[32] Tomasic, above n 29, at 336.

[33] HM Treasury, Statement by the Chancellor of the Exchequer on financial markets, September 17 2007, available from www.hm-treasury.gov.uk.

[34] BBC News, Northern Rock, in facts and figures, 18 February 2008, available from www.bbc.co.uk.

[35] Banking (Special Provisions) Act 2008.

[36] Financial Services Authority *Executive Summary of Review* (Financial Services Authority,London, 2008).

[37] HM Treasury Select Committee *Northern Rock on the Run* (HM Treasury Select Committee, London, 2007) at p.22.

[38] Dilley and Weller, above n 36, at 11.

[39] Federal Bureau Investigation, above n 1.

[40] Federal Bureau Investigation, above n 1.

tightening credit conditions have shed significant new light on the extent to which criminals have exploited the mortgage process to defraud lenders".[41] Indeed, KPMG noted that "the effective prevention, detection and investigation of fraud have rarely seemed more important, as the effects of the global credit crunch continue to be felt".[42] The link between the subprime crisis and mortgage fraud is also illustrated by the fact that during this period of economic uncertainty there has been a 400% increase in the number of mortgage fraud investigations undertaken by the FBI.[43] The increase in suspected instances of mortgage fraud has also been reported by FinCEN.[44] For example, between 2002/2003 there was a 22% increase in mortgage fraud loan SARs, in 2003/2004 the increase was 126%; 47% during 2004/2005; 52% in 2005/2006; 33% in 2006/2007 and 44% in 2007/2008.[45] In April 2008 FinCEN report that "in the calendar year 2006, financial institutions filed 37,313 suspicious activity reports [SARs] citing suspected mortgage loan fraud, a 44% increase from the proceeding year".[46] During the same period, FinCEN has seen a considerable increase of approximately 500% in the number of SARs submitted by depository institutions.[47] The link between the subprime mortgage crisis and organised crime was recognised by the FSA, who in its 2008 Financial Risk Outlook, commented that "organized property fraud is an area where we have seen increased activity. The potential for criminal gain from this type of crime suggests that it is likely to increase unless coordinated action is taken by pubic and private sector agencies and unless the adequacy of systems and controls in financial systems is ensured".[48] Further evidence of the association between the credit crunch and mortgage fraud is illustrated by the point that financial institutions in the UK have reported over 200 suspected cases of mortgage fraud to the FSA.[49] Philip Robinson, Financial Crime and Intelligence Division Director of the FSA stated that as a result of this review "the problem [of mortgage fraud] looks bigger and more widespread than we, and I believe others, once thought".[50] The next part of the paper introduced and then critically considers the measures introduced to combat mortgage fraud in the US.

Part I. The United States of America

There is no single federal statute that applies to mortgage fraud.[51] Jacobsen and Barnhill succinctly summarise the legislative approach to fraud as the "perpetrator's criminal liability is derived either from fraud statutes or statutes that address specific types of mortgage fraud. Perpetrators who run mortgage fraud schemes may be charged with wire fraud, mail fraud,

[41] National Fraud Strategic Authority, above n 15, at 8
[42] KPMG *Fighting Fraud* 25 Summer 2008, at 2.
[43] Heroy, above n 3 at 323.
[44] Financial Crimes Enforcement Network, above n 8, at 3.
[45] *Ibid.*, at 8.
[46] Financial Crimes Enforcement Network, above n 8.
[47] Linn, above n 28, at 7-10.
[48] Financial Services Authority *Financial Risk Outlook 2008* (Financial Services Authority, London, 2008) at p.14. For more examples of mortgage fraud scams see O'Donnell and Planer, above n 6, at 55-57 and H Lax 'Recognizing mortgage fraud' (2007) Michigan Bar Journal November 86 34-38, at 35-38,
[49] Financial Services Authority, Keynote speech by Philip Robinson, Financial Crime and Intelligence Division Director, CML Mortgage Fraud Seminar, 13 February 2008, available from www.fsa.gov.uk.
[50] *Ibid.*
[51] It is important to note that this paper doesn't seek to provide a detailed commentary on the various statutes that criminalise mortgage fraud, but merely to provide a brief overview.

bank fraud, conspiracy, making false statements in loan applications, money laundering, or equity skimming".[52] Wire fraud is defined as developing or attempting to initiate a scheme or pretence to commit fraud for the purpose of obtaining property or money by false representations.[53] If a defendant is convicted of wire fraud, the punishment is a fine and/or imprisonment for up to twenty years. However, if the accused attempts to defraud a financial institution, the fine is $1m and/or a thirty year custodial sentence if found guilty. Bank fraud is committed when a person "knowingly executes, or attempts to execute a scheme to defraud a financial institution, or to obtain any of the moneys, funds, credits, assets, securities, or other property owned by, or under the custody of, a financial institution, by means of fraudulent pretences, representations, or promises".[54] Finally, it is an offence to commit mail fraud if the accused seeks to illegally acquire monies or proceeds via in which the postal system is utilised in the commission of this crime.[55] A detailed discussion of these statutes is beyond the scope of this contribution. The oldest tool utilised by law enforcement agencies in the US to combat financial crime is financial intelligence, and its importance in the battle against mortgage fraud cannot be underestimated. It is to this anti-fraud measure that the chapter now turns to.

The traditional way that to collect financial intelligence is via a currency transaction report or a SAR.[56] The first piece of legislation introduced in the US that sought to utilise financial intelligence was the Currency and Foreign Transactions Act or the Bank Secrecy Act 1970 (BSA 1970).[57] This Act according to Meltzer was introduced to "prevent money laundering of profits resulting from drug sales".58 The Act, in addition to specific regulations from the Treasury Department,59 created a reporting requirement that was prompted by transactions in excess of $10,000.60 The effectiveness of this financial threshold has been questioned due to the process of 'smurfing' or structured payments.61 Congress recognised the problems and enacted the Money Laundering Control Act 1986 (MLCA 1986), which criminalised money laundering and structured payments. Under this Act "banks face the dilemma of either investigating a customer's transaction to ensure that the source of the money is legal or facing liability. If the bank reports the suspicious transaction and it turns out

---

[52] B Jacobsen and M Barnhill 'Drawing the short straw – mortgage fraud and straw buyers' (2008) Utah Bar Journal August 21 9.

[53] This type of fraud can be committed by transmissions over wire, radio, or television communication in interstate commerce, writings, signs, signals, pictures, or sounds for the purpose of executing the scheme or artifice. For a more detailed discussion of wire fraud see J Robinson 'The federal main and wire fraud statutes: correct standards for determining jurisdiction and venue' (2008) Willamete Law Review Sprint 44 479-540.

[54] 18 U.S.C. § 1344 (2006). The Bank Fraud Act was introduced as part of the Comprehensive Crime Control Act (1984). For a more detailed comment on the Bank Fraud Act see M Madia 'The bank fraud act: a risk or loss requirement' (2005) University of Chicago Law Review 72 1145-1471.

[55] 18 U.S.C. § 1341 (2006). For a more detailed discussion about mail fraud see the recent commentary see C Stuart 'Mail and wire fraud' (2009) American Criminal Law Review 46 813-834.

[56] See for example General Accounting Office *Money laundering – needed improvements for reporting suspicious transactions are needed* (1995 Washington) at p.10.

[57] Public Law 91-508, 84 Stat, 1114

[58] P Meltzer 'Keeping drug money from reaching the wash cycle: a guide to the bank secrecy act' (1991) The Banking Law Journal 108(3) 230-255, at 230.

[59] Title 31, section 5313 of the United States Code.

[60] Meltzer, above n 58, at 230.

[61] For a more detailed discussion of the smurfing techniques employed by money launderers see See S. N. Welling, "Smurfs, money laundering, and the federal criminal law: the crime of structuring transactions" (1989) Florida Law Review Spring 41 287-339.

to be incorrect about its suspicion, the bank may be liable under tort law".[62] The usefulness of financial intelligence has been questioned by Benning who took the view that it "produced a large quantity of reports, [yet] produced little useful information".[63] Benning added that "inconsistent reporting standards across financial institutions and agencies made it difficult to discern patterns of activity".[64] Similarly, the Government Accountability Office (GAO) stated that there was no effective administration or control of the information contained in the reports and furthermore that "there is no way of ensuring that the information is being used to its full potential".[65] In response to such criticisms, FinCEN was designated a financial intelligence unit with the purpose of collating and normalizing the SARs regime in 1990.[66] Its primary objective was to "support law enforcement agencies anti-money laundering efforts",[67] which was later expanded to include "responsibility for administration of the BSA 1970".[68] The GAO took the view that "FinCEN is not a traditional law enforcement agency",[69] and added that it aims to "provide government wide intelligence and analysis ... that can be used to aid in the detection, investigation, and prosecution of domestic and international money laundering".[70] Therefore, FinCEN's principal objective is to "enhance US national security, deter and detect criminal activity, and safeguard financial systems from abuse by promoting transparency in the US and international financial systems".[71] Despite its laudable aims, the effectiveness of the reporting systems has been questioned and it has been argued that such reporting obligations are limited because they are the most "least useful for providing intelligence information on possible criminal activity".[72] Furthermore, the "use of information received by law enforcement at federal and state levels is limited and inconsistent".[73]

An important amendment to the BSA (1970) was introduced by the Annunzio-Wylie Anti-Money Laundering Act (1992), which authorised the Treasury Department to compel financial institutions to report any 'suspicious' transactions.[74] The interpretation of this term has limited the effectiveness of these reporting requirements. The GAO took the view that a "specific criteria for determining whether a transaction is suspicious has never been developed".[75] It has been argued "one cannot use a single criterion that will definitively

---

[62] D Alford 'Anti-money laundering regulations: a burden on financial institutions' (1994) The North Carolina Journal of International Law and Commercial Regulation 19 Summer 437-468, at 458.

[63] J Benning 'Following dirty money: does bank reporting of suspicious activity pose a threat to drug dealers?' (2002) Criminal Justice Policy Review 13(4) 337-355, at 337-338.

[64] *Ibid.*, 338.

[65] General Accounting Office, above n 56, at 2.

[66] Benning, above n 63, at 337.

[67] General Accounting Office *Money laundering – FinCEN needs to better communicate regulatory priorities and time lines* (1998 Washington) at p.5.

[68] *Ibid.*

[69] General Accounting Office *Money laundering – progress report on Treasury's financial crimes enforcement network* (1993 Washington) p.1.

[70] See General Accounting Office *Money laundering – a framework for understanding US efforts overseas* (1996 Washington) at p.4.

[71] Will need to reference FinCEN homepage here.

[72] General Accounting Office, above n 56, at 5.

[73] *Ibid.*, at 26.

[74] These measures were introduced by the Treasury Department in 1996.

[75] General Accounting Office, above n 56, at 12.

indicate a connection between a financial transaction and an illegal activity".[76] Harvey noted that "suspicious itself is a wide-reaching term of which there is no objective definition: suspicious is personal and subjective and falls far short of proof based on firm evidence".[77] She added that "in many cases reporting tends to be unusual rather than suspicious and has been driven by the need to be seen to be compliant rather than by concern that laundering activity is taking place".[78] The reporting requirements imposed by the BSA 1970 have imposed significant administrative burdens on financial institutions and they have led to an increased level of record-keeping, report filing, and internal policing requirements. It is questionable however, whether the filing of an SAR will make any difference given the difficulties in securing prosecutions in money laundering offences. It is also possible to argue that the reporting requirements have created a 'needle-in-the-haystack' problem, especially given the large number of SARs annually submitted to FinCEN. Despite such criticisms, the use of financial intelligence is of paramount importance not only to the fight against mortgage fraud, but also money laundering and the financing of terrorism.

It is somewhat to the surprise of the authors that "nonbank lenders, mortgage brokers and other real estate professionals were not subject to the Bank Secrecy Act's provisions, including mandatory mortgage fraud reporting requirements".[79] However, it must be noted that members of the profession are required by statute to have in place an anti-money laundering program.[80] This includes the development of internal anti-money laundering procedures and controls, the appointment of a compliance officer,[81]the creation of an training scheme to encourage employees to detect and prevent money laundering and that an independent audit is carried out to determine the effectiveness of the anti-money laundering procedures.[82] Linn concluded that "regrettably, at the height of the subprime lending boom, trade groups representing non-bank mortgage lenders, mortgage brokers, real estate agents, and other persons involved in real estate closing and settlements, successfully resisted efforts by the Department of Treasury to impose BSA regulations on them".[83] There are a number of possible reasons as to why the federal agencies are reluctant to impose compulsory reporting obligations on the real estate industry, such as cost,[84] the increase of defensive reporting,[85] and increased level of regulation and perhaps, somewhat surprisingly, the real estate industry

---

76 J Rusch 'Hue and cry in the counting-house: some observations on the Bank Secrecy Act' (1988) Catholic University Law Review 37 465-488, at 478-479. For some judicial guidance on the interpretation of this phrase see United States v. Tobon-Builes, 706 F.2d 1092, 1094-95 (11th Cir. 1983).

77 J Harvey 'Compliance and reporting issues arising for financial institutions from money laundering regulations: a preliminary cost benefit study' (2004) Journal of Money Laundering Control 7(4) 333-346, at 335.

78 *Ibid.*

79 Linn, above n 28, at 10.

80 Uniting and Strengthening America by Providing Appropriate Tools Required to Intercept and Obstruct Terrorism Act (2001), s. 352(a).

81 In the United Kingdom this is referred to as a money laundering reporting officer.

82 It has been noted however that the USA Patriot Act does not contain the term "real estate". See A Tellechea 'Economic crimes in the capital markets' (2008) Journal of Financial Crime 15(2) 214-222, at 217.

83 Linn, above n 28, at 10.

84 See for example M Roberts, "Big brother isn't just watching you, he's also wasting your tax payer dollars: an analysis of the anti-money laundering provisions of the USA Patriot Act" (2004) Rutgers Law Review 56(2) 573-602, at 592.

85 A Leong 'Chasing dirty money: domestic and international measures against money laundering' (2007) Journal of Money Laundering Control (10)(2) 141-156, at 141.

felt that they were not at threat from financial crime.[86] This is a naive stance as there is increasing evidence that criminals and terrorists are exploiting this loophole to hide their proceeds of crime and commit fraud. Linn recommended that "extending mandatory fraud reporting requirements to the real estate industry makes sense for another reason. The real estate industry in the US is fragmented, with many participants regulated by a patchwork of federal, state and local agencies. The fragmented nature of the real estate industry in the US, which many now agree was a regulatory weakness during the subprime era, could have been used to some advantage".[87] It is the recommendation of this chapter that the scope of the reporting requirements are extended to incorporate the real estate industry as a matter of urgency given the unprecedented nature of the credit crunch and its inherent links with mortgage fraud.

A legislative attempt to combat mortgage fraud was tabled in April 2007 by Senators Barack Obama and Dick Durbin.[88] The Bill was entitled "Stopping Mortgage Transactions which Operate to Promote Fraud, Risk, Abuse, and Underdevelopment Act".[89] The Bill defined mortgage fraud as "unlawful for any mortgage professional to knowingly execute, or attempt to execute a scheme or artifice - (1) to defraud any natural person, financial institution,[90] or other borrower in connection with the extension of credit that is secured by either real property or personal property that is to be used as a primary dwelling, or "(2) to obtain, by means of false or fraudulent pretences, representations, or promises, any money or property, including without limitation in the form of fees or charges, from a natural person in connection with an extension of consumer credit . . . secured by" either of the same listed in part "(1)."[91] The Bill sought to impose tough criminal sanctions upon people convicted of mortgage fraud – a custodial sentence of 35 years and fines of up to $5m.[92] The proposals also aimed to enlarge the breadth of reports and evidence received by FinCEN. However, the Bill was not signed into law by the President George Bush as it ran out of Congressional time. The most recent legislative attempt to tackle mortgage fraud is the Fraud Enforcement and Recovery Bill. This was originally introduced by the Chairman of the Committee on the Judiciary Patrick Leahy, Senators Grassley and Kaufman and co-sponsored by Senators Klobuchar and Schumer in February 2009. After signing the Bill On May 20th 2009, President Barak Obama stated "the Fraud Enforcement and Recovery Act will protect the American people from giving the federal government new tools and resources to prevent fraud".[93] The aim of this Act was threefold. Firstly, to improve the levels of responsibility and accountability for frauds that had arisen during the financial crisis. Secondly, the Act provided a substantial increase in funding for the Justice Department and other law enforcement agencies to tackle mortgage fraud. In particular the Act empowers the

---

86 For a commentary on these issues in the UK see N Ryder 'The Financial Services Authority, the Reduction of Financial Crime and the Money Launderer – A Game of Cat and Mouse' (2008) Cambridge Law Journal 67(3) 635-653.

87 Linn, above n 28, at 11.

88 Heroy, above n 3 at 343. It is important to note however that this was not the first version of Bill to be introduced by Senators Barack Obama and Senator Dick Durbin, which was originally tabled in February 2006.

89 It is more commonly referred to as the Stop Fraud Act.

90 S. 1222, Sec 2 § 1351(a)(1). As cited in Heroy, above n 3 at 343.

91 S. 1222, Sec 2 § 1351(a)(2). *Ibid.*

92 For a more detailed commentary of the Stop Fraud Act see Heroy, above n 3 at 343-345.

93 The White House, Office of the Press Secretary, May 20 2009, Reforms for American homeowners and consumers – President Obama signs the Families Save their Homes Act and the Fraud Enforcement and Recovery Act, available from www.whitehouse.gov.

government to distribute approximately $500bn for 2010 and 2011 for "additional government enforcement activity".[94] Furthermore, the Department of Justice has been given $330m to investigate any suspected instances of mortgage fraud and to pursue any potential prosecutions that arise from those investigations. Ceresney *et al* stated "even with the increased resources that federal law enforcement agencies are beginning to devote to mortgage fraud, it is unlikely that they will be successful in systematically prosecuting the frauds that may have triggered the credit crisis. The potential amount of fraud in the mortgage industry, coupled with the complexity of fraud investigations and federal resource constraints, makes systematic prosecution difficult".[95] Finally, the Act sought to clarify several problematic areas of the fraud and money laundering statutes.[96] Despite the laudable aims of the Fraud Enforcement and Recovery Act 2009, it has been criticised by several commentators. For example, Walsh and Joslyn writing for the Heritage Foundation questioned the appropriateness the measures and stated that:

> "The faulty premise of the Fraud Enforcement and Recovery Act ... is that criminal activity caused the financial mess America is facing and that criminal prosecution and punishment can fix it. This is precisely the sort of reflexive criminalization that is behind the current over-federalization of crime and that Members of Congress on both sides of the aisle have stated they abhor because it has contributed to the record federal prison population".[97]

Furthermore, they also queried the aptness of creating more legislation to tackle fraud:

> Further, federal law enforcement's two most popular criminal offenses for prosecuting fraud--the federal mail and wire fraud statutes--are so exceedingly broad they can cover an almost unimaginable range of financial wrongdoing. Indeed, general federal fraud statutes, such as the mail and wire fraud statutes, are available to address *any* crimes related to the subprime market and market crisis.[98]

It can be argued that Bush administration largely ignored the problems associated with mortgage fraud and the sub-prime mortgage crisis. One possible reason for this rather lacklustre policy towards mortgage fraud was the administrations' unsuccessful obsession with the 'financial war on terrorism'.[99] The policy towards mortgage fraud has gained significant momentum since the commencement of the Obama administration in January 2009. The introduction of the Fraud Enforcement and Recovery Act 2009 is a welcomed addition to an extensive legislative armoury of the Justice Department. The additional funding

---

94 Kirkland Alert, The Fraud Enforcement and Recovery Act 2009, Kirkland and Ellis LLP.

95 Ceresney *et al.*, above n 21, at 243.

96 Committee on the Judiciary, 111th Congress Report, Fraud Enforcement and Recovery Act of 2009, Mr Leahy. This includes for example important amendments to the False Claims Act following the Supreme Court decision in *Allison Engine Co v United States ex rel, Sanders* 553 U.S. ___ (2008), 128 S. Ct. 2123 (2008). Furthermore, several important amendments were made to several fraud statutes including the definition of 'proceeds' in money laundering statue 18 U.S.C. SS 1956). This was an attempt to overcome the shortcomings of the decision of Supreme Court in *United States v Santos* (No. 06-1005) 461 F. 3d 886, affirmed.

97 B Walsh and T Joslyn 'The Fraud Enforcement and Recovery Act (S. 386): Criminalizing our way out of the financial crisis' No. 2322 March 4, 2009, at 1. A full copy of this can be accessed from http://www.heritage.org/research/legalissues/wm2322.cfm.

98 *Ibid.*

99 For a more detailed discussion of the financial war on terrorism N Ryder 'A false sense of security? An analysis of legislative approaches to the prevention of terrorist finance in the United States of America and the United Kingdom' (2007) Journal of Business Law November 821-850.

for the FBI and other regulatory agencies authorised under the Act is both as welcome as it is essential given the complexity of the fraudulent activity and the subsequent investigation and prosecution by law enforcement agencies. It is extremely difficult to determine the overall effectiveness of the policy adopted in the US to tackle mortgage fraud. Only now are we beginning to understand the extent of the sub-prime mortgage crisis and it is likely that larger instances of suspected mortgage fraud will come to light when more financial institutions collapse or seek further support from the federal agencies.

Part II. The United Kingdom

It is only since 2006 that the problems mortgage fraud have been identified and tackled by the UK government. The UK policy has been significantly influenced by the 2007 Fraud Review,[100] which according to Sarker represented the "first comprehensive and holistic review of fraud and anti-fraud efforts in England and Wales".[101] The legislative framework towards mortgage fraud in the UK can be contrasted with the US because it is contained within a single statute, the Fraud Act 2006. Prior to this Act, the law relating to fraud comprised eight statutory deception offences in the Theft Acts (1968 to 1996) and the common law offence of conspiracy to defraud. This law was "fragmented, disparate and over specific".[102] The Home Office noted that it "is not always clear which offence should be charged, and defendants have successfully argued that the consequences of their particular deceptive behaviour did not fit the definition of the offence with which they have been charged".[103] The Law Commission issued a Consultation Paper in 1999, which distinguished between two forms of a general offence of fraud: one based on dishonesty, and the other based on deception.[104] The Law Commission concluded that while the concerns expressed about existing law were valid they could be met by extending the existing (deception based) offences in preference to creating a single offence of fraud. The Commission reconsidered their conclusions in the light of reactions to the 1999 paper and they issued an informal discussion paper in 2000. This paper accepted the view of respondents that the requirement of dishonesty should be retained and proposed the introduction of a general offence which would cover the infliction, by a false pretence, of any kind of financial loss and the making, by deception, of any financial gain. The Law Commission published a final report in 2002 along with the Fraud Bill.[105] In May 2004, the Home Office proposed a general offence of fraud.[106] The Fraud Act received Royal Assent on November 8th 2006; it overhauled and widened the array of criminal offences available in respect of fraudulent and deceptive behaviour. The Act creates a new general offence of fraud and introduces three possible ways of committing it.[107] Firstly, it makes it an offence to commit fraud by false representation.[108]

---

[100] Attorney General's Office, above n 11, at 2.

[101] R Sarker 'Fighting fraud – a missed opportunity?' (2007) Company Lawyer 28(8) 243-244, at 243.

[102] R Wright 'Developing effective tools to manage the risk of damage caused by economically motivated crime fraud' (2007) Journal of Financial Crime 14(1) 17-27, at 18.

[103] *Ibid*. For a more detailed illustration of this problem see generally R v Preddy [1996] AC 815, 831.

[104] The Law Commission *Legislating the Criminal Code Fraud and Deception, No 155* (The Law Commission: London, 1999).

[105] The Law Commission *Fraud (Law COM No* 276) (The Law Commission: London, 2002).

[106] Home Office Fraud Law Reform – Consultation on proposals for legislation (Home Office: London, 2004).

[107] Fraud Act 2006, s. 1.

[108] Fraud Act 2006, s. 2.

Secondly, the Act makes it an offence to commit fraud by failing to disclose information to another person where there is a legal duty to disclose the information.[109] Thirdly, it makes it an offence to commit a fraud by dishonestly abusing one's position.[110] At this stage it is impossible to determine whether or not the Fraud Act has had an impact on the extent of mortgage fraud or led to an increase in prosecutions.[111] A greater understanding of the UK's policy towards mortgage fraud can be obtained from analysing the measures introduced by the FSA, to which the chapter now turns.

The Financial Services Authority and Mortgage Fraud

In May 1997 the UK government announced that work would begin on the reform of the Financial Services Act 1986.[112] The government sought to implement a new financial regulatory regime which would set basic standards and prevent systematic failure. Under FSMA 2000, the FSA regulates and authorises amongst others, banks, building societies and insurance companies.[113] In order to effectively regulate such a wide range of firms the FSA sets standards and guidance on those standards, with which the firms must comply with. These rules and standards are contained in the FSA's Handbook.[114] Of relevance to this chapter are the statutory objectives of the FSA, and in particular section 6.[115] This requires the FSA to reduce financial crime by ensuring that financial institutions have systems and practices in place to protect them against being used as vehicles by financial criminals. Financial crime is broadly defined and incorporates any offence including fraud or dishonesty,[116] misconduct in, or misuse of information relating to, a financial market;[117] or handling the proceeds of crime.[118] The principal objective of the FSA it to focus on the systems and controls that firms have in place to prevent them from being abused for the purposes of fraud or money laundering.[119] Section 6 states that when the FSA are considering the financial crime statutory objective, they must have regard to the desirability of firms to "being aware of the risk of their businesses being used in connection with the commission of financial crime" and that the firm takes "appropriate measures to prevent financial crime, facilitate its detection and monitor its incidence".[120] The financial crime objective has been deliberately extended to include firms that conduct regulated activities without express authorisation from the FSA.[121]

---

109 Fraud Act 2006, s. 3.

110 Fraud Act 2006, s. 4.

111 For a brief discussion of some early judicial precedent on these offences see B Summers 'Update on recent fraud cases' (2008) Company Lawyer 29(11) 342-344, at 342.

112 H.C. Debs. Col. 508-511, May 20, 1997, Gordon Brown MP.

113 Members of the regulated sector are defined in the Financial Services and Markets Act 2000 (Regulated Activities) Order 2001 S.I. 2001/544.

114 A copy of the FSA Handbook is available from www.fsa.gov.uk.

115 For a general discussion of the statutory objectives of the Financial Services Authority see N Ryder 'Two Plus Two Equals Financial Education – The Financial Services Authority and Consumer Education' (2001) The Law Teacher 35(2) 216-232.

116 Financial Services and Markets Act 2000, s. 6 (3)(a).

117 Financial Services and Markets Act 2000, s. 6 (3)(b).

118 Financial Services and Markets Act 2000, s. 6 (3)(c).

119 A Proctor 'Supporting a risk-based anti-money laundering approach through enforcement action' (2004) *Journal of Financial Regulation and Compliance* 13(1) 10-14, at 11.

120 Financial Services and Markets Act 2000, s. 6(2).

121 This is a criminal offence under the Financial Services and Markets Act 2000, s. 23.

Risked Based Policy towards Financial Crime

The FSA outlined its risk based approach towards financial regulation in 1997 when it stated that it would assume an adaptable method of supervision by targeting specific business practices and the level of risk associated with them.[122] It is necessary to note that the FSA are subject to the principles of good regulation.[123] This requires the FSA to, *inter alia*, use its resources in the most efficient and economic way towards the responsibilities of those who manage the affairs of authorized persons,[124] and to impose burdens on the regulated sector that are proportionate to the benefits.[125] What does this mean in relation to the reduction of mortgage fraud? A firm will be able to allocate its resources in a cost effective and proportionate way so that it can focus on the most relevant risks from mortgage fraud that it faces. In terms of a risk-based approach towards the reduction fraud Doig noted that "the FSA will be looking for firms to demonstrate that they are taking steps to be aware of, and to tackle, fraud risks by being able to identify and report on fraud".[126] The FSA has adopted a two stage policy. Firstly, it has devised a list of services and products that categorise risk status and secondly, it has put in place set of procedures to ensure that firms verify the identity of a client.[127] The risk based approach between the FSA and the regulated sector will vary between the 'highest' and 'lowest' at risk firms.[128] The highest risk firms will benefit from what is best described as a 'continuous relationship' with the FSA in terms of their financial crime obligations, while the lower risk firms will have a 'remote relationship'.[129] In order for this to work, it is essential that firms continuously identify the risks of entering into certain financial transactions which are used in the process financial crime. The FSA hoped that a risk based approach would lift the regulatory burdens imposed on firms and reduce the compliance costs of the regulated sector.[130] The regime introduced by the FSA is not cost effective. The compliance costs for the regulated sector have increased by 60% since the introduction of the FSA regulations.[131] This approach has not worked because the regulated sector is facing spiralling compliance costs as the FSA attempts to reduce financial crime. It is extremely difficult, if not impossible to quantify if the risk based approach towards the reduction of mortgage fraud has worked. What can be concluded is that this approach has

---

122 Financial Services Authority *Financial Services Authority – An Outline* (London, Financial Services Authority, 1997), p. 31.

123 Financial Services and Markets Act 2000, s. 2(3).

124 Financial Services and Markets Act 2000, s. 2(3)(b).

125 Financial Services and Markets Act 2000, s. 2(3)(c).

126 A Doig *Fraud* (Cullompton, Willan Publishing, 2006) at p. 158.

127 M Gill and G Taylor 'The risk-based approach to tackling money laundering: matching risk to products' (2003) Company Lawyer 24(7) 210-213, at 212.

128 According to the FSA the most at risk sections of the financial services industry are international banking and high risk jurisdictions, domestic banking, independent financial advisers, online stockbrocking, spread betting and credit unions. See Financial Services Authority, Press Release, 'Tackling the risk of money laundering in the financial services industry', FSA/PN/100/2001, July 30 2001, available from www.fsa.gov.uk.

129 C Sergeant 'Risk-based regulation in the Financial Services Authority' (2002) Journal of Financial Regulation and Compliance 10(4) 329-335, at 333.

130 See A V M Leong 'Anti-money laundering measures in the United Kingdom: a review of recent legislation and FSA's risk-based approach' (2007) Company Lawyer 28(2) 35-42, at 41.

131 See BBC News, 'Anti-laundering expenses soar', 9 July 2007, available from www.bbc.co.uk, KPMG, Press Release, Banks battle against money laundering as market complexity increases, 9 July 2007, available from www.kpmg.com and P Sproat 'The new policing of assets and the new assets of policing: a tentative financial cost-benefit analysis of the UK's anti-money laundering and asset recovery regime' (2007) Journal of Money Laundering Control 10(3) 277-299.

failed to meet its optimum objective, to reduce the costs of the regulated sector. Therefore, the FSA must seek to produce a more cost effective and streamlined regime by allowing the regulated sector greater flexibility to reduce the extent of fraud mortgage fraud. Since the enactment of FSMA 2000, the FSA has largely concentrated upon tackling the problems caused by money laundering. The development of its fraud policy can be traced to a discussion paper published in 2004.[132] As a result of this discussion paper, the FSA announced its new policy on fraud in October 2004.[133] The FSA has implemented initiatives which include encouraging firms to maintain their anti-fraud systems, amending the FSA Handbook and an increased level of co-operation with firms and trade associations. Furthermore, the FSA has attempted to improve firms and consumers understanding of the risk of fraud and how this can be limited. The next part of the chapter seeks to analyse the specific measures employed by the FSA to limit mortgage fraud including its rule making powers and enforcement powers.

Rule Making Powers

The regulations imposed by the FSA on firms to limit the extent of financial crime are contained in its Handbook,[134] Which provides that firms are under an obligation report 'significant' fraud.[135] The FSA has admitted that "the limited number of reports we receive suggests that many firms are not aware of the requirement or interpret 'significant' very narrowly".[136] Reporting requirements are in integral part of the FSA's policy towards the reduction of financial crime, as they are in the USA. However, the rationale behind some of the obligations under the Handbook must be questioned because it created an additional level of regulation for an area of law which is complicated and fraught with practical difficulties. The FSA imposed the same level of obligations on the regulated sector irrespective of their differing nature and size. The obligations imposed were burdensome and are counterproductive for smaller firms. This resulted in a 'fear factor' amongst firms who might not have the resources or experience to meet their obligations.[137] In 2005, the FSA published a consultation paper outlining its plans to simplify the financial crime under its Handbook.[138] There was strong support from the regulated sector to remove the burdensome regulations and that they should be replaced with high-level requirements for firms to have their own risk-

---

132 Financial Services Authority *Developing our policy on fraud and dishonesty – Discussion Paper 26* (London, Financial Services Authority, 2004).

133 Financial Services Authority *The FSA's new approach to fraud – Fighting fraud in partnership*, Speech by Philip Robinson, October 26 2004, available from www.fsa.gov.uk.

134 Financial Services Authority *Money Laundering Handbook* (London, Financial Services Authority, 2006).

135 Financial Services Authority *Full Handbook – Supervision* (London, Financial Services Authority, 2006) SUP 15.3.17 R.

136 Financial Services Authority, above n 132 at 12.

137 C Nakajima 'Principle-based vs. rule-based regulation: the implications for governance' (2006) Company Lawyer 27(5) 129-130. For example, the first person the FSA fined for breaches of ML was the managing director of a small business which employed only six members of staff with 23 clients. The FSA found no actual evidence of money laundering or that the firm or the managing director had intentionally misled the bank to which they had failed to supply appropriate information about their clients, yet a fine was imposed. See Financial Services Authority, Press Release, 'FSA fines bond broker and managing director for anti-money laundering failures', FSA/PN/115/2005, available from www.fsa.gov.uk.

138 Financial Services Authority *Consultation Paper - 5/10 - Reviewing the FSA Handbook - Money Laundering, Approved Persons, Training and Competence, and Conduct of Business* (London, Financial Services Authority, 2005).

based controls on money laundering.[139] In January 2006 the FSA announced that it was streamlining its Handbook.[140] It was replaced in with a principles-based approach in the Senior Management Arrangements, Systems and Controls, or SYSC part of the Handbook.[141] Part 3 of which now provides that firms must have in place systems and controls which are appropriate for the firm to conduct its business.[142] In particular, a firm is required to "take reasonable care to establish and maintain effective systems and controls for compliance with applicable requirements and standards under the regulatory system and for countering the risk that the firm might be used to further financial crime".[143] Firms are therefore required to carry out regular assessments of the adequacy of the systems they have in place to prevent themselves from being used to further financial crime,[144] allocate a director or senior manager with overall responsibility for establishing and the maintaining of the financial crime.[145] The new regime is intended to provide the regulated sector with an even higher degree of flexibility. This means that firms are able to identify the risks and determine how they can best allocate their resources in areas which are most vulnerable.[146] The FSA has removed the detailed and burdensome rules and replaced them with requirements so that the regulated sector can have their 'own' or 'personal' risk-based controls. This approach might encourage and enable the regulated sector to target their resources more appropriately on activities at risk from financial crime, thus reducing the compliance costs. It is breaches of these obligations under SYSC that has enabled the FSA to utilise its extensive enforcement powers to limit the extent of mortgage fraud.

Enforcement Powers

The FSA has been given an extensive array of enforcement powers, some of which it has utilised to combat mortgage fraud. Enforcement within the context of FSMA 2000 incorporates two broad. Firstly, preventing those who are not authorised to conduct banking or investment business; and secondly, to ensure that those who are authorised to conduct such businesses do so properly.[147] Under FSMA 2000 the FSA has become a prosecuting authority in respect of certain financial criminal offences, such as money laundering. However, the FSA does not have any direct power to prosecute for fraud or dishonesty offences.[148] These powers apply whether or not the entity to be prosecuted is actually regulated by the FSA and they are therefore, the most important aspects of the FSA's obligation to reduce financial

---

[139] Financial Services Authority, Press Release, 'FSA to streamline rules on money laundering', FSA/PN/008/2006, January 26 2006, available from www.fsa.gov.uk. Also see Financial Services Authority, *Policy Statement 06/01 Reviewing our Money Laundering Regime - Feedback on Chapter 2 of CP05/10* (London, Financial Services Authority, 2006) at p. 5.

[140] *Ibid.*

[141] For a more detailed commentary on the FSA Handbook see W Blair and R Brent *Banking and Financial Crime – The International Law of Tainted Money* (Oxford, Oxford University Press, 2008) at pp. 262-266.

[142] Financial Services Authority, above n 135 at SYSC 3.1.1.

[143] *Ibid.*, at SYSC 3.2.6 R.

[144] Financial Services Authority, note 135 above at SYSC 3.2.6 C.

[145] *Ibid.*, at SYSC 3.2.6 H and I.

[146] J Bagge 'The future for enforcement under the new Financial Services Authority' (1998) The Company Lawyer 19(7) 194-197, at 194.

[147] *Ibid.*

[148] The power to prosecute instances of suspected mortgage fraud in the United Kingdom currently lies with the Crown Prosecution Service, the Fraud Prosecution Service and the Serious Fraud Office.

crime.[149] The FSA also has the power to impose a financial penalty where it establishes that there has been a contravention by an authorised person of any requirement imposed under FSMA 2000.[150] The FSA has imposed a series of fines on firms who have breached their anti-money laundering obligations under the FSA Handbook, even where there was no evidence of money laundering.[151] More recently, there been a significant increase in the frequency of financial penalties imposed where it has been determined that a firm has inadequate anti-fraud controls. In March 2006, the FSA fined Capita Financial Administration Limited, or CFAL, £300,000 for poor anti-fraud controls over client identities and account details.[152] After an investigation, the FSA found that CFAL had inadequately considered the threat posed by fraud and had not maintained effective systems and controls to mitigate this risk.[153] The failures by CFAL resulted in a small number of attempted and actual frauds against its customers, which were allegedly facilitated by CFAL employees. Philip Robinson, the FSA Financial Crime Sector leader said that "firms must fully understand the risks they face and have robust anti-fraud controls in place".[154] The FSA concluded that the weaknesses in systems and controls implemented by CFAL contributed to the frauds. They were insufficient and CFAL did not ensure that procedures to mitigate fraud risk were adequately implemented and that fraud awareness training was appropriate.[155] Furthermore, in May 2007 the FSA fined BNP Paribas Private Bank, or BNPP, £350,000 for weaknesses in its systems and controls which allowed a senior employee to fraudulently transfer £1.4m out of the firm's clients' accounts without permission. This was the first time that the FSA has fined a private bank for weaknesses in its anti-fraud systems.[156] The FSA concluded that BNPP did not have an effective review process for large transactions, over £10,000, from clients' accounts. The FSA also determined that BNPPs anti-fraud procedures were not clear about the precise role of senior management in checking significant transfers prior to payment. Therefore, a number of fraudulent transactions were not independently checked. The FSA took the view that "BNPPs failings were serious because they enabled significant fraud to take place and failed to detect subsequent transfers to cover it up for a long period of time".[157] More recently, the FSA fined the Nationwide Building Society £980,000 for "failing to have effective systems and controls to manage its information security risks".[158] The failings highlighted by the FSA related to a stolen laptop from the home of an employee of the building society. Whilst

---

[149] Financial Services and Markets Act 2000, s. 402 (1)(a).

[150] Financial Services and Markets Act 2000, s. 206 (1). Ellinger *et al* noted that "the FSA has imposed heavy 'penalties' on a number of banks for non compliance with the ML Module". See E Ellinger, E Lomnicka and R Hooley *Ellinger's Modern banking Law* (Oxford, Oxford University Press, 2006) at p.113.

[151] See for example, Financial Services Authority Press Release, 'FSA Fines Northern Bank £1,250,000 for money laundering control failings', FSA/PN/084/2003, August 7 2003, available from www.fsa.gov.uk and Financial Services Authority, Press Release, FSA Fines Abbey National £2,320,000 for money laundering control failings, FSA/PN/132/2003, December 10 2003, available from www.fsa.gov.uk.

[152] Financial Services Authority, Press Release, 'FSA fines Capita Financial Administrators Limited £300,000 in first anti-fraud controls case', FSA/PN/019/2006, 16 March 2006, available from www.fsa.gov.uk.

[153] In this instance, the attempted frauds amounted to £417,321 and the actual fraud totalled £328,241.

[154] Financial Services Authority, above n 152.

[155] It must be noted however that once the frauds were discovered an effective remedial programme was implemented.

[156] Financial Services Authority *Financial Services Authority Annual Report 2007/2008* (London, Financial Services Authority, 2008) p 23.

[157] Financial Services Authority, Press Release, 'FSA fines BNPP Private Bank £350,000 for weak anti-fraud controls', FSA/PN/060/2007, 10 May 2007, available from www.fsa.gov.uk.

[158] Financial Services Authority, Press Release, 'FSA fines Nationwide £980,000 for information security lapses', FSA/PN/021/2007, 14 February 2007, available from www.fsa.gov.uk.

undertaking an investigation, the FSA determined that the Nationwide did not have adequate safety measures in place to protect customers from an increased risk of fraud. The FSA Director of Enforcement, Margaret Cole, took the view that "firms' internal controls are fundamental in ensuring customers' details remain as secure as they can be and, as technology evolves, firms must keep their systems and controls up-to-date to prevent lapses in security".[159] This is an illustration of the FSA undertaking immediate and justifiable action against one of the largest providers of mortgages in the UK. It clearly sends a very strong message to all members of the regulated sector.

In December 2007, the FSA fined Norwich Union Life £1.26m for not "having effective systems and controls in place to protect customers' confidential information and manage its financial crime risks".[160] The FSA reported that "these failings resulted in a number of actual and attempted frauds against Norwich Union Life's customers".[161] According to the FSA, the inadequate systems that Norwich Union had in place permitted fraudsters to access and use personal information from customers to "impersonate customers and obtain sensitive customer details from its call centres".[162] Furthermore, the fraudsters were able to obtain confidential customer information including addresses and bank account details. The fraudsters used this information to request the surrender of 74 customers' policies totaling £3.3m in 2006. The level of the fines imposed by the FSA doubtlessly politically satisfying to some, yet it raises an important question, are the fines having any effect? A 2005 study conducted of firms' attitudes towards the FSA regulations revealed that the vast majority of them complied with them not because they perceive it as representing good practice or as combating financial crime, but only because of the threat of sanctions.[163] Approximately two-thirds of UK respondents thought that the level of regulation is too severe for the risks involved in their sector.[164] Therefore, despite the protestations from the regulated sector, it appears that the mere threat of financial sanctions by the FSA compels firms to comply with the regulations. This approach could be described as heavy handed. Nonetheless, it is having the desired effect and it would take a very brave firm to hold up their hands and publicly admit they were not compliant with the FSA regulations aimed at reducing financial crime.

In addition to the ability to impose a financial penalty, the FSA also has the power to ban authorized persons and firms from undertaking any regulated activity.[165] For example, in April 2008, the FSA banned John Paul Keay, who operated as Jack Keay Mortgage Services "for not being competent or capable to perform any functions related to regulated activities, including giving advice".[166] The FSA determined that Mr Keay "failed to maintain adequate control over it, which made the business a target for mortgage fraudsters" and that his business was "used for the submission of mortgage applications containing false

---

[159] *Ibid.*

[160] Financial Services Authority, Press Release, '17 December, FSA fines Norwich Union Life £1.26m', FSA/PN/130/2007, available from www.fsa.gov.uk.

[161] *Ibid.*

[162] Financial Services Authority, above n 160.

[163] M Yeandle, M Mainelli, A Berendt and B Healy *Anti-money laundering requirements: costs, benefits and perceptions* (London, City of London, 2005) p. 44.

[164] R Sarker 'Anti-money laundering requirements: too much pain for too little gain' (2006) *The Company Lawyer* 27(8) 250-251, at 251.

[165] Financial Services and Markets Act 2000, s. 56.

[166] Financial Services Authority *Final Notice to Mr John Paul Keay trading as Jack Keay Mortgage Services*, April 21 2008, available from www.fsa.gov.uk.

information and supported by falsified pay slips, bank statements and employer references".[167] Jonathan Phelan, Head of Retail Enforcement at the FSA, said:

> "Jack Keay's business was used to commit mortgage fraud. We identified many individual failings in what is a very small mortgage broker business. When concerns about mortgage fraud were drawn to his attention by a lender he delegated the task of following this up to his appointed representative and never thought to check on the outcome or make changes to his systems. After the FSA showed him examples of types of falsified documents submitted to lenders through his business, he still failed to demonstrate that he understood the risks".[168]

Another illustration of the FSA using its powers related to Mr Amjad Malik and Mr Tahir Mahmood.[169] The FSA banned two partners of a mortgage broker firm for their involvement in submitting false mortgage applications to lenders. The FSA determined that the partners had submitted bogus loan applications on behalf of clients that contained misleading information relating to their annual income and means of employment.[170] Jonathan Phelan, Head of Retail Enforcement, FSA said:

> "The actions of the these two partners posed a risk to lenders, and banning them supports the FSA's financial crime objective as well as our consumer protection and market confidence objectives. It is part of a wider effort to tackle mortgage fraud, which includes working alongside other authorities such as the police, and acting on information received from lenders and whistleblowers".[171]

In 2008, the FSA has fined and/or banned 12 mortgage brokers for submitting false mortgage applications - Amjad Ali Malik,[172] Tahir Mahmood,[173] Isah Mohammed,[174] Rafiu Akanbi,[175] Erinma Didi Jordan,[176] Byron Brown,[177] Muhammad Adnan Ashraf,[178] Muhammad Asim Iqbal,[179] Mohammed Atif Mayo,[180] Andrew Talai Kiplimo,[181] Mr Keay,[182] Gerard McStravick,[183] Sadia Nasir[184] and Ian Sanderson.[185] In 2007, the FSA only imposed

---

167 *Ibid.*
168 Financial Services Authority, above n 166.
169 Financial Services Authority, Press Release, 'FSA bans mortgage brokers for submitting false loan applications', 21 February 2008, available from www.fsa.gov.uk.
170 *Ibid.*
171 Financial Services Authority, above n 169.
172 Financial Services Authority *Final Notice – Mr Amjad Ali Malik* (London, Financial Services Authority, 2008), available from www.fsa.gov.uk.
173 Financial Services Authority, above n 169.
174 Financial Services Authority *Final Notice – Mr Isah Attayi Mohammed* (London, Financial Services Authority, 2008), available from www.fsa.gov.uk.
175 Financial Services Authority, above n 169.
176 Financial Services Authority Press Release, FSA bans South London mortgage brokers for submitting false loan applications, 9 June 2008, available from www.fsa.gov.uk.
177 *Ibid.*
178 Financial Services Authority, above n 176.
179 *Ibid.*
180 Financial Services Authority, above n 176.
181 Financial Services Authority, Press Release, FSA bans introducer for making false mortgage applications, 5 March 2008, available from www.fsa.gov.uk.
182 Financial Services Authority *Final Notice – Mr John Paul Keay, Trading as Jack Keay Mortgage Services* (London: Financial Services Authority, 2008), available from www.fsa.gov.uk.
183 Financial Services Authority, Press Release, FSA bans Belfast mortgage broker for involvement in fraud, 8 June 2008, available from www.fsa.gov.uk.

five bans were handed down. In 2008, the FSA has prohibited 24 separate brokers and issued fines in excess of £500,000.[186] In the first half of 2009, the level of fines imposed by the FSA has already exceeded this figure.[187] This is clear evidence of the FSA adopting a tougher stance against mortgage fraud. Despite the high levels of fine imposed by the FSA and the ability to ban individuals from offering mortgages, the question that must be asked is why has it taken so long for the FSA to attempt to address the problems associated with mortgage fraud? The FSA clearly prioritized the reduction of money laundering at the expense of other types of financial crime. This tougher stance against mortgage fraud is 'too little to late' and its impact will be minimal with the creation of the NFSA.

Intermediary Fraud Initiative

Another mechanism introduced by the FSA to combat mortgage fraud is an anti-fraud reporting system, which has been referred to as the 'FSA Intermediary Fraud Initiative'. The aim of this scheme is to reduce the extent of mortgage fraud through independent intermediaries. The voluntary scheme has been supported by the CML and has been successfully trialed amongst a number of lenders. The FSA and the CML have agreed anti-fraud reporting criteria, which includes the mortgage provider supplying the FSA with information relating to the name of the intermediary, details of any individuals involved, details of the fraud and evidence, the names of the customers involved and a summary of any investigations. All mortgage lenders have been invited to participate in this voluntary scheme. Doig noted that this is an example of "the FSA encouraging trade associations to work together closely and provide leadership over fraud management".[188] Stephen Bland, Director of FSA's Small Firms Division, said:

> "We very much appreciate the input and co-operation of the CML and lenders in this important initiative. It is the first time we have used information of this type in this systematic way, and it is an example of our strategy of working with the market to supervise small firms working effectively in practice. Mortgage fraud is a serious matter and can lead to criminal proceedings both for intermediaries and mortgage applicants. We are looking to all lenders to help us in the fight against this practice".[189]

Michael Coogan, Director General of the Council of Mortgage Lenders, said:

> "We welcome and support this new, co-ordinated approach to collecting information on fraud. We hope that it will make it easier for the FSA to identify systematic suspicion and act quickly upon it".[190]

---

[184] Financial Services Authority, Press Release FSA bans and fines mortgage broker £129,000 for involvement in mortgage fraud, 7 July 2008, available from www.fsa.gov.uk.
[185] Financial Services Authority, Press Release, FSA fines a mortgage firm £11,900 and bans adviser in relation to false mortgage applications, 15 July 2008, available from www.fsa.gov.uk.
[186] National Fraud Strategic Authority, above n 15, at 16.
[187] BBC, Rising fines for mortgage fraud, BBC news, 20 May 2009, available from www.bbc.co.uk.
[188] Doig, above n 126 at 157.
[189] Financial Services Authority, Press Release, 'FSA and lenders drive to cut mortgage fraud'. 12 April 2006, FSA/PN/039/2006, available from www.fsa.gov.uk.
[190] *Ibid.*

This system is however likely to change with the establishment of the NFSA, as recommended by the Fraud Review.[191] The agency will form an integral part of the government's legislative policy to combat fraud and in March 2007 the government stated that it would establish NFSA in conjunction with a National Fraud Reporting Centre (NFRC). The aim of the NFSA is to "provide the leadership and national coordination needed for anti-fraud efforts to be as effective and efficient as possible. It will provide a managed programme to attack fraud through the entire pipeline of deterrence, prevention, detection, investigation, sanctions and redress for victims".[192] However, its creation must however be questioned because the NFSA will join an already very long list of law enforcement and financial regulatory agencies that aim to tackle financial crime.[193]

Conclusion

Towards the end of the last century money laundering was famously described as the crime of the 1980s and the 1990s. At the start of the new millennium, the mantle was passed from money laundering to the financing of terrorism following the al Qaeda terrorist attacks on the US on September 11th 2001. The financing of terrorism was propelled from resolute obscurity to the top of the international community's financial crime agenda by the ill equipped financial war on terrorism. As we near the end of the first decade of the new millennium, it is bold to argue that mortgage fraud will be the next financial crime of the decade. The extent and frequency of mortgage fraud has been exacerbated by the credit crunch and its full impact is likely to be discussed by both academic commentators and law enforcement agencies long after the completion of this chapter. The US policy towards mortgage fraud has been thrust to the top of the FBI's financial crime strategy. The FBI has been reinvigorated with a generous funding package that will hopefully allow the agency to undertake the necessary investigations into suspected instances of mortgage fraud that have occurred during the credit crunch. The Fraud Enforcement and Recovery Act provide the FBI with an improved arsenal of measures that are aimed to complement the extensive array of statues that criminalise wire fraud, postal and bank fraud. However, it has been argued by some commentators that the offences created by the 2009 Act must be questioned because mortgage fraud was already criminalised by several other statutes. The weakest area of the mortgage fraud policy that must be addressed is the extension of the SARs regime to mortgage providers although questions remain over the general effectiveness of this regime. The overall effectiveness of the policy towards mortgage fraud in the US is extremely difficult to gage. However, it can be concluded that the recent introduction of legislation and the extensive funding guaranteed by federal government have galvanised law enforcement agencies into action. The government has given them the appropriate enforcement tools and they will be under more a higher level of public scrutiny.

In contrast to the measures introduced in the US towards mortgage fraud, the UK's policy has been developed in rather an ad hoc manner. The introduction of the Fraud Act 2006 is a welcome addition to the armoury of prosecutors in the UK and it will hopefully clarify an

---

[191] Attorney General's Office, above n 11, at 2.

[192] *Ibid.*

[193] This includes for example, the Financial Services Authority, the Serious Fraud Office and the Serious Organised Crime Agency.

area of law that has been fraught with difficulties. Furthermore, section 6 FSMA 2000 is an innovative attempt to reduce the impact of financial crime. To date the FSA has been concerned with implementing a risk based policy that aims to prevent and reduce the levels of money laundering. The FSA is beginning to become more actively involved in the prevention of reduction of fraud. The objectives of the risk based policy were two fold. Firstly, to reduce the compliance costs for the regulated sector, and secondly, to lessen the burden on firms. In the first instance, the policy has categorically failed. This is illustrated by a 60% increase in the costs faced by the regulated sector in the last three years. It becomes clear from an examination of the relevant provisions of FSMA that the FSA has extensive investigative and enforcement powers. The FSA has concentrated upon its powers to impose financial sanctions upon the regulated sector. The imposition of financial penalties has had its desired effect, to make the regulated sector comply with the SYSC part of the Handbook. However, it can be concluded that the threat of sanctions has led to a great deal of resentment from the sector and scepticism as to whether the regulations introduced by the FSA are reducing the level of mortgage fraud. The chapter suggests that the success of the enforcement powers could be cynically measured in the total amount of the fine. It is likely that headline figure of a '£2m fine' is politically satisfying to some; it is not a true measure of effectiveness. This chapter concludes that the impact of the policies adopted by the FSA will unfortunately have a minimal impact because organised criminals are using sophisticated methods to commit mortgage fraud.

In: Housing, Housing Costs and Mortgages
Editors: Szilárd Kis and Istvan Balogh, pp. 23-44
ISBN: 978-1-60741-813-9

Chapter 2

VALUATION OF THE IMPACTS OF HOUSING FINANCIAL CRISIS ON LOCAL SUSTAINABLE DEVELOPMENT

***Nava Haruvy*[1,*] *and Sarit Shalhevet*[2,†]**
[1]Netanya Academic College, 1 University Street,
Netanya 42365, Israel
[2]SustainEcon: Environmental Economics Consulting, 126 Thorndike Street,
Brookline, 02446 MA, USA

Abstract

The mortgage crisis in the US has resulted in lower housing costs, as well as greater future income uncertainty. Until the economy recovers from the recession, it is expected that the rate of new buildings will decrease, and the average size of the new houses will be smaller than we have seen during the housing boom, leaving the rural and suburban areas with more open spaces than initially expected, which may be put to beneficial use. At the same time, a reduction in available income and credit, and increased uncertainty regarding future income even among those who have not been affected by the current downturn, have led to reduced spending on everything from luxury goods to food products. Both housing and income uncertainty trends point in the direction of increased crop cultivation by individual households.

For many families in the low and middle-income range, food is a significant part of their total expenses, and a more flexible cost item than other major expenses such as housing and utility costs. This is an especially pronounced problem in fruit and vegetable consumption, as fresh produce tends to be relatively more expensive than "fast foods". As a result, more and more people, especially in rural areas, have begun cultivating crops for self-consumption, or increased their existing level of crop cultivation.

The trend towards increased food self-reliance affects the local sustainable development in many ways, including a variety of social, economic, and environmental impacts. Estimating the monetary value of these impacts is an important tool in regional planning and local policy-making. Economic methods for carrying out these estimates include social impact valuation

* E-mail address: navaharu@netvision.net.il. Tel. 972-52-3611260.
† E-mail address: sarit.shalhevet@gmail.com. Tel. 1-617-8790577.

methods such as the relative housing prices and surveys of willingness to pay to preserve local agricultural crops; and environmental impact valuation methods such as attaching a monetary value to the time lost due to illnesses caused by local environmental impacts. Existing studies show that the value of the social and environmental impacts of local production is much higher than that of the economic impacts; the highest-value social impact is the public benefit from the scenery provided by agricultural crops, which varies greatly by type of crop. As these trends are naturally driven by private economic interests, an economic valuation of the social and environmental impacts of different crops can help local decision-makers to determine how to react to these trends.

Introduction

The mortgage crisis in the US has resulted in lower housing costs, as well as greater future income uncertainty. Until the economy recovers from the recession, it is expected that the rate of new buildings will decrease, and the average size of the new houses will be smaller than we have seen during the housing boom, leaving the rural and suburban areas with more open spaces than initially expected, which may be put to beneficial use. At the same time, a reduction in available income and credit, and increased uncertainty regarding future income even among those who have not been affected by the current downturn, have led to reduced spending on everything from luxury goods to food products. Both housing and income uncertainty trends point in the direction of increased crop cultivation by individual households.

For many families in the low and middle-income range, food is a significant part of their total expenses, and a more flexible cost item than other major expenses such as housing and utility costs. This is an especially pronounced problem in fruit and vegetable consumption, as fresh produce tends to be relatively more expensive than "fast foods". As a result, more and more people, especially in rural areas, have begun cultivating crops for self-consumption, or increased their existing level of crop cultivation. The local and national newspapers, as well as many blogs, have began to report more and more people seeking an increased self-reliance on food supply, especially in fresh produce. The demand for home canning equipment, for example, has increased noticeably, especially in rural areas.

At the same time, on one hand, increased concerns about the impacts of pesticide use on health and about the environmental impacts of food production have raised the level of public preference for fresh produce, and in having organic produce. But on the other hand, the high cost of organic produce has caused even those who consider organic produce as more healthy to compromise by reducing their consumption of organic produce in favor of more conventional produce. These forces increase the attraction of self-grown fresh produce supply even further.

The trend towards increased food self-reliance affects the local sustainable development in many ways, including a variety of social, economic, and environmental impacts. Estimating the monetary value of these impacts is an important tool in regional planning and local policy-making. The economic costs may include the reduced cost of food, but also the value of the additional time spend working on crop cultivation. The value of the social and environmental impacts is harder to estimate, but some economic methods have been developed for carrying out these estimates, including social impact valuation methods such as the relative housing prices and surveys of willingness to pay to preserve local agricultural crops; and environmental impact valuation methods such as attaching a monetary value to the time lost due to illnesses caused by local environmental impacts.

Existing studies show that the value of the social and environmental impacts of local production is much higher than that of the economic impacts; the highest-value social impact is the public benefit from the scenery provided by agricultural crops, which varies greatly by type of crop. As these trends are naturally driven by private economic interests, an economic valuation of the social and environmental impacts of different crops can help local decision-makers determine how to react to these trends.

Research shows that local agricultural crops have social impacts on the local residents, caused by benefits such as noise and temperature reduction, and most of all by the scenic benefits of agricultural crops. These impacts vary greatly by the type of crop. Orchard crops have a high positive effect on people's social amenities, as measured by value of housing as well as by surveys of willingness to pay to preserve local agricultural crops. The valuation varies by type of tree, with spreading, broad-leafed trees such as avocado having the highest value. Field crops have a much lower value, and some field crops that obstruct the scenery, such as corn, do not have any scenic value for the local residents. Growing crops in greenhouses has a negative scenic value and can decrease from the social valuation of the local housing.

Increased local crop cultivation has significant environmental impacts. One of the important impacts is an increase in the use of fertilizers, whose residue can remain in the soil and groundwater for many years. An increase in local pesticide use, machinery and energy use has negative environmental impacts as well. The environmental impacts are measured as the impacts on reducing the average life expectancy, in units of Disability Adjusted Life-Years (DALYs). The monetary valuation of these impacts is calculated based on an estimated value of time, for example, a valuation of health costs and lost income. These impacts are important in measuring the value of local sustainable development, but may differ significantly on the level of global sustainable development, which includes positive impacts such as the reduction in the use of energy for food transportation ("food miles").

Modified Urban Planning

The benefits of urban trees has long been known to urban planners; but urban-agricultural crop cultivation has both positive and negative impacts. Therefore, optimal urban planning should take into account the trend of increased local crop cultivation as an additional component to non-fruit-bearing urban trees. To that aim, our research incorporates different types of planning and impacts into a single urban-agricultural-environmental model:

- Agricultural economic planning: The profit (or household savings) from growing crops, considering the physical limitations of space and other resource availability.
- Urban planning: Includes aesthetic considerations such as scenic value; and physiological considerations such as noise and temperature reduction through increased green spaces. These considerations were incorporating by using the results of research on the physiological impacts of different types of crops on noise and temperature levels; and information on the public preferences for different types of

crops, based on research in psychology, transportation planning, and landscape architecture.

- Environmental planning: Industrial agriculture has developed a reputation as "bad for the environment" because of the extensive use of chemicals that have negative impacts on public health as well as on the air, soil and water resources. The model examined the impact of fertilizers and pesticides on choosing optimal crops, based on existing methods of economic evaluation of environmental impacts (for example see Field, 1994).

The following research examined combinations of agricultural and forestry crops that will optimize either the economic benefits for individuals, or the total public benefits (including both positive and negative impacts on the population), including the tradeoffs between economic and social-environmental impacts. The methodology was based on three components: literature research and interviews; questionnaire for experts in relevant fields; and an optimization model, based mostly on linear planning models for choosing the optimal combination of crops in open area.

Optimization Model for Urban Planning

The model was built in three stage. The first stage was the choice of areas and crops for the case study. The second stage was optimized planning for economic profits; and the third stage incorporated social and environmental impacts and public preferences to reach optimized social benefit planning.

The model in composed of eight sub-models that calculate optimization from different view points. These sub-models are:

- Optimized profits from crop-growing
- Inclusion of positive impacts: noise reduction, temperature reduction, and total positive impacts.
- Inclusion of negative impacts: use of pesticides, fertilizers, and total negative impacts.
- Inclusion of all positive and negative impacts.

Area and Crop Selection

For implementation of the model on a case study area, we chose two areas in central Israel: Elona Regional Council area and Emek Heffer area. The criteria for the choice including areas with land and climate that is suitable for growing a variety of crops, where crops are grown near housing areas, and with a variety of agro-technical, topographical, and urban planning characteristics.

We selected a variety of crops for the case study that would enable to take into consideration a variety of benefit types and interests of the involved parties. The research included a number of orchard types; in most cases, orchards yield the greatest social benefits for the population, but they take a long time to reach a crop-bearing stage, and their planning is relatively inflexible. The research also included a variety of field crops; these crops generally yield few social benefits, but can be grown at lower costs, are more flexible, and can potentially enable the use of wastewater, which is an important environmental consideration. We included several types of vegetables that can be grown either in the open field or in greenhouses. Growing crops in greenhouses is more expensive, and results in large quantities of plastic waste, but has the advantage of higher yield and better quality crops. We also included the option of growing flowers, using gypsophila as a representative local flower. Additionally, we included the alternative options of land use for urban trees or for parks.

Optimization Model Overview

Following the choice of a case study, we constructed an optimization model that calculates the optimal allocation of crops for economic profits, based on economic crop growing budgets. This model was then extended to include social impacts such as scenery and environmental impacts such as increased use of chemicals in household areas.

The target function for the growers is maximizing income; and for society – maximizing the positive social and economic impacts and minimizing the negative ones. The decision variables include the choice of agricultural crops and cultivation methods. The limitations included limits of a reasonable minimum and maximum cultivation area; the parameters included production costs and income, and the possible scenarios included various market conditions and prices for production inputs as well as for the cultivated crops.

When the target function was set as a societal target function that includes the the environmental impacts as well, additional limitations in the model included limitations on the degree of permitted environmental impacts and minimal societal contributions to the local population from each type of social impact.

Types of Impacts

The impacts can be broadly defined under two categories: impacts that are felt mainly by the local population, and impacts that affect a much larger area, and even the entire country, especially in a small country like Israel.

The types of impacts on the immediate geographical surrounding include impacts of the properties of different crop types, such as scenery, blocking noise, impact on temperature, and odor, on the local residents as well as visitors. For example, some crops, like citrus, have scents that are generally considered attractive, while animal husbandry involves scents that are generally disliked. Some crops, especially trees, reduce the level of surrounding noise, while others, like chicken coops, can increase the level of noise in the area. The level of impact depends on the proximity to the residential housing.

The types of impacts on the entire country, or at least on a much larger geographical area, include the impacts of the use of chemicals such as fertilizers and pesticides, and creation and use of wastewater. For example, leaching of nitrogen from fertilizers to the groundwater resources.

Methods for Valuation of the Crops' Impacts

We evaluated the degree of impact of each crop and the economic value of each impact, based on a combination of methods described below.

Methods for Evaluating the Existence of each Impact by Crop

Consultation with experts and questionnaire dissemination. We consulted with experts on open area planning, including experts from the Israeli ministry of environment, and with experts from local regional councils and regional planners. We constructed a questionnaire and conducted several in-depth interviews with decision-makers in these areas. We also consulted with experts on the various types of specific impacts.

- Noise and temperature – use of physiological data. Methods for evaluation the public preferences relate to the existing population, but the decisions made impact future generations as well – preferences of the public may change, but urban trees outlive the existing public (Schiller, 1998). One of the solutions in the use of physiological data, such as the effect of different types of trees on temperature and noise level. For example, experiments measuring the degree of noise blocked by trees found that wide-leaf trees are more effective in blocking noise than needle-leaf type trees (Schiller et al., 2000). Based on consultation with Dr. Schiller, we applied the results of existing research on physiological impacts to estimate the impact of different agricultural crops on the noise and temperature levels.
- Scenic value – we evaluated the public preferences, based on results of surveys in Israel and worldwide on public preferences for different types of scenery.
- Fertilizers – leaching of nitrogen to groundwater. The impact of nitrogen leaching to groundwater was based on previous research, such as Hadas et al., 2000, Harvuy et al., 1999, and Haruvy et al., 2001. Our estimates considered the amount of nitrogen in each type of fertilizer used the the percentage leached to groundwater.
- Pesticides – quantity of active ingredients. Evaluating the damage from pesticides in complex because of the large variety of different chemicals involved, varying levels of exposure and the interactions between different chemicals. Because of the difficulty in directly estimating the damage from pesticides, several proxy variables are often used. Two of the most common are the total amount of active ingredient and the total cost of pesticide use (Swinton and Williams, 1998). More comprehensive evaluations employ the Environmental Impact Quotient (EIQ), which includes the health damage to the farmers and consumers from food consumption as well as from damage to groundwater and the environment. The EIQ is usually directly related to the total amount of active ingredient used.

Methods for Economic Valuation of each Impact

- Willingness-to-pay: We used the results of previous surveys that examined the public willingness to pay for certain characteristics of their environment.
- Hedonic pricing method: There are two main methods to evaluate the impact on housing prices. The first is to ask people such as local residents or real estate agents, and the second is to examine the actual behavior (Field, 1994). An example of the latter method is the hedonic pricing method (HPM). Two types of characteristics impact the price: structural characteristics like the size of the house, the size of the area, and number of rooms; and locational characteristics, which can be positive or negative (Luttik, 2000). Evaluating the impact on housing prices was based on the results of previous research.
- Cost of remediation: We used this method for evaluating the impact of fertilizer use. Ivanier (2001) evaluated the damage to groundwater through the cost of remediation and nitrogen removal. Her research took into consideration two alternative interest rates. In first case, the interest rate was 0 percent, assuming that the weight of future generations is equal to the weight of the present generation, and because the cost of nitrogen removal is already a currently relevant cost, since there has been nitrogen leaching in the area for many years. In the second case, the interest rate was 7.5 percent, and the period of leaching was assumed to be 25 years. In our research we took the first case, of assuming the costs already exist in the present time.
- Total cost of use: We used this method for evaluating the impact of pesticide use. There has been extensive research on the costs of health damages caused to farmers from the use of pesticides (Antle and Pingali, 1994; Pingali et al., 1994; Harper and Zilberman, 1992; Crissman et al., 1994). Some of these examined the relationship between the use of pesticides and complaints relating to known side impacts of these chemicals, and evaluated the cost of medical care of loss of work days as a result of these side effects (Houndekoun and De Groote, 1998). Other researchers evaluated the social benefit to the consumers as a consequence of reducing the use of pesticides, based on willingness to pay surveys (Forster and Mourato, 2000; Fu et al., 1999). These surveys concluded that consumers are aware of the potential damages from pesticides, and are willing to pay more for products that do not include pesticides, in proportion to the amount of damage prevented.

Results

Types of Impacts for Crops by Population Type

Different population groups are impacted differently. In Table 1 we present the impacts on the growers, the local residents, visitors and people who are passing by the area, and the entire country. The type of impact can be positive, varying between + and +++, neutral (0), or negative, varying between - and ---. The number of pluses/minuses represents the degree of influence (minimal, average or large).

Table 1. The impact of each factor on the population

Factor	Growers	Local residents	Visitors	Whole country
Economic value	+	0	0	+ (through employment & prices)
Scenic value	+	+++	++	0
Noise reduction	+	+++	+	0
Temperature reduction	++	+++	+	0
Odors	++	+++	++	0
Fertilizers & Salinity	+++	- - -	- -	- -
Pesticides	+++	- - -	- -	- -
Waste increase	0	- - -	- -	-
Carbon sequestration	+	+	+	+++

Positive Impacts

Lorenzo et al. (2000) conducted a survey in Louisiana on the relative ratings of benefits from urban tress. They concluded that the aesthetic benefits from trees are the most valuable, followed by shade, impact on biodiversity, temperature, privacy, housing value and noise reduction. We examined five of the factors rated as most important: aesthetics (scenery), noise reduction, temperature reduction and shade, and impact on housing prices. These impacts are relevant only for those who at least pass by the area; and excluding scenery, the rest of the impacts are relevant mainly for the local residents.

Noise Reduction

Background

Noise is defined as a sound that is perceived as unpleasant or unwanted by those who hear it. People's sensitivity to noise depends on the noise level, which is measured in decibels (dB), frequency, measured in hertz (Hz), and the context of the sound. For example, scraping nails across a board is a low volume sound that is often perceived as very disturbing, while the loud noise of racing cars is perceived as positive by the viewers (Paulson, 1999). The smallest difference people can feel is about three decibels; and increase of six decibels represents an actual doubling of the noise level, but in practice people perceive an increase of ten decibels as a doubling of the noise level. The level in which hearing may be impaired is 120 – 130 decibels (LaMuth, 1998) and the pain threshold is 130 decibels (Paulson, 1999). A noise level of 140 decibels can cause permanent hearing loss; and alternatively, a constant exposure to a lower level noise of about 85 decibels over a long period of time can also cause permanent hearing loss.

Even at lower levels, noise can have negative impacts such as loss of sleep, reduced productivity, and inconvenience or general annoyance (Levinson, 1996). LaMuth (1998) found that people often rate noise as the main environmental problem factor in their area, sometimes even more than the air pollution and water quality. About a quarter of the population of the European Union report an impairment of their quality of life as a result of noise (EU, 2000).

The Impact of Plants on Noise Reduction

Plant cover has an impact on the noise level. The degree to which plants reduce the level of noise depends on several components: depth of plantation (area); height (a taller plant has a greater impact on noise decrease); density and leaf shape (larger and heavier leaves have greater impact on noise reduction). An orchard with grass cover reduces noise more than an orchard with exposed ground. Every plant reduces noise at different octaves (Levinson, 1996), but this factor was not taken into consideration due to lack of detailed information by crop.

Schiller et al. (2000) examined the level of noise from a source at a fixed noise level in an area free of plants compared with areas with trees of different types. They found that wide-leaf trees have a greater impact on noise reduction than needle-leaf trees, and that leaves closer to ground level increase the degree of noise reduction. Based on the results of these experiments, Dr. Schiller rated the relative degree of noise reduction in the different agricultural crops. The rating depended on several plant parameters: noise, plant height and leaf thickness. For example, avocado trees have a greater impact on noise reduction than plum trees or apple trees, because the leaves of the avocado tree are larger and thicker. We converted Dr. Schiller's relative ratings to actual noise reduction in decibels based on his experiments on forestry trees. The results are presented in Table 2.

Economic Valuation of Noise Reduction

Previous research has evaluated the damage from noise – mainly noise caused by transportation (cars and airplanes). It is difficult to quantify the damage to the population from noise, so the evaluation is usually done based on the hedonic pricing method, examining the reflection of the damage from noise in the housing prices in the area. The commonly used index is the noise depreciation index (NDI), which is the percentage reduction of house price per dB (Levinson, 1996).

There are several limitations in this method. First, the value of the damage depends on the average income per area – the willingness to pay for noise reduction is higher in wealthier populations. Second, the results are biased because beyond a given threshold, people will refuse to buy the house at any price, but this threshold differs for different people (Feitelson et al., 1996).

Research on the impact of noise on housing prices concluded that the total noise from transportation in France is between 0.27 to 0.45 billion dollars, in 1980 prices (Pearce et al., 1984). In more extensive evaluations of the damage, including the impact on housing prices, medical costs, reduces options of land use and cost of lost work days concluded that the annual economic damage from airplanes in the European Union is between 11 to 32 billion dollars (Brussels, 2000).

The level of noise from transportation usually ranges between 50 to 95 decibels (TranSafety, 1997). According to research in the UK, an increase of one decibel in the noise level reduces the value of nearby housing by 0.5 percent. Luttik (2000) found the the noise from transportation in the Netherlands caused a reduction in housing prices by 5 percent. TranSafety publication (1997) quotes research in the US that showed a reduction in housing prices of 0.2 – 0.6 percent for every increase of one decibel in the noise level; and an extensive research in the US that found that housing prices decreased by 0.4 percent for an increase in one decibel of the noise level. Two literature reviews of the impacts of airplane noise on house prices found that an increase of one decibel in the noise level decreases the housing prices by 0.5 – 1 percent (DTLR, 2000). Levinson (1996) summarized a large number of research cases in the US and Europe, and found that the average decrease in housing value is NDI = 0.62.

Based on research in Israel on housing prices (Rosenthal, 1999), we deducted that the reduction in housing value in Israel as a result of an increase of 1 decibel in the noise level would be on average 3825 NIS per house (the exchange rate at the time of the research was approximately 4 NIS = $1). The results in terms of economic value of noise reduction by crop are presented in Table 2.

Table 2. The value of noise reduction by crop: in decibels and in economic value By descending order of monetary value

Crop	Economic value	Noise reduction
	NIS	Decibels
Avocado	19,125	5.0
Eucalyptus	19,125	5.0
Grapefruit	15,300	4.0
Valencia oranges	15,300	4.0
Shamouti oranges	15,300	4.0
Oak	14,344	3.8
Pear	11,475	3.0
Peach	11,475	3.0
Cherry	11,475	3.0
Apricot	11,475	3.0
Plum	11,475	3.0
Apple	11,475	3.0
Pecan	9,563	2.5
Almond	9,563	2.5
Pine	7,650	2.0
Grapevine	7,650	2.0
Olive	7,650	2.0
Park	7,411	1.9
Corn	5,738	1.5
Alfalfa	3,825	1.0
Gypsophila	3,825	1.0
Palm	3,825	1.0
Cotton	3,825	1.0
Cucumber	3,825	1.0
Hay	3,825	1.0
Pasture	3,825	1.0
Combined pasture & field crops	3,825	1.0
Tomatoes	3,825	1.0

Chicken coops, which were not examined here, are considered especially noisy: the level of noise in a chicken coop building during the day ranges between 50 to 90 decibels (Paulson and van Dalfsen, 1999). According to the Israeli ministry of environment, a large percentage of the complaints about noise in rural areas are from poultry farms of different types.

The impact of noise was incorporated in the linear optimization model target function by including the value of the contribution of each crop to the noise reduction, and adding limitations that the crops have to reduce the noise level by at least one decibel on average for the whole area – so that some crops can have a lower impact and others a higher impact, and the average is computed for the whole area. The impact on the housing value is a one-time change, while the model computed annual income. Therefore, the value in the model was computed as the value of the annual income that would have been the result of the increase in housing value, spread over five years at an interest rate of eight percent.

Results

The impact of noise reduction on the value of the housing is larger than the direct economic impact of the crops. In Emek Heffer, the optimized crop allocation when the social impact of noise in included resulted in a significant increase in growing avocado trees, at the expense of field crops and flowers, relative to the optimal crop allocation under economic profit considerations alone. The cost of this reallocation would be on average 3640 NIS per hectare in loss of potential income. In Alona regional council area, since most of the cultivated area was already used for tree plantations, the change in optimal reallocation was minimal, resulting in a small transfer of land from growing persimmon and apples to growing avocado and peaches, with the average profit loss of 30 NIS per hectare.

Temperature Reduction

Background

Plants help to reduce the temperature in the area for three reasons (Urban Vegetation, 1999). First, a decrease in the sun radiation on bodies that are shaded by the plants: the solar energy is partly reflected or absorbed by the plant for photosynthesis. Plants absorb between 60 and 90 percent of the sun's radiation, depending on the plant type and structure. Leaf density is an important component in the plant's ability to absorb radiation. Second, the plant cover changes the type of radiation; the green cover emits less infra-red radiation, reducing the temperature in the parts of the building that face the plants. Third, evapotranspiration processes cause water to evaporate from the land to the atmosphere. The combination of these factors can have a significant impact on total temperature reduction – in Germany the temperature difference between urban areas and nearby parks can is up to seven degrees Celsius (Urban vegetation, 1999).

The benefits of lower temperature are seasonal, and expressed mainly in the summer, and vary by climate. The case study areas in Israel are warm to hot for a large part of the year, so temperature reduction in these areas is more beneficial than in colder climates. Schiller (1998) measured the impact of different crops on the temperature of a given black object under shades of trees of different types and with no plant cover, in different seasons of the year. The measurement was based on the index of thermal comfort, which is a function of temperature, wind speed and humidity. His research examined the degree to which each type of tree reduces the temperature of a black object relative to the same object in an area exposed to direct sunshine. For example, carob trees were found to reduce the body's temperature by six degrees celsius.

The Impact of Plants on Temperature Reduction

Dr. Schiller rated the relative degree of shade and temperature reduction for each crop. We translated the relative rating to actual temperature reduction based on the relationship between the rating of carob trees to their impact on the temperature. The rating of shade provision takes into consideration the actual ability of people to enjoy the shade. For example, the physical structure of avocado trees makes it easier to sit under the tree than the physical structure of a citrus tree does.

Table 3. The value of temperature reduction by crop: in degrees celsius and in economic value. By descending order of monetary value)

Crop	Economic value	Temperature reduction
	NIS	Degrees Celsius
Avocado	1,660	7.5
Oak	1,660	7.5
Grapefruit	1,660	7.5
Valencia oranges	1,660	7.5
Shamouti oranges	1,660	7.5
Pine	1,328	6.0
Olive	1,328	6.0
Carob	1,328	6.0
Pear	996	4.5
Peach	996	4.5
Eucalyptus	996	4.5
Cherry	996	4.5
Palm	996	4.5
Apricot	996	4.5
Pecan	996	4.5
Plum	996	4.5
Almond	996	4.5
Apple	996	4.5
Park	747	3.4
Grapevines	498	2.3
Alfalfa	0	0.0
Gypsophila	0	0.0
Cotton	0	0.0
Cucumbers	0	0.0
Hay	0	0.0
Pasture	0	0.0
Combined pasture & field crops	0	0.0
Tomatoes	0	0.0
Corn	0	0.0

Economic Valuation of Temperature Reduction

Moore (1998) estimated a total national willingness to pay for an change of 4.5 degrees celsius of about 65 billion dollars for the entire US, which translates to $52.55 per person per one degree celsius. The results in terms of economic value of temperature reduction by crop are presented in Table 3.

The temperature change was incorporated into the optimization model by adding the economic value of temperature reduction by crop to the target function, and adding the limitation of a minimal temperature reduction of three degrees celsius on average for the whole area, enabling some crops to contribute less and others more, as long as the minimal condition is reached.

Results

For Emek Heffer, the optimal crop allocation when the plants' impacts on temperature are taken into account are similar to the allocation results when the impact on noise was considered: a significant increase in the area of avocado trees at the expense of field crops and flowers, relative to the allocation based on economic considerations alone. The cost of reallocation in terms of loss of economic income is on average 3360 NIS per hectare. In this case too, the changes of crop allocation in Alona regional council were insignificant.

Scenic Value

The public's preferences for different types of scenery tend to be relatively constant over time. Lindhagen and Horsten (2000) compared surveys of scenery preferences conducted over a period of twenty years and found that there were no significant changes in forestry preferences.

The subject of the public preferences for scenery has been extensive researched by psychologists as well as by landscaper planners. The summary of these research shows the following preferences for different scenery characteristics: Natural scenery is preferable over urban scenery (Ulrich, 1986, Kaplan and Kaplan, 1989, Lamp and Purcell, 1990); a variety of landscapes is preferable to a monotonous landscape (Misgav, 2000) and a variety of plants is preferable to a single plant (Daniel and Shroeder, 1979). The public prefers scenery that includes trees over open space scenery (Brown et al, 1999; Herzon et al., 2000); open low-density planting, although not totally exposed, and scenery with depth and complex arrangements are preferred over a dense plantation (Ulrich, 1986; Kaplan and Kaplan, 1989; Scrinzi and Floris, 2000; Misgav, 2000). There is a preferences for the existence of trails in the area (Brown et al., 1999; Lindhagen and Hornsten, 2000). In pasture areas, the public prefers greater tree cover than the commonly existing coverage (Bullock et al., 1997). Enabling clear visibility of the area is important, and while the shape of the leaves did not matter, the plant height did - the public preference is for medium or tall plants (Scrinzi and Floris, 2000). In cross-cultural studies comparing the preferences between countries, it was universally found that the public prefers tress with expanding round shapes over column and conical shaped trees, as well as trees they are familiar with from their childhood. The relative importance of plan shape is greater than the importance of earlier familiarity with the plant

(Sommer and Summit, 1996; Sommer, 1997). Misgav (2000) surveyed 150 families in Israel and found, in correspondence with the findings in other countries, that the Israeli public prefers planted forested areas over a scenery of low-growing shrubs. The greatest preference was for olive trees, probably due to their local cultural connotations, and the least preferred was the scenery of wild-growing bushes. The public tends to prefer forested, yet carefully designed forests (rather than totally natural ones), that enable depth view and an ability to pass through the area. The least preferred sceneries are the totally open scenery and the dense scenery that does not enable to see through it. Misgav (2000) quotes previous research that shows preference for tall trees, and a scenery with many trees that give the feeling of a shaded area, over sun-exposed areas. High density is liked less than low density due to the visibility limitations and difficulty in passing through the area, but on the condition that the area is not totally exposed. Therefore, the greatest preference is to medium density plantations, followed by low density, and finally by high density areas.

Application to Crop Cultivation in Urban Areas

Field crops that are either low-growing or so tall that the block the visibility through the area would be the least liked by the public. In orchard plantations, a relative thinly spaced planting that enables visibility through the trees and passing through them is preferable. The preference for trees with round and expanding shapes would impact the choice of the preferred crop and lead, for example, to preferring avocado trees over palm trees. The preference for trees that are familiar from one's childhood experience means that optimal planning should take into consideration the crops that have existed over time in that area in creating scenery that would bring the greatest public value. The application of the research results mentioned above to agricultural crop preferences in presented in Table 4.

Valuation of the Scenic Benefit from Agricultural Crops

The scenic benefit includes benefits to visitors and people who are passing by the area, as well as benefits to the local residents. The economic value of the benefits for visitors can be estimated through willingness to pay surveys, or through computing cost of travel expenses, which depends on the number of people who travel to the area and the cost of their travel. The value of the scenery to the local population is calculated by estimating the impact of the scenery on the value of local housing.

Valuation of scenery through the cost of travel: Fleischer and Tzur (1999) surveyed 250 visitors in two areas in Israel. They used surveys to determine the impact of the agricultural scenery on the decision to visit the area, and estimated the cost of the visit depending on where the visitors came from. The concluded that the consumer surplus created by agricultural scenery ranges between $49 to $167 per visitor, depending on the area. The total value of the cost of travel that depended on agricultural scenery was three to seven-fold higher than the economic profits from growing those crops. This value does not have a market price, and does not impact people's decision to grow crops. Therefore, they concluded that in densely populated areas, the optimal area of cultivated land is higher than the existing area in practice.

Table 4. Summary of scenic preferences for different crops. Relative rating ranging from 0 (no scenic value) to 10 (maximum scenic value

Crop	Scenic value
Olive	9.0
Pine	8.0
Oak	8.0
Park	8.0
Avocado	7.0
Grapefruit	6.0
Grapevines	6.0
Cherry	6.0
Valencia oranges	6.0
Carob	6.0
Shamouti oranges	6.0
Pears	5.0
Peaches	5.0
Pasture/low field crops	5.0
Apricot	5.0
Pecan	5.0
Palm	5.0
Almond	5.0
Apple	5.0
Eucalyptus	4.5
Pasture	4.0
Gypsophila	3.0
Palm	3.0
Alfalfa	1.5
Cotton	1.5
Cucumbers	1.5
Hay	1.5
Tomatoes	1.5
Corn	0.5

Valuation of the scenery using the hedonic pricing method (impact on housing prices): Luttik (2000) examined the sales of about 3000 houses in the Netherlands, and found that location is the main determinant of housing prices. Houses at a walking distance (up to 400 meters) from the nearest park received a price premium of six percent, and houses with a view to the park – another eight percent beyond the distance premium, making that a total of fourteen percent price increase for nearby park view. A view of an open space received a price premium of nine percent, and exposure to a view of a variety of sceneries added nine percent to the house price compared with exposure to a monotonous scenery. In contract, view of a building was associated with a price decrease of seven percent. The most significant factor is proximity to water. Proximity of up to one kilometer distance form a lake provided a price premium of seven percent, and a view to the lake added another ten percent over the proximity premium. In a research conducted in Oregon, US, Mahon et al. (2000) found that an increase in the area of nearest wetland by one acre increased the housing price by $24. Decreasing the distance to the nearest water body by 1000 feet increased the house price by $436. The value of the houses was not affected by the type of water body.

Carbon Sequestration

The benefits from carbon sequestration are considered the most important public benefits from forests (Crabtree, 2000), and forests are considered the most economically efficient method for reduction carbon emissions (De Jong et al., 2000). Freeman (2001) calculated the total carbon dioxide emissions and sequestration for forests by type of tree in Israel.

Summary of Public Benefits from Agricultural Crops

A qualitative summary of the contribution of different crops in Emek Heffer shows a high scenic value of olive trees, avocado and citrus trees, followed by the other types of orchards. The contribution of grapevines is lower, because of its low impact on noise and temperature reduction. Pasture has a medium contribution, which springs mainly from its scenic value. Field crops have the lowest contribution to public welfare. When the current crop allocation is compared with the optimization models for maximizing profits and maximizing public benefits.

The results of the optimization model showed that considering the economic aspect alone would lead to a recommendation to increase the areas dedicated to flower growing as much as possible. When the social impacts are taken into account, the results of the model lead to the recommendation to decrease the flower cultivation area, and increase the area devoted to avocado trees beyond the level of its optimal economic profitability.

Negative Environmental Impacts

The damage to society and the environment from using pesticides for crop cultivation in the US is estimated as 2.2 billion dollars a year; this in addition to the direct expenses of four billion dollars on the pesticides themselves (Pimental et al., 1993). The public awareness of the subject has been gradually increasing; surveys of recreational forestry usage conducted over the past twenty years detected a trend of increasing objection to the use of pesticides and fertilizers (Lindhagen and Horsten, 2000).

The main damage from pesticide usage is incurred by the people using the pesticides and those living in the nearby houses. The Israeli ministry of environment had concluded that there should be a distance of 100 – 150 meters from the area of pesticide use to the nearest residential housing, to prevent damage from wind blowing over pesticide residuals.

There are many different types of pesticides with different active ingredients at different risk levels. Direct assessment of the damage from each pesticide is very expensive, so in many cases proxy variables are used to assess the pesticide's environmental impact. The two most important indices are using the quantity of active ingredient per hectare, and using the total costs on pesticides as an indicator of the level of risk; there is a high correlation of approximately 0.7 between these two variables (Swinton and Williams, 1998).

To incorporate the damage from pesticides in the optimization model, we added the cost of pesticide use to the target function (which is set as maximum profit and minimum use of pesticides), and added a limitation on the maximal expenditures on pesticides allowed.

Similarly, to incorporate the damage from fertilizers in the optimization model, we added the cost of remediation to the target function, and added a limitation on the maximal expenditures on treating the nitrogen leaching to groundwater. As the model accounts for the negative environmental impacts by assuming that all the nitrogen from fertilizers that reaches the groundwater must be removed, this is the equivalent of adding a limitation on the total quantity of fertilizer used.

Adding limitations on the damage from pesticides or from fertilizers changes the optimal allocation, increasing the relative area of field crops at the expense of orchards. These adaptations, especially in the case of pesticide damage limitations, reduce the income from the crops by up to 40 percent as compared with the income under the optimal allocation when only economic considerations are taken into account.

Combination of all Social and Environmental Impacts

The final stage was calculating the results of the optimization model when all factors are taken into account – the economic, social and environmental impacts of crop production. The optimal allocation in this case would reduce the income to the growers by 12,310 NIS per hectare, compared with the optimal allocation under economic considerations alone.

The results of the optimization model under the variety of possible considerations are presented in Table 5 and Table 6, for the case study area of Emek Heffer. The results in Table 5 are shown in term of area allocations under the initial, current starting conditions (0), as compared with the optimal allocation for maximizing the growers' profits (A); the optimal allocation when the impact of different crops on noise reduction is taken into account (B.a); when the impact on temperature change is taken into account (B.b), and when all the positive social impacts of crops are taken into account (B.c). The optimal allocation is also shown for the case when the environmental impact of pesticide use for growing each crop is taken into account (C.a); when the impact of fertilizer use is taken into account (C.b); and when both environmental impacts are taken into account, but still not considering the social impacts (C.c). The results for the optimization model when all social, economic and environmental considerations are taken into account are presented in column D.

The results in Table 6 show the economic implications of the results in Table 5. The first rows show the profits to the growers under the current allocation (0); and for each of the options for optimal allocation in the paragraph above in comparison to the current allocation (0) and to the allocation under conditions of maximum profits (A). The following rows show the monetary valuation of the benefits to society under each option, for the current allocation, optimal allocation as compared with current allocation and as compared with allocation under conditions of maximum profits.

Table 5. Optimal crop allocation under different considerations (hectares per crop)
Case study area of Emek Heffer

Total impacts	Optimal allocation under environmental impact considerations*			Optimal allocation under social impact considerations*			Maximum profits	Initial conditions	Crop
	Total environmental impacts	Fertilizers	Pesticides	Total social impacts	Temperature reduction	Noise reduction	Profits to growers	Current allocation	
D	C.c	C.b	C.a	B.c	B.b	B.a	A	0	Model
386	386	385	386	385	385	386	386	771	Cotton
119	119	119	318	359	365	359	436	239	Corn
1627	1932	1865	1462	1444	1442	1444	1423	1275	Corn for animal feed
175	175	175	175	175	175	175	175	351	Corn for silage
37	98	221	97	37	51	37	221	74	Gypsophila
13	13	13	13	13	13	13	13	26	Open-field tomatoes
26	26	26	26	26	26	26	26	52	Greenhouse tomatoes
1	1	1	1	1	1	1	1	2	Open-field cucumbers
56	56	56	56	56	56	56	56	112	Greenhouse cucumbers
139	139	139	139	139	139	139	139	278	Shamouti oranges
80	80	80	80	80	80	80	80	160	Valencia oranges
108	108	108	108	108	108	108	108	216	Grapefruit
50	50	50	50	8	8	8	8	17	Alfalfa
1039	1011	954	1283	1361	1343	1361	1120	584	Avocado
37	37	37	37	37	37	37	37	74	Pecan
338	0	0	0	0	0	0	0	0	Recreational forest
0	0	0	0	0	0	0	0	0	Parks

* Each column shows the optimal allocation when only the impacts mentioned at the top of the column are included in the optimization model.

Table 6. Profits under each allocation (NIS/hectare/year)
Case study area of Emek Heffer

Total impacts	Optimal allocation under environmental impact considerations*			Optimal allocation under social impact considerations*			Maximum profits	Initial conditions	Crop
	Total environmental impacts	Fertilizers	Pesticides	Total social impacts	Temperature reduction	Noise reduction	Profits to growers	Current allocation	
D	C.c	C.b	C.a	B.c	B.b	B.a	A	0	Model
Profits for the growers*									
-2730	5230	8130	6660	5930	5750	5480	9570	460	Total
-3190	4780	7670	6200	5480	5300	5020	9120		Difference from initial state
-12310	-3880	-990	-2460	-3640	-3360	-3640			Difference from profit maximization state
Profit for society*									
82480	-14040	-420	-2470	86280	5490	81250			Initial (current) allocation
93880	2650	7880	4770	111910	12850	105200			Under profit maximization (A)
11400	16690	8300	7240	25630	7360	23950			Difference

* Each column shows the profits when only the impacts mentioned at the top of the column are included in the optimization model.

Conclusion

The importance of open spaces and local agriculture extends far beyond their economic profitability. A large scope of previous research supports the same conclusion as the conclusion from our model, that most of the economic value of agricultural production stems from its social benefits rather than from its direct profits.

The trend of increasing urban gardening and self-food production is generally geared towards the short-term crops, such as herb and vegetable gardening. The optimization model, however, shows that the greatest total welfare to the local population would result from increasing orchard tree crops, beyond the level of their optimal planning for maximum economic profits. Furthermore, the benefit to the local residents varies by type of tree, and is higher for trees with large leaves and wide, spreading shapes, such as avocado trees.

As the research was applied on case studies in Israel, its results would be somewhat different in other countries. However, most of the components of scenic preferences are universal, and have been found to be very similar in the cross-cultural studies quoted in this chapter. One major change may be caused by the factor of "traditional crops" which vary between countries, so that the value of citrus and olive trees, for example, may be higher in Israel than in some other countries due to local cultural factors. Applying the model to optimized urban agriculture in other countries should take into consideration the local climate and the local cultural preferences and their impacts on the relative scenic preferences for different crops.

References

Brown, T. J., Kaplan, R, & Quaderer, G. (1999), Beyond accessibility: Preference for natural areas. *Therapeutic Recreation Journal*, **33**, 209-221.

Brussels (2000), *Deafening Response to Dutch Green's Noise Proposals*. http://ens.lycos.com/ens/oct2000/2000-L-10-20-11.html

Bullock, C. H., & May, J. (1997). Preservation and change in the upland landscape: the public benefits of grazing management. *Journal of Environmental Planning & Management,* **40**, 315-334.

Crabtree, J. R. (2000). a book review of: Steward-Roper, C, Parks, A, (eds). The Living Forest: Non Market Benefits of Forestry. *Forestry,* **73**, 209.

Daniel & Schroeder (1979). Scenic beauty estimation model: predicting perceived beauty of forest landscapes. In: Elsner, G. H., S& Mardon, R. C. (eds), *Our National Landscape*, A Conference on Applied Techniques for Analysis and Management of the Visual Resource, 23-25 April, Nevada, pp. 514-523.

De Jong, B. H. J., Tipper, R., & Montoya-Gomez, G. (2000). An economic analysis of the potential for carbon sequestration by forests: evidence from Southern Mexico. *Ecological Economics,* **33**, 313-27.

Deller, S. C., Tsung-Hsiu S. T., Marcouiller D. W., & English, D. B. K. (2001). The Role of Amenities and Quality of Life in Rural Economic Growth. *American Journal of Agricultural Economics,* **83**, 352-365.

DTLR. (2000). *Valuing the External Costs of Aviation.* Department of the Environment, Transport and the Regions, Transport local government regions, UK. http://www.aviation.detr.gov.uk

E.U. (2000). *Proposal for a Directive of the European Parliament and of the Council, Relating to the Assessment and Management of Environmental Noise.* Commission of the European Communities Report 2000/0194(COD).

Feitelson, E. I., Hurd, R. E., & Mudge, R. R. (1996). The Impact of Airport Noise on Willingness to Pay for Residences. *Transportation Research, Part D: Transport & Environment,* **1**, 1-14.

Field, B.C. (1994). *Environmental Economics - An Introduction.* New York: McGraw-Hill Inc.

Fleischer, A., & Tsur, Y. (1999). *Measuring the Recreational Value of Agricultural Landscape. Working Paper* No. 9911, The Center for Agricultural Economic Research, Rehovot, Israel.

Freeman, D. (2001). *A Model for Analysis of the Impacts of Activities for Environmental Preservation in Agriculture and Forecasts for Emek Heffer.* Report submitted to the Israeli Ministry of Agriculture, Bet Dagan, Israel.

Hadas, A., Hadas, A., Sagiv, B., & Haruvy, N. (2000). Agricultural practices, soil fertility management modes and resultant nitrogen leaching rates under semiarid conditions. *Agricultural Water Management,* **42**, 81-95.

Haruvy, N., Offer, R., Hadas, A., & Ravina, I. (1999). Wastewater irrigation- economic concerns regarding beneficiary and hazardous effects of nutrients. *Water Resources Management,* **13**, 303-314

Haruvy, N., Hadas, A., Ravina, I., & Shalhevet, S. (2000). Cost assessment of averting groundwater pollution. *Water, Science & Technology,* **42**, 135-140

Haruvy, N., Shalhevet, S., & Yaron, D. (2001). Effect of urban development on water quality - environmental concerns. *International Water & Irrigation,* **21**, 24- 32.

Herzon, T. R., Herbert, E. J., Kaplan, R., & Crooks, C.L. (2000). Cultural and developmental comparisons of landscape perceptions and preferences. *Environment & Behavior,* **32**, 323-246.

Ivanier, I. (2001). *M.Sc. in Environmental Science.* The Hebrew University in Jerusalem, Israel.

Kaplan, R., & Kaplan, S. (1989). *The Experience of Nature: A Psychological Perspective.* Cambridge: Cambridge University Press.

LaMuth, C. (1998). *Community Development: Noise.* The Ohio State University Fact Sheet CDFS-190-198.

Lamp, R. J. & Purcell, A.T. (1990), Perception of naturalness in landscape and its relationships to vegetation structure. *Landscape and Urban Planning,* **19**, 333-352.

Levinson, D. M., Gillen, D. & Kanafani, A. (1996),.*The Social Costs of Intercity Transportation: A Review and Comparison of Air and Highway*, University of California at Berkeley.

Lindhagen, A. & Hornsten, L. (2000). Forest recreation in 1977 and 1997 in Sweden: changes in public preferences and behavior. *Forestry,* **73**, 143-153.

Lorenzo, A. B., Blanche, C. A., Qi, Y., & Guidry. M. M. (2000). Assessing Residents' WTP to preserve the community urban forest: A small-city case study. *Journal of Aboriculture,* **26**, 319-337

Luttik, J. (2000). The value of trees, water and open space as reflected by house prices in the Netherlands. *Landscape and Urban Planning,* **48**, 161-167.

Mahan, B. L., Polasky, S., & Adams, R. M. (2000). Valuing urban wetlands: A property price approach. *Land Economics,* **76**, 100-113.

Misgav, A. (2000). Visual preference of the public for vegetation groups in Israel. *Landscape and Urban Planning,* **48**, 143-159.

Moore, T.G. (1998). Health and amenity effects of global warming, *Economic Inquiry,* **36**, 471-488.

Paulson, S., & van Dalfsen, B. (1999). *Management of Noise on Poultry Farms*. Ministry of Agriculture and Food, British Columbia.

Pearce, D., Barde, J. P., Lambert. J. (1984). Estimating the cost of noise pollution in France. *Ambio.,* **13**, 27-28.

Pimental, D., McLaughlin, L., Zepp, A., Lakitan, B., Kraus, T., Kleinman, P., Vancini, F., Roach, W. J, Graap, E., Keeton, W.S., & Selig, G., (1993). Environmental and economic impacts of reducing US agricultural pesticide use. In: Pimental, D., & Lehman, H .(eds). *The Pesticide Question: Environment, Economics and Ethics*, NY: Chapman and Hall, 1993, pp. 223-278.

Rosenthal, G., Efrati, S., Nezer-Ben Harim, A., & Zaban, S. (1999). *Ramat Hanadiv Surroundings: Trends in Economic Development and Policy Tools for Preservation of the Open Spaces*. Ramat Hanadiv, Israel: Yad Hanadiv Foundation Report.

Schiller, G. (1998). Using physiological indices in forestry planning for recreational purposes. *Ecology and Environment,* **5**, 34-44.

Schiller, G., Shaudinitzky, L. H., & Keller, I. (2000). Noise and plantation. *Ecology and Environment*, **6**, 53-57.

Scrinzi, G. & Floris, A. (2000). Featuring and modeling forest recreation in Italy. *Forestry,* **73**, 173-185.

Sommer, R. (1997). Further cross-national studies of tree form preference. *Ecological Psychology,* **9**, 153-160.

Sommer, R., & Summit, J. (1996). Cross-national rankings of tree shape. *Ecological Psychology,* **8**, 327-341.

Swinton, S. M., Williams, M. B., (1998). *Assessing the Economic Impacts of Integrated Pest Management: Lessons from the Past, Directions for the Future.* Staff Paper 98-12, Department of Agricultural Economics, Michigan State University, East Lansing, Michigan.

TranSafety, Inc. (1997). *Factors that Determine the Reduction in Property Values Caused by Traffic Noise.* Road Engineering Journal, October.

Ulrich, R. S. (1986). Human responses to vegetation and landscape, *Landscape and Urban Planning,* **13**, 26-44.

Urban Vegetation. (1999). *The Urban Heat Isles and the Micro-Climatic Variations Brought About by Vegetation.* http:// www.mybestlife.com

In: Housing, Housing Costs and Mortgages
Editors: Szilárd Kis and Istvan Balogh, pp. 45-62
ISBN: 978-1-60741-813-9

Chapter 3

EFFECTS OF BLACKLISTING ON HOUSING PRICES: AN EMPIRICAL STUDY IN HONG KONG

***Yung Yau*[1]**

Department of Public and Social Administration,
City University of Hong Kong, Hong Kong

Abstract

Hong Kong has long suffered from the problem of building dilapidation, particularly in the old districts. Other than stricter enforcement against irresponsible homeowners and intensive public education campaigns, the local government initiated to solve the problem via an incentive approach. In November 2000, the government announced publicly a list of poorly-performing buildings, hoping that the property owners would be motivated to undertake building repair or refurbishment by market forces. As the literature suggested, physical conditions of residential properties, particularly those concerning communal areas and services, might not be fully priced by the market due to information asymmetry. It is envisaged that additional information pumped into the housing market will alter the price gradient between high-quality and low-quality properties as the purchasers will undertake self-protection behaviours in view of the risks associated with the poorly-performing properties. This study aims to empirically examine whether public knowledge of poor conditions of apartment buildings affected the sale prices of these properties based on an analysis of panel data in Hong Kong. Yet, the analysis results showed that properties in blacklisted buildings were not transacted at a discount, compared with those in non-blacklisted buildings before the blacklisting exercise, and the release of public information about the blacklist did not create a relative diminution of the property prices of the blacklisted buildings. Policy implications follow.

Keywords: Apartment properties; hedonic price analysis; information asymmetry; public information; building dilapidation; self-protection

---

[1] E-mail address: y.yau@cityu.edu.hk. Department of Public and Social Administration, City University of Hong Kong, 83 Tat Chee Avenue, Kowloon Tong, Kowloon, Hong Kong.

Introduction

Although housing or residential built environment is an artificial invention of human, it strongly affects human's well-being. Regardless the strong belief in the existence of a direct linkage between housing quality and life quality (e.g. Smith *et al.*, 1988; Muoghalu, 1991; Perry & Felce, 1995), people who attach importance to the quality of their living built environment before catastrophes happen are still the minority. This myopia was vividly illustrated in the outbreak of the Severe Acute Respiratory Syndrome (SARS) in early 2003. Prior to that dreadful epidemic, most homeowners in Hong Kong did not take care of the drainage systems in their buildings. Only after the painful lesson of the SARS outbreak,[2] people started recognizing the essentiality of keeping both the fabrics and services of housing in serviceable conditions. In fact, many buildings in Hong Kong have run into a state of disrepair, which has been well-documented in the Housing, Planning and Lands Bureau (2003), Leung & Yiu (2004) and Yau *et al.* (2008). There exist a number of approaches to tackle the problem of building dilapidation in Hong Kong. For example, the imposition of heavier punishments and strengthening of enforcement actions against homeowners who ignore building care may effectively deal with the problem; social unrest is likely resulted. Propaganda and public education on the importance of building care is certainly a more socially acceptable way-out but its effects become apparent only in the long term.

Other than these approaches, the government attempted to deployed incentives created by the market forces. As early as in April 1997, the Hong Kong government implemented a voluntary Building Safety Inspection Scheme (BSIS) in which building owners of their own accords might appoint qualified building professionals to evaluate the safety performance of their buildings and carry out necessary remedial works as suggested by the professionals (Buildings Department, 2005). After completion of the inspection and remedial works, the Buildings Department would issue a letter of acknowledgement to the owners. It was the government's envision that buildings joining the scheme would receive a good label so their asset and rental values would be enhanced, and more favourable mortgage terms and insurance premiums could be attracted (Buildings Department, 2005).

To optimize the incentive approach, the Housing, Planning and Lands Bureau (2005) proposed a Voluntary Building Classification Scheme (VBCS) after the outbreak of the SARS in 2003. Under the VBCS, buildings would be evaluated and classified with reference to their physical conditions and management characteristics using a predetermined assessment protocol. It was envisaged that good rating received for a building would again be translated into lower insurance premiums, more favourable mortgage terms and thus higher property value. These potential economic gains offer incentives to people to invest in building repair and maintenance. However, incentive approach of such type works only when new information on building information becomes available in the housing market for decision making. Certainly, the availability of new information is only a necessary but not sufficient condition for the effective implementation of the incentive approach. Another necessary condition is that excellent (or poor) building condition is valued by the market.

From the above, the BSIS and the proposed VBCS show their significance if the housing market currently cannot efficiently price building conditions, and needs new information to

[2] The SARS outbreak resulted in 1,755 probable cases of infection and 296 deaths in Hong Kong (World Health Organization, 2003).

be supplied. As analytically suggested by Chau *et al.* (2004) and Lützkendorf & Speer (2005), information asymmetry might bring about the failure of the second-hand housing market in taking property conditions into full consideration in property pricing. However, empirical evidence supporting the argument has been lacking. Besides, whether release of public information on building conditions affects housing value has not been addressed in the existing body of knowledge. Against such backdrop, this study aims to investigate whether public knowledge about poor conditions of domestic buildings in Hong Kong creates measurable effect on the sale prices of the properties in these buildings. A good opportunity for investigation is offered by the blacklisting exercise by the Hong Kong government in November 2000 to condemn the homeowners of 150 buildings for letting their buildings run into dereliction. By means of hedonic price analysis, the author found no significant difference in the selling prices between properties in blacklisted buildings and those in non-blacklisted ones before the release of the building blacklist by the local government. Besides, the release of public information on the blacklist was found to create no change in the price differential between blacklisted and non-blacklisted properties. These results bear noteworthy policy implications regarding building care in Hong Kong.

This article is organized as follows. The theoretical framework bridging the relationship between housing value diminution and the government's blacklisting action is presented in next section. Then, the methodology of the research is detailed and the data are described. Afterwards, results of the analyses are displayed. The analysis results and their implications are discussed before the article is concluded.

Theoretical Framework on Housing Value Diminishment by Blacklisting

To explain the potential effect of the government's blacklisting exercise on housing price, it is useful for one to understand the relationship between condition and price of housing. As asserted by Feijtem & Mulder (2005), value or price has been an ideal measurement of housing quality. In spite of the absence of any empirical support provided by the two scholars, the assertion can still serve as a good starting point for the investigation into the link between these two variables.

Relationship between Property Condition and Property Value

Beyond any reasonable doubt, housing is a composite good, i.e. a good with multiple characteristics, because of different definable attributes such as accessibility, size, and orientation and building condition it possesses. This very nature of housing suggests it should not be valued as if it is a direct object of utility. Founded on Lancaster's (1966) seminal utility theory on composite goods, value of a property can be measured with reference to the property's characteristics since he believed that utility was derived from the characteristics of the goods, and not the goods themselves. In this sense, the value of a composite good should be the sum of the values of its constituent characteristics or featuring attributes. With the application of this concept, literature on the values or implicit prices of various inborn property characteristics like floor level, location, size and service provision is profuse (e.g.

Mok, 1995; So *et al.*, 1997, Yiu & Wong, 2005). Besides, there exists a large body of literature on property value differentials created by external characteristics of housing such as air quality and quietness (e.g. Smith & Deyak, 1975; Espey & Lopez, 2000).

As far as building quality or condition is concerned, Arens (1997) thought that the values of properties with significant physical defects, like cracked slabs or subsoil subsidence, should be discounted with a view to the potential costs of remediation, additional vacancies and extra insurance premiums and monitoring costs. This contention has been widely proven by previous empirical studies. For example, Jimenez (1983) evidenced that price premiums were added to properties with better building conditions in Manila, the Philippines. In northern California of the United States, the presence of substandard structural items in a property was also observed by Murdoch *et al.* (1993) to negatively affect the price of the property. In other literature, physical conditions of dwellings or major building elements (e.g. toilet, kitchen and roof) were often incorporated into hedonic price analyses as dummy variables or indices to control the condition-dependent variations in housing prices (e.g. Butler, 1982; Gamble & Downing, 1982; Kask & Maani, 1992; Bourassa & Peng, 1999). Rather consistently, these variables were found to have statistically significant impacts on property prices. Sometimes, changes in property conditions are implied by some observable acts such as property refurbishment and renovation. For instance, Chau *et al.* (2003) showed that properties in refurbished apartment buildings were sold at a higher price, compared with those not refurbished. In their hedonic price study on two conjoining housing estates in Hong Kong, they discovered an approximately nine percent rise in property values brought about by the refurbishment, signifying a significant positive association between building conditions and housing value.

Self-protection Behaviours in the Housing Market

Although the empirical studies mentioned above provided unambiguous evidence on the condition-value relationship of housing, they did not explain why value diminishment would be caused by poor property conditions. To address this issue, hints can be dug out from the conception of self-protection first put forward by Ehrlich & Becker (1972). In their classic paper, a state-preference model was devised to explain individuals' behaviours under uncertainty using elementary concepts such as indifference curve and expected utility. In their model, there are two states of the world in their model: good state (or well-endowed state) and bad state (or less well-endowed state). In plain words, a bad state is a situation in which an individual suffers a loss, and examples of bad state include fire outbreak, earthquake and collapse of building. When encountering a prospective loss in a bad state, an individual can choose to insure against this loss, or take steps to lower the likelihood that the loss will occur.[3] The latter approach is called self-protection which essentially refers to efforts to reduce the probabilities of bad states given the magnitudes of the corresponding prospective losses.

In the housing market, self-protection behaviours by homebuyers are often observed. For example, flooding creates substantial losses to homeowners in many places in Australia and the United States. In face of the potential losses, homebuyers self-protect themselves by purchasing a house at a discount if the house is located within a flood-prone area if they choose not to take out any insurance policy to indemnify their losses brought about by flooding, or if they would like to ask for a premium cut from insurance companies for the reduced flooding risk.[4] Several hedonic price studies previously examined the values of self-protection measures, like relocating out of harm's way so as to reduce the probability of a loss from a natural hazard, in the housing market. For example, domestic properties located outside earthquake-prone areas in Los Angeles and San Francisco in the United States were found to be sold at a premium (Brookshire *et al.*, 1985). Homes situated outside a floodplain in Baton Rouge of the United States were sold at higher prices than those within the floodplain (Shilling *et al.*, 1985). The same value enhancement effect of self-protection against flooding was also found in other parts of the United States (e.g. MacDonald *et al.*, 1987; Donnelly, 1989; Speyrer & Ragas, 1991).

Besides, findings in other studies concerning human-made hazards manifested that self-protection mitigations were priced in property transactions as well. In the literature, dwelling were found to have higher selling prices when they were sited beyond the influence of potentially hazardous facilities, such as chemical plants (Carrol *et al.*, 1996), landfills (Nelson *et al.*, 1992), and gas pipes (Kask & Maani, 1992).[5] Following this line of thought, buildings with poor conditions entail a higher risk of accident, and thus properties in these buildings should be sold at a lower price, compared with those in well-serviced buildings.

Building Condition and Information Asymmetry

At this stage, perfect information regarding the risks associated with a dwelling was assumed to be available in the housing market. Such information was disseminated via various means, ranging from visual inspection to word of mouth. However, hazards that may adversely affect properties and humankinds are sometimes uncovered until relevant information is disclosed by other parties (e.g. the government or other agencies). For instance, Bernknopf *et al.* (1990) found that after the government's announcement of the hazards regarding earthquake and volcano activities in the Mammoth Lakes area in the United States in the early 1980s, housing prices in that area dropped. Similar results were obtained by Montz (1993) in his study on the effect of the disclosure of flooding risk in New Zealand on housing price. Apart from those studies on natural hazards, there exists plentiful empirical

---

[3] As suggested by Ehrlich & Becker (1972), there is a third alternative in which the individual takes steps to reduce the size of prospective loss from a bad state, given the probability of the occurrence of the bad state.

[4] Self-protection complements market insurance if the latter is available at an actuarially fair rate. To reduce the risk of moral hazard, the premiums of market insurance should reflect truly the amount of self-protection undertaken by an individual for lowering the probability of loss. Any efforts of self-protection perceived to be effective are recompensed by the market in the form of lower premiums. However, as pinpointed by Ehrlich & Becker (1972), the complementary relationship between market insurance and self-protection depends critically on the responsiveness of the premiums of market insurance to the amount of self-protection undertaken by individuals. Also, the efforts paid for self-protection should be observable to market participants.

[5] One should be mindful that locating a residence in the face of hazards is not always self-protective behaviour. For example, locating a residence farther away from the shoreline is a means of self-insurance, but rather for the flood and storm damage in the costal area. This is because the chance of a flood or storm is not reduced by such a location-choice decision. On the other hand, it is a self-protection if a house is sited outside an earthquake-prone zone because the probability of an earthquake in the region where the house is located is lower. In many cases, however, the distinction between these two alternatives is subtle.

research examining the effect of public information about health risk on housing price. For example, Kohlhase (1991) evidenced that health risk associated with a property's proximity to a Superfund site in the United States was not priced by the market until a public announcement about the health risk was made by the local government. Similarly, Gayer *et al.* (2002) studied whether the government's release of information about cancer risks created by hazardous wastes affect the prices of dwellings subject to health risks of different degrees. They found that after the publicity of the new health-risk information, housing in sites with relatively lower risks was sold at a higher price.

Likewise, information on building conditions available in the housing market is rarely perfect. Owing to the problem of information asymmetry,[6] differentials in the conditions among buildings may not be fully observed and reflected in property prices. This situation may be apparent in the second-hand housing market because the sellers, in most cases, grasped more information about the conditions of their properties than the buyers (Chau *et al.*, 2004; Ho *et al.*, 2005). In the absence, the statutory requirement for full disclosure of building information, the seller of a second-hand property may not willingly divulge the defects in the property. The potential buyer cannot easily notice the hidden defects, particularly those connected to common parts or facilities of a building, during a pre-transaction visit or inspection. These defects, including blockage in drainage system and water seepage from the external wall, can be revealed only after prolonged occupation in the property. In this case, second-hand properties are usually sold at a price higher than the reasonable quality-adjusted level. Yet, empirical studies on information asymmetry in the second-hand housing market have been lacking.

Impacts of Information Release on Housing Market

Additional new information pumped into the housing market is crucial for alleviating the problem of information asymmetry in the housing market. However, how does the new information change housing value? To better answer this question, housing is considered a differentiate bundle, H, of various attributes such as size, floor level, condition, amenity facility, accessibility and neighbourhood quality. To put it another way, H is a vector of housing attributes. Assuming that the housing market is perfectly efficient, sellers and buyers have perfect information about all attributes in the housing bundle H of every dwelling in the market. For a particular dwelling d, its equilibrium price, $p(H)$, is generated through the interactive dynamics between consumers' utility-maximization and producers' cost-minimization, and each housing attribute in the bundle is priced implicitly in $p(H)$. The implicit price of housing attribute i can be derived as the partial derivative of $p(H)$ with respect to that attribute. Mathematically,

$$p_{hi}(H) = \frac{\partial p}{\partial h_i} \tag{1}$$

[6] The seller and buyer of a good share identical information about the good in an ideal mode of trade. That means information on the good is symmetric between both parties, be they equally informed or equally uninformed. In reality, nevertheless, markets that allow for such an ideal mode of trade are rare because informational asymmetries of various degrees often exist (Akerlof, 1970; Ong & Brown, 2001; Lützkendorf & Speer, 2005). It is very typical to have sellers knowing more about the goods they sell than buyers.

where $p_{hi}(H)$ denotes implicit price function which is equal to the marginal willingness to pay for a marginal increment in housing attribute *i*. Yet, information is, in reality, imperfect in the housing market. Once the assumption of perfect information is relaxed, the new equilibrium price function, $p(\hat{H})$, is contingent on $\hat{H}$, i.e. the levels of the attributes perceived by the market players. The market players' perceptions depend to a large extent on the availability of information about the attributes in the market. Without the loss of generality, $\hat{h}_j$, the perceived level of housing attribute *j*, is taken as a function of the extent of public knowledge, θ, about the attribute capitalized in the equilibrium price function. Mathematically,

$$\hat{h}_j = g(h_j, \theta) \qquad (2)$$

where h_j is the actual level of housing attribute *j*, and θ falls between 0 and 1. From this function, an attribute cannot be capitalized if its information is completely unknown to the public because $\hat{h}_j = g(h_j, 0) = 0$. At the other extreme which is an ideal situation with perfect information in the market (i.e., $\theta = 1$), the perceived and actual levels of housing attribute *j* coincide such that $\hat{h}_j = g(h_j, 1) = h_j$. This analytical framework suggests that the implicit price for attribute *j* depends on two factors, namely i) the actual level of the attribute and ii) the level of public information about the attribute. Following this line of thought, it is envisaged that the publicity of information about a certain housing attribute to the market changes the implicit price of that attribute unless such information has already been capitalized.

Methodology and Data

To reiterate, the aim of this study is to appraise the effect on property price created by the release of public information about building dilapidation. The housing market in Hong Kong is studied following the theoretical framework detailed above. With a view to the acute problem of building decay in the city, the Hong Kong government announced officially on 4 November 2000 that statutory actions would be carried out against 150 buildings that were seriously dilapidated in the opinion of the Building Authority. It was the intention of the government to coercively make the owners of these buildings to carry out comprehensive repair works to meliorate the health and safety standard of these buildings in one go.[7] The announcement appeared in the headlines in five local daily newspapers on the next day, with the identities of the blacklisted buildings shown.[8] Since the five newspapers reporting the news had very high average net circulations in Hong Kong at that time, press coverage of the news on building blacklisting was considered very wide. The characteristics of these blacklisted buildings are summarized in Table 1.

[7] These blacklisted buildings then became targets for the Co-ordinated Maintenance of Buildings Scheme. Under the scheme, the Buildings Department, in association with six other government departments (namely the Electrical and Mechanical Services Department, Environmental Protection Department, Fire Services Department, Food and Environmental Hygiene Department, Home Affairs Department and Water Supplies Department) assisted the building owners in forming an owners' association and pursuing a comprehensive building management and maintenance programme.

[8] The newspapers were Apple Daily, Ming Pao, Sing Pao, The Sun, and Hong Kong Economic Times.

Table 1. The characteristics of the blacklisted buildings

District		Yau Tsim Mong	Kowloon City	Sham Shui Po	Kwun Tong
Number of buildings		25	24	15	7
Age (years)	Maximum	43.67	43.83	44.92	35.67
	Mean	33.45	31.41	30.67	31.58
	Minimum	17.50	21.08	20.83	27.08
	Standard Deviation	6.25	6.16	7.85	3.95
Number of storeys	Maximum	19.00	24.00	12.00	12.00
	Mean	11.32	12.71	8.60	7.33
	Minimum	6.00	6.00	2.00	5.00
	Standard Deviation	3.09	4.72	2.95	3.61
Number of flats	Maximum	209.00	266.00	126.00	96.00
	Mean	33.45	79.63	49.33	53.67
	Minimum	17.45	6.00	11.00	20.00
	Standard Deviation	6.25	71.94	31.62	35.92

District		Central and Western District	Eastern District	Wanchai	Others
Number of buildings		16	21	10	32
Age (years)	Maximum	41.58	42.08	34.92	47.33
	Mean	30.27	33.40	31.41	31.30
	Minimum	19.92	16.50	21.67	23.67
	Standard Deviation	6.48	8.31	4.38	6.13
Number of storeys	Maximum	26.00	25.00	23.00	19.00
	Mean	11.06	15.38	17.00	8.41
	Minimum	5.00	5.00	11.00	2.00
	Standard Deviation	7.55	6.23	4.62	5.86
Number of flats	Maximum	119.00	373.00	284.00	228.00
	Mean	44.50	141.05	116.20	52.34
	Minimum	5.00	20.00	34.00	6.00
	Standard Deviation	34.35	106.07	75.72	53.08

(1) The blacklisted buildings were identified from Ming Pao (2000).
(2) The characteristics of the blacklisted buildings were obtainable from the Home Affairs Department (2008).

Model Specification

To investigate if the public announcement about blacklisted buildings affected property prices of these buildings, an empirical model is broadly specified as follows:

$$PRICE_k = f(S_k, L_k, T_k, B_k) \tag{3}$$

In Equation (3), the selling price of a property k, $PRICE_k$, is taken as a function of four vectors of determinants, namely S_k, L_k, T_k and B_k. The vector S_k represents structural characteristics of property k, such as building age and floor area. The vector L_k contains locational factors of dwelling k, including vertical location of the property in a building and distance of the building from the nearest mass transit station. T_k is a vector of time dummies which indicate the date of transaction of the property, for controlling the time effects on property price. As for vector B_k which is the focus of this study, it includes a set of dummy variables and their interaction terms. These variables indicate two issues: i) whether the subject property is sited in a blacklisted building or not, and ii) whether the property transaction was undertaken before or after the publicity of the building blacklist.

Founded on the premise of information asymmetry, it is expected that there might be no evident differentials in the implicit prices of building conditions before the government's release of public information because building conditions can be observed only latently. On the other hand, the press coverage which informed the general public about the poor conditions of the blacklisted buildings is expected to pose a negative impact on the equilibrium price of the perceived physical conditions of a property $p(\hat{h}_c)$ because $\hat{h}_c$ is a function of h_c and λ where h_c and $\hat{h}_c$ denote the actual and perceived levels, respectively, of the physical conditions of the subject property (assuming that better conditions mean a higher level). The effect of information release on the price of dwelling c is given by the partial differential of the equilibrium price of the property under information imperfect, $p(\hat{H})$, with respect to λ. Mathematically,

$$\frac{\partial p(\hat{H})}{\partial \lambda} = \frac{\partial p(\hat{H})}{\partial \hat{h}_c} \times \frac{\partial \hat{h}_c}{\partial \lambda}\ . \tag{4}$$

The housing market values goodness in property conditions positively, i.e., $\partial p(\hat{H}) / \partial \hat{h}_c > 0$, and the government's announcement of the identities of poorly-conditioned properties tends to reduce the perceived level of the physical conditions of these properties, i.e., $\partial \hat{h}_c / \partial \lambda < 0$. By this logic, given that the blacklisting exercise provides additional information to the housing market, the blacklisted properties should be sold at a lower price due to the self-protection behaviour of the homebuyers. That means there will be a negative impact on the values of the blacklisted properties, i.e., $\partial p(\hat{H}) / \partial \lambda < 0$.

For the purpose of operationalization, the vectors shown in Equation (3) are expanded to give

$$\begin{aligned} PRICE_{kt} = f(&AGE_{kt}, FLOOR_k, AREA_k, MTRD_k, LISTED_k, \\ &PRELISTING_k, POSTLISTING_k, TIME_{kt};\ \varepsilon_k) \end{aligned} \tag{5}$$

where $PRICE_{kt}$ denotes the transaction price of property k at time t; $TIME_{kt}$ is a vector of monthly time dummies; and ε is the stochastic term. Complete definitions of the variables are reported in Table 2. On account of the lack of any theoretical support, the specification of the empirical model is not known *a priori*. For that reason, various functional forms, including linear, quadratic and semi-log with quadratic terms, are employed for the model estimation.

Descriptions of the Data

To empirically estimate Equation (5) using different functional specifications, transaction data of domestic properties in 23 apartment buildings in the Yau Tsim Mong district were employed. This district was selected for investigation because blacklisted buildings found there were the most among all districts. Also, the confinement to a single district could reduce the locality-related variations of the property characteristics (e.g. topology and income-group mix). Of these 23 buildings, 11 buildings were blacklisted by the Hong Kong government in November 2000. The other 12 buildings serve as controls.

Table 2. Description of the independent variables used in the hedonic price model

Symbol	Measuring Unit of	Description
Age_{kt}	months	The age of the building, which equals the difference between the date of the issue of the occupation permit and the date of the transaction
$Floor_k$	-	The floor level of the transacted property
$Area_k$	square feet	The gross floor area of the transacted property
$MTRD_k$	metres	The distance between the transacted property and the nearest Mass Transit Railway (MTR) station
$Listed_k$	-	A dummy variable that equals 1 when the property was situated in a building which was blacklisted by the government on 4 November 2000 and zero if otherwise
$Prelisting_k$	-	A dummy variable that equals 1 when the property transaction was dated before 4 November 2000 and zero if otherwise
$Postlisting_k$	-	A dummy variable that equals 1 when the property transaction was dated after 4 November 2000 and zero if otherwise

Table 3. Descriptive statistics of the property transaction data

		Maximum	Mean	Minimum	Standard Deviation
Blacklisted Buildings	Property price (HK$ million)	3.05	1.11	0.15	0.54
	Flat size (square feet)	1,170.00	473.17	162.00	170.87
	Floor level	24.00	10.27	1.00	5.33
	Age (months)	514.00	366.07	172.00	78.87
	Distance from MTR station (metres)	105.00	39.95	5.00	35.56
Non-blacklisted Buildings	Property price (HK$ million)	3.60	1.26	0.18	0.54
	Flat size (square feet)	1,031.00	643.80	426.00	166.28
	Floor level	21.00	8.72	1.00	4.49
	Age (months)	503.00	321.67	123.00	129.57
	Distance from MTR station (metres)	175.00	104.25	23.00	54.77
Overall	Property price (HK$ million)	3.60	1.23	0.15	0.54
	Flat size (square feet)	1,170.00	540.58	162.00	188.18
	Floor level	24.00	9.08	1.00	4.73
	Age (months)	514.00	331.89	123.00	121.19
	Distance from MTR station (metres)	175.00	89.46	5.00	57.71

The dataset for property transactions dated between 1 July 1997 and 31 May 2002 were obtained from the Economic Property Research Centre.[9] No significant changes in the conditions of the 28 selected buildings were recorded during that period. Since digestion of the public information released by the government took time, a one-month period immediately after 4 November 2000 was truncated. After the truncation, there were altogether 426 transactions of which 98 (23.00 percent) came from blacklisted buildings. Of the 426 transactions, 368 (86.38 percent) were undertaken before 4 November 2000, with 58 (31.62 percent) being later. The descriptive statistics of the transaction data are summarized in Table 3.

Analysis Results

The estimation results of the hedonic price models of different specifications are shown in Table 4. The adjusted R-squared for the three models ranged from 0.5945 to 0.6373, implying that the estimated models could explain about 60 percent of the variations in the sale price of the properties under investigation.

Table 4. Regression results for the hedonic price model

	Model 1		Model 2		Model 3	
Dependent Variable	**Price**		**Price**		***ln*(Price)**	
	Coefficient	***t*-statistics**	**Coefficient**	***t*-statistics**	**Coefficient**	***t*-statistics**
CONSTANT	-0.0490	-0.2055	0.1383	0.3164	-0.8449	-2.2189**
AGE	-0.0003	-1.1325	-0.0004	-0.2077	-0.0022	-1.2955
AGE^2	-	-	2.11×10^{-7}	0.0696	2.35×10^{-6}	0.9512
FLOOR	0.0004	0.1118	0.0199	1.6621*	0.0076	0.7578
$FLOOR^2$	-	-	-0.0009	-1.7060*	-0.0003	-0.6292***
AREA	0.0017	9.6775***	0.0008	1.2556	0.0020	3.1394***
$AREA^2$	-	-	8.18×10^{-7}	1.4225	-4.55×10^{-7}	-0.8621
MTRD	0.0025	5.7322***	0.0024	1.3267	0.0033	1.8076*
$MTRD^2$	-	-	-5.38×10^{-7}	-0.0475	-1.02×10^{-5}	-0.8968
LISTED×PRELISTING	-0.0479	-0.9266	-0.0586	-1.0679	-0.0508	-1.0276
POSTLISTING	-0.0952	-0.4945	-0.0746	-0.3800	-0.0031	-0.0148
LISTED×POSTLISTING	-0.0659	-0.4205	-0.0588	-0.3782	-0.0524	-0.3801
R-squared	0.6888		0.6937		0.6575	
Adjusted R-squared	0.6357		0.6373		0.5945	
F-statistic	12.9595	***	12.316	***	10.4425	***
Durbin-Watson stat	1.5157		1.5472		1.4976	
No. of observations	426		426		426	

(***), (**) and (*) denote the estimated coefficients of the variables to be significant at the 1 percent level, 5 percent level and 10 percent level, respectively.

The results for the time dummies were omitted, but are available upon request.

All coefficients were estimated with White's Heteroskedasticity-consistent standard errors.

[9] The Economic Property Research Centre was established in 1991 by the Hong Kong Economic Times Limited with the support of the leading real estate agencies in Hong Kong. It provides a database of most property transactions in Hong Kong since 1991. For each transaction record, the Economic Property Research Centre provides details about the transactions such as transaction price, date of transaction, address of subject property, the date of the occupation permit of a building, gross floor area, floor level, *etc.*

Findings on the Control Variables

According to the results of the hedonic price analysis, property age (*AGE*) was found to have no significant impact on the sale price (insignificant even at the 10 percent level) in the three models. As for floor level (*FLOOR*), it did not have show significant association with the sale price (*PRICE*) in Model 1. However, the estimated coefficients of *FLOOR* and $FLOOR^2$ in Model 2 were statistically significant at the 10 percent level but with opposite signs. Given that the estimated coefficient is positive for the first-order term and negative for the second-order term, the effect of floor level on property price increased at a decreasing rate but the rate of change was negligibly small. In Model 3, similar results were obtained except that the estimated coefficient of the first-order term was not statistically insignificant at the 10 percent level. These mixed results look contradictory to the findings of most previous studies in Hong Kong (e.g. Mok, 1995; So *et al.*, 1997; Yau *et al.*, 2008) in which a significant positive correlation between floor level and property price was found. Most probably, this deviation can be explained with the service installations in the buildings under study. In previous empirical research, properties investigated came from relatively new and large-scale housing estates; buildings sampled in the current study fell on the high end of the age spectrum. Lifts were not equipped in many of these old buildings. Therefore, inconvenience might be resulted for the residents because they had to walk upstairs to return home. In these buildings, accordingly, properties at a higher level were not necessarily sold at a higher price.

Moreover, property price was found to increase monotonously with floor area (*SIZE*) in Models 1 and 3 (significant at the 1 percent level). However, no association between these two variables was evidenced in Model 2. Similar results were also returned for the variables concerning the distance between the subject property and the nearest MTR station (*MTRD*). Property price increased monotonously with *MTRD* in Models 1 and 3 (significant at the 1 percent level and 10 percent level, respectively), with no significant relationship spotted in Model 2.

Findings on the Public Information Variables

Bearing in mind the primary objectives of this study, spotlight should be casted on the estimation results for the dummy variable *POSTLISTING* and interaction terms *LISTED×PRELISTING* and *LISTED×POSTLISTING*. The coefficient of the interaction term *LISTED×PRELISTING* indicates whether properties in blacklisted buildings were sold at a lower price, other things being equal, than those in non-blacklisted buildings before the government's announcement of the building blacklist on 4 November 2000. The estimated coefficient of this interaction term was negative but insignificant at the 10 percent level across the three models. That means there was no price differential between those poorly-performing and well-performing properties before the blacklisting exercise.

The coefficient of the dummy variable *POSTLISTING* gives an indication about the change in sale prices of the non-blacklisted properties after the public announcement of the blacklist. The estimated coefficient of *LISTED×POSTLISTING* measures the price differential between the properties in blacklisted buildings transacted after the public announcement and those in non-blacklisted buildings transacted before the announcement. In the three models, the coefficients of the variable and interaction terms were found to be negative but insignificant at the 10 percent level. Most importantly, regardless of the functional form of the model, the difference between the estimated coefficients of the two terms was not statistically significant at the 10 percent level. These results indicate that the difference between blacklisted and non-blacklisted buildings was not valued by the housing market before and after the release of public information about blacklisted buildings.

Implications of the Results and Discussion

Implications of the Results

In many regards, ideal circumstances were offered by the Hong Kong government's blacklisting exercise in 2000 for the investigation of the influence of the release of public information on building dereliction on the housing market. The empirical findings of this research bear far-reaching policy implications with regard to the community management of the building stock in Hong Kong. As aforementioned, the local government proposed to solve the long-lasting predicament of building dilapidation by means of market forces via different schemes such as BSIS and VBCS. Provided that the second-hand housing market suffers from the problem of information asymmetry, building conditions are not fully priced in the existing value league for housing. That provides an impetus for the government to pump more information into the housing market. When the market players are more informed of the conditions of the buildings in the stock, value disparity will be developed between properties with different quality. Properties in better-quality buildings will be rewarded in forms of price premiums, or *vice versa*. By this logic, labelling effects is generated by releasing this sort of information as classes or indexes indicating the physical conditions of the buildings.

To substantiate the government's contention to create a value league which can motivate homeowners to undertake timely building maintenance and repair, additional information provided to the housing should change the condition-value relationship in the first place. The analysis results of this study show no significant difference in the prices between properties in blacklisted and non-blacklisted buildings before 4 November 2000. It is supposed that well-conditioned properties should command higher property value, as evidenced in previous research such as Kask & Maani (1992) and Bourassa & Peng (1999). From these pieces of contradictory evidence, two possible implications can be derived. First, the blacklisting exercise by the Hong Kong government was not prudently conducted. Those 150 buildings blacklisted might not be the worst in terms of physical conditions in the building stock. Alternatively, there might exist a large number of buildings that were badly dilapidated in the opinion of the Building Authority; it is impossible for the government to take actions against all these buildings in one go. For administrative convenience, some of the poorly-performing buildings were blacklisted while some were not. The latter were considered as buildings with better conditions in this empirical study though they were actually in derelict conditions.

However, the above implication does not stand because those non-blacklisted buildings were not selected as the target buildings in the subsequent large-scale building safety campaigns like the Co-ordinated Maintenance of Buildings and Unauthorized Building Works Blitz Operation. Also, there has been no objection raised by the general public and District Councils against the judgements of the Building Authority with regard to the physical conditions of the blacklisted buildings. Accordingly, we move onto the second implication of the analysis results: the difference in physical conditions among buildings, be they blacklisted or non-blacklisted, were not perceived by the housing market in Hong Kong before 4 November 2000. Such a connotation provides a good reason for the local government to manifest the differentiation by instilling more information into the market.

The analysis results, on the other hand, suggested that market players did not response to the publicity of the information about the building blacklist, signifying the inability of the blacklisting exercise in providing new information to the housing market. In other words, the research findings imply that the Hong Kong government's effort to punish the owners of poor-quality housing by blacklisting was in vain. Price differential between properties with poor conditions and good conditions, respectively, was not observed before and after the publicity of the building blacklist. Making a speculation on the reason, the author ascribes this phenomenon to the lack of concern over the importance of building care in the community of Hong Kong. Therefore, the government should dedicate more efforts to foster a culture of building care in the city through more intensive propaganda and public education. This step is of utmost importance and should come before all other incentive schemes such as a territory-wide building classification scheme.

Limitations of the Study

It is beyond doubt that some limitations which may undermine the robustness of research findings exist in this study. What comes first is the small number of observations used in the hedonic price analysis. The constraint primarily roots in the fact that the target group of buildings for the investigation in this study came from the lower end of the quality spectrum. In Hong Kong, transactions of these poor-quality properties are relatively thin. In this regard, possible problem of sample selection bias may occur. Moreover, this study looked into one of the two limbs of the incentive approach only. To put it another way, only the effect of providing information regarding those poorly-performing properties to the market on housing value was focussed; whether there would be a change in the price differential between the properties with superb performance and the others when the government announces a list of honoured properties remains unknown. Theoretically speaking, the condition-value relationship could be non-linear or asymmetric across the quality spectrum. In t his regard, further studies on the labelling effects of good-quality buildings should be warranted.

Conclusion

Facing the ever-serious problems of urban decay and building dilapidation in Hong Kong, a variety of way-outs like stricter enforcement actions and public education are available. Other than these approaches, resort can also be made to the market forces. With the establishment of a value league, properties in buildings with better conditions are valued more than those in dilapidated buildings, installing incentives among property owners to invest in building maintenance and repair. In this process, it is necessary for the housing market to price in the information on building condition. In Hong Kong, information on health and safety conditions of buildings has not been publicly available from large-scale building surveys, as in the situation in the United Kingdom. Market players have to rely heavily on observation and hearsay to obtain information on building conditions. Yet, whether building conditions have already been priced in and whether the release of public information about building conditions adjusts housing price have remained unanswered in the literature. To straddle the existing gaps, this study aims to address these two issues by investigate the housing market in Hong Kong.

This study is made possible because the Hong Kong government officially publicized a list of 150 poorly-performing buildings in November 2000, and this news attracted wide press coverage. Opportunity to study the effect on property price after the government released the building information was offered by this event. Results of the hedonic price analyses suggest that before and after the blacklisting exercise, properties in dilapidated buildings were not transacted at a discount, holding other things constant. In other words, the price gradients between properties in better-performing and derelict buildings before and after the blacklisting exercise were not altered, which is contrary to the government's expectation. Given that there is no punishment in form of value diminishment, owners of dilapidated buildings are not motivated by the market forces to invest in building care. With the long-term benefit of the Hong Kong's community in mind, the local government should think of some other means to tackle the long-lasting building problems in the city.

In spite of the remarkable implications discussed above, the author has to admit that this study is rather preliminary on account of the research limitations like the small number of observations. By this study, nonetheless, it is the author's intention to stimulate more empirical research on the economics of building quality. The findings of the research in this area could offer valuable insights to the public officers in formulating policies with regard to the sustainable management of building stocks in different parts of the world. The author believed that this area of research will grow very fast in the near future because existing building stock has gained the focus of attention in the academia (e.g. Kohler & Hassler, 2002; Augenbroe & Park, 2005; Kohler & Yang, 2007), particularly when urban sustainability is put on the top of agenda in many cities. Other than the effect of building blacklisting, it is also very interesting to study if the values of properties with different degrees of proliferation of unauthorized building works respond to increment in the level of punishment. Besides, changes in the price gradients between properties of different conditions before and after the implementation of a comprehensive building classification scheme can be investigated. Based on the findings of these studies, the responsiveness of the housing market to various measures can be compared, and the public officers can make more informed decisions with regard to the approaches to tackle building problems.

Acknowledgement

The work described in this paper was partially supported by a grant from City University of Hong Kong (Project No. 7200123). The author would like to thank for Miss Stella Yau for the assistance offered in the data collection process.

References

Akerlof, G. A. (1970). The market for lemons: quality uncertainty and the market mechanism. *Quarterly journal of economics,* **84**, 488-500.

Arens, S. B. (1997). The valuation of defective properties: a common sense approach. *The appraisal journal,* **65**, 143-148.

Augenbroe, G., & Park, C. S. (2005). Quantification methods of technical building performance. *Building research and information,* **33**, 159-172.

Bernknopf, R. L., Brookshire, D. S., & Thayer, M. A. (1990). Earthquake and volcano hazard notices: an economic evaluation of changes in risk perceptions. *Journal of environmental economics and management,* **18**, 35-49.

Bourassa, S. C., & Peng, V. S. (1999). Hedonic prices and house numbers: the information of feng shui. *International real estate review,* **2**, 79-93.

Brookshire, D. S., Thayer, M. A., Tschirhart, J., & Schulze, W. D. (1985). A test of the expected utility model: evidence from earthquake risks. *The journal of political economy,* **93**, 369-389.

Buildings Department. (2005). Building Safety Inspection Scheme (voluntary). http://www.bd.gov.hk/english/services/index_exist2_pmb.html.

Butler, R. V. (1982). The specification of hedonic indexes for urban housing. *Land economics,* **58**, 96-108.

Carroll, T. M., Clauretie, T. M., Jensen, J., & Waddoups, M. (1996). The economic impact of a transient hazard on property values: the 1988 PEPCON Explosion in Henderson, Nevada. *Journal of real estate finance and economics,* **13**, 143-167.

Chau, K. W., Ho, D. C. W., Leung, H. F., Wong, S. K., & Cheung, A. K. C. (2004). Improving the living environment in Hong Kong through the use of a building classification system. *CIOB(HK) quarterly journal*, October, 14-15.

Chau, K. W., Leung, A. Y. T., Yiu, C. Y., & Wong, S. K. (2003). Estimating the value enhancement effects of refurbishment. *Property management,* **21**, 13-19.

Donnelly, W. (1989). Hedonic price analysis of the effects of a floodplain on property values. *Water resources bulletin,* **24**, 581-586.

Ehrlich, I., & Becker, G. S. (1972). Market insurance, self-insurance, and self-protection. *The journal of political economy,* **80**, 623-648.

Espey, M., & Lopez, H. (2000). The impact of airport noise and proximity on residential property values. *Growth and Change,* **31**, 408-419.

Feijtem, P., & Mulder, C. H. (2005). Life-course experience and housing quality. *Housing studies,* **20**, 571-587.

Gamble, H. B., & Downing, R. H. (1982). Effects of nuclear power plants on residential property values. *Journal of regional studies,* **26**, 457-478.

Gayer, T., Hamilton, J. T., & Viscusi, W. K. (2002). The market value of reducing cancer risk: hedonic housing prices with changing information. *Southern economic journal,* **69**, 266-289.

Ho, D. C. W., Chau, K. W., Leung, H. F., Cheung, A. K. C., Yau, Y., Wong, S. K., & Lau, S. S. Y. (2005). Assessing the health and safety of residential buildings in Hong Kong. In *Proceedings of the* **2005** *World Sustainable Building Conference*, 27-29 September, Tokyo, pp. 2206-2213.

Home Affairs Department. (2008). Database of private buildings in Hong Kong. http://202.67.130.69/eng/index.php.

Housing, Planning and Lands Bureau. (2003). *Building management and maintenance: consultation paper*. Hong Kong: Government Logistics Department.

Housing, Planning and Lands Bureau. (2005). *Building management and maintenance: Public consultation on mandatory building inspection.* Hong Kong: Government Logistics Department.

Jimenez, E. (1983). The magnitude and determinants of home improvement in self-help housing: Manila's Tondo Project. *Land economics,* **59**, 70-83.

Kask, S. B., & Maani, S. A. (1992). Uncertainty, information and hedonic pricing. *Land economics,* **68**, 170-184.

Kohlhase, J. E. (1991). The impact of toxic waste sites on housing values. *Journal of urban economics,* **30**, pp. 1-26.

Kohler, N., & Hassler, U. (2002). The building stock as a research object. *Building research and information,* **30**, 226-236.

Kohler, N., & Yang, W. (2007). Long-term management of building stock. *Building research and information,* **35**, 351-362.

Lancaster, K. J. (1966). A new approach to consumer theory. *Journal of political economy,* **74**, 132-157.

Leung, A. Y. T., & Yiu, C. Y. (2004). A review of building conditions in Hong Kong. In A. Y. T. Leung, & C. Y. Yiu (Eds.), *Building dilapidation and rejuvenation in Hong Kong* (pp. 11-34). Hong Kong: City University of Hong Kong and the Hong Kong Institute of Surveyors.

Lützkendorf, T., & Speer, T. M. (2005). Alleviating asymmetric information in property markets: building performance and product quality as signals for consumers. *Building research and information,* **33**, 182-195.

MacDonald, D. N., Murdoch, J. C., & White, H. L. (1987). Uncertain hazards, insurance, and customer choice: evidence from housing markets. *Land economics,* **63**, 361-371.

Ming Pao. (2000). The list of 150 buildings in disrepair released. *Ming Pao,* 5 November 2000, A4 [in Chinese].

Mok, H. M. K. (1995). A hedonic approach to pricing of residential properties in Hong Kong. *Hong Kong journal of business management,* **13**, 1-15.

Montz, B. E. (1993). Hazard area disclosure in New Zealand: the impacts on residential property values in two communities. *Applied geography,* **13**, 225-242.

Muoghalu, L. N. (1991). Measuring housing and environmental quality as indicator of quality of urban life: a case of traditional city of Benin, Nigeria. *Social indicators research,* **25**, 63-98.

Murdoch, J. C., Singh, H., & Thayer, M. (1993). The impact of natural hazards on housing values: the Loma Preia earthquake. *Journal of the American Real Estate and Urban Economics Association,* **21**, 167-184.

Nelson, A. C., Genereux, J., & Genereux, M. (1992). Price effects of landfills on house

Ong, S. E., & Brown, G. R. (2001). Information issues in real estate. *Pacific Rim property research journal,* 7, 61-72.

Perry, J., & Felce, D. (1995) Objective assessments of quality of life: how much do they agree with each other? *Journal of community and applied social psychology,* **5**, 1-19.

Shilling, J. D., Benjamin, J. D., & Sirmans, C. F. (1985). Adjusting comparable sales for floodplain location. *The appraisal journal,* **53**, 429-436.

Smith, L., Rosen, K., & Fallis, G. (1988). Recent developments in economic models of housing markets. *Journal of economic literature,* **26**, 29-64.

Smith, V. K., & Deyak, T. A. (1975). Measuring the impact of air pollution on property values. *Journal of regional science,* **15**, 277-288.

So, H. M., Tse, R. Y. C., & Ganesan, S. (1997). Estimating the influence of transport on house prices: evidence from Hong Kong. *Journal of property valuation and investment,* **15**, 40-47.

Speyrer, J. F., & Ragas, W. R. (1991) Housing prices and flood risk: an examination using spline regression. *Journal of real estate finance and economics,* **4**, 395-307.

World Health Organization. (2003). Cumulative number of reported probable cases of SARS. http://www.who.int/csr/sars/country/en.

Yau, Y., Chau, K. W., Ho, D. C. W., & Wong, S. K. (2008). An empirical study on the positive externality of building refurbishment. *International journal of housing markets and analysis,* **1**, 19-32.

Yiu, C. Y., & Wong, S. K. (2005) The effects of expected transport improvements on housing prices. *Urban studies,* **42**, 113-125.

In: Housing, Housing Costs and Mortgages
Editors: Szilárd Kis and Istvan Balogh, pp. 63-92
ISBN: 978-1-60741-813-9

Chapter 4

ECONOMIC GROWTH AND TRANSPORTATION WITH ENDOGENOUS CAPITAL, TIME AND MONEY

Wei-Bin Zhang
Ritsumeikan Asia Pacific University, Japan

Abstract

The purpose of this study is to introduce transportation conditions and money into a growth model with economic geography. The study examines possible effects of transportation conditions and inflation policy on long-term economic growth and geography. The model describes dynamic interactions among capital accumulation, real model, travel time and cost, housing, residential distribution, amenity, and endogenous time distribution among work, travel, and leisure. Although transportation systems are simple in this paper in the light of contemporary literature in transportation research, the paper demonstrates a way to integrating some important models in the literature in transportation research, economic growth theory and urban economics so that the significance of transportation systems upon economies can be properly analyzed.

Keywords: economic growth, capital accumulation, travel cost, travel speed, leisure time, housing rent, land rent, inflation policy, money

1. Introduction

Money and transport systems connect almost all economic activities in modern economic systems. It is well known that relations between economic growth and money have been extensively analyzed in the literature of economic growth since Tobin published his seminar work about growth and money in 1956. Nevertheless, relations between economic growth and transportation systems have been seldom examined in the literature of theoretical economics. As transportation systems connect almost all aspects of human interactions across space, a comprehensive understanding of the role of transportation systems can be achieved only through examining with broad viewpoints. As effects of transportation systems can be properly evaluated only over long period of time, a genuine dynamic approach to interactions, for instance, between transportation systems and economic development is required. Theoretical economics lacks a proper analytical framework for discussing issues related to, for instance, transportation systems and economic growth, transportation conditions and land and housing rents. A main reason for the omission of studying interactions of economic growth and transportation conditions is that the traditional economic growth lacks a suitable analytical framework. In a recent paper, Zhang (2007) has proposed a dynamic growth with transportation systems. The model studies how changes in transportation conditions, such as travel speed and cost, affect economic growth and geography. This paper generalizes Zhang's model by introducing endogenous money into the dynamic system.

Modern analysis of the long-term interaction of inflation and capital formation begins with Tobin's seminal contribution (Tobin, 1965). Tobin deals with an isolated economy in which "outside money" (the part of money stock which is issued by the government) competes with real capital in the portfolios of agents within the framework of the Solow growth model. Since then, many models of growth model of monetary economies are built. In non-monetary growth theory monetary values such as wage, rate of interests, prices of goods and services, land rent are 'fast variables' and are determined by balance conditions of demand and supply of real variables. In frictionless economic systems, issuing money has no effects on economic growth, at least in the long term. Nevertheless, financial assets and paper claims often offer alternatives to hold wealth. In process of exchange and division of labor, money plays an essential role in modern economy. In his well-known paper on long-run effects of inflationary policies, Tobin (1965) showed that an increase in the level of the inflation rate will increase the capital stock of an economy. Sidrauski (1967) constructed an economic model in which no real variable will be affected by the economy's inflation rate. We will address the issues by Tobin and Sidrauski in the alternative framework. Our approach is strongly influenced by the money in the utility (MIU) approach which was initially proposed by Patinkin (1965) and Sidrauski (1967). In this approach, money is held because it yields some services and the way to model it is to enter real balances directly into the utility function. Sidrauski (1967) made a benchmark contribution to monetary economics, challenging Tobin's non-neutrality result. He proposed a framework that explicitly allows for an endogenous treatment of saving behavior. His analytical framework is developed with Patinkin's idea of ensuring a well-defined demand function for money by assuming that the agent's utility is directly affected by money. This approach has been widely applied in monetary growth theory (for instance, Brock, 1974; Turnovsky, 2000).

The objective of this paper is to study growth with economic geography and transport systems. This study deals with a dynamic interaction among capital accumulation, money, land, housing, environment, transportation in an isolated linear economy, by synthesizes the main ideas in the Solow growth model in the neoclassical growth theory, the Alonso urban model and the Muth housing model in the urban economics in an alternative framework to the traditional neoclassical growth theory. The paper is organized as follows. Section 2 defines the basic model. Section 3 guarantees existence of spatial equilibrium. Section 4 simulates the model with the Cobb-Douglas production function. Section 5 examines effects of change in the total productivity of the industrial sector on the spatial equilibrium. Section 6 studies effects of transportation conditions on the spatial equilibrium. Section 7 examines effects of changes in amenity and preference on the spatial equilibrium. Section 8 concludes the study. Appendix A proves the main results in Section 3.

2. The Model

The model is a combination of the basic features of the four key models, the Solow growth model, the Alonso urban model, the Muth housing model in the neoclassical growth theory and urban economics, and the monetary growth model in the MIU approach. Most aspects of the model are similar to the model proposed by Zhang (2007), except that this model introduces money to the spatial economy. As far as urban structures are concerned, we follow the standard residential land-use model. The basic features of this model are that an isolated city state is built on a flat featureless plain. All residents in the economy work in the CBD. People travel only between their homes and the CBD. Travel is equally costly in terms of time and money in all directions. An individual may reside at only one location. The only spatial characteristic of any location that directly matters is the distance from the city center. Since it is complicated to take both space and time in a general equilibrium framework, at this initial stage we simplify the structure of the isolated economic system. The population is homogenous. The households achieve the same utility level regardless of where they locate. All the markets are perfectly competitive. The system is geographically linear and consists of two parts - the CBD and the residential area. The isolated state consists of a finite strip of land extending from a fixed central business district (CBD) with constant unit width. We assume that all economic activities are concentrated in the CBD. We neglect public goods. The households occupy the residential area. We assume that the CBD is located at the left-side end of the linear territory. As we will get the same conclusions if we locate the CBD at the center of the linear system, the specified urban configuration will not affect our discussion.

The system consists of two, industrial and housing, sectors. The industrial production is the same as that in the one-sector neoclassical growth model. We assume that the industrial product can be either invested or consumed. The housing production is similar to that in the Muth model. Housing is supplied with combination of capital and land. We assume that the total labor force is fully employed by the industrial sector. We select industrial good to serve as numeraire. As we assume that the transportation cost of workers to the city is dependent on the travel distance, land rent for housing should be spatially different.

First, we introduce

N —fixed population;

$\overline{N}(t)$ —total labor input at time t;

$K_i(t)$ —capital stocks employed by the industrial sector;

$w(t)$ and $r(t)$—wage rate and rate of interest, respectively; and

$F(t)$ and $C(t)$ —output of the industrial sector and total consumption of the commodity, respectively.

We assume that industrial production is carried out by combination of capital and labor force in the form of $F\left(K_i(t), \overline{N}(t)\right)$, where F is the output of the industrial sector. Assume F to be neoclassical (Burmeister and Dobell, 1970). Introduce $k_i \equiv K_i / \overline{N}$. We have

$$f(k_i) \equiv \frac{F(K_i, \overline{N})}{\overline{N}} = F(k_i, 1)$$

The function, $f(k_i)$, has the following properties

(i) $f(0) = 0$;
(ii) $f(k_i)$ is increasing, strictly concave on R^+, and C^2 on R^{++}; $f'(k_i) > 0$ and $f''(k_i) < 0$; and
(iii) $\lim_{k_i \to 0} f'(k_i) = \infty$ and $\lim_{k_i \to +\infty} f'(k_i) = 0$.

Markets are competitive; thus labor and capital earn their marginal products, and firms earn zero profits. The rate of interest, $r(t)$, and wage rates, $w(t)$, are determined by markets. Hence, for any individual firm $r(t)$ and $w(t)$ are given at each point of time. The production sector chooses the two variables, $K_i(t)$ and $\overline{N}(t)$, to maximize its profit. The marginal conditions are given by

$$r + \delta_k = f'(k_i), \quad w = f(k_i) - k_i f'(k_i), \tag{1}$$

where δ_k is the depreciation rate of physical capital.

We now describe housing production and behavior of households. First, we introduce

L — fixed (territory) length of the isolated state;
ω — distance from the CBD to a point in the residential area;
$R(\omega,t)$ and $R_h(\omega,t)$ — land rent and housing rent at location ω;
$k(\omega,t)$ and $s(\omega,t)$ — wealth owned by and saving made by a household at location ω, respectively;
$c(\omega,t)$ — consumption of a household at location ω;
$T(\omega,t)$ and $T_h(\omega,t)$ — work time and leisure time of a household at location ω;
$n(\omega,t)$ and $L_h(\omega,t)$ — residential density and lot size of a household at location ω;
$K_h(t)$ — capital stocks employed by the housing sector; and
$K(t)$ — total capital stock of the economy.

The total labor input, $\overline{N}(t)$, is the sum of the labor input over the space. According to the definitions of $n(\omega, t)$, $T(\omega, t)$ and $\overline{N}(t)$, we have

$$\overline{N}(t) = \int_0^L n(\omega, t) T(\omega, t) d\omega. \tag{2}$$

Residential housing assets play a dual in the economy. First, residential housing assets are used as a durable consumption good. They are the source of housing services. Residential housing assets are used as a mechanism for the intertemporal transfer of wealth, which generates both rents and capital gains through housing appreciation. It is well known that Muth introduces a commodity "housing" rather than land in describing dwelling conditions. Housing is produced with land and non-land inputs. Households have a derived demand for land, dependent on both preferences for housing and technical characteristics of housing production function. We follow this approach in explaining decision making of dwelling sites of households. The housing industry supplies housing services by combining land and capital. Let us denote $c_h(\omega,t)$ housing service received by the household at location ω. We specify the housing service production function as follows

$$c_h(\omega,t) = k_h^{\alpha_h}(\omega, t) L_h^{\beta_h}(\omega, t), \ \ \alpha_h + \beta_h = 1, \ \ \alpha_h, \beta_h \geq 0, \tag{3}$$

where $k_h(\omega,t)$ is the input level of capital per household at location, ω. Here, we assume that housing capital can be instantaneously adjusted. All the characteristics of houses such as the size of a lot and the size of a house can be changed instantaneously without costs. Hence the capital-land ratio is always perfectly adjusted.[1]

The marginal conditions are given by

$$r + \delta_k = \frac{\alpha_h R_h c_h}{k_h}, \ \ R = \frac{\beta_h R_h c_h}{L_h}, \ \ 0 \leq \omega \leq L. \tag{4}$$

According to the definitions of L_h and n, we have

$$n(\omega,t) = \frac{1}{L_h(\omega,t)}, \ \ 0 \leq \omega \leq L. \tag{5}$$

The total capital stocks employed by the housing sector is equal to the sum of the capital stocks for housing over space at any point of time. The relationship between $k_h(\omega,t)$ and $K_h(t)$ is thus given by

---

[1] Our approach is mainly based on Anas (1978), even though the Anas housing production also includes the labor input. Further issues related to the durability of real estates and its costly conversion and replacements are also discussed by Anas. See also Fischer et al (1996), Arnott (1980), Arnott et al (1999) and Glaeser and Gyourko (2005) for introducing more realistic aspects of housing market to the growth model. A recent literature review is referred to Lin et al (2004).

$$K_h(t) = \int_0^L n(\omega,t)k_h(\omega,t)d\omega. \tag{6}$$

Each worker may get income from land ownership, wealth ownership and wages. In order to define incomes, it is necessary to determine land ownership structure. It can be seen that land properties may be distributed in multiple ways under various institutions.[2] To simplify the model, we assume the absentee landownership. This means that the income from land rent is spent outside the economic system.

We assume that agents have perfect foresight with respect to all future events and capital markets operate frictionless. The government levies no taxes. Money is introduced by assuming that a central bank distributes at no cost to the population a per capita amount of fiat money $M(t) > 0$. The scheme according to which the money stock evolves over time is deterministic and known to all agents. With μ being the constant net growth rate of the money stock, $M(t)$ evolves over time according:

$$\dot{M}(t) = \mu M(t), \quad \mu > 0.$$

At t the government brings $\mu M(t)$ additional units of money per capita into circulation in order to finance all government expenditures via seigniorage. Let $m(t)$ stand for the real value of money per capita measured in units of the output good, that is, $m(t) = M(t)/P(t)$. The government expenditure in real terms per capita, $\tau(t)$, is given by

$$\tau(t) = \frac{\dot{M}(t)}{P(t)} = \frac{\mu M(t)}{P(t)} = \mu m(t).$$

The representative household receives $\mu m(t)$ units of paper money from the government through a "helicopter drop", also considered to be independent of his money holdings. Consumers make decisions on choice of lot size, consumption level of commodity as well as on how much to save. Let $\overline{m}(\omega, t)$ and $k(\omega, t)$ stand for respectively the per capita real money

[2] There are three often-applied assumptions in the literature of urban economics. They are the absentee landownership, the public ownership, and the equally shared landownership. The absentee landownership assumption means that land is owned by absentee landlords who spend their land incomes outside the economic system. This may also be interpreted as that the government spends the income from land on public goods such as military and households equally benefit from the public goods. If the public goods enter the utility in the following way, $H(g)U(x)$ where $H(g)$ is a function of the public goods, g being independent of location and x is the vector of the other factors that affect the utility, the model is mathematically identical to the interpretation just described. In the case of the public ownership, for instance as accepted in Kanemoto (1980), the city government rents the land from the landowners at certain rent and sublets it to households at the market rent, using the net revenue to subsidize city residents equally. The equally shared landownership means that the land is equally shared by the population and the income from the land is equally shared among the population.

balances and wealth (excluding land) owned by the typical household in at location ω. Each household at ω obtains the real income

$$y(\omega, t) = r(t)k(\omega, t) + w(t)T(\omega, t) - \pi(t)\overline{m}(\omega, t) + \mu m(t), \quad 0 \le \omega \le L. \tag{7}$$

The disposable income is given by

$$\hat{y}(\omega, t) = y(\omega, t) + a(\omega, t), \tag{8}$$

where

$$a(\omega, t) \equiv k(\omega, t) + \overline{m}(\omega, t).$$

At each point of time, a consumer at location ω distributes the total available income among holding money, $\overline{m}(\omega, t)$, consuming housing goods, $c_h(\omega, t)$, saving, $s(\omega, t)$, consumption of goods, $c(\omega, t)$. A household also decides the time distribution among work, leisure and travel to work. It is assumed that the travel time from the CBD to the residential location is only related to the distance and neglect any other effects such on technological change, infrastructure improvement, and congestion on the travel time form the CBD to the residential area. Let T_0 and $\Gamma(\omega)$ respectively stand for the total available time and the time spent on traveling between the residence and CBD. We should require that the travel time increases in ω. We have

$$T(\omega, t) + T_h(\omega, t) + \Gamma(\omega) = T_0.$$

It should be remarked that in the literature of transportation research there are many empirical and theoretical studies on interactions between travel behavior and land use patterns.[3] The size and shapes of cities are interacting with daily activities. At this stage of the research, we try to make transport systems and land use pattern as simple as possible because of analytical difficulties. Issues related to economic growth, land use patterns and transport choice will be examined in future.

We assume that travel cost, $\Gamma_c(\omega)$, is dependent only on the distance.[4] The travel cost increases in ω. The budget constraint is given by

$$(1 + r(t))\overline{m}(\omega, t) + R_h(\omega, t)c_h(\omega, t) + c(\omega, t) + s(\omega, t) + \Gamma_c(\omega) = \hat{y}(\omega, t).$$

This equation means that the consumption and saving exhaust the consumers' disposable personal income. Substituting equation (8) into the budget constraint yields

---

[3] See, for instance, Banister (1999), Boarnet and Crane (2001), Srinivasan and Ferreira (2002), Maat et al. (2005) and Buchanan et al. (2006).

[4] In reality, transport mode is an endogenous variable, which implies that like housing, transportation service should enter the utility function. Transportation cost is actually related to income (see, for instance, Train and McFadden, 1978, Rietveld et al, 2003, De Palma et al, 2005). If we assume a linear relation between transportation cost and income, then our analysis will not be affected.

$$(r(t) + \pi(t))\overline{m}(\omega, t) + w(t)T_h(\omega, t) + R_h(\omega, t)c_h(\omega, t) + c(\omega, t) + s(\omega, t) = \overline{y}(\omega, t), \tag{9}$$

where

$$\overline{y}(\omega, t) \equiv (1 + r(t))k(\omega, t) + w(t)[T_0 - \Gamma(\omega)] + \mu m(t) - \Gamma_c(\omega).$$

The variable, $\overline{y}$, is the "potential" available income for the household at location ω as the term, $w(T_0 - \Gamma(\omega))$, is the potential wage income. Location choice is closely related to the existence and quality of such physical environmental attributes as open space and noise pollution as well as social environmental quality. We assume that utility level, $U(\omega, t)$, of the household at location ω is dependent on $\overline{m}(\omega, t)$, $T_h(\omega, t)$, $c_h(\omega, t)$, $s(\omega, t)$, and $c(\omega, t)$ as follows[5]

$$U(\omega, t) = \theta(\omega, t)\overline{m}^{\varepsilon_0}(\omega, t)T_h^{\sigma_0}(\omega, t)c^{\xi_0}(\omega, t)c_h^{\eta_0}(\omega, t)s^{\lambda_0}(\omega, t), \quad \varepsilon_0, \sigma_0, \xi_0, \eta_0, \lambda_0 > 0, \tag{10}$$

in which ε_0, σ_0, ξ_0, η_0, and λ_0 are a typical person's elasticity of utility of real money balance, leisure time, industrial goods, housing, and saving at ω. We call ε_0, σ_0, ξ_0, η_0, and λ_0 propensities to hold real money balance, to use leisure time, to consume goods, to consume housing, and to hold wealth, respectively.

As argued by Glaeser et al (2001), consumption amenities have increasingly played more important role in urban formation. Public services, accessibilities, local transportation systems, pollution, and human relations such as discrimination all involve externalities and affect amenities. We incorporate amenity into the consumer location decision by assuming that amenity is a function of residential density.[6] Distance from the CBD reflects two elements: the inconvenience of the distance and the value of the amenity of the surrounding area. The urban dynamics is influenced by many changing characteristics of environmental quality such as air quality, levels of noise pollution, open space, and other physical and social neighborhood qualities at each location. Environmental quality can be reflected in part by its effect on the location choice of the individual. Many kinds of externalities may actually exist at any location. Some may be historically given, such as historical buildings and climate; others such as noise and cleanness, may be endogenously determined by the location of residents. Households may prefer a low-density residential area to a high one, as there tend to have more green, less noise, more cleanness and more safety in a low-density area. Nevertheless, there are other factors, such as social interactions, which may make high-density area attractive. We consider that residential

[5] This utility function is applied to various dynamic economic models. A comprehensive explanation of the utility function and its relations to the traditional approaches in economic dynamic analysis are provided by Zhang (2005, 2006).

[6] This study does not take account of externalities for producers. For instance, firms often prefer to locate to other firms. An explicit introduction of externalities will make the spatial structure far more complicated. In the literature of urban economics, various externalities have been analyzed (see, Henderson, 1974, Upton, 1981, Abdel-Rahman, 2004).

densities may have positive or negative agglomeration effects. We specify the amenity, $\theta(\omega, t)$, at ω as follows

$$\theta(\omega, t) = \theta_1 n^{\vartheta}(\omega, t), \ \theta_1 > 0.$$

The function, $\theta(\omega, t)$, implies that the amenity level at location ω is related to the residential density at the location.

For simplicity, we restrict the analysis to the case that all households obtain the same level of utility at any point of time. This also comes out of our assumption that the population is homogeneous and people can change their residential location freely without any transaction costs and time delay. The conditions that households get the same level of utility at any location at each point of time is represented by

$$U(\omega_1, t) = U(\omega_2, t), \ 0 \le \omega_1, \omega_2 \le L.$$

It should be noted that we neglect possible costs for migration. Maximizing $U(\omega, t)$ subject to the budget constraint (9) yields

$$\overline{m} = \frac{\varepsilon \overline{y}}{r + \pi}, \ T_h = \frac{\sigma \overline{y}}{w}, \ c = \xi \overline{y}, \ c_h = \frac{\eta \overline{y}}{R_h}, \ s = \lambda \overline{y}, \tag{11}$$

where

$$\varepsilon \equiv \rho \varepsilon_0, \ \sigma \equiv \rho \sigma_0, \ \xi \equiv \rho \xi_0, \ \eta \equiv \rho \eta_0, \ \lambda \equiv \rho \lambda_0, \ \rho \equiv \frac{1}{\varepsilon_0 + \sigma_0 + \xi_0 + \eta_0 + \lambda_0}.$$

The above equations mean that the real money balance, housing consumption, consumption of the good and saving are positively proportional to the available income.

According to the definition of $s(\omega, t)$, the wealth accumulation for the household at location ω is given by

$$\dot{a}(\omega, t) = s(\omega, t) - a(\omega, t), \ 0 \le \omega \le L. \tag{12}$$

As the state is isolated, the total population is distributed over the whole urban area. The population constraint is given by

$$\int_0^L n(\omega, t) d\omega = N. \tag{13}$$

The total consumption, $C(t)$, is given by

$$\int_0^L n(\omega, t)c(\omega, t)d\omega = C(t). \tag{14}$$

The national real balance is equal to the sum of the real money balances of all the households. That is

$$\int_0^L \overline{m}(\omega, t)n(\omega, t)d\omega = Nm(t). \tag{15}$$

The assumption that capital is fully employed is given by

$$K_i(t) + K_h(t) = K(t). \tag{16}$$

The total capital stocks employed by the production sectors is equal to the total wealth owned by all the households. That is

$$\int_0^L k(\omega,t)n(\omega,t)d\omega = K(t). \tag{17}$$

We have thus built the dynamic growth model with endogenous spatial distribution of real money balance, wealth, consumption and population, capital accumulation and residential location. We now examine dynamic properties of the system.

3. The Spatial Equilibrium

This section examines equilibrium of the spatial dynamics. We are only concerned with equilibrium of the dynamic system because it is difficult to find out explicit expressions of the motion of the system. The following lemma shows that the system has at least one equilibrium point. The lemma also provides the procedure to determine the equilibrium values of all the variables. The procedure is important for simulation.

Lemma 1

The equilibrium value of the capital density, k_i, of the industrial sector is determined by

$$H(k_i) - [\lambda f'(k_i) + \lambda\mu - \lambda\delta_k - \varepsilon]\frac{N}{\varepsilon} = 0, \tag{18}$$

where

$$H(k_i) \equiv \left[\left(\frac{f}{f'} + \overline{\alpha}k_i - 1\right)\frac{(\delta + \mu + f')}{f / f' + \overline{\alpha}k_i} - \frac{\xi_1}{\lambda}\right]\left(\frac{\xi + \varepsilon}{\lambda} + \delta_k - \frac{\overline{\alpha}f' - \delta}{f / f' + \overline{\alpha}k_i}\right)^{-1} N.$$

$$\xi_1 \equiv \xi + \lambda + \varepsilon, \ \overline{\alpha} \equiv \frac{\xi_1}{\alpha_h \eta} > 0.$$

For a positive solution k_i, r and w are determined by (1). The real money per capita, m, is determined by the following equation

$$\left[T_0 N - N\left[\int_0^L \frac{d\omega}{\Gamma_0^{\beta_0}(\omega, m)}\right]^{-1}\int_0^L \frac{\Gamma(\omega)}{\Gamma_0^{\beta_0}(\omega, m)} d\omega\right]\frac{1}{m} = H_0(k_i),$$

where

$$\Gamma_0(\omega, m) \equiv [wT_0 + \mu m - w\Gamma(\omega) - \Gamma_c(\omega)], \ H_0(k_i) \equiv \frac{H(k_i)}{k_i} - \left(\frac{\alpha_h \eta}{k_i f'} - \frac{\sigma}{w}\right)\left(\frac{H(k_i) + N}{\lambda}\right).$$

The real money per capita at location ω is given by $\overline{m}(\omega) = r_0 \Gamma_0(\omega)$, where

$$r_0 \equiv \left[\left(\frac{r + \mu}{\varepsilon}\right) - (1 + r)\left(\frac{\lambda r + \lambda \mu}{\varepsilon} - 1\right)\right]^{-1}.$$

The equilibrium values of all the other variables are determined by the following procedure: $n(\omega)$ by (A19) and (A20) $\rightarrow$ $\overline{y}(\omega)$ by (A17) $\rightarrow$ $R_h(\omega)$ by (A15) $\rightarrow$ $T_h(\omega)$, $c(\omega)$, $c_h(\omega)$ and $s(\omega)$ by (11) $\rightarrow$ $T(\omega) = T_0 - T_h(\omega) - \Gamma(\omega)$ $\rightarrow$ $k_h(\omega)$ by (A14) $\rightarrow$ $k(\omega)$ by (A10) $\rightarrow$ K by (A8) $\rightarrow$ $\overline{Y}$ by (A2) $\rightarrow$ $\overline{N}$ by (A3) $\rightarrow$ $K_i = k_i \overline{N}$ $\rightarrow$ $K_h = K - K_i$ $\rightarrow$ $F = F(K_i, \overline{N})$ $\rightarrow$ $L_h(\omega) = 1 / n(\omega)$ $\rightarrow$ $c_h(\omega) = k_h^{\alpha_h}(\omega) L_h^{\beta_h}(\omega)$ $\rightarrow$ $R(\omega)$ by (4) $\rightarrow$ $c(\omega)$ and $s(\omega)$ by (11).

As it is difficult to interpret conditions for existence of meaningful equilibrium, we will simulate the model to illustrate the behavior of the model. Before simulation, we examine some properties of the model. From equation (A18), we have

$$\frac{n(\omega_1)}{n(\omega_2)} = \left(\frac{\Gamma_0(\omega_2, m)}{\Gamma_0(\omega_1, m)}\right)^{\beta_0}, \quad (19)$$

where $\beta_0 = (1/\eta_0\rho - \beta_h)/(\vartheta/\eta_0 - \beta_h)$. As $1/\eta_0\rho - \beta_h$ is positive, the sign of β_0 is the same as that of $\vartheta/\eta_0 - \beta_h$. We see that $\Gamma_0(\omega, m)$ falls in ω. As $\Gamma_0(\omega_2)/\Gamma_0(\omega_1) < 1$ in the case of $\omega_1 < \omega_2$, we have $n(\omega_1) > n(\omega_2)$ if $\beta_0 < 0$. The residential density is higher nearer the CBD. As $L_h(\omega) = 1/n(\omega)$, the land size per household rises in the distance from the CBD. As travel costs more as the residence is further away from the CBD, it is reasonable to observe the declination of the residential density as the distance from the CBD increases. Yet, if $\beta_0 > 0$, the residential density distribution is inverse to the case of $\beta_0 < 0$, that is, the further the residential location is away from the CBD, the higher the density is. To see why this happens, from the definition of β_0 we see that the parameter becomes positive only when $\vartheta - \eta_0\beta_h > 0$. A positive ϑ means that as the residential density rises, the local attractiveness is increased. The condition, $\vartheta > \eta_0\beta_h$, implies that the individual welfare is positively strongly affected by, for instance, social interactions among local people and the propensity to use land is low. As people highly evaluate interacting with each other among locals, the urban residential density becomes higher further away from the CBD. In this study, we limit our examination to the case of $\beta_0 < 0$.

By equations (A15) and (A17), we have

$$\frac{R_h(\omega_1)}{R_h(\omega_2)} = \left(\frac{\Gamma_0(\omega_2)}{\Gamma_0(\omega_1)}\right)^{(\beta_0 - 1)\beta_h}, \tag{20}$$

where we use (19). We have $R_h(\omega_1) > R_h(\omega_2)$ if $\omega_1 > \omega_2$. The housing rent is higher nearer the CBD. By

$$\bar{y}(\omega) = \left(\frac{r + \mu}{\varepsilon}\right) r_0 \Gamma_0(\omega, m),$$

we see that $\bar{y}(\omega)$ falls in ω. From equations (11), we see that the leisure time, $T_h(\omega)$, and consumption level of the industrial goods, $c(\omega)$, fall in the distance. From $R_h(\omega)c_h(\omega) = \eta\bar{y}(\omega)$ and (20), we have

$$\frac{c_h(\omega_1)}{c_h(\omega_2)} = \left(\frac{\Gamma_0(\omega_1)}{\Gamma_0(\omega_2)}\right)^{\beta_h\beta_0 + \alpha_h}.$$

Under the requirement of $\beta_0 < 0$, the housing consumption per household rises (decreases) in distance if $\beta_h\beta_0 + \alpha_h > 0$ ($\beta_h\beta_0 + \alpha_h < 0$). As

$$T(\omega) = T_0 - \Gamma(\omega) - \frac{\sigma \bar{y}(\omega)}{w},$$

the work time may either fall or rise in distance.

It is observed that as we get closer to the city center, not only the population density but also the capital intensity per square miles increase. Buildings tend to be higher near the center. We now explain this phenomenon. The capital-land ratio, $k_h(\omega, t)/L_h(\omega, t)$, is given by

$$\frac{k_h(\omega, t)}{L_h(\omega, t)} = k_h(\omega, t) n(\omega, t) = \frac{N \alpha_h \eta \bar{y}(\omega)}{(r + \delta_k) \Gamma_0^{\beta_0}(\omega, m)} \int_0^L \Gamma_0^{\beta_0}(\omega, m) d\omega,$$

where we use equations (A14) and (A20). We have the following corollary.

Corollary 1

The capital-land ratio decreases in distance from the CBD.[7]

4. Spatial Equilibrium by Simulation

So far our analyses have been conducted with general form of the production function. To simulate the model, we examine the spatial equilibrium by specifying the production function in the Cobb-Douglas form

$$F = AK_i^{\alpha} \bar{N}^{\beta}, \ \alpha + \beta = 1, \ \alpha, \beta > 0, \tag{21}$$

where A is the productivity of the industrial sector. We have $f = Ak_i^{\alpha}$. By equation (18), we solve

$$\frac{\bar{\alpha} \lambda \alpha^2}{\varepsilon} \left(\frac{f}{k_i} \right)^2 + \alpha^* k_i - \left(\frac{\xi + \delta_k \lambda}{\varepsilon} \right) \alpha_0 \alpha f - \frac{\alpha_1 f}{k_i} - \mu_0 = 0, \tag{22}$$

where

$$\mu_0 \equiv \left(\frac{\lambda \mu - \lambda \delta_k}{\varepsilon} \right) \delta + \mu, \ \alpha_0 \equiv \frac{1}{\alpha} + \bar{\alpha},$$

$$\alpha^* \equiv \left[(\delta + \mu) - \frac{\xi_1}{\lambda} - \left(\frac{\xi + \varepsilon}{\lambda} + \delta_k \right) \left(\frac{\lambda \mu - \lambda \delta_k}{\varepsilon} - 1 \right) \right] \alpha_0,$$

$$\alpha_1 \equiv \alpha + \alpha \delta \frac{\lambda}{\varepsilon} - \alpha \bar{\alpha} \left(\frac{\lambda \mu - \lambda \delta_k}{\varepsilon} - 1 \right).$$

[7] This result is also explained in the Muth model (see Fujita, 1999: Section 3.7).

In this case, we have

$$H(k_i) = \left[\left(1 - \frac{1}{\alpha_0 k_i}\right)\left(\delta + \mu + \frac{\alpha f}{k_i}\right) - \frac{\xi_1}{\lambda}\right]\left(\frac{\xi + \varepsilon}{\lambda} + \delta_k - \frac{\overline{\alpha}\alpha f / k_i - \delta}{\alpha_0 k_i}\right)^{-1} N.$$

From this equation, we determine k_i. Once we solve this equation, according to Lemma 1, we can solve all the other variables in the system. It is straightforward to solve the other location-independent variables as follows

$$r = \alpha A k_i^{-\beta} - \delta_k, \quad w = \beta A k_i^{\alpha}.$$

To solve the location-dependent variables, we specify the travel cost and time functions as follows

$$\Gamma(\omega) = \nu\omega, \quad \Gamma_c(\omega) = \nu_c \omega, \quad \nu, \nu_c > 0, \quad 0 \le \omega \le L. \tag{23}$$

Both travel time and cost are assumed to be linearly related to the distance. By equations (23) and (A21), for $\beta_0 \neq -1$ we solve

$$T_0 N - \nu N \left[\int_0^L \frac{d\omega}{\Gamma_0^{\beta_0}(\omega, m)}\right]^{-1} \int_0^L \frac{\omega}{\Gamma_0^{\beta_0}(\omega, m)} d\omega = m H_0(k_i), \tag{24}$$

where we use $w_0 \equiv \upsilon w + \upsilon_c$ and

$$\Gamma_0 = w T_0 + \mu m - w_0 \omega, \quad H_0(k_i) = \frac{H(k_i)}{k_i} - \left(\frac{\alpha_h \eta}{\alpha f} - \frac{\sigma}{w}\right)\left(\frac{H(k_i) + N}{\lambda}\right).$$

From equation (24), the average real money holding is determined. Following Lemma 1, we determine all the other variables at equilibrium as follows

$$\overline{m}(\omega) = r_0 \Gamma_0(\omega), \quad n(\omega) = n(\omega) = \frac{N}{\Gamma_0^{\beta_0}(\omega, m)}\left[\int_0^L \frac{d\omega}{\Gamma_0^{\beta_0}(\omega, m)}\right]^{-1}, \quad \overline{y}(\omega) = \left(\frac{r + \mu}{\varepsilon}\right) r_0 \Gamma_0(\omega, m),$$

$$R_h(\omega) = \eta^{\beta_h}\left(\frac{r + \delta_k}{\alpha_h}\right)^{\alpha_h} n^{\beta_h}(\omega)\overline{y}^{\beta_h}(\omega), \quad T_h(\omega) = \frac{\sigma \overline{y}(\omega)}{w}, \quad c(\omega) = \xi \overline{y}(\omega), \quad c_h(\omega) = \frac{\eta \overline{y}(\omega)}{R_h(\omega)},$$

$$s = \lambda \bar{y}(\omega),\ T_i(\omega) = T_0 - T_h(\omega) - \Gamma(\omega),\ k_h(\omega) = \frac{\alpha_h \eta \bar{y}(\omega)}{r + \delta_k},\ k(\omega) = \left(\frac{\lambda r + \lambda \mu}{\varepsilon} - 1\right)\bar{m}(\omega),$$

$$K = H(k_i)m,\ \bar{Y} = \frac{K + mN}{\lambda},\ \bar{N} = T_0 N - \int_0^L n(\omega)\Gamma(\omega)d\omega - \frac{\sigma \bar{Y}}{w},\ K_i = k_i \bar{N},\ K_h = K - K_i,$$

$$F = F(K_i, \bar{N}),\ L_h(\omega) = \frac{1}{n(\omega)},\ R(\omega) = \frac{\beta_h R_h(\omega) c_h(\omega)}{L_h(\omega)}.$$

To simulate the model, we specify values of the parameters as follows

$$A = 1.3,\ N = 10,\ L = 5,\ \alpha = 0.3,\ \alpha_h = 0.45,\ \varepsilon_0 = 0.05,\ \eta_0 = 0.1,\ \xi_0 = 0.11,\ \sigma_0 = 0.2,$$

$$\lambda_0 = 0.75,\ \vartheta = -0.2,\ \mu = 0.02,\ T_0 = 1,\ \upsilon = 0.01,\ \upsilon_c = 0.02,\ \delta_k = 0.06. \tag{25}$$

The population is fixed at 10 units and the urban size is fixed at 5 units. The total productivity is specified with 1.3. We specify α with 0.3 partly because some empirical studies with the Cobb-Douglas production function uses this value. The propensities to consume goods and consume housing are respectively specified at 0.11 and 0.1, which implies that the ratio between the expenditures on goods and housing is 1.1. The propensity to use leisure and to hold money are respectively specified at 0.2 and 0.05. The amenity parameter, $-\vartheta$, is negative. This implies that the households prefer to living in an area with low residential distribution. The total available time is fixed at unit and $\nu = 0.01$ means that the total travel time from the CBD to the other end of the system will use 5 per cent of the total available time. The travel cost per unit of distance is specified at $\nu_c = 0.02$. The depreciation rate is specified at 0.06.

We plot equations (22) and (2.3) in Figure 1. For the given parameters, the equations have unique solutions.

Following Lemma 1 under (25), we calculate the equilibrium values of the location-independent variables as follows

$$k_i = 1.100,\ f = 1.338,\ w = 0.936,\ r = 0.305,\ m = 0.368,\ \bar{N} = 6.203,\ K = 8.891,$$

$$K_i = 6.824,\ K_h = 2.067,\ F = 8.298,\ C = 1.843,\ S = 12.568. \tag{26}$$

The share of the capital employed by the housing sector is lower than the capital stocks employed by the industrial sector. The total labor input, $\bar{N}$, is equal to 6.2. As the total potential labor input is equal to 10,[8] about 38 per cent of the potential labor is used for leisure and travel. The rate of interest is about 36.5 per cent. We now plot the equilibrium values of the location-dependent variables as in Figure 2. The residential density, consumption of goods and housing consumption decline in distance. Both the housing rent and land rent fall in distance. The input of capital per household falls and the lot size increases in distance. The physical wealth and real money holdings per household decline in distance. Work time rises and leisure time decline in distance.

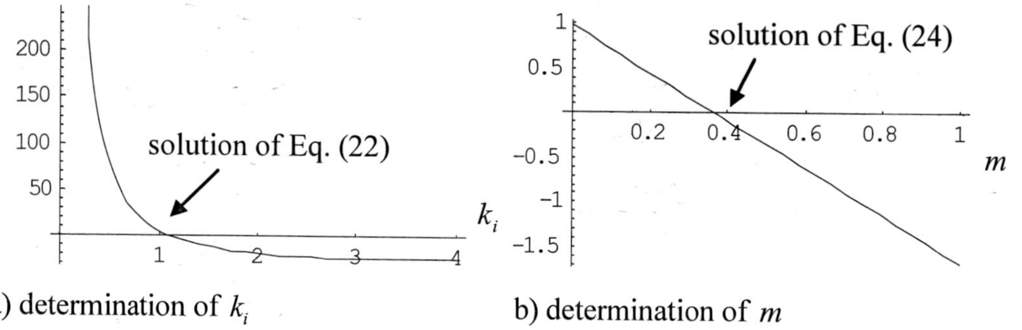

Figure 1. Determination of Capital Intensity and Average Real Money Holding.

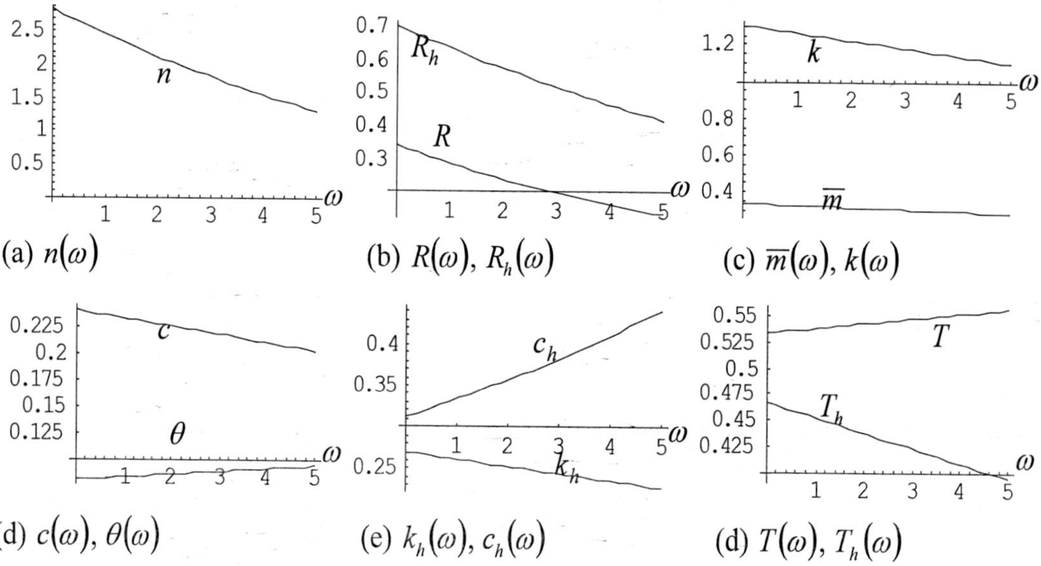

Figure 2. The Equilibrium Values of the Location-Dependent Variables.

[8] The "potential labor input" is the labor input if all workers spend all their available time on working without traveling and enjoying leisure. In this study, we neglect other possible relations between work time and work efficiency.

Let F_h stand for the total output of the housing sector. That is

$$F_h \equiv \int_0^L R_h(\omega) c_h(\omega) n(\omega) d\omega .$$

It can be shown that $F_h = \eta \overline{Y}$. The national output, Y, is given by

$$Y = F + F_h = 9.973.$$

The shares of the industrial and housing sectors in the national output are given by

$$\frac{F}{Y} = 0.832, \quad \frac{F_h}{Y} = 0.168.$$

The housing sector's share is 16.8 per cent.

5. Technological Change and Spatial Equilibrium

The previous sector studies the equilibrium structure of the economic geography. First, we examine effects of change in the total productivity. We introduce a symbol, $\overline{\Delta}$, by which a variable $\overline{\Delta} x$ stand for the change rate of the variable x in percentage due to changes in value of a parameter value. That is

$$\overline{\Delta} x \equiv \frac{x(A) - x(A_0)}{x(A_0)} \times 100,$$

where $x(A)$ stands for the value of the variable, x, with the parameter value A and $x(A_0)$ stands for the value of the variable, x, with the parameter value A_0. We now allow the total productivity to be changed from 1.3 to 1.5. The simulation results are given in (27) and plotted in Figure 3. As the productivity is improved, the capital intensity, the output per work time, the wage rate, the wealth per capita, the total capital stocks, the output per work hour, the wage rate, the capital stocks employed by the industrial sector, the total labor time, the total consumption level, the total output of the industrial sector, and the national output are all increased. The average real money holding, the capital stocks used by the housing sector, and the rate of interest fall as the productivity is increased. From Figure 3a the residential density falls near the CBD and rises far away from the CBD. This implies that the urban residenyial density becomes fatter over space. The leisure time rises and the work time falls at any location as the technology is improved. The consumption level, wealth and real money holding per household at any location are increased. The amenity is slightly affected. The land rent, rent of housing, housing rent, and housing consumption per capita are increased as technology is improved.

$$\bar{\Delta}k_i = 1053,\ \bar{\Delta}f = 1890,\ \bar{\Delta}w = 1890,\ \bar{\Delta}r = -9.07,\ \bar{\Delta}m = -1339,\ \bar{\Delta}N = 6.51,\ \bar{\Delta}K = 1313,$$

$$\bar{\Delta}K_i = 17.72,\ \bar{\Delta}K_h = -2.05,\ \bar{\Delta}F = 26.63,\ \bar{\Delta}C = 5.37,\ \bar{\Delta}S = 5.37,\ \bar{\Delta}Y = 23.07. \tag{27}$$

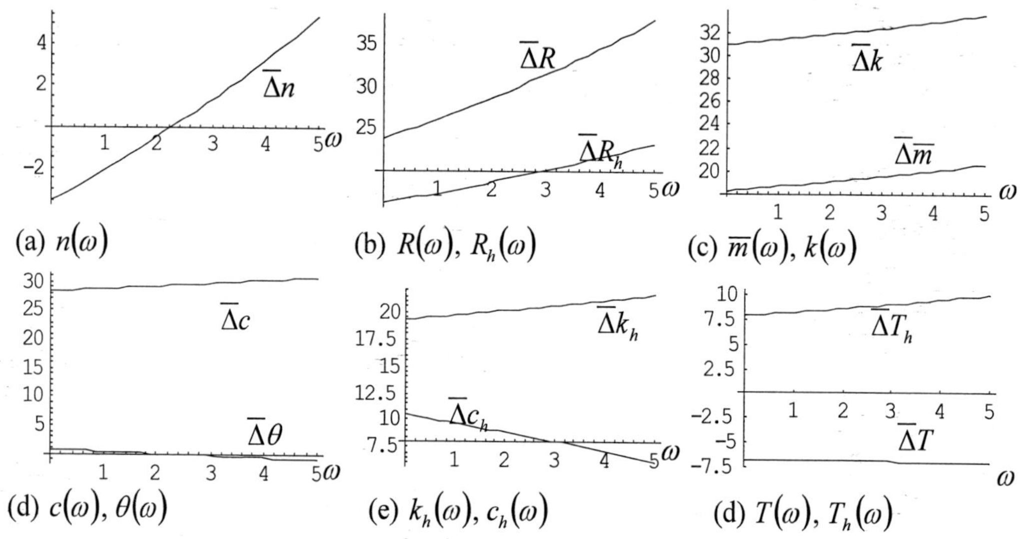

Figure 3. Technological Change and Spatial Equilibrium.

6. Transportation Conditions and Spatial Equilibrium

Improvement in transportation conditions and economic growth affect urban pattern formation and land use patters.[9] Improvement in transportation systems will bring a wide range of benefits to individuals and society. Some benefits are direct and some are indirect. As our growth model explicitly takes account of travel time and costs, we can examine issues related to effects of changes in transportation conditions upon the economic structure and spatial formation. First, we examine the spatial equilibrium structure when the travel speed, $1/v$, is changed. Let the parameter, v, falls from 0.01 to 0.08. The effects on the space-independent variables are given in (28). A decrease in v implies an increase in the travel speed. The variables,

[9] Knowles (2006) examines how transport innovations have changed the role of transport in shaping space over a long historical period. Knowles studies effects of cheaper and faster transport on spatial development at local, national and international levels, impacts of fixed links in removing transport barriers, effects of intermodality on land/sea transport systems, environmental externalities in increasingly mobile societies as well as social exclusion resulting from restricted access to transport. Although this paper considers the simplified transport, it provides some insights into the issues by analyzing exogenous changes in the parameters related to transport technology. It can be seen that our analytical framework should enable use to deal some of the important issues addressed by Knowles by extending the model to analyze transportation systems as an endogenous part of the economic system.

k_i, f, w, and r are not affected by changes in the travel speed. From Lemma 1, we see that the capital intensity of the industrial sector is not affected by the travel speed. As the output level of per unit labor input, the rate of interest and the wage rate per unit of labor input are uniquely determined by the capital intensity and technology of the industrial sector, we see that the change in the speed has no effects on these variables. Although these variables are not affected, a household's income from wage and the total output will be affected because these variables are also affected by the change in the time distribution. The variables, m, $\overline{N}$, K, K_i, K_h, F, C, S and Y, are increased in the same proportion. We provide the simulation results for the space-dependent variables as in Figure 4. As the travel time at fixed location to the urban center is reduced, the household at that location will increase leisure time and work time. Under the given preference for leisure time, we see that different from the case of technological improvement in the industrial sector, as the travel is sped up, the total work input is increased due to the increase in the total work time. As the total labor input is increased, the output is increased. The increase in the output increases the savings and the capital stocks. We see that as a consequence of the improvement in travel speed, the macroeconomic performance of the economy is improved.[10] As transportation conditions are improved, the residential density falls near the CBD and rises far away from the CBD. The land rent and rent of housing rise and fall where the residential density falls and rises. The consumption level of goods, capital stock and real money holding per household at any location are increased. The amenity and consumption of housing rise near the CBD and fall far away from the CBD.

$$\overline{\Delta}k_i = \overline{\Delta}f = \overline{\Delta}w = \overline{\Delta}r = 0, \ \overline{\Delta}m = \overline{\Delta}\overline{N} = \overline{\Delta}K = \overline{\Delta}K_i = \overline{\Delta}K_h = \overline{\Delta}F = \overline{\Delta}C = \overline{\Delta}S = \overline{\Delta}Y = 0.43. \tag{28}$$

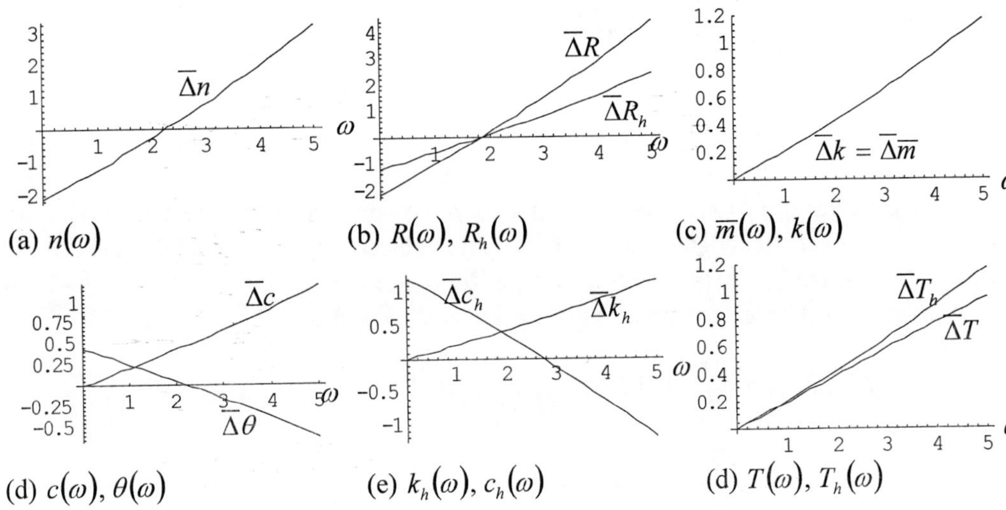

Figure 4. Change in Travel Speed and Spatial Equilibrium.

[10] A limitation of our model is that we don't take account of the costs for improving the transportation system. If we take account of the costs (which are paid by tax income either on households or the production sector), the conclusions for the macroeconomic performance may not be always positive.

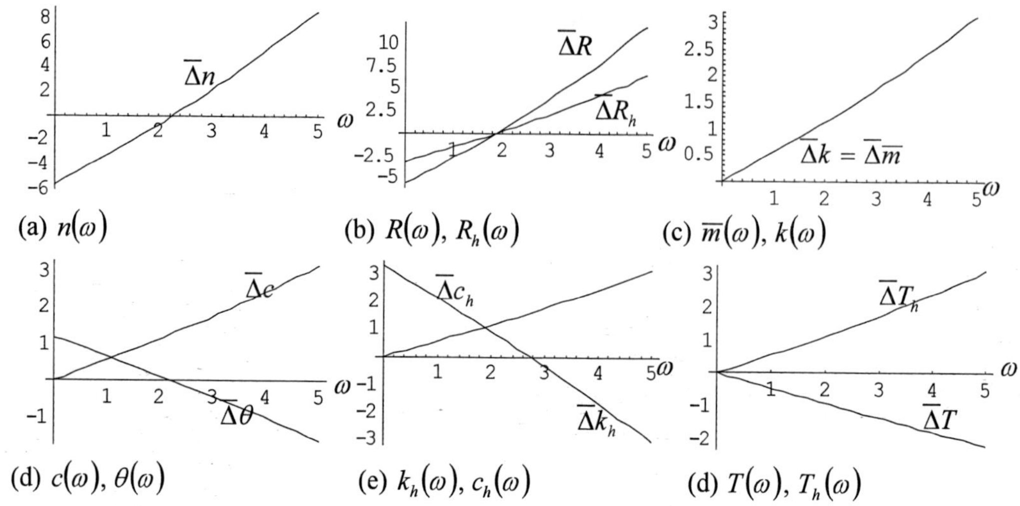

Figure 5. Travel Cost and Spatial Equilibrium.

We now allow the travel cost per unit of distance, v_c, to fall from 0.05 to 0.015. The effects on the space-independent variables are given in (29). The variables, k_i, f, w, $\bar{k}$ are not affected by the travel cost. The capital intensity of the industrial sector is not affected by the travel speed. As the output level of per unit labor input, the rate of interest and the wage rate per unit of labor input are uniquely determined by the capital intensity and technology of the industrial sector, the change in the cost has no effects on these variables. The simulation results for the other variables are plotted in Figure 5. As travel cost falls, the total labor, real money holding per household, total capital stocks, two sectors' capital stocks, the total output and total consumption are a;; reduced slightly in the same proportion. As people pay less for traveling the same distance, the household at a location becomes relatively richer as an immediate consequence of the change in travel cost. As people prefer to live in residential area with higher level of amenity which is negatively related to the residential density, some people will move away from the area near the CBD. As the population is redistributed so that the total work time is reduced, we see that the aggregated variables are reduced as travel cost is reduced. The residential density, land rent, and rent of housing become lower near the CBD and higher far away from the CBD. The leisure time at any location is increased and

$$\bar{\Delta}k_i = \bar{\Delta}f = \bar{\Delta}w = \bar{\Delta}r = 0, \ \bar{\Delta}m = \bar{\Delta}N = \bar{\Delta}K = \bar{\Delta}K_i = \bar{\Delta}K_h = \bar{\Delta}F = \bar{\Delta}C = \bar{\Delta}S = \bar{\Delta}Y = -0.06. \tag{29}$$

7. Amenity, Preference and Spatial Equilibrium

In the amenity function, $\theta_1 n^{\vartheta}(\omega)$, the parameter, θ_1, has no impact on the spatial equilibrium. We describe possible effects of amenity on the spatial equilibrium by how the system reacts to change in the parameter. We now increase ϑ from -0.2 to -0.1. The effects on the space-independent variables are given in (29). The variables, k_i, f, w and r not affected. The variables, m, $\overline{N}$, K, K_i, K_h, F, C, S and Y, are increased in the same proportion. We see that if residents react the local environment more positively, then the total labor input is slightly increased. The total capital stocks, the stocks employed by the industrial sector, the total output of the industrial sector, and the national output are all slightly increased. The effects on the location-dependent variables are plotted in Figure 6. The residential density, land rent, and rent of housing rise near the CBD and fall far away from the CBD. Because of the residential redistribution, the total labor supply is increased. The leisure time and work time are almost not affected. The consumption level of goods and amenity are increased. Physical wealth and real money holding at each location are almost not affected.

$$\bar{\Delta} k_i = \bar{\Delta} f = \bar{\Delta} w = \bar{\Delta} r = 0, \ \bar{\Delta} m = \bar{\Delta} N = \bar{\Delta} K = \bar{\Delta} K_i = \bar{\Delta} K_h = \bar{\Delta} F = \bar{\Delta} C = \bar{\Delta} S = \bar{\Delta} Y = 0.2. \tag{29}$$

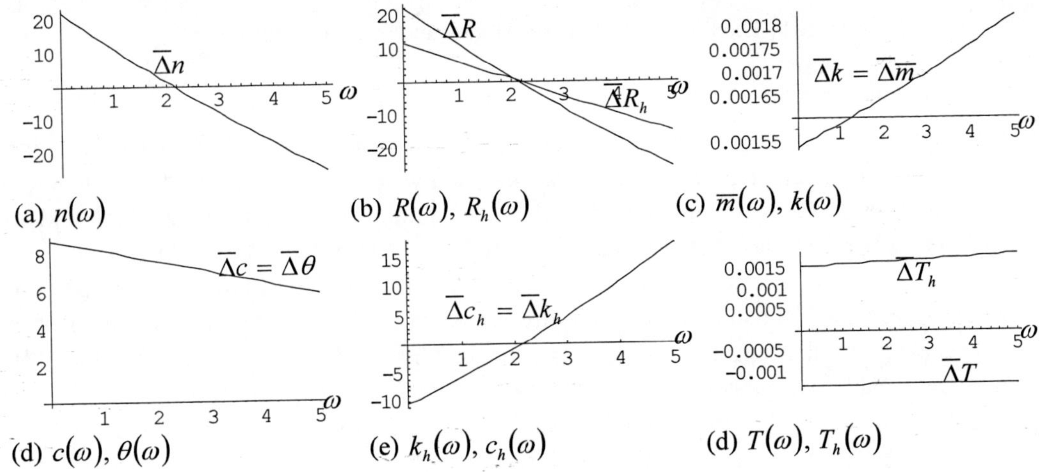

Figure 6. Amenity and Spatial Equilibrium.

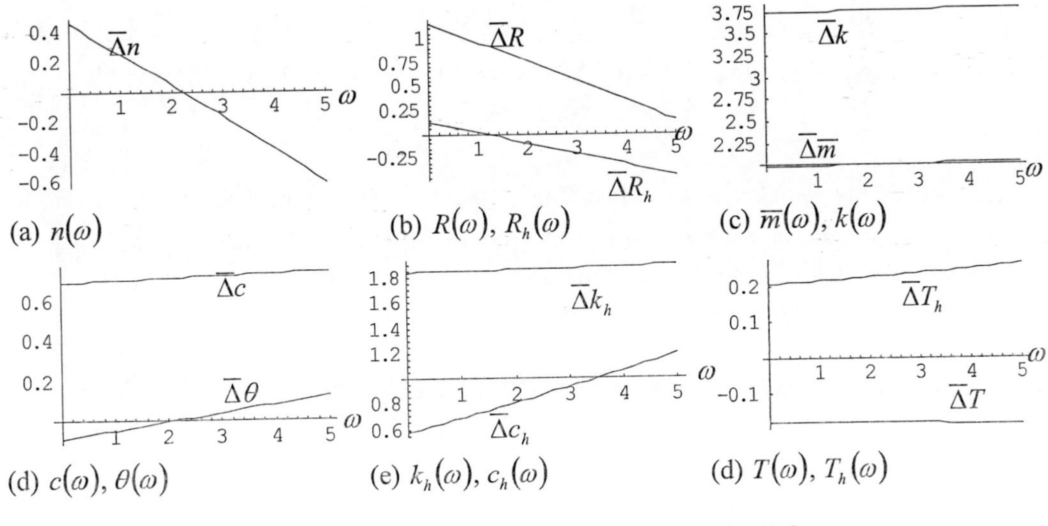

Figure 7. The Propensity to Save and Spatial Equilibrium.

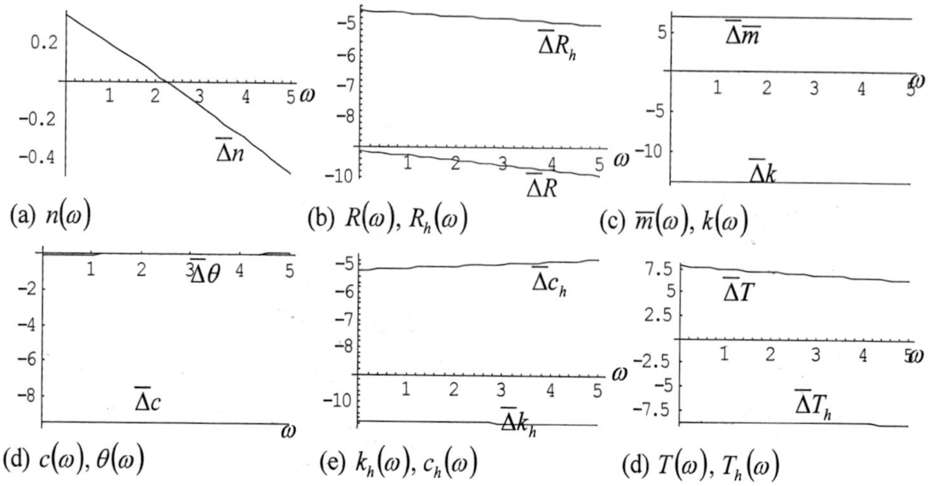

Figure 8. The Propensity to Hold Money and Spatial Equilibrium.

We now consider a case that the propensity to own wealth, λ_0, rises from 0.75 to 0.77. The effects of change in the propensity to save on the location-independent variables are given by (30). The capital intensity, output per work time, and wage rate are increased and the rate of interest falls. The total consumption, total capital stocks employed by the housing sector, and real money holding per household are reduced. The total work time, the total physical capital and total output are increased. The time-dependent variables are plotted in Figure 7. The residential density rises near the CBD and falls fra away from the CBD. The land rent is increased over the entire urban area but the rent of housing rises near the CBD and falls far away from the CBD. The physical wealth, real money holding, the consumption level of goods, and consumption lvel of housing are increased. The amenity falls near the CBD and rises far away from the CBD. The work time per capita falls and leisure time is increased.

$$\overline{\Delta}k_i = 1.64, \ \overline{\Delta}f = \overline{\Delta}w = 0.49, \ \overline{\Delta}r = -1.35, \ \overline{\Delta}m = -2.77, \ \overline{\Delta}N = 1.38, \ \overline{\Delta}K = 2.15,$$

$$\overline{\Delta}K_i = 3.04, \ \overline{\Delta}K_h = -0.79, \ \overline{\Delta}F = 1.88, \ \overline{\Delta}C = -1.91, \ \overline{\Delta}S = 0.71, \ \overline{\Delta}Y = 1.24. \tag{30}$$

We increase the propensity to hold money, ε_0, from 0.05 to 0.06. The effects are respectively represented in (31) and Figure 8. The capital intensity, output per work time and wage rate are reduced. The total work time and output are reduced. The average real money holding and total consumption level are increased.

$$\overline{\Delta}k_i = -2.02, \ \overline{\Delta}f = \overline{\Delta}w = -0.61, \ \overline{\Delta}r = 1.72, \ \overline{\Delta}m = 28.06, \ \overline{\Delta}N = \overline{\Delta}K = -3.75,$$

$$\overline{\Delta}K_i = -5.70, \ \overline{\Delta}K_h = 4.34, \ \overline{\Delta}F = -4.33, \ \overline{\Delta}C = \overline{\Delta}S = 5.84, \ \overline{\Delta}Y = -2.62. \tag{31}$$

We also simulate the effects when σ_0 rises from 0.2 to 0.23. The variables, k_i, f, w and r, are not affected. The variables, m, $\bar{N}$, K, K_i, K_h, F, C, S and Y, are reduced in the same proportion, -5.2. The residential density rises near the CBD and falls far away from the CBD. The land rent, rent of housing, per capita physical wealth, per capita consumption level, and real money holding fall over space. The leisure time is increased and the work time is increased. The amenity is slightly affected. We represent the effects of change in the inflation policy, μ, from 0.02 to 0.03 as in (32) and Figure 9. We see that money is not neutral in this model.

$$\bar{\Delta}k_i = 0.31,\ \bar{\Delta}f = \bar{\Delta}w = 0.09,\ \bar{\Delta}r = -0.26,\ \bar{\Delta}m = -7.63,\ \bar{\Delta}\bar{N} = 1.06,\ \bar{\Delta}K = 0.69,$$

$$\bar{\Delta}K_i = 1.36,\ \bar{\Delta}K_h = -1.53,\ \bar{\Delta}F = 1.15,\ \bar{\Delta}C = \bar{\Delta}S = -1.74,\ \bar{\Delta}Y = 0.66. \tag{32}$$

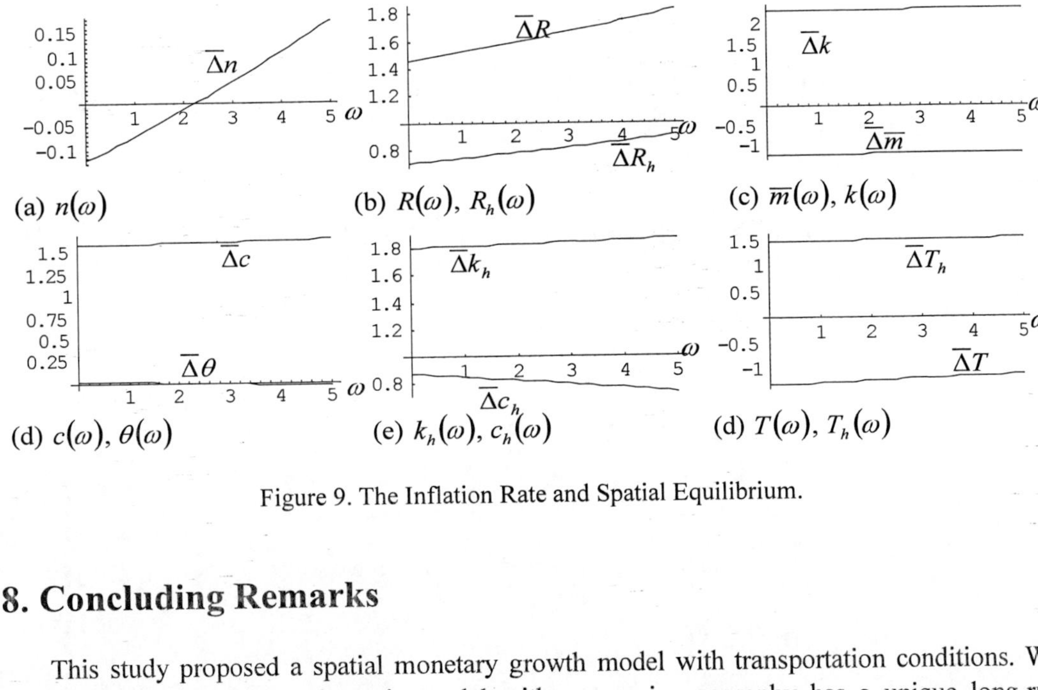

Figure 9. The Inflation Rate and Spatial Equilibrium.

8. Concluding Remarks

This study proposed a spatial monetary growth model with transportation conditions. We simulated the model. The dynamic model with economic geography has a unique long-run equilibrium point. We also analyzed changes in the total productivity of the industrial sector, transportation conditions, amenity, inflation policy and preference on the spatial equilibrium. As we are mainly concerned with implications of transportation systems for economic development, this paper is concerned with simple transportation systems. Many limitations of this model become apparent in the light of the sophistication of the literature of transportation research. It is important to examine implications of various transportation network structures for economic growth and development. As capital accumulation is endogenous in our model, our study makes it possible to introduce dynamics among infrastructure development, transportation systems, and economic growth, even though resulted models may become analytically less tractable. In this paper, we assume that urban land use is concentrated on residential use. Actually, production and transportation use land. For instance, Solow and Vickery (1971) examine use of urban land for transportation in a similar spatial setting as in this study. We may consider that at each location, land is used either for transportation and housing as follows: $L_H(\omega) + L_T(\omega) \le 1$, where $L_H(\omega)$ and $L_T(\omega)$ are respectively the ratios of land devoted to housing and transportation. We may thus treat travel time to the CBD at ω as a function of the residential density and transportation conditions from the CBD to the location.

Appendix: Proving Lemma 1

We are concerned with existence of equilibrium. First we define the total disposal income as

$$\bar{Y} \equiv \int_0^L \bar{y}(\omega) n(\omega) d\omega.$$

Multiplying the equations in (11) by $n(\omega)$ and then integrating the resulted equations from 0 to L with respect to ω, we obtain

$$mN = \frac{\varepsilon \bar{Y}}{r + \pi}, \quad C = \xi \bar{Y}, \quad (r + \delta_k)\frac{K_h}{\alpha_h} = \eta \bar{Y}, \quad S = \lambda \bar{Y}, \tag{A1}$$

where we use equation (15) and $R_h c_h = (r + \delta_k) k_h / \alpha_h$ from equations (4). By equation (12), we have $s(\omega) = a(\omega)$. From $s(\omega) = a(\omega)$, we have

$$S = K + mN,$$

where we use $a = k + \overline{m}$. From this equation and $S = \lambda \bar{Y}$, we solve

$$\bar{Y} = \frac{K + mN}{\lambda}. \tag{A2}$$

From $T_h = \sigma \bar{y} / w$ and the time constraint, we have

$$T_0 - \Gamma(\omega) - T(\omega) = \frac{\sigma \bar{y}(\omega)}{w}.$$

Multiplying the above equation by $n(\omega)$ and then integrating the resulted equations from 0 to L with respect to ω, we obtain

$$\overline{N} = T_0 N - \int_0^L n(\omega)\Gamma(\omega)d\omega - \frac{\sigma\overline{Y}}{w}. \tag{A3}$$

It should be noted that the national production is equal to the national consumption and national net saving. That is

$$C + S - K - mN - (\mu - \pi)mN + \delta_k K = F.$$

Substituting equations (A1) into the above equation yields

$$(\xi + \lambda + \varepsilon)\overline{Y} = F + \delta K + (\delta + \mu + f'(k_i))mN, \tag{A4}$$

where we use $r + \delta_k = f'(k_i)$ in equations (1) and $\delta \equiv 1 - \delta_k$. Insert equation (A2) in equation (A4)

$$\left(\frac{\xi + \lambda + \varepsilon}{\lambda}\right)(K + mN) = f'\overline{N} + \delta K + (\delta + \mu + f'(k_i))mN. \tag{A5}$$

From $r + \delta_k = f'(k_i)$ and $(r + \delta_k)K_h = \alpha_h \eta \overline{Y}$ in (A1), we have

$$f'(k_i)K_h = \alpha_h \eta \overline{Y}. \tag{A6}$$

Substituting equation (A4) into equation (A6) yields

$$\overline{\alpha} f' K = (f + \overline{\alpha} f' k_i)\overline{N} + \delta K + (\delta + \mu + f')mN, \tag{A7}$$

where we use $K_h = K - K_i$. From equations (A5) and (A7), we delete $\overline{N}$ and obtain

$$K = H(k_i)m, \tag{A8}$$

where

$$H(k_i) \equiv \left[\left(\frac{f}{f'} + \overline{\alpha} k_i - 1\right)\frac{(\delta + \mu + f')}{f/f' + \overline{\alpha} k_i} - \frac{\xi_0}{\lambda}\right]\left(\frac{\xi + \varepsilon}{\lambda} + \delta_k - \frac{\overline{\alpha} f' - \delta}{f/f' + \overline{\alpha} k_i}\right)^{-1} N.$$

We should require $H(k_i) > 0$. Equation (A8) determines the ratio, K/m, as a unique function of k_i.

Inserting equation (A2) and $\pi = \mu$ in the first equation in ((A1), we solve

$$\frac{K}{m} = \left(\frac{\lambda r + \lambda \mu}{\varepsilon} - 1\right)N.$$

Substituting equation (A8) and $r + \delta_k = f'(k_i)$ into the above equation yields

$$\Omega(k_i) \equiv H(k_i) - [\lambda f'(k_i) + \lambda \mu - \lambda \delta_k - \varepsilon]\frac{N}{\varepsilon} = 0. \quad \text{(A9)}$$

As we should require $H > 0$, we should also require

$$f'(k_i) > \delta_0 \equiv \delta_k + \frac{\varepsilon}{\lambda} - \mu.$$

As f' falls in k_i, to maintain the above inequality we should require $0 < k_i < k_i^*$, where $k_i^* = +\infty$ if $\delta_0 \le 0$ and $f'(k_i^*) = \delta_0$ if $\delta_0 > 0$.

Assume that the equation, $\Omega(k_i) = 0$, has a positive unique meaningful solution, $k_i > 0$. Once we determine k_i, then by equations (2) we immediately solve r and w as functions of k_i. Hence, in the rest of Appendix, we can treat k_i, r and w as parameters.

At equilibrium from equations (11) and (12) we have $\lambda \bar{y}(\omega) = a(\omega)$. Inserting this equation in $\bar{m}(\omega) = \varepsilon \bar{y}(\omega)/(r + \mu)$, we have

$$k(\omega) = \left(\frac{\lambda r + \lambda \mu}{\varepsilon} - 1\right)\bar{m}(\omega). \quad \text{(A10)}$$

From the definition of $\bar{y}(\omega)$, $\bar{m}(\omega) = \varepsilon \bar{y}(\omega)/(r + \mu)$, and $a = k + \bar{m}$, we have

$$\left(\frac{r + \mu}{\varepsilon}\right)\bar{m}(\omega) = (1 + r)k(\omega) + w[T_0 - \Gamma(\omega)] + \mu m - \Gamma_c(\omega). \quad \text{(A11)}$$

From equations (A10) and (A11), we solve

$$\bar{m}(\omega) = r_0 \Gamma_0(\omega), \quad \text{(A12)}$$

where

$$r_0 \equiv \left[\left(\frac{r+\mu}{\varepsilon}\right) - (1+r)\left(\frac{\lambda r + \lambda \mu}{\varepsilon} - 1\right)\right]^{-1}, \ \Gamma_0(\omega, m) \equiv \left[wT_0 + \mu m - w\Gamma(\omega) - \Gamma_c(\omega)\right].$$

Substituting equations (11) into $U(\omega)$ in (10) and then using $U(0) = U(\omega)$, we have

$$\frac{R_h(\omega)}{R_h(0)} = \left[\frac{n(\omega)}{n(0)}\right]^{\vartheta/\eta_0} \left[\frac{\bar{y}(\omega)}{\bar{y}(0)}\right]^{1/\eta_0 \rho}. \quad \text{(A13)}$$

From $R_h(\omega)c_h(\omega) = \eta \bar{y}(\omega)$ and $(r + \delta_k)k_h = \alpha_h R_h c_h$, we have

$$k_h(\omega) = \frac{\alpha_h \eta \bar{y}(\omega)}{r + \delta_k}. \quad \text{(A14)}$$

Substituting $c_h = k_h^{\alpha_h} L_h^{\beta_h}$ into $(r + \delta_k)k_h = \alpha_h c_h R_h$, we have

$$R_h(\omega) = \eta^{\beta_h} \left(\frac{r + \delta_k}{\alpha_h}\right)^{\alpha_h} n^{\beta_h}(\omega) \bar{y}^{\beta_h}(\omega). \quad \text{(A15)}$$

Substitute equation (A15) into equation (A13)

$$1 = \left[\frac{n(\omega)}{n(0)}\right]^{\vartheta/\eta_0 - \beta_h} \left[\frac{\bar{y}(\omega)}{\bar{y}(0)}\right]^{1/\eta_0 \rho - \beta_h}. \quad \text{(A16)}$$

From $\bar{m}(\omega) = \varepsilon \bar{y}(\omega)/(r + \mu)$ and equation (A12), we have

$$\bar{y}(\omega) = \left(\frac{r + \mu}{\varepsilon}\right) r_0 \Gamma_0(\omega, m). \quad \text{(A17)}$$

Insert this equation in equation (A16)

$$n(\omega) = \left[\frac{\Gamma_0(0, m)}{\Gamma_0(\omega, m)}\right]^{\beta_0} n(0), \quad \text{(A18)}$$

where

$$\beta_0 \equiv \frac{1/\eta_0 \rho - \beta_h}{\vartheta/\eta_0 - \beta_h}.$$

Integrating equation (A18), we obtain

$$n(0) = \frac{N}{\Gamma_0^{\beta_0}(0, m)} \left[\int_0^L \frac{d\omega}{\Gamma_0^{\beta_0}(\omega, m)} \right]^{-1}. \quad \text{(A19)}$$

Insert equation (A19) in equation (A18)

$$n(\omega) = \frac{N}{\Gamma_0^{\beta_0}(\omega, m)} \left[\int_0^L \frac{d\omega}{\Gamma_0^{\beta_0}(\omega, m)} \right]^{-1}. \quad \text{(A20)}$$

From $K = K_i + K_h$ and equation (A8), we obtain

$$k_i \overline{N} + K_h = H(k_i) m.$$

Insert (A3) and (A6) into the above equation

$$T_0 N - \int_0^L n(\omega) \Gamma(\omega) d\omega - \frac{\sigma \overline{Y}}{w} + \frac{\alpha_h \eta \overline{Y}}{k_i f'(k_i)} = \frac{H(k_i)}{k_i} m.$$

Insert equation (A2) into the above equation and then dividing the two sides of the resulted equation by m, we have

$$\left[T_0 N - \int_0^L n(\omega) \Gamma(\omega) d\omega \right] \frac{1}{m} = H_0(k_i) \equiv \frac{H(k_i)}{k_i} - \left(\frac{\alpha_h \eta}{k_i f'} - \frac{\sigma}{w} \right) \left(\frac{H(k_i) + N}{\lambda} \right), \quad \text{(A21)}$$

where we also use $K / m = H(k_i)$. Insert equation (A20) in (A21)

$$\left[T_0 N - N \left[\int_0^L \frac{d\omega}{\Gamma_0^{\beta_0}(\omega, m)} \right]^{-1} \int_0^L \frac{\Gamma(\omega)}{\Gamma_0^{\beta_0}(\omega, m)} d\omega \right] \frac{1}{m} = H_0(k_i). \quad \text{(A22)}$$

Equation (A22) contains a single variable, m. We have thus proved Lemma 1

References

Abdel-Rahman, H.M. (2004) The City System Paradigm: New Frontiers, in *Urban Dynamics and Growth: Advances in Urban Economics*, edited by Capello, R. and Nijkamp, P. Amsterdam: Elsevier.

Anas, A. (1978) Dynamics of Urban Residential Growth. *Journal of Urban Economics* **5**, 66-87.

Arnott, R.J. (1980) A Simple Urban Growth Model with Durable Housing. *Regional Science and Urban Economics* **10**, 53-76.

Arnott, R., Braid, R., Davidson, R. and Pines, D. (1999) A General Equilibrium Spatial Model of Housing Quality and Quantity. *Regional Science and Urban Economics* **29**, 283-316.

Banister, D. (1999) Planning More to Travel Less. Land Use and Transport. *Town Planning Review* **70**, 313–38.

Boarnet, M.G. and Crane, R. (2001) *Travel by Design: The Influence of Urban Form on Travel*. Oxford: Oxford University Press.

Brock, W.A. (1974) Money and Growth: The Case of Long Run Perfect Foresight. *International Economic Review* **15**, 750-77.

Buchanan, N., Barnett, R., Knigham, S., and Johnston, D. (2006) The Effect of Urban Growth on Commuting Pattens in Christchurch, New Zealand. *Journal of Transport Geography* **14**, 342-54.

Burmeister, E. and Dobell, A.R. (1970) *Mathematical Theories of Economic Growth*. London: Collier Macmillan Publishers.

De Palma, A., Kilani, M. and Lindsey, R. (2005) Congestion Pricing on a Road Network: A Study Using the Dynamic Equilibrium Simulator METROPOLIS. *Transportation Research A* **39**, 588-611.

Fischer, M.M., Button, K.J. and Nijkamp, P. (1996, edited) *Regional Housing and Labour Markets*. Cheltenham: Edward Elgar.

Fujita, M. (1999) *Urban Economic Theory – Land Use and City Size*. Cambridge: Cambridge University Press.

Glaeser, E.L. and Gyourko, J. (2005) Urban Decline and Durable Housing. *Journal of Political Economy* **113**, 345-75.

Glaeser, E.L., Kolko, J., and Saiz, A. (2001) Consumer City. *Journal of Economic Geography* 1, 27-50.

Henderson, J.V. (1974) The Sizes and Types of Cities. *American Economic Review* **64**, 640-56.

Kanemoto, Y. (1980) *Theories of Urban Externalities*. Amsterdam: North-Holland.

Knowles, R. D. (2006) Transport Shaping Space: Differential Collapse in Time–space. *Journal of Transport Geography* (in press).

Lin, C.C., Mai, C.C. and Wang, P. (2004) Urban Land Policy and Hosing in an Endogenously Growing Monocentric City. *Regional Science and Urban Economics* **34**, 241-61.

Maat, K., van Wee, B., and Stead, D. (2005) Land Use and Travel Behaviour: Expected Effects From the Perspective of Utility Theory and Activity-based Theories. *Environment and Planning B* **32**, 33–46.

Patinkin, D. (1965) *Money, Interest, and Prices: An Integrating of Monetary and Value Theory*, 2nd edition. New York: Harper and Row.

Rietveld, P., Button, K. and Nijkamp, P. (2003, edited) *Urban Transport*. Cheltenham: Edward Elgar.

Sidraski, M. (1967) Rational Choice and Patterns of Growth in Monetary Economy. *American Economic Review* **57**, 534-44.

Solow, R.M. and Vickrey, W.S. (1971) Land Use in a Long Narrow City. *Journal of Economic Theory* 3, 430-47.

Srinivasan, S. and Ferreira, J. (2002) Travel Behavior at the Household Level: Understanding Linkages with Residential Choice. *Transportation Research D* **7**, 225–42.

Tobin, J. (1956) The Interest Elasticity of the Transactions Demand for Money. *Review of Economics and Statistics* **38**, 241-47.

Train, K. and McFadden, D. (1978) The Goods/Leisure Tradeoff and Disaggregate Work Trip Mode Choice Models. *Transportation Research* **12**, 349-53.

Upton, C. (1981) An Equilibrium Model of City Sizes. *Journal of Urban Economics* **10**, 15-36.

Turnovsky, S.J. (2000) *Methods of Macroeconomic Dynamics*. Mass., Cambridge: MIT Press.

Zhang, W.B. (2005) *Economic Growth Theory*. Hampshire: Ashgate.

Zhang, W.B. (2006) *Growth with Income and Wealth Distribution*. London: Macmillan.

Zhang, W.B. (2007) Economic Geography and Transportation Conditions with Endogenous Time Distribution amongst Work, Travel, and Leisure. *Journal of Transport Geography* (in press).

In: Housing, Housing Costs and Mortgages
Editors: Szilárd Kis and Istvan Balogh, pp. 93-108
ISBN: 978-1-60741-813-9

Chapter 5

ESTIMATES OF HOUSING COSTS AND HOUSING DIFFICULTIES: AN APPLICATION ON ITALIAN METROPOLITAN AREAS*

Carmelo Maria Torre[1, a], Paola Perchinunno[b] and Francesco Rotondo[1]

[1]Department of Architecture and Urban Planning, Polytechnic of Bari, via Orabona 4, 70125 Bari, Italy

[2]Department of Statistical Science, University of Bari, Via C. Rosalba 53, 70100 Bari, Italy

Abstract

The paper shows a reasoning about how economic estimates and geostatistical analyses can support the necessary decision making process started with new national policies on social housing. The decision about priorities of housing policies, the dissemination of funding in the different parto of Italy can be helped by regional and local economic analyses.

In this light the role of evaluation is examined, in order to show which kind of approach can be referred to each dimension, context and level. After a general introduction explaining the main aspects of the National Housing Plan, an example of integrate assessment of rent market and difficulty in housing access is shown. The result is a scaling that profiles some Italian metropolitan reality, and identify the geographical general/local differentiation among cities/part of cities. All the examples are aiming to demonstrate that only an integrate, multilevel approach, supported by appropriate analysis can succeed in improving policies for increase supply and quality of housing stock.

Keywords: housing costs, economic policies, scan statistics, hot spots

---

* The contribution is the result of joint reflections by the authors, with the following contributions: C. M. Torre (paragraph 1, 2.3. and 4) to P. Perchinunno (paragraph 2.1, 2.2), and to F. Rotondo (paragraph 3.1 and 3.2).

[a] E-mail address: torre@poliba.it

[b] E-mail address: {s.montrone; mabil; p.perchinunno}@dss.uniba.it

1. Introduction

When compared to other European Union (EU) countries, Italy is characterised by one of the highest degree of housing ownership. 74% of Italian households are owned by resident families, the second highest percentage after Luxembourg (75%) in Western Europe. If we consider the ownership without mortgage, Italy ranks first.

According to the Italian Bureau of Statistics (ISTAT, 2004), an average 30% of family expenditure is devoted to their household. Among elderly people, that percentage increases up to 45%, in case of singles, and up to 36% for couples.

According to EFILWC (2006) that produced the first European survey of the social dimension of housing in the European Union (depicted in Figure 1), Italy is at the same time a country with a high degree of ownership (more less the 68%), and a low degree of social housing tenancy (5%)

Social/aided housing represents less than 5% of the total stock of owned/rented households, and the fourth worst result after Spain (2%), Greece (2%) and Luxembourg (1%) in western Europe. A strong correlation is apparent between high degrees of ownership and low degrees of social housing, whereas there seems not to be a general direct relationship between welfare system and social housing supply. Data about France, Germany, Italy, Spain, Sweden and UK (2003) show a various distribution of household conditions, quality, tenancy and ownership.

Home-owning is a main preoccupation of Italian families, who invest most of their savings to that purpose, with the aim of securing heritage for future generations (Guiso and Visco, 1994) However, the traditional consideration of household as a non-renounceable family asset clashes with the increase of around 40% in non-deflated price of households from 2000 to 2005 (Cannari and Faiella, 2006). The increasing trend followed a static period between 1996 and 1999, framed in a more general economic recession.

At the same time, in the Italian context the perception of heaviness of housing cost is the most relevant in Europe, as a research inside the EU fourth framework program demonstrates (ECHP, 2002).

Over the last five years of the previous millennium, a relevant survey attributed the perception of heaviest financial burden due to housing costs to Italian renters and low-income owners in the whole EU-15 (ECHP, 2002), as shown in Figure 2. The gloomy perspective on housing costs is due to low-income renters (pessimistic answers being more than 50% of the sample) rather to than low-income owners (for whom the pessimistic answers are more than 40% of the sample).

In Italy, another reason behind the growing attention to ownership costs lies in the loss of real purchasing power (13% of loss for employees from 2001 to 2007).

Finally, the most recent survey of the Italian Institute Censis and ISTAT about Italian Households expenditure, confirmed that the contemporaneous increase of cost of life with the increase of mortgage rates push the average percentage of cost devoted to house owning upper the threshold of 40% of family balance.

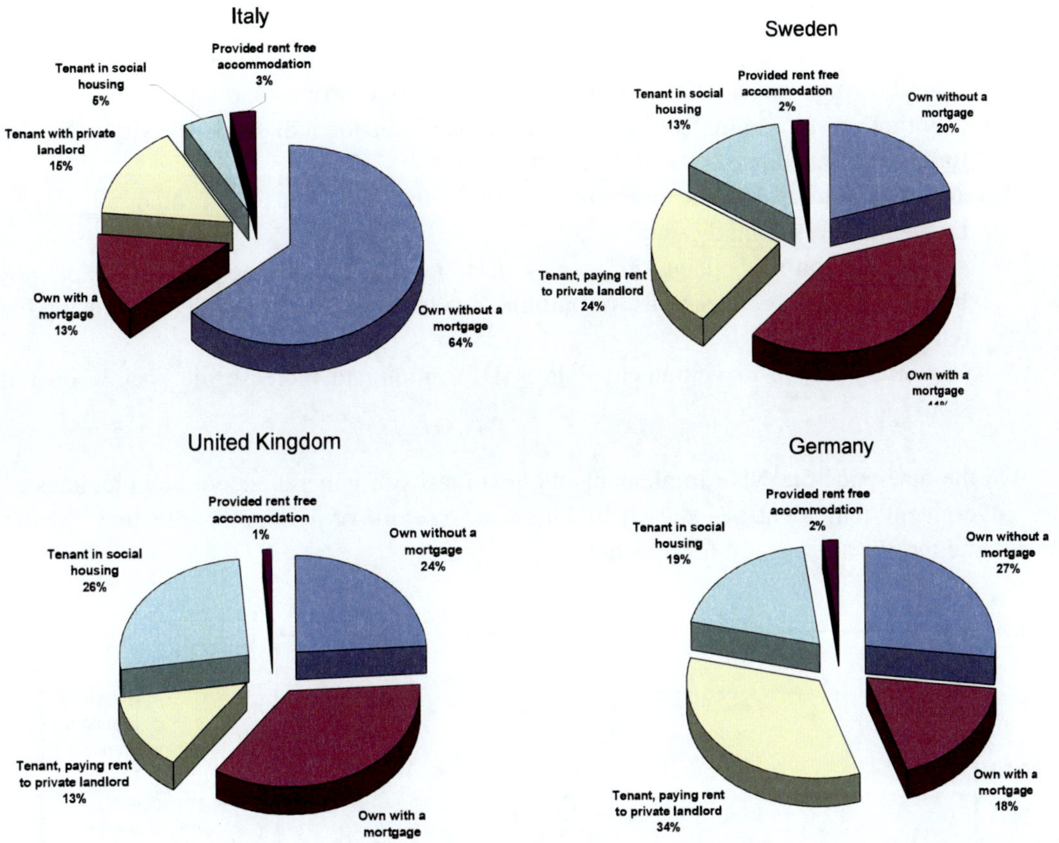

Figure 1. Distribution of the social housing stock in some EU countries (adapted after EFLWC, 2006).

The preoccupation of owning a house increases with the increase of economic difficulty of families, and with the availability of low cost homes for low income families.

The issue of housing costs has become more relevant in European Policies since the enlargement from fifteen to twenty-seven member states, against the background of aiming at higher social cohesion, a main hindrance being in fact the equalisation of living and housing costs (SOCOHO, 2004).

The OECD (2005) re-consideration of housing ownership cost as a factor related to inflation causes in the balance of European households is a further evidence of that renewed attention.

Just in the last two years The debate about housing accessibility and ownership conditions is gaining momentum in the Italian context as well , due to ever increasing prices over the last years in all metropolitan real estate markets.

In order to deal with the question, in fact the general financial programme provided by the Italian Government (with the national act 133/2008) set the basis of the "National Housing Plan" (NHP). The NHP guidelines identify on one side five tasks to increase the offer of low-rent dwellings, that are at the core of the government policies:

1. constitution of an integrate system of real estate funds (REF), in order to acquire and to build new residential estate, provided to increase the housing offer. Such system should involve financial and estate companies, public-private partnership;
2. quantitative and qualitative increase of the public residential stock, usually suffering for high maintenance costs of its heritage;
3. aid to private real estate operating investors in social housing, promoting project financing of residential estate;
4. aid to cooperative housing companies (CHC), which represent the most important Italian no-profit organisations for building residential estate, if devoted to housing for rent;
5. support to Urban Development Plan (UDP) aiming to increase the social housing stocks.

On the other side the NHP implements the main tasks of general economic guidelines of the government that identifies the main interested sectors of Italian People that can be considered mostly needing aid for housing.

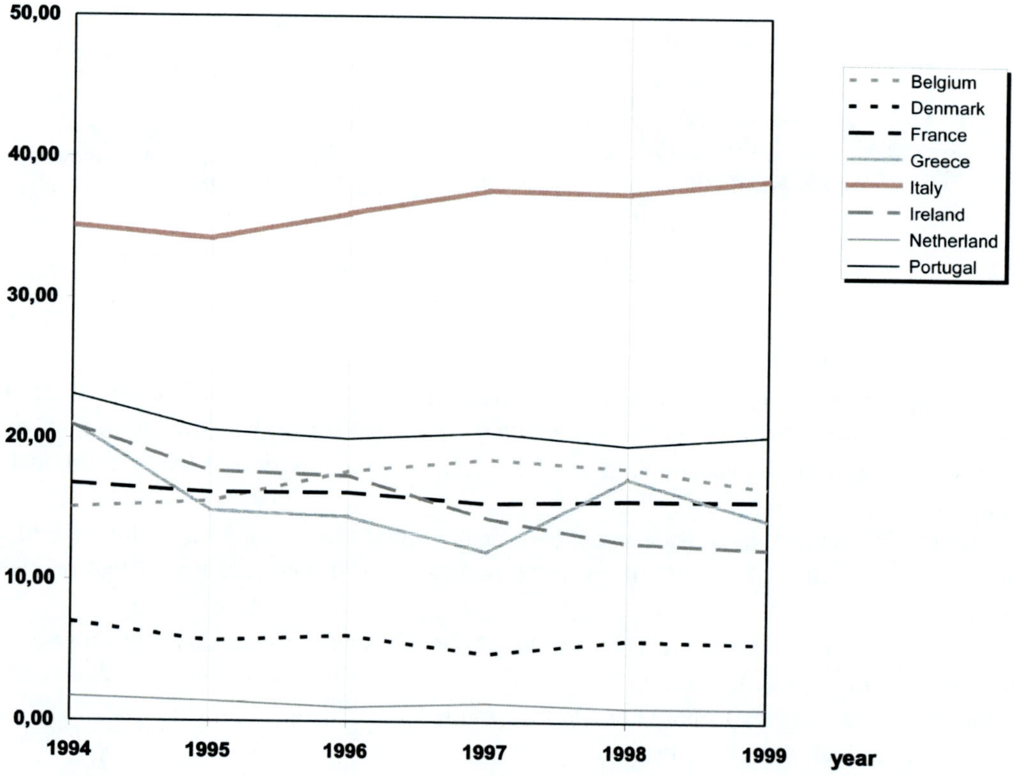

Figure 2. Percdentage of families suffering "perceived heaviness" of housing cost in EU Countries (adapted after ECHP, 2002).

The identified targets are:

- low income families,
- young couples,
- university students,
- elderly people,
- long-term migrants
- people subjected to tenancy eviction.

To apply the NHP on the above target of population it becomes necessary on one hand to know about costs of living in a house for families, and on the other hand, how many families in a city find the difficulty in renting of buying a home because of their condition of social deprivation.

In some recent speech, the Italian Premier, Mr. Silvio Berlusconi, showed the possibility to build in the short term many hundreds of thousands of homes.

This intention brings to mind the experience of Swedish Million Homes Programme, pain and delight of Welfare State among Sixties and Seventies in Sweden (Borgegård and Kemeny, 2004). That programme is reminded and as the biggest plan of social housing in the history of Europe (1.006.000 homes in nine years), and, as a consequence, tha cause of the first transition from dwelling shortage to dwelling surplus, accompanied with relevant costs of refurbishment of the housing stock (Hall and Vidèn, 2005).

Looking abroad, in the same time as Italy, UK, by the support of the National Housing Corporation (HC), started with the affordable housing programme (since April 2008), which in some way seems to be similar to the Italian NHP, according to the policies of refurbishment of the existing housing stock. HC in the meanwhile is promoting studies about the impact of credit crunch and market changes have been on the supply, or on the demand for, and about the affordability of low cost homes ownership (CCHPR, 2008).

To conclude this introduction we can say that the attitude of European Countries that are paying attention to housing inequalities is oriented towards tree different tools:

a) financial leverage, to make more attractive for investors and entrepreneurs the production of social housing stock on rent, or to renew the existing,
b) inclusive planning to realize new integrate settlements and increase the supply of homes,
c) direct funding to weak part of homeless people.

These tree tools are not neutral or indifferent respect to the socio-economic context of cities.

The financial leverage need a minimum critical mass to be effective and attractive. Direct financing, instead, can rich single target, but often without guarantee about a good result.

Planning for rehabilitation and integration need a physical-spatial contiguity and recurrence of similar state of difficulty, and needs an active role of local authorities, collaborating with the central or the regional ones.

This means that some evaluation of which instrument could be useful, as it is tried to show in the following pages.

The aim of this work is to integrate Economic Evaluation and Statistical Methods to identify geographical hot spots of the presence of urban housing discomfort connected with low-value properties and a low presence of residential facilities.

According to this scope, the paper describes on one hand the way to investigate the spatial localisation of social-residential discomfort in each metropolitan district, by the use of spatial fuzzy clustering and the identification of hot spot condition, and on the other hand, the way to intersect the profile of the obtained dissemination of residential discomfort with the heaviness of the housing ownership cost in each metropolitan area.

The following paragraph, therefore, describes the utilised indicators to describe the social-residential discomfort in a sample of Italian Metropolitan Areas.

After the description of indicators, the way to combine in a fuzzy complex profile and the way to emphasise the hot spot of discinfort are shown.

Finally, after the description of the way to calculate the housing ownership cost in the Italian context, a comparison between the evidence of statistics and the estimate of heaviness of ownership is described.

2. The Identification of Social and Housing Difficulty Indices

2.1. A Multidimensional Approach for the Identification of Urban Difficulty

At the city level, policies can be addressed by investigating condition of unavailability of housing services and quality, to understand better some peculiar aspect of distribution of housing difficulty.

The presence of a varied range of definitions on the theme of urban discomfort underlines the necessity of no longer relying on a single indicator but on a group of indicators. The different scientific research pathways are consequently directed towards the creation of *complex indicators*, sometimes going beyond dichotomized logic in order to move towards a classification which is "*fuzzy*" in nature, in which every unit belongs to the category of discomfort with a range from 1 (*maximum discomfort*) to 0 (*absence of discomfort*), the values of discomforts represent in practices different levels of *"urban poverty"*. Classifying the populations of home residents simply as either *poor* or *non-poor* constitutes an excessive simplification of reality, negating all shades of difference existing between the two extremes of high level well-being and marked material impoverishment. Urban poverty/housing discomfort are certainly not that kind of attribute which can characterize an individual in terms of presence or absence, but rather is manifested in a range of differing degrees and shades (Cheli and Lemmi, 1995).

2.2. Identifying Indicators of Social and Housing Difficulty

With regards to the choice of difficulty indices there is, therefore, a consideration of various aspects associated to educational levels, to working conditions and to housing conditions along with the quality of housing. The indices were chosen with the aim of identifying the level of residential poverty and were calculated in order to align elevated levels on the indices with elevated levels of poverty.

The various indices were classified into *two sets*:

- *Social difficulty of residents*, related to the conditions of the resident population within the various census sections (educational qualifications, working conditions, overcrowding);
- *Housing difficulty,* related to the housing conditions of dwellings occupied by residents in the various census sections (housing status, lack of functional services such as landline telephone and heating systems).

A particular index tied to *social difficulty* of the resident population, the *index of lack of progress to high school diploma,* is obtained by elaborating the ratio between the total resident population aged 19 or over who have not achieved a high school diploma and the total resident population of the same age. Such an evaluation presupposes that poverty is in some way tied to levels of schooling, at the very least in cultural terms. Another important index as a measure of poverty, tied to occupational dynamics, is the *rate of unemployment*, understood as resulting from the ratio between the population aged 15 or over in search of employment with respect to the total labour force of the same age group. A further measure is the *index of overcrowding*: the ratio between the total number of residents and size of dwellings occupied by residents. Connected to the phenomena of *housing difficulty* is the evaluation of the *classification of housing status* (in rented accommodation, homeownership, usufruct or free use). In particular, it is evident that homeownership is an indicator inversely correlated to poverty. A measure of poverty is, therefore, represented by the *incidence of the number of dwellings occupied by rent-payers* with respect to the total number of dwellings occupied by residents. Finally, aspects of residential poverty associated with the *availability of functional services* are considered in the analysis, including goods of a certain durability destined for communal use such as the availability of landline telephone or the presence of heating systems. Consistent with the aim of identifying aspects related to poverty, the *incidence of the number of dwellings deprived of services* was calculated for each residence (landline telephone and heating system) with respect to the total number of dwellings occupied by residents.

The different indices of social and housing difficulty were calculated both for individual sections of some metropolitan areas in Italy: Bologna, Firenze, Milano, Torino, Genova, Roma, Cagliari, Bari and Napoli. Table 1 shows average indexes of household poverty for each city.

The analysis of urban poverty in the above mentioned cities, shows that the percentage of people over 19 years who have not achieved a *high school diploma* ranges from 44.8% in Roma to 58.5% in Napoli. As regards to the *unemployment rate* we can see very low percentages in Northern Italy cities (Bologna 4.3%, Firenze 5.2% and Milano 5.5%) and higher scores in Southern Italy cities (Cagliari 17.6%, Bari 19.5% and Napoli 30.5%).

This index highlights the serious social and economic difficulties occurring in some areas. With regard to the *overcrowding rate*, an average of less than 3 inhabitants per 100 square meters is observed in some cities (Bologna and Firenze for example), at variance with Napoli where the largest rate of about 4 people on average for every 100 square meters of housing occurs.

Table 1. Average of indexes in some Italian metropolitan areas, 2001

	Educational qualifications	Working conditions	Over-crowding	Housing status	Lack of landline telephone	Lack of heating system
Bologna	49.0%	4.3%	2.6%	27.5%	9.5%	0.2%
Firenze	50.5%	5.2%	2.6%	24.4%	7.0%	1.1%
Milano	44.9%	5.5%	2.8%	34.0%	11.3%	0.3%
Torino	54.0%	8.1%	3.0%	32.2%	14.8%	0.6%
Genova	55.8%	8.3%	2.8%	24.2%	10.9%	1.5%
Roma	44.8%	10.9%	3.0%	23.5%	9.4%	2.2%
Cagliari	47.5%	17.6%	2.7%	18.9%	15.2%	23.5%
Bari	54.9%	19.5%	3.4%	29.4%	16.8%	10.2%
Napoli	58.5%	30.5%	4.1%	44.2%	16.9%	33.1%

Source: Our elaboration of the data from the Population and Housing Census, 2001.

As regards to the *typology of occupation*, the percentage of the dwelling occupied by renters ranges from a minimum of 18.9% of residents rent in Cagliari to a maximum of 44.2% in Napoli. As regards to the incidence of *dwellings deprived of landline telephone*, scores vary from a minimum of 7.0% in Firenze to a maximum of 16.8% in Bari and of 16.9% in Napoli. Even stronger is the difference with respect to *dwellings with no heating system*: these percentages are close to zero in Northern Italy cities (because of the lower temperatures), whereas higher percentages are observed in Southern Italy (23.5% in Cagliari and 33.1% in Napoli).

2.3. The Estimate of the Ownership Cost

The geography of poverty in the urban context does not give a complete information about the ability of families in accessing to the residential stock.

The depicted statistics, in fact, offers a detailed information about the spatial concentration of areas of difficulty, but they do not provide a measure of the possibility to find an appropriate accommodation in the housing market.

The equilibrium of demand and offer, and the counterbalance between rent and sale of dwellings varies from a city to another: it can be measured in a general way by the relationship between ownership costs and real rents of houses, or income of families.

The idea is that, after the construction of profile which put on evidence the variability of the dissemination of difficulty inside each metropolitan area, the ownershio cost could be an appropriate integration in a decision making process at the national level, to address priorities and to discriminate among urgent condition in the different metropolises.

The housing ownership cost represents the annual cost of households Endershott & Slemrod, 1983). The household is the place of production of "lodging service", compensated by the home rent.

Poterba (1984), in a highly quoted paper defines household as an asset, valuable in the market by referring to the cost of realisation, the cost of owning and the imputable rent. He identified some main contributions to the composition of housing cost, which was expressed as follows in its original formulation:

$$R = P(\delta + k + (1-\theta)(i-\mu) - \pi_H)$$

where R is the imputable rent of household, and P is the real price of household,

i is the lost interest obtainable with alternative investment to the buying of the household, if necessary corrected with the reduction of taxes on income deriving from mortgage discount,

1-θ is the incidence of taxation of property, paid with a marginal rate θ,

k represents the repair costs,

δ represents the depreciation of households in the market,

π represents the inflation.

The equilibrium between housing services cost and benefit implies that the former equals the imputed rent of owner-occupied households.

Himmelberg et al. (2005) propose a newer formulation of $R = P_t u_t$ (measured at the time t) with the following six component at the time *t*:

$$P_t u_t = P_t r^{rf} + P_t \omega_t - P_t \tau_t (r_t^m + \omega_t) + P_t \partial_t - P_t g_{t+1} + P_t \gamma_t$$

a) the cost of foregone potential not earned by investing differently that in a house, related to risk-free (denoted by the apex *rf*) interest rate r_t^{rf} (considered in opportunity cost terms).
b) the yearly cost of property taxes, ω_t.
c) the tax deductibility of mortgage interest r_t^m (denoted by the apex *m*) and property taxes on income taxation, $P_t\tau_t(r_t^m+\omega_t)$.
d) the repair costs expressed as a fraction δ_t of home value.
e) the expected capital gain (or loss) during the year from *t* to *t+1*, g_{t+1}
f) the additional risk premium $P_t\gamma_t$, to compensate homeowners for the higher risk of owning *vs*. renting.

The hypothesis of equilibrium in the housing market implies that the expected annual ownership cost should not rise up the annual cost of renting. In this case we should expect a decrease of house prices or a reduction of yearly housing sales. The converse happens if annual ownership costs fall. This naturally correcting process implies a "no arbitrage" condition which states that the one-year rent must equal the sum of the annual costs of owning. Using the above equation, we can summarize this logic by equating annual rent with the annual cost of ownership.

Some scholars (Nakagami. & Pereira, 1993) highlighted, by observing trends in different markets, that such standard formulations of ownership costs tend to undervalue the "bequest value". The estimate of ownership costs could be overvalued in co-presence of low taxation of property assets and high taxation of financial assets. It means that in such cases the bequest value represents a transferable (fiscal, but not only) advantage from the present generation to the future one.

The difference between user cost and actual rent could be a measure of the *misperception* of advantages/disadvantages deriving from owning/renting a household (Case & Shiller, 1988) or a way to provide forecasts about "bubbles" (Stigliz, 1990)

Haurin and Chung (1988) introduce a "survival function" and a "hazard function" of maintaining property; such functions are related to a time variation of components of housing costs.

Stein (1995) and, more recently, Harding and others (2004) found that even a small variation of the ownership cost could correspond to relevant changes in the real estate market.

As regards Italy, the estimete of ownership cost is not an easy task, especially due to the lack of transparency of real estate market transactions..

As regards the opportunity cost of alternative investments, national stocks have been taken in consideration.

The annual repair costs has been deducted from data provided by the national association of home builder (ANCE) and from geographical variation of costs provided by the national bureau of statistics (ISTAT).

As regards taxation costs, the municipal property tax (ICI) has been considered; ICI in fact provides a realistic information (if compared with the taxation of personal income, that is based on an obsolete cadastral system).

In the same way, as regards the deductibility from taxation, the maximum reduction of ICI has been considered.

The capital gain/loss referable to housing asset has been appraised on the basis of reports provided by the above mentioned real estate consultancy firms. Finally the risk of owning versus renting has been derived from an elaboration of housing insurance costs.

As regards the quality of data acquisition and elaboration, save for some relevant Research Institutions (such as the Study Center at the Bank of Italy, or the National Bureau of Statistics - Istat), there is hardly any attention paid to non statistical approaches to those questions. A main difference between Italy and the USA is the relative homogeneity of imputed rent, in the same way of other items related to construction costs and taxation. Unlike USA, in the Italian context the variability of fiscal legislation is very limited at a local scale, and estimates based on time-series surveys are very difficult, also for the lack of transparency in real estate market.

Italian tradition of real estate appraisal is the counterpart of economic studies, in developing reflections on rental costs in real estate market, and can play a relevant role in analysis of implication in housing policies.

For instance, reminding Appraisal Institute studies, Simonotti (2006) uses the addiction method to formulate the imputed rent, quite similarly to the above mentioned Poterba (1984). Further back, than Poterba, Forte and de Rossi (1976) gave a definition of imputed rent in the real estate market, as "pendulum" waving around the value of a more or less stable centre of 4%, according to traditional economics contribution (risk-free rate, fiscal policies, demand-offer equilibrium). Again, the conceptual reminding of the *bequest value* quoted by Nakagami and Pereira (1993), seems to correspond with the concept of *social complex values* of Italian built housing heritage (Fusco Girard, 1987) Starting again from the nine metropolitan cities of above (Bari, Bologna, Cagliari, Firenze, Genova, Milano, Napoli, Roma and Torino) we set a comparison between ownership costs and rents, based on the analyses carried out by the most important Italian real estate consultancy firms (e.g. Gabetti, Nomisma, FIAIP).

If theory works and data are truly effective, those places where the gap between ownership costs and rent is small, should be in a peak condition. In that condition owners should decide among the alternative of renting at an higher price, or to sale. Turin, for example, has been affected by an increase of rents, and maybe by a contraction of the demand, due to an external factor, represented by the seek for profitable short-term rents, in occasion of the Winter Olympic Games. In this case Turin represents a exception among great urban areas (Rome, Naples, Florence Milan) where the existence of a consistent demand of university students and commuters contributes to have high middle-term rents.

3. The Identification of Hot Spots of Housing Discomfort and Social Difficulty in Bearing Housing Costs

3.1. A Model Based Scan Statistics

The second steps in statistical analysis is to go further, by the introduction of a physical reference to urban spaces characterised by discomfort.

Scan statistics are used to detect and evaluate clusters in a temporal, spatial or space-time setting. This is done by gradually scanning a window across time and/or space, noting the number of observed and expected observations inside the window at each location. In the SaTScan software, the scanning window is either an interval (in time), a circle or an ellipse (in space) or a cylinder with a circular or elliptic base (in space-time). Multiple different window sizes are used. The window with the maximum likelihood is the most likely cluster, that is, the cluster least likely to be due to chance. A *p*-value is assigned to this cluster (Block 2007).

Table 2. Comparison between ownership cost and rent in some metropolitan areas, year 2004-2005

City	Ownership Cost				Rent				Shift rent own. cost
	central	semi centr	periph.	average	central	semi centr	periph.	average	
Bari	5.1	5.4	5.4	5.3	5.3	5.6	6.2	5.7	8.2%
Bologna	4.1	4.6	4.6	4.5	4.4	4.7	4.7	4.6	3.3%
Cagliari	5.0	5.1	5.3	5.1	5.8	5.5	5.8	5.7	11.3%
Firenze	4.0	4.0	4.1	4.1	5.1	5.3	5.5	5.3	30.9%
Genova	4.7	4.8	5.4	5.0	5.2	5.5	6.2	5.6	13.7%
Milano	4.1	4.0	4.4	4.1	4.6	5.0	5.3	5.0	19.9%
Napoli	4.5	4.7	5.0	4.7	5.7	6.0	6.3	6.0	27.8%
Roma	4.3	4.5	4.8	4.5	6.2	6.4	7.2	6.6	45.5%
Torino	4.7	4.7	4.8	4.7	4.7	4.8	4.9	4.8	1.5%

In this case, with the use of the SaTScan model a possible identification of hot spots of discomfort has been obtained from the data generated by a fuzzy analysis starting from two sets of indicators (the first for social difficulty, the second for housing difficulty). SaTScan operates by locating a circular window of arbitrary radius, and calculating the probability of urban difficulty, inside the circle, or the probability of urban difficulty, outside the circle, and consequently by optimizing the dimension of the radius (Montrone et al., 2009)

3.2. Geographical Clustering of Social and Housing Difficulty

Of the four cities analyzed in the previous chapter was made the territorial representation only in some cities, which are considered significant for high homogeneity or heterogeneity of the data resulting from the application fuzzy. In particular, have been represented the cities with some situations of greater social and housing difficulty (as Napoli, Bari and Cagliari) and cities with less discomfort (as Bologna). In detail, for every city we have identified a different number of clusters, composed of a different number of census sections, where the identification of difficulty is given by the inside average; the higher the average value, the higher is the level of poverty. A further aspect of interest is given by the *p*-value, that is the probability of the critical region of the test, where the lower the values shown, the better defined is the cluster.

The interpretation of data analysis shows that the value of inside averages (included in the interval 0-1) are very high, except for Bologna. Optimal values are shown also by *p*-values. Among the different clusters, someone are strongly discriminating, whereas others show a non-significant *p*-value for the reason that we have few cases inside the area or a strong variability is apparent, although around a high value of the inside average (Table 3). The different clusters are shown on a map by a shades of green ranging from maximum degree of social and housing difficulty (the darkest grey) to minimum degree (the lightest grey) so that the represented reality is immediately understandable (Figure 3).

In detail, two critical areas are observed in *Bari*: the *old centre* of the city, called “San Nicola”, Madonnella and Carrassi. We have two secondary clusters as well (characterised by a lower average of 0.41), which can be identified with areas in which intense council housing took place during 60s (Stanic, San Girolamo, Carbonara and Ceglie).

In *Cagliari* we have two areas of strong deprivation, where an average of 0.8 is observed. In particular, are identified the areas of Manna-Barracca and Levante. In the west side of the city, instead, data can give a misperception, due to the existence of a relevant amount of touristic houses.

A different situation occurs in *Bologna*, where low average values are observed (ranging from a minimum of 0.23 to a maximum value of 0.44). Areas in which some deprivation is present are located in the Northern city, particularly in Borgo Panigale, Navile and San Donato areas.

The situation in *Napoli* is much more critical, for the reason that there is a wide area with high average values (ranging from a minimum value of 0.6 to a maximum of 0.7). In particular, we can see the presence of areas of maximum deprivation, like as Scampia, Piscinola, Pianura and Bagnoli, where known and serious problems of urban decay occurs.

Also, we can see another large area comprising Secondigliano, Miano, S. Pietro Paterno, Poggioreale, Barra, S. Giovanni a Teduccio, Ponticelli, S. Carlo Arena and S. Lorenzo.

Starting from identified clusters concerning social and housing difficulties, it could be possible to obtain useful indications for planning urban regeneration policies, making decisional process more transparent and scientifically supported.

In order to go more in depth, as regards the city of the geographically described in the sample, we compared the incidence of ownership costs with the pro-capita income. The result shows the highest incidence of ownership in the poorest context (Table 4).

The result apparently is homogeneous with the above statistical approach; but it should be better tested, by analysing the distribution of pro-capita income with family income. In fact, Bologna is well known as a city with a higher family rate of employment (mostly two employed people for each family); that makes the heaviness of home ownership decrease. The same is not true for Bari, Cagliari and Napoli.

Table 3. Description of clusters referring to social and housing difficulty sets

Cluster	Number of cases	Inside average	Outside average	*p*-value
Bari				
1	69	0.67	0.27	0.0010
2	322	0.41	0.26	0.0010
3	158	0.41	0.27	0.0020
4	21	0.58	0.28	0.0040
5	10	0.58	0.29	0.6220
6	8	0.58	0.29	0.9999
Cagliari				
1	505	0.34	0.20	0.0010
2	24	0.71	0.24	0.0010
3	5	0.77	0.25	0.0130
4	2	0.93	0.25	0.3240
5	6	0.60	0.25	0.7440
6	2	0.79	0.25	0.9850
Bologna				
1	84	0.23	0.11	0.0010
2	12	0.33	0.11	0.0700
3	33	0.24	0.11	0.3780
4	2	0.44	0.11	0.9830
5	3	0.38	0.11	0.9850
6	9	0.37	0.11	0.9980
Napoli				
1	2,226	0.60	0.37	0.0010
2	104	0.65	0.48	0.0010
3	58	0.61	0.48	0.6930
4	58	0.61	0.48	0.9890

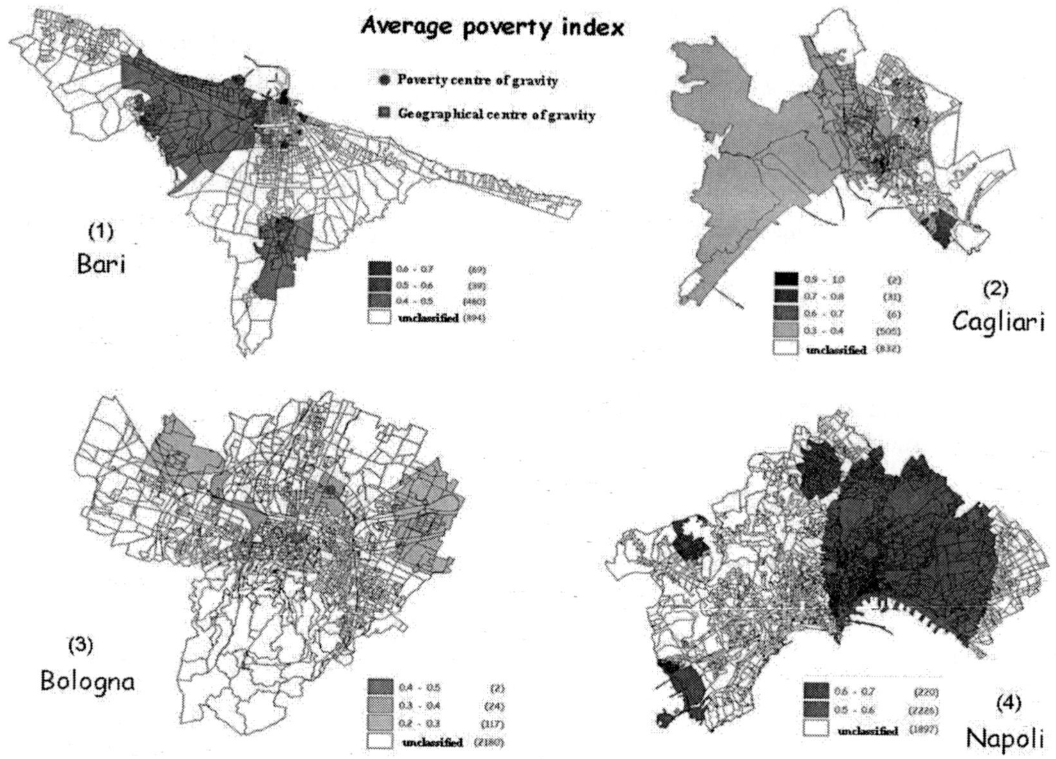

Figure 3. SaTScan model for the identification of Hot Spots of social and housing difficulty in different cities of Italy: Bari (1), Cagliari (2), Bologna (3) and Napoli (4).

5. Conclusion

This paper shows by different ways the need to manage with urban residential discomfort, social dimension of poverty and heaviness of costs of housing, using statistical approaches, economic vision and spatial and time relationship. In order to show such need, the examples refer to the description of some geo-statistical profiles of urban discomfort considered as a structural indicator of the access of affordable housing, and to the ability of forecasting market trends and accessibility of housing rents/sales by ownership costs.

Table 4. Comparison between ownership cost, rent and income in some metropolitan areas, year 2005

City	pro-capita Income	Ownership cost	own. cost/pro capita income	Size of poorty (cluster 5+6 from table 3)
Bari	22112	7761,3	35.1%	18
Bologna	25801	8251	32.0%	12
Cagliari	24163	6409	26.5%	8
Napoli	21968	8737	39.8%	116

The preliminary question leading towards the identification of town planning and architectonic solutions to the problem of urban regeneration, at a time when there is a lack of public resources for investment, focuses on the identification of areas with the highest level of urban poverty in order to direct the choices of political decision-makers in a transparent, well thought-out and objective manner. The authors believe that the model used in this study is able to provide relevant data for the identification of such areas. Using the SaTScan methodology to find the hot spots of social and housing difficulty, provides certain considerations for future research in housing policies now relevant in the European Countries' agenda.

Information obtained by the hot spots could be possible useful indications for planning equitable urban and housing policies.

Secondly, even if geo-statistical analysis give a good representation of the dichotomy among northern and southern metropolitan cities, by describing different profiles, further information should be added to address policies towards a support for rents or an alternative incentive to acquiring properties.

It is clear that a high level of homeownership quality often is accompanied by a condition of limited small poverty areas in the urban area.

In the same is clear that those city that are right places of urban regeneration, can be well-identified by discomfort analyses, and should be simultaneously interested by relocating an offer for affordable home-renting more than for home buying, due to an existing small economic ability to exercise the *right to buy*.

The ownership cost analysis, finally, is just a try to open to new field of investigation for planners and real estate researchers in this direction. Some lection can be learned from our reasoning. The first one is that the question of housing management, a crosses various economic and spatial level. A great effort about new knowledge on prices, costs, family conditions is needed, to identify correctly the target of housing policies.

References

Block, R. (2007). Software Review: Scanning for Clusters in Space and Time. *Social Science Computer Review,* **25(2)**: 272-278.

Borgegård L. E. & Kemeny J. (2004) Sweden: High-rise housing for a low-density country. In R. Turkington, R. van Kempen and E. Wassenberg (eds.) *High-rise housing in Europe: current trends and future prospects* (pp.31-48). Delft: Delft University press.

Cannari, L. & Faiella, I. (2004). *House prices and housing wealth in Italy*, Rome: Bank of Italy, Mimeo.

Case, K. E. & Shiller R.J. (1988) The Behavior of Home Prices in Boom and Post-Boom Markets. *New England Economic Review, November,* **88**: 29-46.

CCHPR (2008) *Low Cost Home Ownership: Affordability, Risks and Issues*. Cambridge: Cambridge Centre of Housing and Planning Research.

Cerioli, A. & Zani, S. (1990) A Fuzzy Approach to the Measurement of Poverty. In: C. Dagum, & M. Zenga (Eds.), *Income and Wealth Distribution, inequality and Poverty* (pp. 272-284). Berlin: Springer Verlag.

CENSIS – ISTAT (2005) *Indagine sui consumi degli Italiani*. Roma: Istituto Nazonale di Statistica.

Cheli, B. & Lemmi, A. A (1995) Totally Fuzzy and Relative Approach to the Multidimensional Analysis of Poverty. *Economic Notes* **24(1)**, 115--134.

Dubois, D. & Prade, H. (1980). *Fuzzy sets and systems.* Boston: Academic Press.

ECB (2003) *European Central Bank Report on structural factors in the EU housing markets.* Frankfurt au Main: European Central Bank Publications.

ECHP (2002) *European Community Household Panel Report on subjective Evaluation of Housing Conditions.* Luxemburg: Office for Official Publications of the European Communities.

EFILWC (2006) *First European Quality of Life Survey of the European Foundation for the Improvement of Living and Working Conditions: Social dimensions of housing.* Luxembourg: Office for Official Publications of the European Communities.

FIAIP (2005) *Rapporto annuale sul mercato immobiliare.* Bologna: Osservatorio immobiliare Fiaip.

Forte, C. & de' Rossi, B. (1974) *Principi di economia ed Estimo.* Rome, Italy: Etas Libri.

Fusco Girard, L. (1987) *Risorse architettoniche e culturali. Strategie di conservazione e metodi di valutazione.* Milan, Italy: Franco Angeli.

Gabetti & Nomisma (2005) *Report on Italian Real Estate Market.* Milano: Gabetti.

Guiso L. & Visco I. (1994) *Saving and the accumulation of wealth. Essays on Italian Household.* Cambridge: Cambridge University Press.

Hall. T. and Viden, S. (2005) The Million Homes Programme: a review of the great Swedish planning project. *Planning Perspectives*, **20 (3)**, 301-328.

Harding, J. P., Rosenthal S. S. & Sirmans C. F. (2004). Depreciation of Housing Capital and the Gains from Homeownership, WP, Syracuse, (NY): Syracuse University Press.

Haurin D. R. & Chung E.C. (1998). The Demand for Owner-Occupied Housing: Implications from Intertemporal Analysis. *Journal of housing economics* **7**: 49–68.

Hendershott, P. & Slemrod, J. (1983). Taxes and the User Cost of Capital for Owner-Occupied Housing. *AREUEA Journal, Winter,* **10 (4)**: 375-393.

Himmelberg, C., Mayer, C. & Sinai, T. (2005). Assessing High House Prices: Bubbles, Fundamentals and Misperceptions. *Journal of Economic Perspectives*, **19(4)**: 67-92.

Kuldorff, M. (1997) A spatial scan statistics. *Communication in Statistics: Theory and Methods*, **26**: 1481-1496.

Montrone S., Perchinunno P., Rotondo F., Torre C. M. & Di Giuro A.(2009) Identification of Hot Spots of Social and Housing Difficulty in Urban Areas: Scan Statistic for Housing Market and Urban Planning Policies. In: B. Murgante, G. Borruso, & A. Lapucci (Eds.) *Geocomputation and Urban Planning* (pp.57-78). Berlin Heidelberg: Springer Verlag.

Nakagami, Y. & Pereira A.M. (1993). Housing Costs and Bequest Motives. *Journal of Urban Economics,* **33(1)**: 68-75.

Patil, G.P. & Taillie, C. (2004). Upper level set scan statistic for detecting arbitrarily shaped hotspots. *Environmental and Ecological Statistics* **11**: 183-197.

Poterba, J. (1984) Tax Subsidies to Owner-occupied Housing: An Asset Market Approach. *Quarterly Journal of Economics* **99**: 729-52.

Simonotti, M. (2006) *Metodi di valutazione immobilare.* Palermo, Italy: Dario Flaccovio Editore.

Stein, J. (1995). Prices and Trading Volume in the Housing Market: A Model with Downpayment Effects. *Quarterly Journal of Economics* **110** : pp. 379-406.

Stiglitz, J. E. (1990). Symposium on Bubbles. *Journal of Economic Perspectives* **4(2)**: 13-18.

In: Housing, Housing Costs and Mortgages
Editors: Szilárd Kis and Istvan Balogh, pp. 109-120
ISBN: 978-1-60741-813-9

Chapter 6

WILLINGNESS TO PAY FOR THE ADDED COST OF INNOVATIONS IN HOUSING

Kevin M. Simmons and Daniel Sutter
Austin College, UT – Pan American

Abstract

Innovations in housing add value to the buyer but increase the cost of production. While innovations may increase the homes function or save money in the long run, it is an open question as to whether or not builders can recoup the additional cost. This paper examines several methods to test a buyer's willingness to pay for new features. The case of innovations designed to mitigate and protect residents from certain natural hazards is used to illustrate market acceptance of the added cost to construct safer homes.

Introduction

The year 2008 will likely be noted as one of the sharpest drops in housing values in history. Many issues have conspired to bring about this fall in prices, and some home building companies will not survive the downturn. Those that do survive will face tighter profit margins and have to carefully balance trade-offs in construction practices as well as the features they offer to home buyers.

A house can be thought of as a "bundle" of products and services. All homes must include some of these features, while building codes and local ordinances mandate others. These basic attributes cannot be altered and form a floor on the cost to construct the home. Beyond these basic structural processes the cost to build the home is determined by the components that are included. Builders must decide which set of components will appeal to their customers but also at a price that enables them to maximize their profits. Most of the time these decisions must be made before a home is sold making the trade-off more sensitive to the price their customers are ultimately willing to pay.

Homebuyers rarely express directly how much they are willing to pay for specific features. Rather they typically choose between available homes featuring different bundles of components at a price for the entire home rather than a menu of options and prices for each component. Given all of the various components of the bundle, buyers can rarely choose their perfect home, and seldom face a choice between homes which differ in only one component. Overcoming the disconnect between how buyers "value" a home and cost considerations is a challenge that home builders must meet if they hope to survive.

In this paper, we will review ways that people place value on items generally. We then proceed to discussing techniques that attempt to parse a willingness to pay for features that often do not have a direct price. Finally, we provide examples of how much people are willing to pay for housing features which minimize damage from natural disasters. This example can be generalized to help firms determine how much they can charge for specific housing components and perhaps assist them in making construction decisions consistent with profit maximization.

Expected Utility

Economists use the term "utility" to describe the enjoyment that people receive from consuming a product or service. This concept is quite useful in assessing the benefit received from something even if no direct monetary gain can be established. When someone is considering a purchase, a process weighing the benefits of the purchase versus the costs is inevitable. This process may not be obvious to the individual but plays out nonetheless at a subconscious level. When the consumption involves uncertainty, economists apply the concept of "expected utility" (von Neumann and Morgenstern 1944).

Consider an example which has obvious monetary benefits and costs. A person is in the market for a new car. She plans to drive the car 50 miles a day, five days a week, for a total of 250 miles per week or 1000 miles per month. Two models are equally attractive to her but the first gets 20 miles to the gallon while the second gets 25. At a gasoline price of $2.50 per gallon the second car will save 120 gallons per year or $300 annually. Assuming she plans to drive this car for 3 years and the resale is roughly equal, the more efficient car is only worth about $900 to this customer. Any price difference above $900 will cause her to choose the less efficient car.

To use the concept of expected utility does not require a monetary comparison. Benefits and costs are not always compared with dollars and cents. An example could be the "safety" associated with one product versus another. Let's return to our example of someone considering two different cars. This time let's assume that everything is equal except that one model has more airbags than the other and costs about $1000 more. If our consumer "values" the added safety enough that she is willing to pay the additional cost, we must assume that she places a value on the additional airbags of more than $1000. But if someone were to ask her, independent of this purchase, how much safety was worth to her, she may not be able to place a dollar value on that benefit.

Reasons for Buying a Home

Families purchase homes for various reasons but their motivation can be summarized into four essential elements; shelter, location, safety and status. A fundamental need for all individuals and/or families is shelter. The need for shelter seems obvious but consider for a moment how much we empathize with stories describing increased homelessness in our communities. For those of us fortunate enough to be able to have a "roof over our head" the mere thought of living on the streets is frightening. Homeownership gives families a sense of place, much more than simply renting a place to live. In the years since 1960, homeownership rates have increased from 62.1% to 68.9% in 2005.[1]

Beyond shelter, the reasons for purchasing a particular property vary by individual family. Perhaps the most compelling reason is location. A job change may require that the family move from one city to another and the purchase of a home in the new town is required. Within a particular community, location still matters. Access to shopping, entertainment, transportation networks and schools play a large role in any home purchase decision.

Once a location has been established, other reasons begin to influence the decision. Safety is one that is usually considered with expected crime rates of one neighborhood versus another. This concern is universal. No one desires to live in a community with a high probability of becoming the victim of criminal activity. But other elements of safety are also important, including proximity to earthquake fault lines and exposure to environmental pollutants. Finally, families may consider the status of one neighborhood compared to another. In most cities, there are neighborhoods which require homebuyers to pay a premium for the opportunity to live there. It could be the strength of a homeowners association that enforces restrictions which keep property values up or just the "prestige" of a particular zip code. For some families this status has value and they are willing to pay for the added status the neighborhood affords. In all of these criteria, the family is pursuing a home which will enable them to increase the expected utility of owning a home.

From Innovation to Market Adoption

Engineers are constantly creating new construction practices or inventing devices to increase efficiency or build safer or more user friendly homes. The incorporation of these innovations into the actual finished product ultimately depends upon their acceptance by the industry, consumers and code enforcement officials. Some of these innovations yield easily observable benefits for the consumer while others are visible only to the home builder. Convincing home buyers of the value of the latter type of innovation may be difficult. In these cases the home buyer will be unable to see the improvement once wallboards are installed, and would have to take the builder's word about the value (or even existence) of the innovation.

Such problems of trust of a seller are not unique to home building; the problem of "lemons" for instance, pervades the market for used cars, which has provided the name economists apply to the problem (Akerlof 1970). Markets overcome lemons problems through the development of reputation or by brand name capital of sellers. But in some markets reputation does not suffice and regulation plays a role. In the construction industry these regulations are of course building codes. The code development process becomes the means to certify the hidden components of construction, and the code enforcement process assures home buyers that homes possess the specified components.

[1] ^ "US Census Bureau, homeownership rate since 1960".

But the building code process does not work automatically, that is, codes do not enforce themselves. Field work by insurers and engineers after Hurricane Andrew revealed that shoddy construction practices prevalent in Florida throughout the 1970s and 1980s had contributed substantially to damage. The reviews estimated that perhaps 25% of the damage in Andrew was due to poor building practices (Mileti 1999) and that homes built after 1980 sustained significantly greater damage (Fronstin and Holtmann 1994). South Florida had what was regarded by experts as a model building code, so the problems arose from enforcement deficiencies. The deficiencies stemmed from several factors, including the acceptance by local officials of materials and practices which did not meet code requirements and an insufficient number of inspectors given the rapid growth of Florida during this period. Officials in Florida began crafting new codes that included innovations to protect structures against hurricane force winds. The hurricane seasons of 2004 and 2005 proved to be a significant test of the new Florida Building Code and show striking improvements in the ability of homes constructed under the new code to survive hurricane force winds.[2]

Florida's experience demonstrates that building codes can be based to improve home safety. But codes have limits as a general means of incorporating housing innovations. Excessive building codes encourage builders to look for ways to cut corners in an effort to reduce their cost of construction. Communities experiencing rapid growth may have difficulty enforcing codes, and communities may seek to not enforce codes as a means of attracting growth. Also by requiring inclusion in all homes, codes are an ineffective means to implement innovations which will appeal to some but not all home buyers. Including what should be optional features in codes will raise cost for builders more than value to buyers. For most housing innovations, builders will need to rely on the market to choose which innovations customers are willing to pay for and which ones will not survive. Economists generally prefer markets as the most efficient mechanism for allocating goods. At it's core, markets decide which products consumers really want, the price consumers will pay and which firms are best able to provide the goods to their customers.

New innovations must appeal to the preferences of homebuyers to be adopted in the housing market. Some innovations are designed to reduce the costs of home ownership, for instance energy efficient appliances or increased attic insulation. Most of the appeal to the homebuyer is lower utility bills and the task of the construction firm is to provide credible information to their customers verifying the potential energy savings. Some consumers may be convinced to adopt these measures based on a commitment to energy conservation. This objective is more nuanced making the sales pitch somewhat complicated. Regardless of the challenges, a market ensures that "better mousetraps" will be adopted, not because of mandates from local officials but because home builders want to provide what their customers demand.

Reliance on markets to disseminate new innovations into the housing market should not imply that government and insurance companies cannot influence which products will be demanded by consumers. When a product is coincident with overall goals of society, say energy efficiency, government can offer tax reductions for the purchase of these products. At the federal level, tax credits for energy efficient appliances have successfully increased the use of the products. State governments can also use tax credits to encourage adoption of

[2] http://aec.ihs.com/news/2005/florida-building-codes-hurricane-resistance.htm

certain innovations; in 2002 Oklahoma passed a 10% (or 100 square feet) credit on property taxes to homeowners installing a FEMA approved tornado shelter.

Insurance companies have a strong incentive to encourage their customers to install products that will survive a disaster. One of the most expensive natural events to insurance companies is a hailstorm. Roofing material manufacturers have developed roofing shingles that can withstand most hail stones. In Texas homeowners are offered a discount on their homeowners insurance policy for hail-resistant shingles. Using incentives like tax credits or discounts on required homeowners insurance have the effect of lowering the price to consumers making adoption by the market more likely.

Placing Value on Housing Attributes

The previous sections briefly summarized some of the basic criteria for how people decide to buy a particular home. We next consider in more detail how they may value particular home attributes. These values in turn determine which housing innovations are adopted in the market and which are not. As discussed earlier, homebuyers may not always use a monetary rule as their criteria but some innovations lend themselves to a simple benefit / cost analysis that can be monetized so we will begin with an approach that does consider dollars spent to expected cost savings.

Consider a potential home buyer who has found two homes that are equally attractive to her in every way except one. One home has an energy efficient HVAC system which will save the homeowner $1,000 per year in heating and cooling costs, while the other does not. The additional price that this buyer would be willing to pay for the energy efficient home will depend on the expected life of the HVAC system and the value to her of the lower future energy costs. Economists use the term "discount rate" to quantify individuals' impatience, or preference for receiving a benefit today as opposed to the same benefit in the future. In the case of our homebuyer, she weighs the up front cost of the more efficient HVAC unit against the expected benefit across time of the lower electric bills. The amount of premium she is willing to pay reflects her preference for money over time, the more impatient one is the lower the utility of future reduced electric bills. In practice the discount rate will be the interest rate at which the buyer could borrow, say the interest rate which would be paid on the mortgage of the house or loan for purchase of the appliances.

The home buyers willingness to pay for the energy efficient HVAC will depend on several additional factors. One will be whether the home buyer finds the claims about energy savings credible, or if she thinks changing energy prices might affect the dollar value of the reduced energy use. Also of relevance are any incentives which might be available for the purchase of energy efficient appliances, such as relates from the local electric company or tax incentives.

Homeowners will make a similar decision on features that can be added to existing homes. Staying with our example of energy efficiency, consider the installation of a radiant barrier. Radiant barriers have become a popular treatment to older homes, particularly in areas with hot summers, and high air conditioning costs. The radiant barrier is sprayed to the attic side of an existing roof. By providing some insulation between the temperature of the roof, which gets very hot in the summer, and the attic, temperatures in the attic remain low. Air conditioning this home becomes easier for two reasons; first lower attic temperatures keep the conditioned portions of the home cooler and secondly, since most duct work is in the attic there is less cooling loss from the unit to the register into each room. How much is a homeowner willing to pay to have a radiant barrier installed? Once again, she will compare the costs of the barrier against the reduced utility bills. If the present value of the reduced bills exceeds the price, the homeowner will have the barrier installed. If the installations must be financed, the relevant interest rate for discounting will be the rate paid on the financing loan.

Now let's examine an example that does not provide such a clear cut comparison of costs versus benefits, hail resistant shingles. One of the largest claims for property insurers is the cost to replace roofs damaged by hail. Recently, shingle manufacturers have developed roofing materials that provide some "give" when struck by a hail stone. For most hail storms, this ability to absorb the blow protects the shingle from damage and enables the homeowner to avoid roof replacement after a storm. What is the homeowner willing to pay for shingles that provide this protection? We can first consider this question assuming that the home owner would pay the full amount of the roof replacement out-of-pocket, and then consider how insurance interacts with the decision. The willingness-to-pay for shingles will depend on four factors. The first, most importantly, is the cost of the roof replacement. This is a financial consideration similar to what we discussed earlier but it has a difference and that leads us to the second point. The second is the probability of a damaging hailstorm. In some parts of the country, hailstorms are common and most residents assume that they will be affected sooner or later, but the homeowner must still make a decision as to the likelihood of being hit by hail. Third, the homeowner must weigh how much the inconvenience of replacing a roof is worth to her. Even with full insurance against the monetary cost of the roof repairs, having a roof replaced is an inconvenient interruption of life that most people would like to avoid. The inconvenience value must be added to the cost of roof repairs to get the households full cost of a loss. Finally, since the roof repair occurs in the future, the homeowner's impatience or discount rate also affects the willingness-to-pay.

Insurance coverage obviously complicates but does not fundamentally alter this decision. With insurance, part of the loss from roof repair will be paid by the homeowner's insurance policy. The amount the homeowner would pay would depend on their policy deductible. Also of relevance is whether the homeowner receives any reduction in their insurance premium for installation of the hail resistant shingles. Most insurance companies find it advantageous for their customers to buy roofs with hail resistant shingles.

For attributes that do not have an obvious benefit/cost relationship, it is a challenge to determine how a potential buyer would "value" the attribute. For many years social scientists have worked to develop methods to accurately determine how much someone is willing to pay for something that does not have a direct cost. An example of this difficulty would be placing a value on the enjoyment of a national park by an individual. Entry fees do not attempt to completely pay for the operations and upkeep of a national park. Most visitors would say that the visit was certainly worth more to them than the entrance fee. But the important question becomes exactly how much people would be willing to pay for the park. Methods developed by economists for use in such situations include the survey method, the contingent valuation method, and the hedonic price method. Basic surveys and surveys using the contingent valuation method are based on the simple approach of asking people directly what a good is worth to them. Formally, this is known as a "stated preference" approach. The person simply states to the researcher how much they would be willing to pay to visit a park like the Grand Canyon or Yellowstone. The method is simple to implement but some economists have concerns with the reliability of the "stated" value. No one is actually spending money. The respondent to the survey simply gives a guess as to what the park visit is worth. This response does not cost her anything and in no way obligates her to actually part with anything of monetary value. Strategically the respondent might have an incentive to exaggerate and indicate that visiting Yellowstone was a priceless experience to help preserve the park. At a minimum, people do not have to think carefully about how much they would really be willing to pay for the park.

The contingent valuation method has been developed by researchers to limit any bias in such surveys (Mitchell and Carson 1989). The survey must be carefully designed to elicit valuable information. For instance, a respondent might be asked about their willingness to pay for a visit to Yellowstone under several different scenarios concerning management of the park or availability of parts of the park. At a minimum this causes the respondent to consider different possible prices for different outcomes but it does not completely remove the bias inherent when no actual cash transaction takes place.

In contrast to stated preference methods, other methods use market revealed values, or "revealed preference" methods. The most reliable revealed preference methodology of relevance for the housing market is the hedonic pricing method (Rosen, 1974). Hedonic pricing methods assume that the price of a house implicitly depends on all of the various component features of a home. With detailed enough data on the sales price and features of a large number of homes in a market, researchers can apply econometric techniques to estimate the shadow price or implicit value potential buyers are willing to pay for a particular attribute. The individual components can be priced out even if they do not have a specified price. This is particularly useful in residential real estate because the quoted price of an individual house is for a package, without attempting to break out the additional cost for each item within the house. While new homes may be able to price individual components before they are installed, older homes do not have that luxury. Even when a new home builder gives clients the option of upgrades, this does not completely determine how much the client would be willing to pay for the upgrade, simply how much the builder will charge for the upgrade. Hedonic models can estimate a reasonable range of the willingness to pay for various features.

To use the hedonic pricing approach, the researcher needs the actual sales price of the home, a detailed list of features each sold home possesses, as well as information on non-structural attributes that may influence the price. For instance, the quality of neighborhood schools may influence the selling price as well as other issues like crime rates, access to transportation networks etc. Once the data is compiled, the researcher uses a statistical method which compares or regresses how changes in the sales price of an individual home varies with changes in the attributes the individual home possesses. Given that a sufficient number of transactions are available to the researcher, the amount of change, on average, in sales price given changes in the presence or non-presence of a particular attribute will tell the researcher how much that attribute is worth to buyers. A model which includes as much information as possible about each home will provide a much more accurate assessment of the value of each attribute since the researcher can control for the presence of all elements of home that help buyers determine the price they are willing to pay.

Real World Example: Disaster Mitigation

To illustrate how innovations in housing can be valued, we next consider features that reduce or mitigate the effects of a disaster which may occur at some time in the future. Natural disasters are low probability, high consequence (LPHC) events, and many researchers express concern that residents ignore the possibility of being affected and consequently under prepare for disasters (Camerer and Kunreuther 1989, Meier 2006). Wind storms such as tornadoes or hurricanes can cause a great deal of damage to residential structures. Tornadoes can produce winds in excess of 300 miles per hour as was documented in the May 3, 1999 tornado which struck the Oklahoma City metro area. The key to reducing damage to a home in hurricane winds is maintaining the integrity of the roof structure. Most homes are designed for wind speeds up to 120 miles per hour, but winds in a Category 3 hurricane on the Safir-Simpson scale can exceed this threshold. But the structural integrity of homes can be improved to survive major hurricanes. Homes engineered with continuous wind load connections and impact resistant shutters on exterior wall openings (windows and doors) will be likely to sustain less damage in a hurricane. Winds in the strongest tornadoes can exceed 200 mph, and winds in an EF-5 tornado (on the Enhanced Fujita Scale) may approach 300 mph. Few structures will ever be designed to survive an EF-5 tornado, and so for tornadoes the concern is less about the survival of the structure but more about minimizing injuries or death. It is possible to provide a small area within the home to protect the residents from the risk of injury or death. Damage reduction can be a significant concern in weaker tornadoes (EF-0 through EF-2) which rarely kill residents of single family homes but which do damage homes. Again measures exist to enhance the structural integrity of homes exposed to tornadoes. But for both hurricanes and tornadoes the structural enhancements will increase the cost to build the home. If residents do indeed ignore the possibility of being harmed by a natural disaster, they will perceive no value added to a home from features meant to mitigate the damage or protect the occupants. Our concern is to determine whether home buyers are willing to pay an increase in sales price for the added protection these enhancements provide.

An Anecdotal Example

The May 3, 1999 tornado which destroyed over 2300 buildings in the Oklahoma City metro area significantly affected a local builder, Home Creations.[3] The owner, Jalal Farzaneh, contacted the engineering department at the nearby University of Oklahoma for suggestions on how he could build homes which may survive these storms. The answer prompted him to redesign several components of his production process at a reasonable cost, low enough that he did not increase the price of his homes. These structural enhancements would not prevent the destruction of the home from an EF-4 or EF-5 tornado. They would, however, greatly reduce the damage from a smaller tornado. Since over 90% of tornadoes are less than an EF-3, these enhancements go a long way toward reducing property damage. We interviewed Mr. Farzaneh a few years after the tornado. He reported that once buyers became aware of the structural improvements and the effect these improvements had on the homes ability to survive a small tornado, sales increased dramatically. Home Creations was so pleased with

[3] http://www.homecreations.com/

the effect on sales that they later instituted a program to provide tornado safe rooms, built to FEMA standards, as an option to their customers at cost. While these innovations did not translate into higher prices for the firm, they did give Home Creations an edge for customers. This indicates that potential home buyers do place a value on the protection that finds it's way, not into increased prices, but into increased sales.

Empirical Evidence

Examples such as Home Creations illustrate the potential value of mitigation innovations for housing. Systematic empirical studies, however, provide better evidence of willingness to pay for the increased cost associated with mitigation. A number of empirical studies employing either the contingent valuation or hedonic price methods have investigated natural hazards and mitigation in housing.

As discussed, some observers suspect that housing markets ignore the risk of natural hazards altogether. Yet a number of hedonic price studies have documented the influence of exposure to natural hazards on house prices, with homes less exposed to risk being worth more, everything else equal. For example, Brookshire et al. (1985) found that homes in Los Angeles and San Francisco located in designated seismic risk zones sold for a discount, indicating that buyers perceived earthquake risk. Beron et al. (1997) found that the discount for homes located in seismic zones declined after the 1989 Loma Prieta earthquake, since damage from the quake was not a extensive as many experts had expected from a quake of this magnitude. Shilling, Benjamin and Sirmans (1985), MacDonald, Murdock and White (1987) and Spreyer and Ragas (1991) examined the influence of location in a flood plain on home prices in three different Louisiana cities and found that homes in the flood plains sold for approximately 6% less than comparable homes outside of the flood plain. Carbone et al. (2006) and Hallstrom and Smith (2005) examined the impact of Hurricane Andrew on housing markets in Miami-Dade and Lee counties in Florida. Houses located in areas of the counties prone to storm surge flooding increased in price less than other homes. All of these studies show that vulnerability to hazards reduces home prices, which shows that markets do not ignore risk. And individual hazards can affect home prices as well. Ewing et al. (2006) found that severe windstorm events (powerful tornadoes and hurricanes) reduced house prices in the affected cities by up to 2% in the quarter of the event, even though the storms had no permanent impact on prices.

Surveys are a relatively simple and inexpensive way to provide a sense of whether a new innovation has value to potential customers. The May 3, 1999 Oklahoma tornadoes inspired researchers in addition to firms like Home Creations. Several surveys examined the value of a tornado saferoom or shelter. A saferoom is a small area within a home which is engineered beyond the structural integrity of the overall home. Shelters can be installed underground thus protecting residents. While engineers have advocated this idea for years, it did not gain traction until one home in Del City, Oklahoma was featured by FEMA[4] in a visit that President Clinton made to the disaster site after the May 1999 tornado. This home was completely destroyed except for a closet that had been "super engineered" by the homeowners when they built the house. FEMA and the state of Oklahoma began a campaign

[4] http://www.fema.gov/pdf/rt/rt_ok99.pdf

to educate residents and also provided grants of up to $2000 for homeowners who retrofitted their home to include a FEMA approved saferoom or shelter.[5]

A number of papers analyze surveys of willingness-to-pay for tornado shelters or safe rooms (Ozdemir and Kruse 2000, and Miller, Morgan and Womack 2001, Ozdemir 2005, Ewing and Kruse 2006). The surveys were conducted with residents of Oklahoma and Texas soon after the 1999 tornado. The surveys found that residents were indeed willing to pay an additional cost for a saferoom of approximately $2500. Lower priced versions of a FEMA approved shelter could be purchased for about $2000 so the results indicate that the willingness to pay for this innovation was viable, at least for moderate priced shelters. In addition, residents perceive the importance of verification of the quality of shelter construction. Ewing and Kruse (2006) find that residents of Tulsa were willing to pay an extra $600, or 25% of the total willingness-to-pay, for a shelter certified by the National Storm Shelter Association.

Surveys, however, do not provide the rigor that could be obtained when actual transactions are available for examination. Several hedonic studies have documented that individual mitigation innovations have value. The authors conducted such a study in Oklahoma City based on 2005 sales data (Simmons and Sutter, 2007). The six years prior to 2005 witnessed two strong tornadoes in the Oklahoma City metro area, the May 3, 1999 F-5 tornado and an F-4 in May 2003 which followed a very similar path to the one four years earlier. This history with tornadoes and the aggressive campaign to educate and encourage residents to adopt shelters (through the 2000 Oklahoma Saferoom Initiative and 2002 property tax abatement measure) provides an ideal opportunity to test for a value of shelters. A hedonic price model was employed, using sales price data and home characteristic data from the Oklahoma County tax assessor's office. A tornado shelter was found to increase the price of the home by about 3.5% on average. The average sales price of homes in the study was approximately $120,000 and thus home buyers valued shelters at roughly $4,200. The authors similarly found a 5% premium for community shelters on the rental price of lots in manufactured home parks in Oklahoma (Simmons and Sutter 2008). Thus a wide segment of the market values shelters, both home buyers and potential home buyers.

Tornado shelters protect family members against a risk of death and thus might be viewed differently by home buyers from innovations to protect the home against property damage. Yet hurricane shutters, permanently installed steel curtains which can be deployed to protect windows, doors and other exterior openings from flying debris, can substantially reduce damage, both directly and by averting wind pressure induced damage to roofs. Using the hedonic price method, Simmons, Kruse and Smith (2002) found that homes with hurricane shutters on a barrier island of a Gulf coast city sold at a premium to those without. The premium was again about 5% of the sale price for an average priced home.

Conclusion

Attempts to offer potential homebuyers the features they desire in residential real estate is a challenge that requires construction companies to be innovative in their market plans. Builders need to discern which features buyers are willing to pay enough extra for to cover

[5] http://www.fema.gov/plan/prevent/saferoom/resinit.shtm

their cost. To provide a product that appeals to the largest number of potential customers, home builders must learn which innovations will be profitable. Knowledge of how customers form their preferences is the first step. A necessary second step, however, is determining what value customers place on one innovation versus another. This second step allows the firm to choose among features that may be attractive to customers but also at a price equal to the value buyers place on them. Companies that are able to choose the set of features that not only appeal to their customers but also enable them to maximize their profits will ultimately prevail.

References

Camerer, C.F., and Kunreuther, H. (1989), "Decision Processes for Low Probability Events: Policy Implications," *Journal of Policy Analysis and Management*, **8**(4), 565-592.

Carbone, J.C., Hallstrom, D.G., and Smith, V.K. (2006), "Can Natural Experiments Measure Behavioral Responses to Environmental Risks?" *Environmental and Resource Economics*, **33**(3), 273-292.

Ewing, B.T., and Kruse, J.B. (2006), "Valuing Self Protection: Income and Certification Effects for Safe Rooms." *Construction Management and Economics*, 24(10), 1057-1068.

Ewing, B.T., Kruse, J.B., and Wang, Y. (2007), "Local Housing Price Index Analysis in Wind-Disaster-Prone Areas." *Natural Hazards*, **40**(2), 463-483.

Federal Emergency Management Agency. 2000. *Design and Construction Guidance for Community Shelters*. Publication #361, Washington DC.

Fronstin, P. and Holtmann, A.G. (1994). "The Determinants of Residential Property Damage Caused by Hurricane Andrew," *Southern Economic Journal*, **61**(2), 387-397.

Hallstrom, D.G., and Smith, V.K. (2005), "Market Responses to Hurricanes." *Journal of Environmental Economics and Management*, **50**(3), 541-561.

MacDonald, D. N., Murdock, J. C. and White, H. L. (1987), "Uncertain Hazards, Insurance, and Consumer Choice: Evidence from Housing Markets," *Land Economics*, **63**, 361-371.

Mileti, D.S. (1999), *Disasters by Design*. Washington DC: Joseph Henry Press.

Miller, D., Morgan, D., and Womack, C. (2002). "Buying Tornado Safety: What Will it Cost?", *Southwestern Economic Proceedings*, **29**(1), 35-45.

Mitchell, R.C., and Carson, R.T. (1989), *Using Surveys to Value Public Goods: The Contingent Valuation Method*. Washington DC: Resources for the Future.

Newmann, J. and Morgenstern, O. (1944), *Theory of Games and Economic Behavior*. Princeton, NJ. Princeton University Press.

Ozdemir, Ozlem. 2005. "Risk Perception and the Value of Safe Rooms as a Protective Measure from Tornadoes: A Survey Method." In B.T. Ewing and J.B. Kruse (eds.) *Economics and Wind*. Nova Science Publishing, pp. 89-104.

Ozdemir, O., and Kruse, J.B. (2000). "Relationship Between Risk Perception and Willingness-to-Pay for Low Probability, High Consequence Risk: A Survey Method", Working Paper, Texas Tech University.

Rosen, S., (1974). "Hedonic Prices and Implicit Markets: Product Differentiation in Pure Competition", *Journal of Political Economy*, **82**(1), 34-55.

Shilling, J. D., Benjamin, J.D., and Sirmans, C.F. (1985), "Adjusting Comparable Sales for Floodplain Location," *Appraisal Journal*, **53**, 429-436.

Simmons, K.M., Kruse, J.B., and Smith, D.A., (2002), "Valuing Mitigation: Real Estate Market Response to Hurricane Loss Reduction Measures," *Southern Economic Journal*, **68**(3), 660-671.

Simmons, K.M., and Sutter, D. (2007a). "Tornado Shelters and the Housing Market," *Construction Management and Economics*, **25**, 1119-1126.

Simmons, K.M., and Sutter, D. (2007b). "Tornado Shelters and the Manufactured Home Parks Market," *Natural Hazards*, **43**(3), 365-378.

Spreyer, J. F., and Ragas, W. R. (1991). "Housing Prices and Flood Risk: An Examination Using Spline Regression," *Journal of Real Estate Finance and Economics*, **4**, 395-407.

In: Housing, Housing Costs and Mortgages
Editors: Szilárd Kis and Istvan Balogh, pp. 121-133
ISBN: 978-1-60741-813-9

Chapter 7

AN EXERCISE DEMONSTRATING THE OPERATION OF FREE MARKETS: EXPLAINING HOUSING PRICE DIFFERENTIALS WITHIN A HISTORIC LANDMARK DISTRICT

Richard J. Cebula[1], Patricia E. Gaynor[2] and Michael Toma[1]
[1]Armstrong Atlantic State University, Georgia, USA
[2]Appalachian State University, North Carolina, USA

Abstract

This study provides an example of the operation of free markets by applying a hedonic pricing model to explain housing price differentials ***within*** a historic landmark district. By considering home sales solely within such a district, in principle the market experiment transpires within an institutionally homogenous framework, i.e., all sales share a common characteristic in that they occur within a land area designed as "historic." This exercise demonstrating the operation of free markets involves in the Savannah Historic Landmark District, which is located in and adjacent to the downtown of Savannah, Georgia. Estimating the model in semi-log form reveals that the natural log of the *real* sales price of a house in this particular environment was positively affected by the number of bathrooms, fireplaces, rooms, stories in structure, garage car spaces, and square feet of finished living space, the presence of a custom kitchen, a deck, a private courtyard, an exterior construction of brick or stucco, an underground sprinkler system, and whether or not the house was new. The *real* sales price was negatively affected by the presence of a rental apartment on the premises and by an exterior of either vinyl or wood siding. Listing a house for sale during the peak selling season from May through July also acts to raise the *real* sales price of the house. Finally, the analysis also demonstrates that property taxes are capitalized into housing prices. Ultimately, the analysis demonstrates the efficiency of free markets within a model which systematically permits the evaluation of a host of housing characteristics within a somewhat homogeneous context.

Introduction

Hedonic pricing models have been applied by researchers to a wide variety of circumstances in recent years. For example, the hedonics framework has been applied to the issue of flood hazard and hurricane damage (Bin & Polasky, 2004; Harrison, Smersh & Schwartz, 2001), the impact of air quality, environmental, and safety issues (Decker, Nielsen & Sindt, 2005; Dotzour, 1997; Garrod & Willis, 1992; Murdoch, Singh & Thayer, 1993; Smith & Huang, 1993), and the issue of over-education and under-education in a dynamic labor market (McMillen, Seaman & Singell, 2007). Hedonic pricing has been used frequently in explaining housing prices (Dotzour, 1997; Murdoch, Singh, & Thayer, 1993; Harrison, Smersh, & Schwartz, 2001).

A National Historic Landmark District is one of the 2430 districts that is recognized by the U.S. government for its historic significance. The Savannah Historic Landmark District is in fact one of the largest such districts in the U.S. The area designated in this case roughly corresponds to the city limits of the city of Savannah, Georgia, prior to the Civil War.

This study seeks to provide an example of the operation of free markets by applying a hedonic pricing model to explain housing price differentials *within* the context of a given, heretofore essentially overlooked historic landmark district. By considering home sales solely within such a district, in principle the market experiment transpires within an institutionally homogenous framework, i.e., all sales share a common characteristic in that they occur within a land area designed as "historic." This exercise demonstrating the operation of free markets involves in the Savannah Historic Landmark District, which is located in and adjacent to the downtown of Savannah, Georgia, and which effectively has not previously been formally studied in this fashion.

In a broader context, aside from being the first and only study to date to apply the hedonic pricing model to the Savannah Historic Landmark District, this study differs from the existing literature on hedonic pricing models as applied to historic district home transactions in several ways. First, this study makes use of a substantially larger data set of *actual* house sale transactions *within* a historic district than most previously published research on the topic, albeit that this study is restricted *solely* to houses *within* the historic district being studied. Indeed, the intent of the present study in part is to examine how the *free market* operates and one of many possible ways to do this is to focus strictly within the Savannah Historic Landmark District. Doing so permits us to identify price-determining characteristics of houses within a *homogeneous* area, i.e., houses in the analysis *all* share the *common trait* of being *within* the Savannah Historic Landmark District. Such a focus is pertinent to any and all persons/parties who find an inherent value to home ownership in such a district; indeed, such ownership might well imply being a tangible part of "history." Another potentially unique aspect of the present study is the consideration of a variable that captures the seasonal variation of house sale prices within a historic district within the hedonic pricing model. This variable allows us to expressly model a recurring pattern in monthly data that is not accounted for in previous research on house prices within historic districts. Finally, another facet of the present study is that in its investigation of housing sales over the six-year period from 2000 through 2005, each housing sale price has been appropriately adjusted using an index of *housing* prices *per se* over the study period. The result is that each and every housing price observation is expressed in 2005 dollars, i.e., in completely comparable terms. The use of a *housing price index* rather than the national or a regional consumer price index, as in the existing hedonic literature on historic districts, is justified because a broadly-based CPI, by definition, incorporates the prices of *all* household consumption goods and services, many of which are entirely unrelated to the prices of single-family homes.

In the next section of this study, the hedonic pricing model is provided, and the data are described. Following conventional practice in the literature, the model is estimated in semi-log form. The empirical results of a variety of model specifications are summarized in the subsequent section of the study. In addition, the overall empirical results are interpreted. The conclusion provides a summary of the results. An underlying theme that is manifested in the estimates is that the free market paradigm functions in a remarkably systematic and efficient fashion.

Framework for the Empirical Analysis

This section of the study provides the framework within which the hedonic pricing model is applied strictly to housing sales within the Savannah Historic Landmark District. The underlying theory and summaries of many pertinent empirical results of applied hedonic pricing models are described in Dotzour (1997), Murdoch, Singh, & Thayer (1993), and Harrison, Smersh, & Schwartz (2001), and thus are not reviewed in great detail here. The basic premise is that a house represents a bundle of both desirable and undesirable attributes to utility-maximizing consumers, all of which contribute to the market value of the house as revealed through a market transaction, i.e., a home sale. The hedonic pricing model decomposes the transaction price into various components such as interior and exterior features, or other traits of the house that affect the sale price. The estimated parameters of the model provide information about the relative contribution (statistical significance and magnitude of effect) of any given house feature.

In the present study, the hedonic pricing model takes the following general form:

$$\text{lnRSALESPRj} = f(\text{Ij}, \text{Ej}, \text{Oj}) \tag{1}$$

where:

lnRSALESPj = the natural log of the *real* price of house j, where the price of the jth house is expressed in 2005 dollars;
Ij = a vector of interior physical characteristics for house j;
Ej = a vector of external physical characteristics for house j; and
Oj = a vector of other factors associated with house j.

The present study applies the hedonic model to home sales in the Savannah Historic Landmark District over the six-year period from 2000 through 2005. Data for 678 home sales during this time frame in the district were obtained from the Savannah Board of Realtors' Multiple Listing Service (mls). A full information set is available on all data categories and forms of variables used in the model for 593 of these 678 sales. Although the vast majority of the 593 observations represent re-sales of existing homes, a number of sales (40) were newly built structures. In order to permit comparison of sales prices across the time period, all housing prices were converted to and expressed in 2005 dollars using the price index for single-family homes from the U.S. Census Bureau (2007, Table 710). The mean price of a house sold in the Savannah Historic Landmark District from 2000 to 2005, expressed in 2005 dollars, was $377,305.70.

Table 1. Variables in the Analysis

RSALESPR= the price of house j expressed in 2005 dollars
lnRSALESPR= the natural log of the price of house j expressed in 2005 dollarsBATHS= the total number of baths (full plus half) in house j
FIREPLACES= the number of fireplaces in house j
ROOMS= the total number of rooms, other than bedrooms, such as a bonus room, den, family room, great room, loft, separate living room, study, separate dining room, or sunroom
SQFT= the total number of square feet of finished living space in house j
lnSQFT=the natural log of the total number of square feet of finished living space in house j
CUSTKIT= a binary variable = 1 when house j had a customized kitchen and = 0 otherwise
APT= a binary variable indicating whether house j had a rental apartment within its structure (= 1 if yes, = 0 otherwise)
BRICK= a binary variable indicating whether house j had a primarily or completely brick exterior (= 1 if yes, = 0 otherwise)
DECK= a binary variable indicating whether house j had an exterior deck (=1 if yes, = 0 otherwise)
CRTYD= a binary variable indicating whether house j had a private courtyard (=1 if yes, = 0 otherwise)
SPRINKLER= a binary variable indicating whether house j had an underground sprinkler system (= 1 if yes, = 0 otherwise)
STORIES= the number of stories/floors present in house j
STUCCO= a binary variable indicating whether house j had a stucco exterior (=1 if yes, =0 otherwise)
GARAGESP= the number of garages spaces on house j's premises
SIDING= a binary variable indicating whether house j had a wood or vinyl exterior (=1 if yes, = 0 otherwise)
POOLTUB= a binary variable indicating whether house j had its own hot-tub or pool (=1 if yes, = 0 otherwise)
NEW= a binary variable indicating whether house j was new at the time of sale (=1 if yes, = 0 otherwise)
WARRANTY= a binary variable indicating whether house j had a home warranty in effect at the time of sale (= 1 if yes, = 0 otherwise)
SEASON = a binary variable indicating whether house j was first listed during the prime Savannah selling season of May through July (= 1 if yes, = 0 otherwise)
PROPTX = annual property tax for house j paid to city and county government

Table 2. Descriptive Statistics

Variable	Mean	Standard Deviation
lnRSALESPR	12.48	0.895
BATHS	2.715	1.828
FIREPLACES	2.81	2.66
ROOMS	1.599	1.517
SQFT	2,329	1,492
CUSTKIT	0.137	0.504
APT	0.068	0.252
BRICK	0.277	0.448
DECK	0.176	0.38
CRTYD	0.3097	0.4627
SPRINKLER	0.055	0.227
STORIES	2.189	0.839
STUCCO	0.114	0.318
GARAGESP	0.23	0.58
SIDING	0.14	0.347
POOLTUB	0.02	0.14
NEW	0.058	0.24
WARRANTY	0.074	0.26
SEASON	0.25	0.435
lnSQFT	7.61	0.61
PROPTX	6,735.53	3,758.14

There were a variety of interior and exterior physical characteristics available for each house sold as well as other factors associated that were available and expressly included in the analysis. These factors are listed and formally defined in Table 1. Basic descriptive statistics for each of the variables considered in the analysis are provided in Table 2. Naturally, for each of the impacts of the explanatory variables on housing price in the model, the expected sign is proffered under the assumption of *ceteris paribus*.

The interior physical characteristics of house j include: BATHS, the *tota*l number of baths (full plus half baths); FIREPLACES, the total number of fireplaces; ROOMS, the total number of listed rooms (other than bedrooms) such as bonus rooms, dens, and so forth; SQFT, the number of square feet of finished interior living space; CUSTKIT, the presence of a customized kitchen; and APT, whether or not there exists an apartment unit within the house. The number of *bedrooms per se* was *omitted* because it was very highly correlated with the variables SQFT, FIREPLACES, *and* BATHS. Additionally, there was very little variation in the number of bedrooms in the sample. The mean number of bedrooms was approximately 2.98, with a standard deviation of 0.32.

As observed in the literature (Dotzour, 1997; Murdoch, Singh, & Thayer, 1993; Harrison, Smersh, & Schwartz, 2001), the real sales price (RSALESPR) of house j is expected to be an increasing function of the number of desirable internal (as well as external) physical housing characteristics. For example, RSALESPR is expected to be an increasing function of the number of bathrooms and fireplaces. It also is expected to be an increasing function the number of listed rooms (as defined above), the square footage of finished living space, and the presence of a custom kitchen. In addition, since the presence of an apartment in the house reduces the number of square feet of available living space (for the principal resident/owner) within house j, and reduces privacy of the resident/owner of the house, RSALESPR is expected to be a decreasing function of the presence of an apartment within the house.

The exterior physical characteristics of house j include: BRICK, whether or not the exterior is made principally of brick; DECK, whether the house has a deck; CRTYD, whether or not the house has a courtyard; SPRINKLER, whether or not the house has an underground sprinkler system; STORIES, the number of stories; STUCCO, whether or not the house exterior is of stucco construction; GARAGESP, the number of garage car spaces that are part of the house; SIDING, whether or not the house exterior is made of vinyl or wood siding; and POOLTUB, whether or not the house has a hot-tub or a swimming pool.

Consistent with the existing literature, the RSALESPR of house j is expected to be an increasing function of whether or not the house exterior is brick and the number of stories of the structure. Similarly, the RSALESPR is expected to be an increasing function of the presence of other house features, including a deck, the presence of a pool or hot-tub, and the number of garage spaces. It also is hypothesized here that whereas a stucco exterior may enhance RSALESPR, an exterior construction of vinyl or wood siding would reduce RSALESPR. Finally, the presence of a private courtyard is expected to enhance the RSALESPR for house j, as would the presence of an underground sprinkler system.

Several other idiosyncratic factors associated with house j include: NEW, whether or not the house was new at the time of sale and WARRANTY, whether or not the house had a one-year home warranty in effect as of the date of closing. As suggested in Decker, Nielsen & Sindt (2005), a *new* house is often considered highly desirable because in part it is in need of little or no repair and generally cleaner and brighter and equipped with new and modern appliances; hence, a *new* house *per se* is expected to command a higher sales price. Accordingly, it is argued here that a "new" house will tend to command a greater market price. Similarly, it is hypothesized that houses that have a one-year home warranty will be more appealing and hence will command a higher price.

Initial Empirical Results

This section provides the initial results of empirically estimating the hedonic model outlined above. In each of the estimates, the White (1980) procedure is adopted to correct for heteroskedasticity. Initially, five estimates are provided, the original model and four variations thereof. In column (a) of Table 3, all 17 of the estimated coefficients exhibit the hypothesized signs, with ten statistically significant at the one percent level, five statistically significant at the five percent level, and only two (those for the variables WARRANTY and POOLTUB) failing to be significant at the ten percent level. The coefficient of determination indicates that the model explains over three-fifths of the variation in the dependent variable (lnRSALESPR). Finally, the F-statistic is significant at far beyond the one percent level, evidence of the overall strength of the model.

Table 3. OLS Estimates of the Hedonic Pricing Model (for lnRSALESPR)

Variable	(a)	(b)	(c)	(d)	(e)	(f)
Constant	+11.07	+11.07	+11.08	+11.03	+11.04	+8.6
BATHS	+0.108	+0.108	+0.109	+0.1099	+0.111	+0.104
	(+4.38)	(+4.38)	(+4.38)	(+4.48)	(+4.48)	(+4.32)
FIREPLACES	+0.054	+0.054	+0.054	+0.056	+0.056	+0.052
	(+4.47)	(+4.48)	(+4.46)	(+4.66)	(+4.65)	(+3.99)
ROOMS	+0.037	+0.037	+0.039	+0.034	+0.036	+0.027
	(+2.29)	(+2.34)	(+2.47)	(+2.15)	(+2.32)	(+1.96)
SQFT	+0.00008	+0.00007	+0.00008	+0.00007	+0.00008	-------
	(+2.21)	(+2.19)	(+2.15)	(+2.03)	(+1.98)	
CUSTKIT	+0.096	+0.103	+0.103	+0.10	+0.107	+0.108
	(+1.98)	(+2.13)	(+2.14)	(+2.02)	(+2.24)	(+2.54)
APT	-0.19	-0.196	-0.197	-0.173	-0.178	-0.204
	(-2.42)	(-2.51)	(-2.52)	(-2.19)	(-2.27)	(-2.76)
BRICK	+0.248	+0.252	+0.249	+0.249	+0.25	+0.229
	(+3.94)	(+4.00)	(+3.96)	(+3.98)	(+4.01)	(+3.75)
DECK	+0.155	+0.154	+0.154	+0.153	+0.152	+0.17
	(+3.55)	(+3.57)	(+3.55)	(+3.52)	(+3.51)	(+3.92)
CRTYD	+0.231	+0.236	+0.24	+0.231	+0.24	+0.26
	(+5.13)	(+5.30)	(+5.34)	(+5.16)	(+5.37)	(+5.75)
SPRINKLER	+0.193	+0.185	+0.186	+0.182	+0.175	+0.185
	(+2.78)	(+2.69)	(+2.72)	(+2.65)	(+2.58)	(+2.64)
STORIES	+0.209	+0.208	+0.208	+0.213	+0.212	+0.19
	(+3.34)	(+3.35)	(+3.35)	(+3.39)	(+3.40)	(+3.81)
STUCCO	+0.336	+0.339	+0.337	+0.342	+0.343	+0.329
	(+5.15)	(+5.19)	(+5.20)	(+5.26)	(+5.31)	(+5.35)
GARAGESP	+0.109	+0.1066	+0.1088	+0.111	+0.11	+0.11
	(+3.54)	(+3.46)	(+3.53)	(+3.58)	(+3.56)	(+3.68)
SIDING	-0.164	-0.165	-0.166	-0.15	-0.152	-0.134
	(-2.35)	(-2.36)	(-2.36)	(-2.12)	(-2.13)	(-1.97)
POOLTUB	+0.149	-------	-------	+0.15	-------	-------
	(+0.90)	)		(+0.93		
NEW	+0.302	+0.299	+0.31	+0.288	+0.298	+0.31
	(+4.09)	(+4.03)	(+4.26)	(+3.80)	(+3.94)	(+4.20)
WARRANTY	+0.081	+0.091	-------	+0.07	-------	-------
	(+1.38)	(+1.64)		(+1.20)		
SEASON	-------	-------	-------	+0.12	+0.122	+0.123
				(+2.44)	(+2.48)	(+2.53)
lnSQFT	-------	-------	-------	-------	-------	+0.349
						(+4.22)
R^2	0.62	0.62	0.62	0.62	0.62	0.63
adjR^2	0.61	0.61	0.61	0.61	0.61	0.62
F	54.62	58.01	61.79	52.24	58.7	60.43

Based on estimate (a) in Table 3, the *real* sales price of houses in the Savannah Historic Landmark District (expressed in natural log form) is a positive function of the number of bathrooms, fireplaces, rooms (other than bedrooms), garage spaces, stories in structure, and the number of square feet of finished living space in the house. In addition, the presence of a custom kitchen, a deck, a private courtyard, or an underground sprinkling system adds to the sales price. An exterior construction of brick or stucco, and "new" construction also tend to increase the sale price of the house. Undesirable house features that reduce the natural log of the real sales price are the presence of a rental apartment and an exterior of vinyl or wood siding.

In estimate (b) of Table 3, the model is re-estimated but with the altogether statistically insignificant variable POOLTUB dropped from the model. Overall, the results in column (b) are nearly identical with those in column (a), except that the coefficient on the variable WARRANTY is now not only positive (as before) but also statistically significant at the ten percent level. Thus, there is very modest support for the positive role that a home warranty might play in contributing to the price of a house. Of course, given that null hypothesis, H_o, can be only barely rejected at the ten percent level for variable WARRANTY, this finding is not compelling. However, the results for the remaining 15 explanatory variables are robust.

In estimate (c), the marginal variable WARRANTY has been omitted from the model (along with variable POOLTUB), and the results for all 15 estimated coefficients remain very robust. All 15 exhibit the hypothesized signs, with 11 being statistically significant at the one percent level, two being statistically significant at the two percent level, and two being statistically significant at the three percent level. These results strengthen the conclusions stated above for estimates (a) and (b). Although the coefficients of determination as well as the adjusted coefficients of determination are negligibly different among the estimates, the F-statistic rises moving from estimate (a) to estimate (b) to estimate (c). The results for the 15 "core" hedonic variables appear very robust and consistent.

Estimate (d) returns to the original model inclusive of variables WARRANTY and POOLTUB but adds a new variable, one that fits into the "other factors" category, namely, the variable SEASON. SEASON is a binary variable for houses placed on the market during the "prime" selling season in the Savannah market, namely, from May through July. This variable takes a value of unity if the house was listed during the peak selling season and takes a value equal to zero otherwise. The coefficient on this variable is expected to be positive since during this season home buyers in the Savannah housing market are highly active, a factor related to the ending of the Spring term and the beginning of the Fall term in the local school systems. In estimate (d), all 18 coefficients exhibit the hypothesized signs, with 11 statistically significant at the one percent level and five statistically significant at beyond the five percent level. The same variables found to be statistically significant in estimates (a) through (c) are significant in estimate (d); in addition, the variable SEASON is positive as expected and statistically significant at the two percent level.

Finally, estimate (e) omits the two insignificant variables from estimate (d), namely WARRANTY and POOLTUB. In this case, all 16 of the estimated coefficients exhibit the expected signs, with 11 statistically significant at the one percent level, three statistically significant at the 2.5 percent level, and two statistically significant at the five percent level. These results clearly are consistent with the parameter estimates of the basic model, including the apparent statistical significance of the additional variable SEASON.

A number of observations meriting discussion are provided next. First, with the exceptions of WARRANTY and POOLTUB, all of the estimated coefficients have the expected signs and are statistically significant across the estimated models. Equally interesting, if not more so, is the relative consistency of the coefficients across estimates. In most cases, the estimated coefficient on each of the 15 core statistically significant variables, as well as that for the control variable SEASON, exhibits remarkably little variation from one estimate to the next. Finally, because of these circumstances, it is with a high degree of confidence that we can describe the contribution of each of these explanatory variables to the real sales price (in natural log form) of houses *within* the Savannah Historic Landmark District.

As for the specific contributions of the statistically significant variables on LnRSALESPR, there are 16 effects that can be summarized in the analysis so far; each result is to be understood as reflecting the free market valuation placed on houses located strictly *within* the Savannah Historic Landmark District, such that for persons/economic agents interested in solely in intra-district housing price determinants, these results are presumably useful. In a semi-log functional form with the dependent variable being expressed in natural log terms, a one unit change in an independent variable has a percentage change effect on the dependent variable that is given by one hundred multiplied by the estimated coefficient, *ceteris paribus*. On the other hand, when interpreting the coefficients on dummy variables, we follow the procedure outlined in Maddala (1999).

Accordingly, with respect to the interior features of house j, if other variables are held constant (remain the same), the presence of an additional full or half bathroom causes the real sale price of house j to increase by 11.1 percent. This factor generates the largest positive sales price response for interior features. By comparison, holding all other independent variables constant, the presence of a custom kitchen yields a positive price change of 11-12 percent over the real sales price of houses without a customized kitchen. This is followed by more modest price increases for a fireplace (5.6 percent) and number of rooms (3.6 percent). Other things equal, the presence of an apartment has a relatively large negative price effect, with those houses with an apartment selling at roughly 19 percent *less* than those without this feature. The effect of the SQFT variable on the real sale price of house j is handled somewhat differently because the scale of measurement is per square foot. In particular, the real housing price rises by roughly \$30.18 (in 2005 dollars) for each additional square foot of finished living space, which lies at the midpoint of the range for other similar studies (Dotzour, 1997; Murdoch, Singh, & Thayer, 1993; Harrison, Smersh, & Schwartz, 2001).

Regarding the sales price response of house j to exterior features, the cladding type of house j exercises the largest effect. For example, a house with stucco cladding has a roughly 38 percent sale price *premium* over those that do not. A brick exterior results in a 28 percent *increase* in sales price, while a wood or vinyl siding results in a roughly 16 percent *discount* in sales price. A relative comparison across exterior cladding types can be made by subtracting the percentage figures just provided. For example, if house *m* is of brick cladding and if house *n* is of wood or vinyl cladding, house *m* sells (theoretically) at a 44 percent premium over house *n*. The presence of a courtyard adds a roughly 26-27 percent change to the sales price of a house, whereas the presence of a sprinkler system adds roughly 20 percent. A one unit increase in the number of stories in house j adds 21 percent to the sales price. Lastly, the presence of a deck has a 16-17 percent positive effect on sales price, and a one-unit change in the number of garage spaces exercises a positive 11.0 percent impact on sales price.

As for the sales-price response of house j to other non-interior and non-exterior features, if house j is of new construction, it sells with a premium of 33 percent as compared to other existing houses. Finally, a house that is sold during the primary selling season from May through July commands a sale price premium of 13-14 percent. Demand peaks during this season, and home buyers pay a sizeable premium as a result.

Before closing out this section of the study, we refer the reader to column (f) of Table 3, where the variable SQFT has been replaced in the model by its natural log, i.e., lnSQFT. Although the vast majority of related studies typically adopt a variable comparable to SQFT, expressing the SQFT variable in natural log form has been occasionally undertaken as well (Maddala, 1999). The result of substituting lnSQFT for SQFT in the model is shown in column (f) of Table 3 to exercise relatively mild impacts on most of the results. The main exception is that the elasticity estimate for variable lnSQFT is +0.349. This finding implies that, say, a ten percent increase in the square footage of living space *per se* would elevate the housing price by roughly 3.5 percent. It is possible that adopting this form of the square footage variable might be interpreted as more useful/realistic than adopting its level. That, of course, is for the reader to judge. Aside reducing the statistical significance levels (and magnitudes) of the ROOMS and SIDING variables, however, the substitution of lnSQFT for SQFT does *not* appear to materially alter the impacts of any of the *other* variables in the analysis.

Conclusion and Further Analysis

This study provides an example of the operation of free markets by applying a hedonic pricing model to explain housing price differentials within the context of a given historic landmark district. By considering home sales solely within such a district, in principle the market experiment transpires within an institutionally homogenous framework, i.e., all sales share a common characteristic in that they occur within a land area designed as "historic." This exercise demonstrating the operation of free markets involves in the Savannah Historic Landmark District, which is located in and adjacent to the downtown of Savannah, Georgia, and which effectively has not previously been formally studied in this fashion. Estimating the model in semi-log form reveals that the natural log of the real sales price of a house in this particular environment was positively affected by the number of bathrooms, fireplaces, rooms (other than bedrooms), stories in structure, garage car spaces, and square feet of finished living space, the presence of a custom kitchen, a deck, a private courtyard, an exterior construction of brick or stucco, an underground sprinkler system, and whether or not the house was new. The natural log of the *real* sales price was negatively affected by the presence of a rental apartment on the premises and by an exterior of either vinyl or wood siding. Listing a house for sale during the peak selling season from May through July also acts to raise the *real* sales price of the house. In addition, there is a positive real sales price effect for a house designated as a Historic National Landmark.

Table 4. Two Alternative Estimates: Property Taxation

Variable	(a)	(b)
Constant	+11.14	+7.53
BATHS	+0.12	+0.13
	(+3.42)	(+3.32)
FIREPLACES	+0.59	+0.054
	(+4.72)	(+4.19)
ROOMS	+0.034	+0.025
	(+2.19)	(+1.92)
SQFT	+0.0001	-------
	(+2.41)	
LnSQFT	-------	+0.452
		(+4.70)
CUSTKIT	+0.08	+0.077
	(+1.98)	(+1.91)
APT	-0.157	-0.183
	(-1.97)	(-2.44)
BRICK	+0.24	+0.223
	(+3.88)	(+3.38)
DECK	+0.153	+0.163
	(+3.58)	(+3.88)
CRTYD	+0.21	+0.23
	(+4.62)	(+5.06)
SPRINKLER	+0.178	+0.188
	(+2.60)	(+2.72)
STORIES	+0.197	+0.169
	(+3.13)	(+3.40)
STUCCO	+0.339	+0.327
	(+5.33)	(+5.51)
GARAGESP	+0.099	+0.098
	(+3.02)	(+2.97)
SIDING	-0.129	-0.105
	(-1.80)	(-1.65)
NEW	+0.307	+0.305
(+3.99)	(+4.18)	
SEASON	+0.103	+0.092
	(+2.14)	(+1.96)
PROPTX	-0.00004	-0.00003
	(-2.46)	(-2.92)
R^2	0.67	0.67
$AdjR^2$	0.64	0.64
F	54.35	57.74

Providing more detail, this study focuses on houses sold within this historically designated area for the six-year period 2000 through 2005. In order to make all housing prices comparable, they are all expressed in 2005 dollars, using an index of *housing price inflation*, as described above. The basic model consists of 17 potential factors that could influence *real* housing prices. Furthermore, two of the estimated models include a control variable (SEASON) for the listing of a house for sale during the prime-selling season in Savannah. Estimates from five semi-log variations on the basic model are presented in this study.

Before closing, this study would somehow seem incomplete if property tax liabilities were ignored. To remedy this situation, the models from columns (e) and (f) from Table 3 are expanded to include the property tax paid on house j (PTXj). Based on the theory in Tiebout (1956) and the empirical analysis in Oates (1969) and the conventional wisdom, property taxes should, at least to some degree, be capitalized by the free market into housing prices. Ergo, the expected impact of higher *real* property taxes on house j on the real sales prices of house j is negative, *ceteris paribus*. As shown in columns (a) and (b) of Table 4, the estimated coefficient on the *real* property tax variable is negative in both estimates while being statistically significant at the two percent level in column (a) and at the one percent level in column (b). Hence, inclusion of this variable does not materially alter the conclusions of the analysis, whereas the variable does demonstrate that property taxes are capitalized into housing prices—further evidence of the efficiency of free markets.

References

Bin, O., & Polasky, S. (2004). Effects of Flood Hazards on Property Values: Evidence before and after Hurricane Floyd, *Land Economics*, **80**, 490-500.

Decker, C.S., Nielsen, D.A., & Sindt, R.P. (2005). Is Pollution a Homogeneous Determinant of Value? *The Appraisal Journal*, **73**, 183-96.

Dotzour, M.G. (1997). Groundwater Contamination and Residential Property Values, *The Appraisal Journal*, **65**, 279-87.

Garrod, G., & Willis, K.G. (1992). The Environmental Economic Impact of Woodland: A Two State Hedonic Price Model of the Amenity Value of Forestry in Britain, *Applied Economics*, **24**, 715-28.

Harrison, D.M., Smersh, G.T., & Schwartz, A.L. (2001). Environmental Determinants of Housing Prices: The Impact of Flood Zone Status, *Journal of Real Estate Research*, **21**, 3-20.

Maddala, G.S. (1999). *Introduction to Econometrics*. New York: Prentice-Hall.

McMillen, D.P., Seaman, P.T., & Singell, L.D. (2007). A Mismatch Made in Heaven: A Hedonic Analysis of Over-education and Under-education, *Southern Economic Journal*, **73**, 901-930.

Murdoch, J., Singh, H., & Thayer, M. (1993). The Impact of Natural Hazards on Housing Values: The Loma Prieta Earthquake, *American Real Estate and Urban Economics Association Journal*, **21**,167-84.

Oates, W.E. (1969). The Effects of Property Taxes and Local Public Spending on Property Values: An Empirical Study of Tax Capitalization and the Tiebout Hypothesis, *Journal of Political Economy*, **77**, 957-971.

Smith, V.K., & Huang, J.C. (1993). Hedonic Models and Air Pollution: Twenty-five Years and Counting, *Environmental and Resource Economics*, **3**, pp. 381-394.

Tiebout, C.M. (1956). A Pure Theory of Local Expenditures, *Journal of Political Economy*, **64**, 416-424.

U.S. Census Bureau, (2007), *Statistical Abstract of the United States, 2007*. Washington, D.C.: U.S. Government Printing Office.

Reviewed by Stephen M. Renas, Wright State University

In: Housing, Housing Costs and Mortgages
Editors: Szilárd Kis and Istvan Balogh, pp. 135-146
ISBN: 978-1-60741-813-9

Chapter 8

THE FUNCTION OF MORTGAGES IN FACILITATING BANK LENDING

Guanghua Yu[*]
Faculty of Law, The University of Hong Kong

I. Introduction

North claims that "the inability of societies to develop effective, low cost enforcement of contracts is the most important source of both historical stagnation and contemporary underdevelopment in the Third world."[1] Some evidence in China and elsewhere is consistent with North's claim.[2] Enforcement of contracts, however, can be carried out by informal or formal means.[3] The economic theory of self-enforcing contracts suggests that a contract is self-enforcing either because the expected future gains from adhering to the contract exceed the current gain from a violation of the contract or because there are extra-legal means of enforcement (such as norms established between relatives and closely-knit social networks).[4] It is obvious that self-enforcing agreements are not feasible if the sequence of occasions for

---

* Associate Professor, Faculty of Law, The University of Hong Kong; S.J.D., University of Toronto, 1996; J.D., University of Toronto, 1993; LL.M., Osgoode Hall Law School, York University, 1988; B.A.; Shanghai Maritime University, 1985. The author thanks the University of Hong Kong for a Small Project Grant.

1 North, D. (1990). Institutions, Institutional Change and Economic Performance. New York: Cambridge University Press, at 54.

2 Yu, G. & Zhang, H. (2008). Adaptive Efficiency and Financial Development in China: the Role of Contracts and Contractual Enforcement. *Journal of International Economic Law*, 11(2), 459-494; Bernstein, L. (1992). Opting Out of the Legal System: Extralegal Contractual Relations in the Diamond Industry. *Journal of Legal Studies*, 21, 115-157 (The change of resorting to formal dispute resolution in the diamond industry supports the hypothesis that in the presence of a credible formal legal regime, when the need arises to go beyond the ethically derived, extra-legal norms that govern the transactions, it seems likely that the formal law will be more frequently used); Johnson, S., McMillan, J., & Christopher, W. (2002). Courts and Relational Contracts. *Journal of Law, Economics and Organization* 18, 221-275 (finding that effective courts foster the establishment of new relations and court enforcement is more important when the supplier involves specialized inputs).

3 For a review of the role of informal and formal contracts in economic development, see Trebilcock, M. J., & Leng, L. (2006). The Role of Formal Contract Law and Enforcement in Economic Development. *Virginia Law Review* 92, 1517-1580.

4 Telser, L. (1980). A Theory of Self-enforcing Agreement. *Journal of Business,* 53(1), 27-44, at 42.

transactions has a definite known last period.[5] In addition, highly uncertain conditions are not conducive to self-enforcing agreements.[6] In the modern world, however, unexpected things occur very frequently. The Asian financial crisis, the recent US financial crisis, significant change of cost conditions resulting from commodity price fluctuation are some of the unexpected events which are likely to affect the payoff of contractual parties. To support exchanges, contractual parties may take hostage from the other contractual party.[7] If hostage is used, non-performance by a contractual party will result in the loss of or harm to the hostage.

This chapter argues that hostage used in informal contracts normally only deal with two contractual parties. Build upon and enforced by the formal law, the device of mortgages can cope with multiparty conflict of interest. Section II of this essay explains this thesis. Section III uses evidence of increasing use of mortgages in China to show the role of mortgages in facilitating bank lending. Conclusions follow in Section IV.

II. The Device of Mortgages and Formal Law

When the present value of the expected future benefits from maintaining an agreement exceeds that of the expected benefits from a violation of the agreement, the agreement becomes "self-enforcing." According to Telser, the only recourse of the non-breaching party in a self-enforcing agreement is to terminate the agreement.[8] Williamson shows that "the use of hostages to support exchange is widespread and economically important.[9] Using hostages to support bilateral foreign relations in China can be traced back to 720 B.C.[10] Viewed from the perspective of using hostage, the expected future stream of benefits from maintaining a self-enforcing agreement can be viewed as hostage. Violation of such an agreement will result in the loss of the hostage. That is the termination of the agreement and the resulting loss of the expected future stream of benefits.[11]

Klein and Leffler deal with the issue of quality guarantee in sales transactions.[12] A major finding of their paper is that "market prices above the competitive price and the presence of non-salvageable capital are means of enforcing quality promises."[13] If the seller cheats by lowering the quality standard in a transaction, the spread of complaints of consumers will result in reduced sales or loss of sales. When reduced sales or loss of sales occur, the seller will either lose the market price above the competitive price or suffer loss on the non-salvageable asset investment. Viewed from that perspective, market price of the seller above the competitive price and the loss of benefits from using the non-salvageable asset because of

[5] Id., at 44.
[6] Id.
[7] Williamson, O. (1983). Credible Commitments: Using Hostage to Support Exchange. *American Economic Review*, 73, 519-540.
[8] Telser, supra note 4, at 27.
[9] Williamson, supra note 7, at 537.
[10] Yang, L. S. (1952). Hostages in Chinese History. *Harvard Journal of Asiatic Studies,* 15, 507-521.
[11] For a similar view in the context of international trade relations, see Yarbrough, B. V., & Yarbrough, R. (1986). Reciprocity, Bilateralism, and Economic 'Hostage': Self-enforcing Agreements in International Trade. *International Studies Quarterly*, 30(1), 7- 21, at 11.
[12] Klein, B., & Leffler, K. B. (1981). The Role of Market Forces in Assuring Contractual Performance. *The Journal of Political Economy* 89(4), 615-641.
[13] Id., at 618.

the reallocation for the next best alternative can be regarded as hostage. Advertising[14] and developing products with brand names[15] normally indicate that a company is investing in non-salvageable assets and the presence of a current and future price premium.

Klein argues that a franchisor acting as a franchisee's landlord can discipline an opportunistic franchisee by imposing a sunk-cost penalty on him. Franchisors can better

> ...assure quality by requiring franchisee investments in specific ... assets that upon termination imply a capital loss penalty larger than can be obtained by the franchisee if he cheats. For example, the franchisor may require franchisees to rent from them short term (rather than own) the land upon which their outlet is located. This lease arrangement creates a situation where termination can require the franchisee to move and thereby impose a capital loss on him up to the amount of his initial non-salvageable investment. Hence a form of collateral to deter franchisee cheating is created.[16]

In business franchising, the hostage may be the capital cost of the vulnerable sunk investment.[17] Alternatively, the hostage may be the value of future above-normal profit earnings for the franchisee.[18] Termination of the franchising contract will result in both types of loss. Empirical evidence on franchising relations in the United Kingdom, however, does not strongly support the view that termination of the franchising contract will necessarily result in the loss of location specific investment.[19] Lease termination is subject to very careful private regulation including the inclusion of arbitration clause, renewal, or buy back of franchisee's assets.[20] The purpose of lease control by the franchisor is rather due to the high cost in finding a suitable new site.[21]

The term "mortgage" refers to a transaction whereby a debtor or a third party ("mortgagor") uses certain property ("mortgaged property") as security for an obligation without the transfer of the possession of such property. If the debtor fails to fulfill his or her obligation, the creditor ("mortgagee") has priority over the mortgaged property.[22] Viewed from the perspective of hostage, mortgaged property can be considered as hostage. This is so because the failure of performing the obligation by the debtor will lead to the disposition of the mortgaged property. When the mortgaged property chosen to secure debt consists of assets whose value in the borrower's business exceeds their market value, the harm to a borrower that defaults under a mortgage contract is the loss of the idiosyncratic value. Since the particular mortgaged property may be used to secure several debts, default on any of the debts will result in the loss of the hostage. Put it another way, the probability of losing the hostage in mortgage contracts is greater than in other simple bilateral contracts.

---

14 Id., at 630.
15 Id., at 632.
16 Klein, B. (1980). Transaction Cost Determinants of 'Unfair' Contractual Arrangements. *American Economic Review Proceedings,* 70, 356-62, at 359.
17 Id.
18 See Klein, B., Crawford, R.A., & Alchian, A. A. (1978). Vertical Integration, Appropriable Rents and the Competitive Contracting Process. *Journal of Law and Economics,* 21, 297-326.
19 Dens, A. W. (1993). A Case-Study Analysis of Franchise Contracts. *The Journal of Legal Studies,* 22(2), 367-393.
20 Id., at 372.
21 Id., at 376.
22 For a discussion of the roles of secured debt in alleviating adverse selection problems and moral hazard problems, see Triantis, G. G. (1992). Secured Debt Under Conditions of Imperfect Information. *Journal of Legal Studies,* 21, 225-258.

The above discussion on the hostage used in self-enforcing contracts and in mortgage contracts raises a very important question on the institutional difference between simple self-enforcing contracts and mortgage contracts. After all, a simple bilateral mortgage contract is also self-enforcing. When a piece of mortgaged property is used to secure separate debts, the mortgagor faces several secured creditors, mortgagees. The device of mortgages, however, can be used to deal with multiple creditors. The rest of this section will explain why the device of mortgages is different from simple bilateral self-enforcing contracts.

Williamson has remarked:

> The study of contract in both law and economics has mainly emphasized legal rules and technicalities. Such an orientation is supported by the implicit assumption that the courts "work well." Whether they work well or poorly, however, requires a comparative institutional assessment.[23]

I take Williamson's suggestion to carry out a comparative institutional assessment to examine the mortgage regime.

In Telser's simple bilateral contract model discussed previously, each contractual party calculates whether s/he is better off continuing or terminating the relation with the other party. S/he terminates the contractual relation if and only if the current gain from termination exceeds the present value of the expected gains from continuing. Such a self-enforcing model becomes problematic, however, when it is extended to multilateral agreements. Discussing in the context of international trade, Beth Yarbrough and Robert Yarbrough have observed that "delicate balancing of costs and benefits may be difficult to accomplish with large numbers of participants."[24] Different rounds of negotiating multilateral trade agreements show how long and difficult it is to reach trade agreements. In mortgage contracts, a debtor may face numerous creditors. Furthermore, when a mortgage contract is enforced upon default, the relations between the borrower and secured creditors normally come to an end as far as the particular mortgaged property is concerned.

Klein and Leffler's model deals with promises on quality which cannot be verified by a court. If consumers expect the product to be of high quality but the seller offers a low-quality product to the unsuspecting buyers, the seller can reap a short-run profit. "Cheating will be prevented and high quality products will be supplied only if firms are earning a continued stream of rental income that will be lost if low quality output is deceptively produced."[25] In their model, a single breach on quality can exact a heavy cost through the costless communication of the breach on the market. As discussed, market prices above the competitive price and the presence of non-salvageable capital are means of enforcing quality promises. Their model, however, does not deal with multiple transactions when one party faces numerous creditors. In the latter case, contractual devices have to deal with not only relations between the debtor and other creditors but also relations between creditors. In some other cases, legal devices also need to regulate the relations between secured creditors and purchasers for value in good face.

While Klein and Leffler focused on market forces in contract enforcement, Avner Grief's study of the relations between the Maghribi merchants and their overseas agents in the

[23] Williamson, supra note 7, at 537.
[24] Yarbrough and Yarbrough, supra note 11, at 20.
[25] Klein and Leffler, supra note 12, at 617.

Mediterranean during the late medieval Commercial Revolution shows how a non-market reputation-based institution worked.[26] In his study, information sharing and multilateral punishment enabled credible commitment of agents to merchants ex ante and effective fulfillment of contractual obligations ex post.[27] Similar to Klein and Leffler, Grief does not deal with problems arising from multiple bilateral contractual relations.

In the case of mortgage, a mortgagor may use the same collateral to borrow money from different creditors. When the mortgagor defaults and the value of the collateral is unable to satisfy the claims of all the mortgagees, each mortgage has the incentive to seize the collateral and realize its right ahead of other creditors. This collective action problem faced by creditors requires a third party enforcement regime. To solve the priority issue, most countries have developed a formal regime. The normal rule is that the order of priority of the several mortgagees must be ascertained, and the first in priority paid in full before anything is given to those who rank below him in priority.[28] So far we have not seen an informal regime which is able to solve the priority competition issue among mortgages efficiently.

The administration of the formal regime of mortgage law requires a functional court system. In addition, a separate registration system must be established so that mortgaged property can be registered. Such a registration system serves an important purpose of recording the sequence of all mortgaged property of a particular mortgagor. With this registration system, potential mortgagees, trade or financial creditors, can easily search whether a particular debtor has used the same asset to secure debts before. Without a registration system, creditors will have great difficulty finding out whether the debtor has used the same asset to secure debts. When creditors face great uncertain, they will either reduce credit or lend at a higher interest rate. In either case, the cost of capital formation will be higher.

If a country cannot establish a registration system and a formal legal system, the device of secured debt has to be foregone. Economists claim the importance of the device of secured debt. First, secured debt may solve the debt erosion problem. As a secured lender can usually perfect its security interest easily when there is a registration system, it enjoys priority over subsequent lenders. As a result, the debtor cannot issue subsequent debt of equal or higher priority. Therefore, unless the secured creditor is under-secured, the opportunity to redistribute wealth by the debtor through subsequent debt financing is effectively neutralized.[29] In addition, security interests make the substitution of high-risk for low-risk assets after obtaining the loan more difficult.[30] After obtaining the loan, the borrower may have the incentive to substitute projects with more variable cash flow for projects with less variable cash flow. As creditors are not able to share the upside benefits from the borrower's asset substitution but must bear the downside risk, asset substitution transfers wealth from creditors to the debtor. If the debt is secured, however, those secured assets cannot be easily

---

[26] Grief, A. (1993). Contract Enforceability and Economic Institutions in Early Trade: The Maghribi Trader's Coalition. *American Economic Review*, 83, 525-548.

[27] Id.

[28] Fairest, P.B. (1980). *Mortgages* (2nd Edition) London, United Kingdom: Sweet & Marwell, at 103 and 130; Art. 199 of the Law on Real Property in China, available at http://www.chinalawinfo.com; Duncan, W. D. and Willmott, L. (1996). *Mortgages Law in Australia* (2nd Edition). Sydney, Australia: The Federation Press, at 142-46.

[29] Schwartz, A. (1981). Security Interests and Bankruptcy Priorities: A Review of Current Theories. *Journal of Legal Studies*, 10, 1-37, at 31-33.

disposed of without permission of the secured creditor. Furthermore, secured debt can ameliorate the underinvestment problem.[31] Some profitable projects will not be undertaken by a borrower which can use only equity or unsecured debt to finance them but will be undertaken if they can be financed with secured debt. Besides, secured interests over specific assets impair their marketability. This is so because the transfer of secured assets not made in the ordinary course of the debtor's business passes title to the purchaser subject to the perfected security interest.[32] Therefore, secured debt makes it difficult for the debtor to transfer wealth from secured creditors to itself. As secured debt serves important purposes of alleviating the above examined moral hazard problems, the inability of establishing a secured debt regime including mortgages results in a dead-weight social loss.

Williamson argues for the importance of using hostages to support exchange in informal contractual settings. He also cites Klein and Leffler's point that requiring franchisees to rent from the franchisor the outlet can reduce opportunistic behaviors on the part of the franchisee.[33] When the franchisee cheats on quality of the good or price, the franchisor can require the franchisee to move and "thereby impose a capital loss on him up to the amount of his initial non-salvageable investment on the outlet."[34] As discussed previously, Dnes's empirical study in the United Kingdom does not support Williamson's view.[35] While hostages can be used to support exchange, they may also be abused. When a formal legal regime is used to enforce law and contracts, using hostages to support exchange becomes unnecessary. Under a formal legal regime such as the law of mortgages, abuse of the hostage, the mortgaged property is carefully regulated.

In the United Kingdom, a mortgagee is under a duty to take reasonable care to obtain the true market value of the mortgaged property.[36] A building society has a duty "to take reasonable care to ensure that the price for which the property is sold is the best price that can be reasonably obtained."[37] Obviously, the law tries to solve the problem that the mortgagee may not have the incentive to sell the mortgaged property at a reasonable price, causing harm to the mortgagor or other mortgagees. In Australia, "a receiver owes duties to the mortgagor, primarily to exercise powers in good faith not sacrificing the mortgagor's interest recklessly, to act strictly within the conditions of appointment, to account to the mortgagor for surplus after the discharge of securities and, if property is to be sold, a duty to obtain the best possible price."[38] In China, the Law on Real Property also requires that the sale of mortgaged property mush be done with reference to the market price.[39]

This section explains that the device of mortgages requires the support of a formal legal regime. Under a formal legal system, the use of hostages to support exchange becomes unnecessary. In addition, a formal legal system solves the problem of abusing the hostage relatively well. As the device of mortgages can solve many types of moral hazard problems

---

30 Smith, C. W., & Warner, J. B. (1979). Bankruptcy, Secured Debt, and Optimal Capital Structure: Comment. *Journal of Finance*, 34, 247-251, at 250.

31 René M. Stulz, R. M., & Johnson, H. (1985). An Analysis of Secured Debt. *Journal of Financial Economics*, 14, 501- 521, at 515-18.

32 Triantis, supra note 22, at 247.

33 Williamson, supra note 7, at 529.

34 Id.

35 Dnes, supra note 19.

36 Cuckmere Brick Co. Ltd. v. Mutual Finance Ltd., [1979] Ch. 948.

37 Fairest, supra note 28, at 98.

38 Duncan and Willmott, supra note 28, at 94.

39 Law on Real Property, supra note 28, Art. 195(3).

after the debtor obtains the loan and secures well the principal and interest, secured debt of mortgages is widely used in many developed countries. The increasing use of mortgages of real property in China also provides empirical evidence that mortgages facilitates bank lending. The precondition of developing a formal legal regime of mortgages is, however, the improvement in defining and enforcing property rights.

III. Mortgages and Bank Lending in China

In the last 10 years or so, as economic reform reaches a more mature stage in China, secured lending, particularly the device of mortgages, has become more widespread. In a recent study, Haselmann and his colleagues examined the relationship between reform of bankruptcy law and collateral law and behavioral changes by banks in their lending activities.[40] One of the findings of their study is that "collateral law designed to protect individual creditors' claims is of greater importance for expanding bank lending than is bankruptcy law, which is aimed at establishing a collective enforcement regime."[41] One implication of this study is that if mortgage contracts are legally enforceable, their adoption will increase bank credits as well as the quality of these credits. The rest of this section will provide the evidence of the increasing use of mortgages in the context of China's economic transition. During this transition, efforts have been made to better define and enforce property rights of real property.

The following table shows a relatively close correlation between the GDP growth rate and the growth rate of fixed asset investment. Higher growth rate of fixed asset investment are more likely to result in higher growth rate of GDP in the same year. This is true for all years except 1998. On the other hand, lower growth rate of fixed asset investment are more likely to result in lower growth rate of GDP in the same year. The best examples are 1989, 1990, and 1999.

This table also confirmed the importance of investment in urban housing property in China's economic development. When fixed asset investment plays a very important role in China's economic development, the increasing proportion of investment in urban housing property in total fixed asset investment explains the growing importance of investment in urban housing property. The last column of the above table reveals that the proportion of investment in urban housing property in total fixed asset investment has been doubled since 1997 compared with that in the period from 1986 to 1996. Viewed from the property rights perspective, it is very difficult to have such a considerable increasing amount of investment in urban housing property without clear definition and enforcement of property rights in the property law system. The easy search of titles of land-use rights and housing property and of the burden of mortgage in such real property in large cities in China has significantly facilitated transactions in real estate assets.

---

[40] Haselmann, R. F. H., Pistor, K., & Vikrant, V. (2006). How Law Affects Lending 1 (Columbia Law and Economics Working Paper No. 285), available at http://ssrn.com/abstract=846665. (last visited on September 20, 2007).

[41] Id, at 2.

GDP, Fixed Asset Investment, and Investment in Urban Houses
Unit: 100 Million Yuan

Year	Gross Domestic Product (GDP)	GDP Growth Rate % (calculated at constant prices)	Total Investment in Fixed Assets	Growth Rate of Total Investment in Fixed Assets %	Investment in Urban Housing	Investment in Urban Housing in Total Fixed Asset Investment %
1986	10275.2	8.8	3120.6	22.7	219	7.0
1987	12058.6	11.6	3791.7	21.5	240	6.3
1988	15042.8	11.3	4735.8	25.4	-	-
1989	16992.3	4.1	4410.4	-7.2	359	8.1
1990	18667.8	3.8	4517.0	2.4	321	7.1
1991	21781.5	9.2	5594.5	23.9	406	7.25
1992	26923.5	14.2	8080.1	44.4	411	5.1
1993	35333.9	14	13072.3	61.8	637	4.9
1994	48197.9	13.1	17042.1	30.4	1446	8.5
1995	60793.7	10.9	20019.3	17.5	1303	6.5
1996	71176.6	10	22974.0	14.8	1407	6.1
1997	78973.0	9.3	24941.1	8.8	3509	14.1
1998	84402.3	7.8	28406.2	13.9	3799	13.4
1999	89677.1	7.6	29854.7	5.1	3718	12.5
2000	99214.6	8.4	32917.7	10.3	3608	11.0
2001	109655.2	8.3	37213.5	13.0	5616	15
2002	120332.7	9.1	43499.9	16.9	5319	12.2
2003	135822.8	10	55566.6	27.7	5078	9.1
2004	159878.3	10.1	70477.4	26.6	8919	12.6
2005	183084.8	10.2	88773.6	26.0	10727	12.1

Source: Except for the last two columns, the data of this table come from the China Urban Construction Statistical Yearbook (China Architecture & Building Press, 2005) at 171. The data on investment in urban housing property come from various years in the China City Statistical Yearbook (Beijing: China Statistical Press).

The move towards market orientation in allocating land use rights on the primary market provides good evidence of the improving definition and transfer of land use rights. While administrative allocation of free land use remains, that proportion has been decreasing. The allocation of land use rights with fee payment has been more and more relied upon. There are three main methods of allocating land use rights in the latter case.[42] They include agreement between the relevant governmental authority and the land user, auction whereby the governmental authority publically sells the land use rights to the person who is willing to pay the highest price, and bidding where the government authority invites potential users to submit bids and the person who is willing to pay the highest price is normally chosen. In

[42] Provisional Regulation on the Allocation and Transfer of State-owned Land Use Rights in Urban Areas, issued by the State Council on May 19, 1990. This Regulation is reprinted in the Collection of the Laws of the PRC, 1764 (Jilin: Jilin People's Press, 1990-1992). Later laws and regulations have followed these three methods of allocating land use rights with fee payment and to some extent have restricted the allocation of free land use.

1993, 152,676 hectares of land were allocated nationwide.[43] Among them, around 89,750 hectares were allocated by administrative methods for free use (*huabo*), accounting for 58.78%[44] while around 62,926 hectares were allocated through auction, bidding or agreement, occupying the remaining 41.22% (*churang*). In 2001, allocation of land through auction, bidding, or agreement accounted for 55.5 % of the total allocation of 164,000 hectares.[45] Since then, allocation of land-use rights through *churang* has taken a dominant position.[46]

Among the three methods of allocating land with pay, the method of agreement (*xieyi churang*) is becoming less significant. In 1987-88, allocation of land with pay through agreement accounted for 96.7% of the total area.[47] The percentage of 81.2% of the total land allocation in terms of size through agreement in 1992 remained very high.[48] Since 2002, allocation of land-use rights through auctions and/or biddings have began to increase. The percentage of land allocation through auctions and/or biddings was 15% in 2002, 33% in 2003 and 50.9% in 2007 respectively.[49] Higher prices in obtaining land-use rights for urban development reveal that users including developers have confidence in the security of their investment in real estate. Clear definition and transferability of property rights in real estate through contracts are the precondition for investment.

Formal property law not only affects the security of investment in real estate but also influences the way people finance their investment in real property. Palomar observed that "when land titles and land tenure are secure, landholders may utilize their property rights as collateral for loans."[50] As the Chinese economy possesses strong characteristics of a dual economy in the sense that urban cities are relatively highly developed while rural areas are underdeveloped, a brief comparison between the outcomes resulting from the formal property law on land use is helpful.

Whereas the definition, transfer, and registration of property rights of land and housing property in urban areas are relatively certain as discussed in the previous part, things are different in rural areas. There were restrictions on the conversion of rural land to land for non-agricultural use from 1987 to 2006. The dominant concern behind the restrictions is the worry about the quick depletion of arable land in a country with a huge population. Restrictions began to increase when the economy started to grow at a fast rate in the middle of 1980s. The 1986 Law on the Administration of Land still provided three methods of converting rural land to land for non-agricultural use.[51] First, when state-owned enterprises and collectively–owned enterprises in urban areas establish joint enterprises (*lianying qiye*) with collectively-owned enterprises in rural areas and need to use collectively-owned land in rural areas, these joint enterprises may convert the rural land to state-owned land after giving compensation to

---

[43] Liu, S. (2008). Property Rights in Land and Real Estate Market Development in China. A lecture delivered at the School of Law of Renmin University, available at http://www.civillaw.com.cn/article/default.asp?id=41228 (last visited on November 10, 2008).

[44] Id.

[45] Id.

[46] Id. In 2003, allocation of land use rights through *churang* accounted for 74.79% of the total 258,860 hectares allocated to users. In 2006, allocation of land use rights through *churang* amounted to 71.5% of the total allocated land of 204277 hectares.

[47] Id.

[48] Id.

[49] Id.

[50] Palomar, J. (2002). Land Tenure Security as a Market Stimulator in China Contents. *Duke Journal of Comparative and International Law*, 12, 1-74, at 10-11.

farmers or the collectively-owned enterprises in the rural area may use the land use rights as equity contribution after obtaining governmental approval.[52]Second, housing construction in rural areas, construction related to the establishment of village (township) enterprises, construction of village (township) public infrastructure, or construction of village (township) public utilities or welfare projects can be carried out after obtaining governmental approval.[53] Third, when non-rural residents in urban areas have to use collectively-owned land in rural areas for the purpose of housing construction, they may use land in rural areas after obtaining governmental approval.[54] A Circular of the State Council in 2006 prohibited the conversion of land for agricultural use to land for non-agricultural use by means of leasing instead of expropriation which has been subject to stricter control.[55]

In the 1998 Law on the Administration of Land, the third method discussed under the 1986 Law on the Administration of Land is no longer possible.[56] Related to the abolishment of this method of converting land from agricultural use to non-agricultural use in this law, using rural land for residential purposes both for farmers and urban residents is very restrictive. The 1986 Law on the Administration of Land provides that those farmer applicants who have sold or let their houses shall not be eligible for additional land for building houses.[57] The 1998 Law on the Administration of Land further adds a provision that each household shall only have one piece of household land (*Zhaijidi*).[58] Various governmental regulations or rules have also prohibited the purchase of rural houses by urban residents.[59]

The very restrictive approach to the conversion of land from agricultural purpose to non-agricultural purposes and to the purchase of rural houses by urban residents turned many transactions into illegal or informal transactions. Despite some exceptions created by some local governments, using rural land as mortgage asset to finance various projects becomes very difficult.[60]

The picture is very different in urban areas where land title and land tenure are relatively secure. The registration and search of land-use rights or housing title and mortgages of such assets are relatively easy. The statistical data of mortgages related to land-use rights and housing property in urban China provide strong empirical evidence on the role of formal law

---

[51] The Law on the Administration of Land is reprinted in the Collection of the Laws of the PRC 1872 (Jilin: Jilin People's Press, 1949-1989).

[52] Id., Art. 36.

[53] Id., Art. 37.

[54] Id., Art. 41.

[55] Circular of the State Council on Strengthening the Control of Land, available at http://www.gov.cn/ztzl/jqtdtk/content_379776.htm (last visited on November 14, 2008).

[56] The 1998 Law on the Administration of Land is reprinted in the collection of the Laws of the PRC, 2051 (Jilin: Jilin People's Press, 1998).

[57] The 1986 Law on the Administration of Land, supra note 164, Art. 38.

[58] Art. 62.

[59] Circular of the General Office of the State Council on Strengthening the Administration of Land Transfer and the Prohibition of Speculation and/or Sale of Land, issued in 1999 and available at http://www.bjtd.com/article_view.asp?article_ID=330 (last visited on November 14, 2008); Decision of the State Council on the Deepening of Reform and Strict Administration of Land, issued in 2004 and available at http://www.people.com.cn/GB/shizheng/1026/3078631.html (last visited on November 14, 2008); Huang Songyou, "People's Court Shall not Support the Purchase of Rural Houses by Urban Residents," a speech delivered at the Civil Adjudicative Work Conference held on April 9, 2007, available at http://big5.xinhuanet.com/gate/big5/news.xinhuanet.com/legal/2007-04/10/content_5955994.htm (last visited on November 14, 2008).

[60] Liu Shouying, supra note 43.

of property rights in China's economic development. The following table shows the mortgage of land use rights in urban areas.

Mortgage of Land-use Rights in Urban China[61]

Year	Total Land Turnover on the Secondary Market (hectares)	Mortgage of Land-Use Rights (hectares)	Transfer of Land-Use Rights (hectares)	Leasing of Land-Use Rights (hectares)	Percentage of Mortgaged Land in Total Land Turnover
2001	2290000	2140435	139304	10261	93.7%
2002	372672	288821	66757	17272	77.5%
2003	1185168	1102207	69633	9055	93%
2004	3565376	3422761	66842	79876	96%

The above table shows that the mortgage of land-use rights plays a significant role in financing investment in the real estate sector in urban China. There is a positive correlation between the growth of real estate loans and the growth of real estate investment as reflected in the following table. It goes without saying that without the mortgages, the amount of loans from banks would have been considerably smaller.

In addition to the evidence on the mortgage of land-use rights in urban area, the increasing use of home mortgage for financing the purchase of housing property through bank loans has also stimulated economic growth. From 1999 to 2004, the average annual property development and home mortgage loans grew by 49%.[62] By the end of 2004, the outstanding residential mortgage loans reached 1.6 trillion yuan, 83 times the amount in 1997.[63] In 2005, the outstanding mortgage loans amounted to 1.84 trillion yuan, accounting for 10% of the GDP in that year.[64]

With the high rate of economic development in China, the value of land-use rights and/or housing property has also increased rapidly. The increasing value of such real estate in turn induces people to devote more resources to define or enforce their property rights. The following table on the increasing number of legal disputes dealt with by courts in China from 1987 to 2001 provides strong empirical evidence.[65] The trend is particularly obvious from 1991.

The discussion in this section shows the close correlation between policy and legal changes related to land-use rights and housing in urban areas and China's high rate of bank lending. As urban residents in the past did not have ownership rights in their housing property which used to be small and crowed, reform in this area tend to be less difficult compared with reform of large state-owned enterprises, education reform or health care reform. The reform of the real estate market has obviously made most urban residents better off. The adoption of pay for using land through auction, bidding, or agreement has considerably increased the revenue of local governments. This in turn has provided great incentives for local governments to attract investment to their local areas. The relative easy transfer of land-use

[61] Id.
[62] Liu, L. (2007). Housing Market in Urban China, Master Thesis 61 (University of Nevada, Reno).
[63] Cheng , supra note 62.
[64] Liu, supra note 63.
[65] The numbers in this table are compiled by the author based on the China Legal Yearbook from 1988 to 2002. Beijing, China: Law Press.

rights in land and housing and the growing use of mortgages have also facilitated investment on the part of enterprises or individuals.

Correlation between Real Estate Loans and Real Estate Investment[66]

	1999	2000	2001	2002	2003	2004
Growth of real estate loans	39%	117%	35%	42%	37%	23%
Growth of real estate investment	14%	19%	27%	24%	30%	28%

Real Property Disputes Dealt with by Chinese Courts

Year	Numbers
1987	71110
1988	68664
1989	68229
1990	55704
1991	53938
1992	58782
1993	67736
1994	82341
1995	94234
1996	109822
1997	120732
1998	140993
1999	155782
2000	165799
2001	172750

V. Conclusion

This chapter explains that the device of mortgages requires the support of a formal legal regime. As secured debt of mortgages is able to solve many moral hazard problems, the institution of mortgages promotes bank lending. China's economic transition has provided a good test case on whether formal law plays any role in its economic development. The evidence in this essay is consistent with North's claim that an effective and low cost third party enforcement regime of contracts is critical to economic development. To invest and enter into contracts to buy and sell real property requires a formal property law system. The law of mortgages is an important part of the property law. The increasing use of mortgages in bank lending in China provides positive evidence that the formal law of contract and property contributes to China's economic development.

66 Cheng, J. Reviews on Housing Finance in China. Available at http://www.adb.org/PRCM/speech-pres/pboc-jiansheng.pdf (last visited on November 15, 2008).

In: Housing, Housing Costs and Mortgages
Editors: Szilárd Kis and Istvan Balogh, pp. 147-157
ISBN: 978-1-60741-813-9

Chapter 9

EFFECTS OF CHANGES IN FINANCIAL REGULATION ON DEFAULT RISK EXPOSURE OF MORTGAGES AND THE HOUSING MARKET CYCLE

***Ling T. He*[*] *and K. Michael Casey*[†]**
Department of Economics and Finance
University of Central Arkansas, Conway, AR 72035, USA

Abstract

The purpose of this study is to examine effects of financial regulation and deregulation on default risk exposure of mortgages and the past housing bubbles. Our findings suggest that financial deregulation in the early 1980s, along with other macroeconomic factors, encouraged reckless mortgage lending and thus helped create the real estate bubble in the late 1980s. The crash of the real estate market prompted two regulation acts which raised capital requirements for financial institutions. As a result, mortgage lending became more prudent. However, policy loopholes opened a door for subprime mortgage lending in early 2001. The significantly weakened default risk exposure in mortgages triggered another round of housing market appreciation. This bubble burst in 2006. The possible solutions to fix the loopholes in regulations are discussed.

Introduction

The cause of the recession beginning in 2008 has been attributed to the housing bubble and subsequent collapse of the mortgage market. Increasing homeowner defaults triggered the crisis that rapidly expanded to include major banks and other purchasers of derivative securities based on residential mortgages. The bulk of the defaults started in the adjustable rate mortgage market and quickly expanded into subprime mortgages. While these symptoms

[*] E-mail address: linghe@uca.edu. (501) 450-5334.
[†] E-mail address: mcasey@uca.edu. (501) 450-5335.

of a failed system are easy to recognize it becomes more problematic to trace the symptoms back to the root cause or causes. It is the premise of this paper that changes in financial regulation, coupled with periods of easy monetary policy, created the real estate bubble and the overextension of credit in this market.

To fully understand the impact of regulation or deregulation on the mortgage markets it becomes useful to review the past several decades of changing legislation and monetary policy. The period from 1972 to 2005 can be subdivided into three distinct regulatory time periods. The period from 1972 to July 1989 was characterized by legislation and monetary policy that encouraged not only overall inflation but more specifically home price inflation.

Two pieces of legislation in the early 1980s encouraged housing price inflation. The Depository Institutions Deregulation and Monetary Control Act of 1980 (DIDMCA) and Garn-St. Germain Depository Institutions Act of 1982 (GSDIA) both set the stage for the housing bubble by encouraging financial institutions to become more aggressive in underwriting mortgages. The major provisions of these pieces of legislation made mortgages more readily available by reducing restrictions on lenders via more lenient capital standards and greater ability to compete for deposits. Alternatives to traditional mortgages were also allowed with the passage of GSDIA. These changes in regulation encouraged the abandonment of risk assessment procedures traditionally followed by lenders in order to make homeownership available to a larger segment of the population. These practices resulted in defaults and subsequent bank failures.

The next period begins with this real estate bubble bursting and a return to more prudent real estate lending. This second period runs from August 1989 to December 2000 and indicates lenders reverted back to lending practices where mortgage rates were priced according to default risk.

The last period begins in January 2001 when the pendulum swung back to more lax lending practices and easy monetary policy. Beginning in early 2001 money from the dot.com stock market bubble began pouring into markets offering higher returns. Much of this money found its way into the mortgage market. Low mortgage rates and the rapid expansion of the secondary mortgage market once again provided fuel for housing price appreciation. Mortgage securitization exploded during this time period as did the use of credit default swaps (CDS) which is essentially default insurance on mortgage backed securities. The CDS market actually became very speculative and resulted in a total dollar volume of more than $30 trillion by the end of 2008. The end result of this last time period has many similarities to the period ending in July 1989. In other words history repeated itself only on a grander scale.

Regulation or deregulation often has long-term unintended consequences. It is our premise that there have been very specific regulatory and monetary causes of the past real estate bubbles. The following history of financial regulation and deregulation provides the background information to support our position. We follow this history with some policy recommendations designed to prevent history from repeating itself. Perhaps even some of these recommendations are transferable to other financial markets.

Table 1. Summary Statistics (in Percent, except for t-values)

	Period of January, 1972 through July, 1989								
	MORT	NHS	EHS	STA	PER	PRICE	CPI	DEF	TERM
Mean	0.1771	0.3326	0.2480	0.1598	0.0206	0.7740	0.5272	0.0268	0.1253
Std. Dev	3.0253	7.8860	3.7614	8.8343	7.2475	3.1653	0.3491	1.2319	3.3809
Correlation coefficient of MORT	100	-48.77	-30.99	-25.27	-41.57	-3.27	34.66	-7.95	-18.51
t-value		(-8.06)[a]	(-4.71)[a]	(-3.76)[a]	(-6.61)[a]	(-0.47)	(5.34)[a]	(-1.15)	(-2.72)[a]

	Period of August, 1989 through December, 2000								
	MORT	NHS	EHS	STA	PER	PRICE	CPI	DEF	TERM
Mean	-0.1802	0.4446	0.4278	0.2662	0.2517	0.3066	0.2473	-0.0916	0.3808
Std. Dev 2.5746	6.7733	4.5676	6.6195	4.8116	3.5583	0.1682	0.8119	2.3069	
Correlation Coefficient of MORT	100	-16.57	6.31	4.21	0.02	1.06	-5.49	20.32	-47.57
t-value		(-1.95)[b]	(0.73)	(0.49)	(0.19)	(0.12)	(-0.64)	(2.41)[a]	(-6.28)[a]

	Period of January, 2001 through December, 2005								
	MORT	NHS	EHS	STA	PER	PRICE	CPI	DEF	TERM
Mean	-0.2191	0.5463	0.5613	0.6526	0.5777	0.7272	0.2077	0.1213	0.4877
Std. Dev	3.3002	5.1998	2.8501	6.4302	3.4269	4.0408	0.2868	1.0575	3.0063
Correlation Coefficient of MORT	100	-5.55	18.16	-28.34	-7.07	6.70	8.06	14.49	-46.36
t-value		(-0.42)	(1.41)[c]	(-2.25)[b]	(-0.54)	(0.51)	(0.62)	(1.11)	(-3.98)[a]

MORT =Percentage changes in mortgage rates.
NHS =Percentage changes in new home sales.
EHS =Percentage changes in existing home sales.
STA =Percentage changes in new home starts.
PER =Percentage changes in housing permits.
PRICE =Percentage changes in the median sales prices of new homes sold.
CPI =Percentage changes in Consumer Price Index.
DEF =Default risk premium.
TERM =Term risk premium.
Superscripts of a, b and c indicate the one, five, and ten percent significance level, respectively.

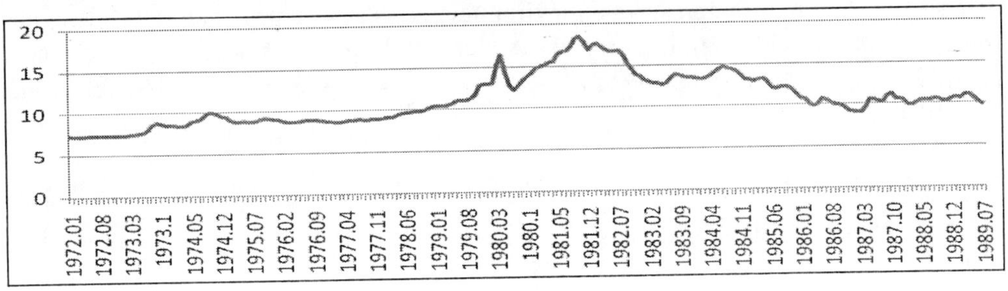

Figure 1. Mortgage rate (%).

Inflationary and Financial Deregulation Period (January of 1972 through July of 1989)

In 1970s the monthly average of percentage changes in CPI was as high as 0.68% which was fueled by soaring oil prices and growing government spending and accompanied by sluggish and negative economic growth. The phenomenon is known as "stagflation." The staggering inflation started to decline in 1980s, therefore, the average monthly rate reduced to 0.53% over the pre-FIRREA period. In such an inflationary environment, interest rates for 30-year fixed rate mortgages increased, on the average, about 0.18% every month during the same period (Table 1 and Figure 1). The correlation coefficient for changes in CPI and mortgage rates (34.66% with a t-value of 5.34) indicates a significant linear relationship between the two variables. As inflation began to retreat in 1980s, the housing market was getting ready to be a new engine for GDP growth. The real estate boom started in the mid1980s and peaked in 1989.

The real estate escalation was propelled by financial sector deregulation which started in 1980 with the passage of the Depository Institutions Deregulation and Monetary Control Act and accelerated with the passage of the Garn-St. Germain Depository Institutions Act in 1982. The Monetary Control Act stimulates mortgage lending through the following regulations:

- Lowering mandatory reserve requirements that banks must keep in noninterest earning accounts at the Federal Reserve Banks.
- Raising the federal deposit insurance coverage from $40,000 to $100,000 per insured account.
- Allowing all types of depository institutions to access the Federal Reserve Discount Window for credit advances.
- Preempting state usury laws limiting rates lenders could charge on residential mortgages.
- Permitting federal credit unions to originate residential mortgages.

The Garn-St. Germain Depository Institutions Act of 1982 was entitled "An Act to revitalize the housing industry by strengthening the financial stability of home mortgage lending institutions and ensuring the availability of home mortgage loans." As the title suggested, the aim of the Act was to invigorate the housing industry by addressing depository institutions' serious financial problems evolving from intense competition among financial institutions in the high interest rate environment. As the most important deregulation legislature on the U.S. banking industry, the Act contains numerous provisions to enhance the competitiveness and lending power of all types of depository institutions. The following are highlights of provisions of the Act:

- Authorizing banks and savings institutions to offer the Money Market Deposit Account without interest rate ceiling, in order to compete more effectively with money market mutual funds.
- Providing flexibility and authority to the federal regulatory agencies to approve interstate acquisitions of failed financial institutions.

- Offering capital (net worth) assistance to troubled depository institutions specialized in home mortgage lending.
- Overriding state restrictions on enforcement by lenders of due-on-sale clauses in most mortgages in which the borrowers agree to pay off mortgages in full when houses are sold, in order to allow lenders to make timely adjustments on mortgage interest rates.
- Allowing depository institutions to make alternative mortgages, including adjustable rate mortgages, in addition to traditional fixed rate mortgages.

As a result of the deregulation in financial sector, paying higher interest rates on deposits become a powerful competitive tool to attract deposits among depository institutions; on the other hand, competition to make more mortgages kept mortgage rates at lower and more stable levels after 1982 (Figure 1) and caused mortgage lending activities, in general, to be less prudent. Many researchers, such as Kane (1985, 1989) and Eichler (1989), sensed some serious maturity mismatching problems for savings institutions when they saw the dramatic increase in short-term interest rates in the late 1970s. Traditionally, short-term deposits are the major funding sources for saving institutions, while regulatory policies encourage financial institutions "to make long-term fixed-rate mortgages to facilitate home ownership in the country" (Gupta and Misra, 1999). When interest rates spiked and became volatile, the profitability of savings institutions took a big hit. As capital levels declined, "some savings institutions inappropriately extended loans with excessive risks to compensate their weak performance," and used some accounting and appraisal methods to hide their financial problems (Madura and Wiley, 2000). The recklessness in mortgage lending is indicated by the marginal exposure of mortgage rates to default risk. The linear relationship between alterations in mortgages rates and default risk premium is trivial, as suggested by an insignificant correlation coefficient of -7.95% or -0.0795 (Table 1). The negligible amount of default risk exposure of mortgage rates may play an important role in creating the real estate bubble in the late 1980s. The high inflation in the 1970s and strong demands for residential homes stimulated by the loose mortgage lending led to the phenomenal increase in housing prices. The median sales prices of new homes sold appreciated by 0.774% every month, on average, over the sample period.

The significant negative correlation coefficient (-18.51%) between changes in mortgage rates and term risk premium reflects the fact that the average of actual maturities of mortgages is shorter than the nominal maturities, ranging from ten to fifteen years. The shorter actual maturities are caused by either earlier amortization related to home sales or refinancing when mortgage rates fall. During the sample period, local savings institutions and credit unions were major players in mortgage lending business. Therefore, mortgage rates were closely associated with local residential real estate markets. The changes in mortgage rates were highly and negatively correlated with variations in new and existing home sales, housing permits and starts (Table 1). These significant correlations were also the result of less developed financial markets for mortgage backed securities. Although mortgage securitization was invented and expanded in the sample period, its exploding growth, equipped with extensive applications of new information technology, occurred only after 1989.

The housing bubble started to burst in the second quarter of 1989. The crash of housing markets wreaked havoc on depository institutions, especially those heavily involved in aggressive mortgage lending. By 1989, 234 savings institutions were declared by regulators as technically insolvent, additional 122 institutions were insolvent based on generally accepted accounting principles, and other 136 only appeared solvent due to goodwill on their balance sheet (Madura and Wiley, 2000). This large scale of failures in savings and loan industry triggered a series of responses from the U.S. government. One of the serious outcomes was the Financial Institutions, Reform, Recovery and Enforcement Act (FIRREA) passed in August 1989.

Bank Reform and Securitization (August 1989 through December 2000)

The FIRREA, known as the bailout bill, provided government funds to insolvent savings and loan associations and demanded sweeping changes in the examination and supervision of savings institutions. As a result, it dramatically changed the thrift industry and considerably enhanced its federal regulation. The major provisions of the Act include:

- Creating the Resolution Trust Corporation (RTC) to close or merge hundreds of insolvent savings institutions, and establishing the Resolution Funding Corporation (RETCORP) to borrow from private capital markets to fund RTC activities.
- Requiring savings institutions to meet minimum capital requirement: tangible asset of 1.5% of total assets; core capital, the sum of tangible capital and goodwill, equal to 3% of total assets; and risk-based capital equal to 6.4% of risk-weighted assets (rising to 8% after January 1, 1993). Goodwill was excluded from core capital after 1994.
- Creating the Bank Insurance Fund (BIF) and the Savings Association Insurance Fund (SAIF) under the administration of the Federal Deposit Insurance Corporation. The Federal Savings & Loan Insurance Corporation (FSLIC), along with the Federal Home Loan Bank Board (FHLBB), was abolished.
- Founding the Office of Thrift Supervision (OTS) to charter, regulate, examine, and supervise savings institutions.
- Creating the Federal Housing Finance Board (FHFB) as an independent Agency to oversee the 12 federal home loan banks.
- Authorizing Fannie Mae and Freddie Mac to support mortgages for low- and moderate-income families.
- Forming the Appraisal Subcommittee (ASC) to provide oversight and input to the Appraisal Foundation, in order to promulgate the Uniform Standards of Professional Appraisal Practice and the minimum requirements for appraisal licensing in states. Members of ASC were from the various federal mortgage regulatory agencies.

The minimum capital requirements contained in FIRREA were further expanded by the Federal Deposit Insurance Corporation Improvement Act (FDICIA) of 1991. Its Section 38 specified capital categories and ratio requirements based on international capital standards

(Basel Committee). Moreover, Section 39 required regulators to establish standards defining safety and soundness in operations and management; asset quality, earnings, and stock valuation; and compensation. As soon as serious capital or safety and soundness problems in financial institutions were discovered, FDICIA required the FDIC to use prompt corrective action and least cost resolution to intervene in restructuring banks and thrifts that failed to meet minimum capital requirements and merging insolvent financial institutions into healthy ones.

The federal regulations on minimum capital requirements, stands of safety and soundness, inspection and supervision, and stands of professional housing appraisal practice restrained reckless mortgage lending in the early 1980s. Those regulations compelled banks and thrifts to adjust their risk tolerance levels and carefully analyze risk factors involved in mortgage lending. Mortgage rates over the period of August 1989 to December 2000 reflect the shift in mortgage lending from reckless to prudent. The coefficient of correlation between mortgage rates and default risk premium reaches 20.32 % with a t-value of 2.41 which indicates a one percent statistical significance level (Table 1). The result evidently suggests that financial deregulations in the early 1980s and regulations in the late 1980s and the early 1990s are relevant to changes in the default risk exposure of mortgages and mortgage lending behavior.

Inflation during this period dropped drastically. The average monthly change of CPI was only 0.25%, in contrast to 0.53% for the first period (1972 to the mid of 1989). The huge decline in inflation was also echoed in continuously falling mortgage rates. The mortgage rates dropped by 0.18% every month, compared with a monthly increase of 0.18% for the first period. Falling mortgage rates can stimulate mortgage refinancing which can effectively shorten the actual maturities of mortgages. The increase in mortgage refinancing pushed the negative relationship between mortgage rates and term risk premiums to an even higher level with the correlation coefficient jumping to -47.57%, from -18.51% for the first period.

Another prominent development during the 1990s was the rapid growth and expansion in securitization of increasing variety of assets. The process was invigorated by spectacular innovations in information technology and advances in financial theories and applications. The securitization of mortgages changed real estate exposure of mortgage rates and funding sources for mortgage lending. With the rapid expansion of securitization of mortgages, more and more local mortgage lenders (banks, thrifts, and mortgage companies) quickly sold their mortgages to big financial institutions that packaged mortgages and issued mortgage-backed securities (MBS). The major players are U.S. government or government-sponsored agencies: the Government National Mortgage Association (Ginnie Mae), the Federal National Mortgage Association (Fannie Mae) and the Federal Home Loan Mortgage Corporation (Freddie Mac). According to Securities Industry and Financial Market Association, by the end of 2000, the total amount of MBS outstanding reached $3.6 trillion, about 21% of the total U.S. bond market. Since local mortgage originators did not hold mortgages for a long time, the real estate risk exposure of mortgage lending reduced considerably. The correlations between mortgage rates and five housing factors diminishes by a considerable amount ranging from 50% (new home sales and the median sales prices of new home sold) to 80% (existing home sales, home starts and permits), compared with the first period. Mortgage securitization brought more funds from other parts of the country and even the globe to finance local mortgage lending. This change in funding sources surely modified the equilibrium equation for mortgage rates and reinforced the shrinking process in the housing market risk exposure of mortgages.

Subprime Mortgages and the Housing Bubble (January 2001 through December 2005)

According to the National Bureau of Economic Research (NBER), the first U.S. economic recession in the twenty-first century began in March 2001 and ended in November 2001. It lasted for eight months only. Nonetheless, the stock market predicted the recession almost one year earlier. The monthly NASDAQ composite index reached the highest level of 4,696.69 in February 2000 and plummeted thereafter. In March 2001 the index was only 1,840.26. The collapse of the stock market followed the bust of dot-com bubble. As a result, investors started to shift their investment focus from dot-com stocks and high tech sectors to real estate markets. Housing market data can verify this important alteration in investments. Three real estate variables in Table 1 for the third period, the median sales prices of new home sold, housing permits and starts, are more than doubled, in contrast to that for the second period. Furthermore, the monthly growth rates for existing and new home sales jump by 20-30% over the same interval. The strong demand for real properties was bumped up by easy liquidity available during the period.

The monthly inflation over the period of 2001 to 2005 averaged about 0.21%. The mild inflation provided the Federal Reserve Bank with an excellent opportunity to utilize an easy monetary policy to stimulate economic growth. The Fed continuously lowered the effective funds rate from 6.54% in July 2000 to 0.98% in December 2003, although it came back to 4.16% in December 2005. The low funds rate pushed mortgage rates down to about 6% during the period (Figure 2). Overall, the mortgage rates declined about 0.22% per month. The falling mortgage rates provoked ongoing refinancing by home owners. Therefore, the negative correlation between changes in mortgage rates and term risk premium during the period remained very strong (46.36%).

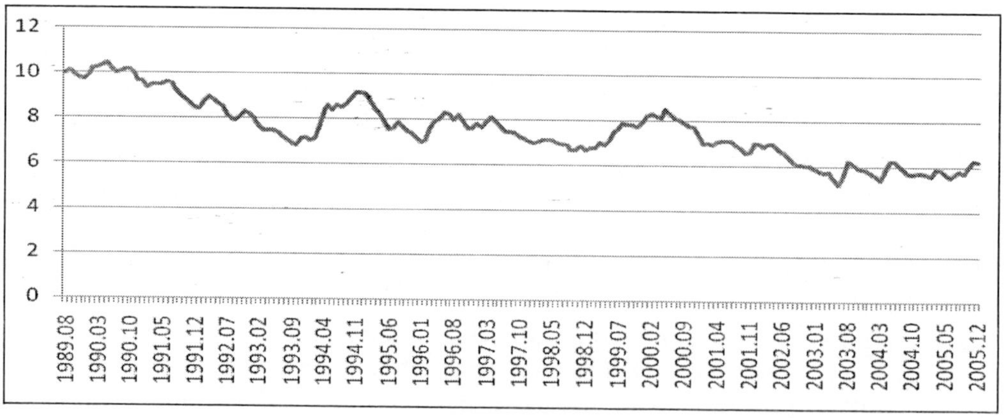

Figure 2. Mortgage rate (%).

The combination of strong demand for mortgages and easy liquidity stimulated the subprime mortgage lending which had appeared in the past real estate boom cycles. Subprime mortgage borrowers normally have credit scores below 620 on a scale of 300 through 850. The lower credit scores of subprime borrowers may reflect their poor credit histories associated with payment delinquencies, charge-offs, and even bankruptcies. Therefore, subprime mortgages have a much higher default rate than that of prime mortgages. Many subprime mortgages originated during this period were adjustable-rate mortgages (ARM) with very low teaser rates initially to attract subprime borrowers. The rates would increase considerably after some initial period. The rate hike can trigger payment default which may lead to a home foreclosure. In fact, it was the major reason that caused painful consequences for both homeowners and many financial institutions after the mid 2006. The irresponsible subprime mortgage lending eroded mortgage underwriting standards significantly in the period of 2001 to 2005, which was known for booming real estate markets. For example, practices such as using automated mortgage underwriting procedures to avoid appropriate credit review and documentation in originating subprime mortgages; lowering cash down payment from conventional 20% to 5%, 2%, even 0%; and creating interest-only mortgages which allow borrowers to pay only interest on mortgages for a period of five to ten years emerged. Our empirical result also suggests that mortgage lending became more irresponsible, compared with the second period. The coefficient of correlation between mortgage rates and default risk premium reduces from 20.32% in the second period to 14.49% in the third period. The correlation in the later period is statistically insignificant. An obvious motivation behind the reckless mortgage lending is rooted in the fact that most mortgage lenders could sell their mortgages immediately after origination, thanks to the well developed mortgage-backed securities market and keep lucrative fees. The wild mortgage lending activities incited irresponsible borrowings and eventually helped create a housing bubble at the end of the third period.

Conclusion

Our analysis indicates that financial deregulations and regulations have apparent influence on default risk exposure of mortgages and housing market cycles. It may not be difficult to understand the relationship between financial deregulations and creating asset bubbles, including a housing bubble. However, the fact that the housing bubble formed in the post-FIRREA period raises an interesting regulatory question, that is, why did two regulation acts, FIRREA and FDICIA, fail in preventing financial institutions from reckless mortgage lending during the period of 2001 to 2005? In order to make sure that the financial institutions are healthy and engage in prudent loan lending, both FIRREA and FDICIA put rigorous capital requirements on financial institutions. Nonetheless, those required capital ratios may not work as initially designed in some extreme economic situations, because they are essentially inflexible and not forward looking.

During a period with high economic growth, fast appreciation in asset prices may easily inflate the required capital ratios for financial institutions. The high ratios make financial institutions look healthy and encourage them to make more loans to pursue more profits, thus help create asset bubbles. On the other hand, in an economic downturn, depressed asset prices can dramatically slash the capital ratios over a relatively short period of time. The deteriorated ratios place heavy regulatory pressure on financial institutions and force them to hoard cash to preserve capital and thus aggravate the shortage of liquidity in a depressed time.

The self-defeating effect of financial regulations may be minimized by allowing more flexible previsions which authorize regulators to adjust required capital ratios to more appropriately reflect real economic conditions.

Further, results of our analysis suggest that future changes in financial regulation should focus on risk control on financial activities, in order to reduce the chance for harmful financial turmoil. The following policy changes may be helpful in this regard.

Require "skin in the game." Lenders historically have been reluctant to loan money to borrowers who do not put some of their own money at risk. This process of having something at stake is known as putting "skin in the game" in many circles. In other words you need to have something at risk in order to properly evaluate the probability of success or failure. The practice of mortgage originators earning substantial fees and then being able to immediately package and sell these mortgages on the secondary market removed their interest in originating good loans. The overarching theme of any legislation should be to not encourage asset bubbles by creating incentives to abandon traditional risk assessment methods and consistent risk pricing.

Limit the size of financial institutions. Additional consideration should be given to limiting the size of financial institutions so that any one failure does not have the ability to devastate the economy. Risk by definition means there is a possibility of failure. Confinement of failures to smaller spheres of influence would ensure that the economic malaise could not spread far. Evidence of this principle can be seen with the small regional bank failures that have been allowed to occur. The demise of any one of these smaller entities impacts only those stakeholders and investors who knew (or should have known) and understood the risks of their market.

Regulate and limit the use of derivative securities. The explosion of the CDS market was driven purely by speculation. Persons writing credit default swaps were driven by bonus motives and many did not consider the long-term impact of this type of exposure. In many cases the individuals likely had no incentive to care about the long-term impact.

Appendix: Data Description

The data used in this study covers a period of January 1972 through December 2005. The variability of data dictates the sample period. The data set contains the following monthly series:

CPI: the percentage changes in the U.S. Consumer Price Index for all urban consumers: all items. The index is seasonally adjusted (Bureau of Labor Statistics).

EHS: the percentage changes in existing residential home sales (National Association of Realtors).

Mort: the percentage changes in interest rates for 30-year fixed rate mortgages (Federal Home Loan Mortgage Corporation).

NHS: the percentage changes in new residential home sales (U.S. Census Bureau).

PER: the percentage changes in new housing permits (U.S. Census Bureau).

PRICE: Median Sales Prices for New Homes Sold (U.S. Census Bureau).

STA: the percentage changes in new housing starts (U.S. Census Bureau).

Seasonally adjusted annual rates are used for monthly series of EHS, NHS, PER , and STA. The following are monthly return series:

CORP: the monthly returns on long-term corporate bonds (Stock, Bonds, Bills, and Inflation 2005 Yearbook, Ibbotson Associates).

LONG: the monthly returns on long-term U.S. government bonds (Stock, Bonds, Bills, and Inflation 2005 Yearbook, Ibbotson Associates).

SHORT: the monthly returns on one-month U.S. Treasury Bills (Stock, Bonds, Bills, and Inflation 2005 Yearbook, Ibbotson Associates). According to Fama and French (1993), $SHORT_{t-1}$ is the proxy for "the general level of expected returns on bonds."

DEF_t $CORP_t$ - $LONG_t$. It represents the default risk premium (Fama and French, 1993).

$TERM_t$ $LONG_t$ - $SHORT_{t-1}$. It is the maturity risk premium and measures unexpected changes in interest rates (Fama and French, 1993).

References

Bennett, P., R. Peach, and S. Peristiani. 2001. "Structural Change in the Mortgage Market and the Propensity to Refinance," *Journal of Money, Credit, and Banking* 33, pp. 955-975.

Fama, E., and K. French. 1993. "Common Risk Factors in the Returns on Stocks and Bonds," *Journal of Financial Economics* **33**, pp. 3-56.

Fratantoni, M. and S. Schuh. 2003. "Monetary Policy, Housing, and Heterogeneous Regional Markets," *Journal of Money, Credit, and Banking* **35**, pp. 557-589.

Eichler, N. 1989. The Thrift Debacle, Berkeley, CA, University of California Press.

Gupta, A. and L. Misra. 1999. "Failure and Failure Resolution in the US Thrift and Banking Industries," *Financial Management* **28**, pp. 87-105.

Kane, E.J. 1985. The Gathering Crisis in Deposit Insurance, Cambridge, MA, MIT Press.

Kane, E.J. 1989. The S&L Insurance Mess: How Did it Happen? Washington, DC, Urban Institute Press.

Madura, J. and M.K. Wiley. 2000. "The Impact of the Financial Institutions Reform, Recovery and Enforcement Act on the Risk of Savings Institutions." *The Financial Review* **35**, pp. 145-168.

In: Housing, Housing Costs and Mortgages
Editors: Szilárd Kis and Istvan Balogh, pp. 159-170
ISBN: 978-1-60741-813-9

Chapter 10

THE IMPACT OF RISING HOME PRICE ON THE INCOME ELASTICITY OF HOUSING DEMAND

Zhu Xiao Di
Joint Center for Housing Studies, Harvard University, USA

Abstract

Income elasticity is a classical measurement in economics. For many years economists have earnestly studied the income elasticity of housing demand, even though little consensus has ever been reached. Part of the difficulty came from the fact that housing is both a consumption and investment at the same time. Many studies have been devoted to disentangling these two components, but no one has tried to measure the income elasticity of housing demand over time to observe any notable change. Because of the dual motives to purchase a home, most economists do agree that housing demand is best measured as home price rather than home size. The recent housing boom in the United States, however, dramatically inflated home price and widely increased housing costs. When home price is inflated flatly, one may have a reason to expect a suppressed income elasticity of housing demand, because a relatively smaller percentage change in home price can adequately reflect the same amount of difference in the absolute price of homes purchased. On the other hand, given the investment motive of owning homes, it is reasonable to expect that a higher income elasticity of housing demand should correspond to a higher home price appreciation. In fact, a study by Turner (2003) using selected metropolitan data from the 1985 to 1995 American Housing Surveys (AHS) did find that "families are less likely to own and housing demand is reduced during episodes of relatively high, anticipated house-price volatility," i.e. uncertainty in home price appreciation. So, which hypothesis is correct? Using the national data from the 1985 to 2007 AHS survey data, my study found evidence to support both hypotheses described above, though at different times. In addition, it discovered another powerful factor that has a strong impact on the income elasticity of housing demand. That is, cash inflows from the equity market to the real estate due to the market crash in 2000 depressed the income elasticity of housing demand drastically. This is not surprising though, because in theory, as Hoyer (1998) pointed out a long time ago, "in broad terms a declining immediate correlation between changes in income and consumption reflects more liberal capital markets." In short, this chapter examines one important impact of changing home prices, which not only fits the theme of the entire book,

Housing, Housing Costs and Mortgages, but adds some theoretical flavor to a perhaps highly practical-sounding title.

Introduction

As a classical measurement in economics, economists have studied the income elasticity of housing demand for many years, yet little consensus has ever been reached. Part of the difficulty came from the fact that housing is both a consumption and investment at the same time. As owner-occupied housing has both consumption and investment components of it, purchasing such a home satisfies both incentives simultaneously. Income elasticity of housing demand is therefore much more complicated than that of most other consumer goods.

Many studies have been devoted to disentangling these two components, (such as in Ranney, 1981; Henderson and Ioannides, 1983; Fu, 1995; Brueckner, 1997; and Lin and Lin, 1999), and the study in 1999 even estimated the ratio of consumption to investment motives roughly to be one to three. Economists have studied income elasticity of housing demand for long (such as in Reid, 1962; Muth, 1965; Winger, 1968; DeLeeuw, 1971; Carliner, 1973; Polinsky and Ellwood, 1979; Goodman & Kawai, 1982; Glennon, 1989; Goodman, 1990), because it is "of concern to policy makers and planners and to all who are involved in forecasting the demand for housing" (Wilkinson, 1973). Recently there was even an attempt of using it to detect whether a housing bubble existed (Fernandez-Krans and Hon, 2006).

Because of the dual motives to purchase a home, most economists do agree that housing demand is best measured as home price rather than home size. The recent housing boom in the United States, however, dramatically inflated home price and widely increased housing costs. When home price is inflated flatly, one may have a reason to expect a suppressed income elasticity of housing demand, because a relatively smaller percentage change in home price can adequately reflect the same amount of difference in the absolute price of homes purchased. For example, if housing price inflated from a range of 200,000 to 300,000 to a range of 300,000 to 400,000, then it would only take 25 percent increase to cover the range from lower to upper end, instead of 50 percent increase as it would have been before the price inflation. Thus the measured income elasticity also becomes flatter. If there was such a reduction in the income elasticity of housing demand, we should be able to detect it by using the same source of data to measure the income elasticity of housing demand over time. Namely, when house price inflates over time, income elasticity decreases as a result. On the other hand, given the investment motive of owning homes, it is reasonable to expect that a higher income elasticity of housing demand should correspond to a higher home price appreciation. In fact, a study by Turner (2003) using selected metropolitan data from the 1985 to 1995 American Housing Surveys (AHS) did find that "families are less likely to own and housing demand is reduced during episodes of relatively high, anticipated house-price volatility," i.e. uncertainty in home price appreciation. In other words, income elasticity decreases as house price does not appreciate well, which is just the opposite of the previous hypothesis. So, which hypothesis is correct and true?

In the past, various researchers have found the income elasticity of housing demand to range from 0.89 to 1.46, "suggesting that households are willing to devote a relatively large portion of their extra income to buying more housing" (Clark and Dieleman, 1996). These traditional models do not account for the possibility that households may own two or more homes, and some researchers have already pointed out these shortcomings (Hansen et al. 1998). The recent study by Belsky et al. (2007) filled in the blank by including second-home ownership in the equation. This chapter therefore follows the footprint of that study, using the same national data of the AHS but repeatedly from 1985 to 2007, focusing on homebuyers rather than all homeowners to catch a more accurate account on the income elasticity of housing demand.

From such a follow-up using a consistent source of data over more than decades, it is expected to be able to test both hypotheses above on the net impact of housing market dynamics, especially that of an inflated housing price, on the income elasticity of housing demand. It is fairly remarkable already though that despite the fact that so many researchers have studied the income elasticity of housing demand, not even one single study has ever tried to measure it repeatedly over time. For that matter alone, this chapter will uniquely contribute to the current literature. In addition to the two hypotheses described above, testing them may also lead to other discoveries regarding other possible major factors significantly influencing the income elasticity of housing demand.

Data and Methodology

Every two years, the Census Bureau conducts the AHS surveys at the national level for HUD, interviewing about 50,000 households each time. I focused on homebuyers and their reported purchasing price is the dependent variable in my OLS regression models. In each survey, these are the buyers who purchased and moved to a new primary residence within the 2 years prior to the survey (for 1985, it is only those who bought homes within 12 months of the survey). There are several merits in taking this approach. The recent purchasing price is usually accurately remembered and reported and ties closely to the reported household income at the time.

As Belsky et al. (2007) explained in their paper, estimated permanent household income is a better variable than current income to determine the income elasticity of housing demand. In this chapter, just as in theirs, I followed the methodology of Wachter and Megbolugbe (1992) and performed a Box-Cox transformation on the dependent variable of the permanent income regression with $\lambda = 0.5$. I then re-transformed the predicted value before including it in the housing demand models (see Appendix tables in Belsky et al. (2007).

The permanent household income variable and the dependent variable were then run through logarithmic conversions to make the sample distribution more normal. Such transformations can reduce the sample size as they automatically dropped observations with zero or negative values. To avoid this problem, I assigned a value of $1 to negative or zero values before performing the logarithmic transformation.

The national AHS survey contains detailed household information including current household income, age, race/ethnicity, educational attainment of household heads, and family type. Unfortunately, the dataset lacks geographic detail. While about 100 metropolitan areas are specified, in most cases the number of observations is far too small to create a meaningful hedonic price index. Instead, to control for differences in the costs of housing and non-housing goods across areas, I have to rely on the interaction of the four census regions and three types of metropolitan status: cities, suburbs, or non-metro, just as in Belsky et al. (2007). This provides 12 categories—an admittedly crude control for housing price differences across the country but nevertheless worth using. These variables appear in the models as dummies to represent those living in Northeast cities, Northeast suburbs, Northeast non-metro, Midwest cities, Midwest suburbs, Midwest non-metro, South cities, South suburbs, South non-metro, West cities, West suburbs, or West non-metro.

I constructed all other variables also consistent with Belsky et al. (2007). If a household was not headed by a non-Hispanic white, I coded it as a minority household. I also created age categories to classify the household head as under 35, 35-44, 45-54, or 55-64. Because seniors have largely reduced income after retirement, I excluded them in my models on income elasticity of housing demand. A set of six dummy variables flags various types of households: married without children, married with children, single parents, other family type, single person, and other non-family type.

Education is a key predictor in estimating permanent household income in modeling work and researchers often use it as a proxy for permanent income if they do not take a first step to estimate permanent household income. Since in both Belsky et al. (2007) and this chapter we have estimated permanent income, we do not include education variables anymore, otherwise it would be redundant and interfering.

Between 1985 and 1995, the AHS data had a variable to flag the ownership of properties other than primary residence. In more recent AHS data, however, this variable was dropped. So in my models I can only include the variable for earlier years, but I did check that excluding this variable does not fundamentally affect my model results. It only slightly increases the coefficient for the independent variable of permanent income, simply due to one fewer controlled variable in the model. In other words, the level of income elasticity of housing demand after 1995 is a little bit inflated compared to that in years before then. Because of focusing on homebuyers rather than all homeowners, the estimates of income elasticity of housing demand in this chapter appear to be somewhat higher than reported elsewhere in literature. Table 1 displays some basic descriptive statistics of means or percentages on all the variables used in the models.

OLS Regression Model Results and Discussions

Table 2 shows model estimates and fits by presenting coefficients and R-squares for every other year between 1985 and 2007 when AHS data were collected. Figure 1 illustrates the income elasticity of housing demand for each data collection year between 1985 and 2007.

Table 1. Sample Characteristics (Share or Means of Variables Used)

	1985	1987	1989	1991	1993	1995	1997	1999	2001	2003	2005	2007
Sample Size	1894	3931	3327	3148	3228	3433	3000	3552	3042	2953	2855	2126
Purchasing Price (in 2007 dollars)	133104.40	137220.50	155640.00	145235.80	140418.60	147134.10	142244.60	173379.60	151026.20	161494.40	184864.00	191826.10
Purchasing Price (log)	11.43	11.44	11.54	11.49	11.48	11.52	11.49	11.71	11.63	11.72	11.78	11.80
Current Household Income (in 2007 dollars)	74719.74	76858.60	77947.34	74226.62	73259.06	75429.23	73315.41	88233.39	88655.65	80839.19	76488.21	78667.02
Permanent Household Income (in 2007 dollars)	62873.22	70230.46	72115.22	68675.69	67316.86	67817.10	67834.52	77239.10	80427.54	76397.39	72557.40	73584.70
Permanent Household Income (log)	10.98	11.10	11.13	11.08	11.06	11.07	11.06	11.18	11.21	11.17	11.11	11.11
Age under 35	50.11	45.03	45.78	44.47	42.50	40.72	40.80	38.43	42.47	43.04	41.16	40.36
Age 35-44	29.20	29.92	29.40	29.89	31.16	31.17	31.20	31.64	30.01	28.01	27.08	26.53
Age 45-54	11.72	14.37	14.79	14.99	17.16	18.18	18.43	18.86	17.36	17.95	19.44	20.13
Age 55-64	8.98	10.68	10.04	10.64	9.17	9.93	9.57	11.06	10.16	11.01	12.33	12.98
Minority	13.31	12.62	15.33	15.28	16.79	19.78	20.17	21.90	22.75	25.43	26.65	26.15
Married Couple without Children	27.19	27.04	26.60	26.33	26.49	26.45	27.33	27.96	26.33	25.63	25.67	26.25
Married Couple with Children	42.71	42.74	41.21	40.18	39.03	38.63	37.63	37.33	36.03	33.59	33.80	30.71
Single Parent	7.13	7.12	7.97	7.43	8.74	9.29	8.80	8.02	9.50	9.58	9.46	9.41
Other family Household	3.96	4.43	4.27	5.05	4.71	4.72	3.87	4.34	4.77	4.77	4.38	4.66
Single Person Household	12.99	13.76	14.19	15.31	14.78	14.86	16.30	16.64	17.32	18.86	19.68	21.45
Other Non-Family Household	6.02	4.91	5.77	5.69	6.26	6.06	6.07	5.72	6.05	7.55	7.01	7.53
New England City	4.17	3.54	3.88	3.21	2.66	3.52	2.83	3.58	2.83	3.22	3.50	2.87
New England Suburb	9.35	7.56	8.15	6.13	7.50	8.80	5.73	7.91	6.34	6.47	6.94	6.21
New England Non-metro	4.65	6.46	4.60	6.26	4.31	3.52	5.00	4.67	5.03	3.83	4.31	4.23
Midwest City	6.97	4.48	6.67	4.86	7.56	7.57	6.07	6.19	5.85	5.76	6.48	4.89
Midwest Suburb	12.51	9.90	11.99	10.93	12.36	14.30	11.53	13.15	11.21	12.67	11.63	11.57
Midwest Non-metro	7.50	9.56	7.09	10.39	7.71	7.37	9.13	7.83	8.02	8.43	6.94	6.73
South City	9.40	7.38	9.17	7.59	9.36	7.40	7.73	6.39	7.20	7.92	8.83	7.53
South Suburb	15.79	12.80	14.40	12.52	15.83	15.58	13.87	13.23	15.91	14.32	16.78	21.31
South Non-metro	8.82	16.54	10.64	14.74	11.62	11.21	15.73	13.20	15.35	14.19	12.78	15.90
West City	7.29	6.31	7.66	6.23	7.13	6.55	6.23	7.94	6.64	7.28	6.90	5.13
West Suburb	9.50	9.29	10.70	10.01	9.54	10.11	11.27	11.80	11.51	11.55	10.65	10.54
West Non-metro	4.07	6.21	5.05	7.15	4.43	4.05	4.87	4.11	4.11	4.37	4.27	3.10
Second-home Ownership	17.95	11.88	9.83	14.49	12.52	12.79						

Table 2. Model Coefficients and R-square

	1985	1987	1989	1991	1993	1995
Sample Size	1894	3931	3327	3148	3228	3433
Intercept	-6.0254	-6.5824	-8.34344	-6.58777	-6.9457	-6.2718
Permanent Household Income (log)	1.54311	1.61532	1.76929	1.60903	1.64327	1.57937
Age 35-44	0.02308	0.01949	-0.04556	0.05786	0.01808	-0.0159
Age 45-54	-0.0554	-0.2364	-0.19479	-0.05344	-0.0366	0.02326
Age 55-64	0.14119	0.008	0.20467	0.10928	0.17753	0.14983
Minority	0.21793	0.20454	0.17111	0.18835	0.11525	0.128
Married Couple with Children	0.18572	0.09961	0.12147	-0.0004901	0.11528	0.10427
Single Parent	0.43878	0.53812	0.48006	0.36149	0.46941	0.48094
Other family Household	-0.0016	0.26787	-0.04383	-0.01455	-0.0053	0.03678
Single Person Household	0.32189	0.47307	0.53628	0.4876	0.49745	0.42026
Other Non-Family Household	0.3011	-0.2297	-0.1596	-0.17119	-0.1259	0.04046
New England Suburb	0.33545	0.00757	0.1192	0.15388	0.15466	0.23872
New England Non-metro	0.51007	0.08014	0.12117	0.17462	0.23349	-0.2087
Midwest City	0.10531	-0.2877	-0.18051	-0.11624	-0.0304	-0.113
Midwest Suburb	0.0947	-0.1416	-0.09345	0.01453	-0.0138	0.03111
Midwest Non-metro	0.01912	-0.3048	-0.26461	-0.11486	-0.2134	-0.2046
South City	0.37438	-0.0126	-0.10226	0.0236	-0.0763	0.05892
South Suburb	0.20789	-0.1178	-0.0003402	0.07454	-0.0091	0.14465
South Non-metro	0.39124	-0.1623	-0.04957	0.05309	-0.0875	-0.0526
West City	0.47433	0.0813	0.17356	0.23765	0.2584	0.30768
West Suburb	0.4073	0.09501	0.24164	0.32077	0.20764	0.36225
West Non-metro	0.54351	-0.025	0.14263	0.21397	0.15911	0.20858
Second-home Ownership	0.11413	0.21859	0.21726	0.14621	0.17763	0.177
R-squares	0.2935	0.2923	0.2764	0.2717	0.2675	0.2078
	1997	1999	2001	2003	2005	2007
Sample Size	3000	3552	3042	2953	2855	2126
Intercept	-6.8496	-5.6551	0.1	-1.87156	-2.2285	-0.9922
Permanent Household Income (log)	1.63583	1.51805	1.03585	1.19634	1.25916	1.14396
Age 35-44	0.03624	-0.0554	-0.06798	-0.07555	-0.068	0.0121
Age 45-54	-0.0342	-0.2872	-0.12963	-0.10434	-0.2533	-0.0645
Age 55-64	0.34134	0.17718	0.08297	-0.03483	-0.0705	0.14
Minority	0.08358	0.18787	0.13287	0.16202	0.23516	0.16515
Married Couple with Children	0.0132	0.11183	-0.01823	-0.07342	-0.0503	0.02673
Single Parent	0.50953	0.639	0.19049	0.2688	0.20144	0.14712
Other family Household	-0.0533	0.17238	-0.07482	0.18706	0.12805	-0.3178
Single Person Household	0.5172	0.50784	0.24245	0.29098	0.3658	0.38585
Other Non-Family Household	-0.1584	0.1847	-0.2083	-0.05112	-0.1633	-0.2625

Table 2. Continued

	1985	1987	1989	1991	1993	1995
New England Suburb	-0.0065	0.05011	-0.14608	0.10845	0.01131	0.0665
New England Non-metro	-0.0724	0.0572	-0.10997	-0.00304	-0.1522	0.0132
Midwest City	0.09461	0.09588	-0.06709	0.04975	-0.0184	-0.2627
Midwest Suburb	0.06512	0.18335	-0.12347	0.22624	-0.1555	-0.1384
Midwest Non-metro	-0.1812	0.18186	-0.33842	-0.02904	-0.2787	-0.2951
South City	0.0688	0.22621	-0.09211	0.07981	-0.1387	-0.5731
South Suburb	0.1198	0.09324	-0.11922	0.16902	-0.0119	0.02596
South Non-metro	-0.0689	0.08743	-0.2208	0.08371	-0.0172	-0.1203
West City	0.19774	0.47267	-0.03625	0.43285	0.14619	0.22053
West Suburb	0.26723	0.32908	0.04018	0.24268	0.10151	0.28273
West Non-metro	0.10437	0.36419	-0.08944	0.43654	0.03916	0.13535
R-squares	0.1715	0.1998	0.143	0.1592	0.147	0.1804

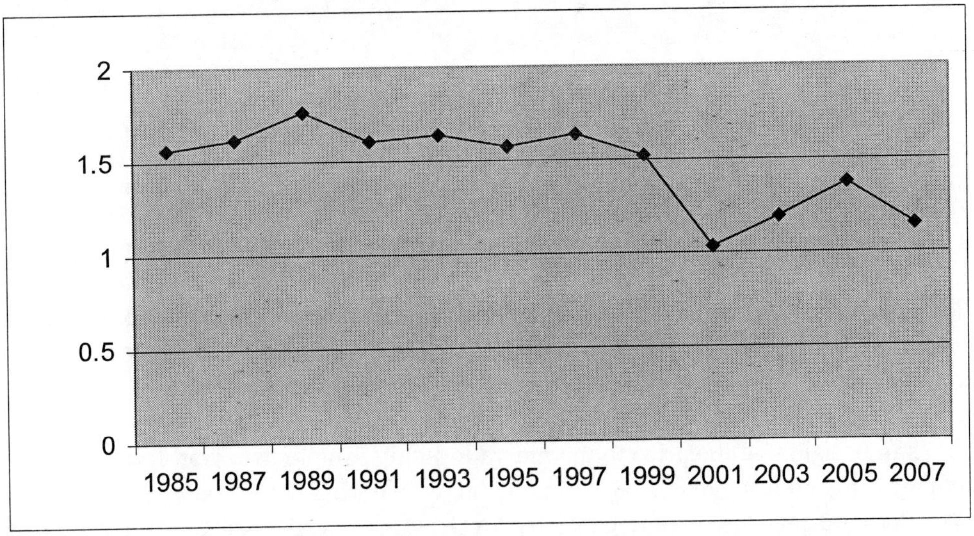

Figure 1. Income Elasticity of Housing Demand.

On first blush, it looks like that the level of income elasticity of housing demand seems to be fairly steady except for a notable dip in 2001 and it recovers about half way by 2003. Other than that incidence as an exception, the two hypotheses both seem to hold some truth. Based on Turner (2003) that elasticity goes up and down with investment prospect, it is plausible to see that elasticity went up between 1985 and 1989 and dropped in 1991 during the previous housing market downturn. It is also expected to see that dip again in 2007 during the recent housing market downturn. Because of the quite inflated home price during recent housing boom, however, it is not surprising to see somewhat lower level of the elasticity during the boom than that of earlier years. I checked that if I took out second-home ownership variable from the models for the early years (1985 to 1995), the level of income elasticity of housing demand during those early years would be even slightly higher. I left it in the model partly because it substantially improved the model with a much higher R-square. This observation of suppressed income elasticity of housing demand suggests that not only Turner

(2003) was right but the other hypothesis is also true and that the impact of the rising and inflated home price is even greater than the influence of a good prospect of home price appreciation.

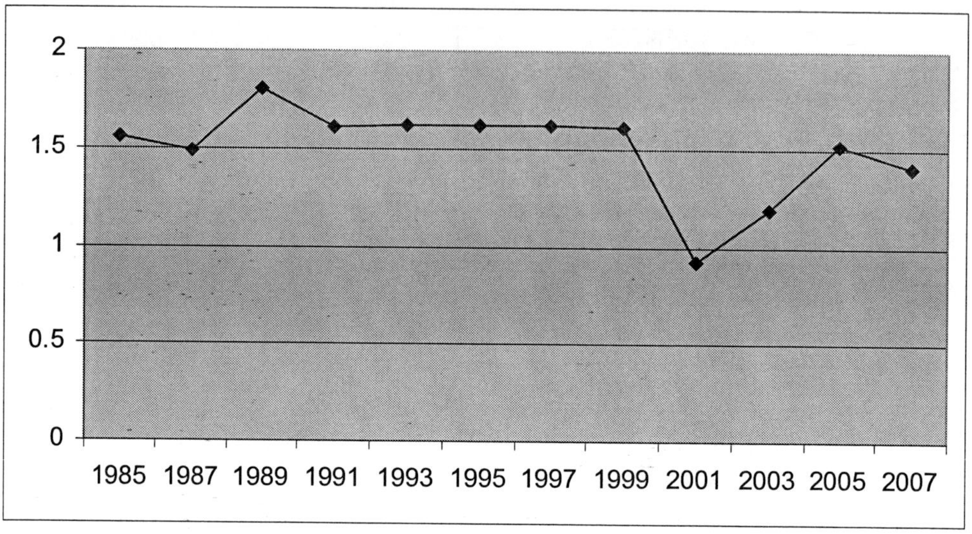

Figure 2. Income elasticity after adjusted by home price to permanent household income ratio.

The recent growth in home price fundamentally shifted the relationship between housing price and household income and made the price to income ratio much higher than it used to be. For many decades, the ratio of median home price to median household income has remained at about 2.5 or less, but the recent housing boom pushed that ratio to as high as 3.5 or more. No wonder such a rising price made us observe a reduction in the level of income elasticity of housing demand during the last housing boom.

It has to be said that the price to income ratio in my sample data is in fact different from the actual world and has a much less dramatic increase during the recent years of the housing boom. After adjusting the income elasticity level by the actual price to income ratio in my sample, indexed with 1985 as 100 percent base point,[1] the level of income elasticity during recent years tills up a little but not as much. When we look at the revised levels of income elasticity of housing demand, we find that the general pattern for the middle years between 1991 and 1999 becomes even flatter (see Figure 2).

The most dramatic drop occurred in 2001, and by 2003 it was only recovered about half way. This is not expected from my two initial hypotheses. What could have possibly caused the drastic reduction in the level of income elasticity of housing demand? It dawned on me when I recalled what have happened to the Wall Street in the year of 2000. After years of great expansions pushed by stocks of companies in the high technology industry, the equity market crashed in 2000. Lots of liquid investment money consequently moved to the real estate market. In fact, the continued growth in the housing market after 2000 prevented the whole country from a serious economic recession. The money injected into the real estate market dwarfed the effect of household income on housing demand and these additional

[1] See Appendix Tables.

resources pushed down the level of income elasticity of housing demand dramatically. Such an understanding of the reduction on the level of income elasticity of housing demand from its normal level should be plausible because it fits the general rule of income elasticity. As Hoyer (1998) pointed out long time ago, "in broad terms a declining immediate correlation between changes in income and consumption reflects more liberal capital markets." When desperate investors from the Wall Street liquidated whatever was left of their investment and bought homes, the relationship between home price and household income became less relevant. Those who saved more and harvested in the heydays of the equity market might be able to buy more housing even if their household income was not that high.

This discovery has two-fold meanings. First, we are reassured that the income elasticity of housing demand is a stable measurement over time in general, and although it could be affected by housing market cycles from time to time their actual impact is relatively small. Therefore, it can be used as a tool for forecasting housing demand as some researchers have long hoped for. This is important because it demonstrates that out of the two most important key factors in determining homeownership in the United States—household income and household wealth—household income is still the dominant factor. In contrast, for example, in China, household income is less relevant and many households are more dependent on capital gains to trade up for better housing.

Second, factors outside of housing market cycles sometimes may have stronger impact on the level of income elasticity of housing demand than variables typically monitored within the housing industry, such as home price and its ratio to household income. Knowing the effects of such external factors is helpful and those who want to apply the income elasticity of housing demand in forecasting market demand are well-advised to pay attention to these external factors, and before settling on the income elasticity number of a particular year to use they would better check the numbers for other years as well to make sure that is not an atypical year.

Conclusion

This chapter uses cross-sectional AHS national data from 1985 to 2007 to follow up over time changes in the income elasticity of housing demand measured as purchasing price of primary residence by recent homebuyers. It deepens our understanding of the dual motives of both consumption and investment in purchasing owner-occupied housing. I find that, while both initial hypotheses still hold some truth at different times, the single one most important factor that could dramatically change the income elasticity of housing demand is actually something outside of the housing industry. During the post-2000 equity market crash, the more liberal capital markets caused the money to flow into the real estate market.

In our current situation, the greediness to make quick money while irresponsibly shipping risks to others has melted down the Wall Street after the subprime mortgage crisis brought down the housing market. In its aftermath, how and how much capital will flow and what else may strongly affect the income elasticity of housing demand is largely unknown at this point, but it should not be surprising if its impact turns out to be huge, as we have already checked the pattern of change over twenty years in this chapter and seen how large that impact could be. The bottom line is that income elasticity of housing demand is a measurement that is generally quite stable and can be used as a variable in any efforts to calculate or forecast housing demand, except for external factors might have strong and extreme impact that temporarily distort this measurement. Therefore, caution should be used and it is well advised to select different years overtime for a repeated measurement before blindly settling on any given year as the single number to apply in practical use.

Appendix

Table A.

	Price to permanent income ratio	Index by price to permanent income
1985	2.117	1.000
1987	1.954	0.923
1989	2.158	1.019
1991	2.115	0.999
1993	2.086	0.985
1995	2.170	1.025
1997	2.097	0.991
1999	2.245	1.060
2001	1.878	0.887
2003	2.114	0.999
2005	2.548	1.203
2007	2.607	1.231

Table B.

	Original income elasticity	Income elasticity adjusted by home price to permanent household income index
1985	1.563	1.563
1987	1.615	1.491
1989	1.769	1.804
1991	1.609	1.607
1993	1.643	1.619
1995	1.579	1.619
1997	1.636	1.620
1999	1.518	1.610
2001	1.036	0.919
2003	1.196	1.195
2005	1.259	1.515
2007	1.144	1.409

References

Belsky, Eric; Di, Zhu Xiao, and McCue, Dan. 2007. Multiple-Home Ownership and the Income Elasticity of Housing Demand, Chapter 14 in *Land Policies and Their Outcomes*, edited by Gregory K. Ingram and Yu-Hung Hong, Lincoln Institute of Land Policy, Cambridge, Massachusetts.

Brueckner, J. K. 1997. "Consumption and Investment Motives and the Portfolio Choices of Homeowners." Journal of Real Estate Finance and Economics, **15**(2), 159-180.

Carliner, Geoffery. 1973. Income Elasticity of Housing Demand. *The Review of Economics and Statistics*. **55**(4), 528-532.

Clark, W. A. V., & Dieleman, F. M. (1996). *Households and housing : choice and outcomes in the housing market*. New Brunswick NJ: Center for Urban Policy Research Press, Rutgers University.

DeLeeuw, F. 1971. The Demand for Housing. *Review of Economics and Statistics,* February Issue.

Fernandez-Kranz, Daniel and Mark T. Hon. 2006. "A Cross-Section Analysis of the Income Elasticity of Housing Demand in Spain: Is There a Real Estate Bubble?" *The Journal of Real Estate Finance and Economics*, Vol. 32, No. 4. pp. 449-470.

Fu, Y. "Uncertainty, Liquidity and Housing Choices." *Regional Science and Urban Economics*, **25**(2), 1995, 223-36.

Glennon, D. 1989. Estimating the Income, Price, and Interest Elasticities of Housing Demand. *Journal of Urban Economics*. **25**, 219-229.

Goodman, Allen C. and Kawai, Masahiro. 1982. Permanent Income, Hedonic Prices, and Housing Demand: New Evidence. *Journal of Urban Economics.* **12**(2), 214-237.

Goodman, Allen C. 1990. Demographics of Individual Housing Demand. *Regional Science and Urban Economics*. Vol 20. pp. 83-102.

Hansen J.L.; Formby J.P.; Smith W.J. 1998. Estimating the Income Elasticity of Demand for Housing: A Comparison of Traditional and Lorenz-Concentration Curve Methodologies. *Journal of Housing Economics.* **7**(4), 328-342.

Henderson, J. V., and Y. M. Ioannides. "A Model of Housing Tenure Choice." *American Economic Review*, **73**(1), 1983, 98-113.

Hoyer, Morten Malle, 1998. "The Income and Price Sensitivity of Private Consumption." *Monetary Review*, 4th Quarter, 1998, Danmarks Nationalbank.

Lin, C. and Sue-Jing Lin. 1999. "An Estimation of Elasticities of Consumption Demand and Investment Demand for Owner-Occupied Housing in Taiwan: A Two-Period Model." *International Real Estate Review*, **2**(1), 110-125.

Muth, R. F. 1965. The Stock Demand Elasticities for Non-Farm Housing. *The Review.* **47**, November Issue.

Polinsky, A. Mitchell, and Ellwood, David T. 1979. An Empirical Reconciliation of Micro and Grouped Estimates of the Demand for Housing. *The Review of Economics and Statistics*. **61**(2), 199-205..

Ranney, S. I. "Inflation Expectations and the Demand for Housing." *American Economic Review*, **71**(3), 1981, 324-33.

Reid, M. 1962. *Housing and Income*. Chicago: University of Chicago Press.

Turner, T. M. 2003. “Does Investment Risk Affect the Housing Decisions of Families?” *Economic Inquiry*, **41**(4), 675-691.

Wachter, Susan M. and Megbolugbe, Isaac F. 1992. Racial and Ethnic Disparities in Homeownership. *Housing Policy Debate.* **3**(2), 333-370.

Wilkinson, R. K. 1973. “The Income Elasticity of Demand for Housing.” *Oxford Economic Papers*, New Series, Vol. 25, No. 3, pp. 361-377.

Winger, A. 1968. Housing and Income. *Western Economic Journal.* **6**(June 1968), 226-232.

In: Housing, Housing Costs and Mortgages
Editors: Szilárd Kis and Istvan Balogh, pp. 171-179
ISBN: 978-1-60741-813-9

Chapter 11

HOUSING COSTS AMONG LOW-INCOME RENTERS AND HOMEOWNERS: "RENT V. BUY" AND THE HIDDEN COSTS OF LOW-INCOME HOMEOWNERSHIP

***Russell N. James III*[1], *Cliff A. Robb*[2], *Andrew T. Carswell*[1] *and Jorge H. Atiles*[1]**
[1]University of Georgia, USA
[2]University of Alabama, USA

Abstract

Much government policy in recent years has been directed at increasing homeownership among low-income households. Many have argued for the unconditional acceptance of increasing low-income homeownership as an important policy goal. However, evidence from household expenditures in the Consumer Expenditure Survey suggests many difficulties of this conceptually appealing target. Low-income homeowners are more likely to purchase homes with proportionally higher "hidden" ownership costs such as maintenance and utilities. Further, tax policies direct homeownership benefits towards high-income households, often generating no tax deductions for low-income households. Because of these distinctions, currently available consumer information on "rent v. buy" calculations can be particularly misleading for low-income households. Government policies mandating increased lending to low-income households combined with the realities of housing costs differences for these households may have ultimately contributed to the current mortgage default crisis.

Introduction

Housing constitutes the largest expenditure category in the typical American family's household budget (Gieseman & Rogers, 1986). The impact of consumer housing decisions can dwarf many other consumer expenditure decisions. Consequently, it is vital that consumers and consumer educators be well informed about the realities of housing choices and housing costs. Mistakes about housing costs can lead to misallocation of resources (Brueckner, 1997) or, in some cases, foreclosure. Because of the variety of initial and ongoing expenses associated with homeownership, families in rented housing are particularly vulnerable to miscalculating the costs of homeownership.

The consequences of lower-income families shifting from renting to owning based upon inappropriate comparisons can include increased default rate and poor financial outcomes for families. Further, the failure to incorporate the unique housing circumstances commonly facing lower-income homebuyers may have contributed to the mispricing of low-income mortgage backed securities and the resulting global financial difficulties.

Consumers may mistakenly believe that simply comparing current monthly rent with potential monthly mortgage payments provides an adequate measure of affordability. Recent increases in mortgage foreclosures suggest that consumers are making miscalculations in their ability to meet the costs of homeownership (Goldstein, 2004). Estimating the total costs of homeownership, as compared to renting, can be a challenging task. Some costs, such as mortgage interest, property taxes, and property insurance are obvious and usually known in advance. However, other costs may be less obvious and much more variable.

For those making the tenure switch from renter to homeowner, accounting for these costs can be daunting. Aside from the initial homeownership expenses, home maintenance and repair costs rarely concern renters, but can be a major source of expenditure for homeowners. Low-income homebuyers may be subject to even larger costs, to the extent they are more likely to purchase older homes with more repair needs. Certain utilities, such as water or trash, are commonly included in rent payments, but must be paid for separately by homeowners. There are demonstrated effects of volume discounting and economies of scale that renters enjoy regarding energy costs that elude homeowners (Rong, 2006; Linneman & Voith, 1991). Thus, even renters who do pay "pass through" or proportional water bills in multifamily housing may benefit from volume discounting for the apartment building as a whole. Because rented housing is often in multifamily structures, tenants may enjoy much lower heating and cooling bills (Rong, 2006). The presence of neighboring units above, below, or beside one's apartment unit dramatically reduces the energy needed to maintain climate control. In addition, owned homes are often substantially larger than rented units (Linneman & Voith, 1991). This size generates additional energy costs for climate control, as well as the need for additional furnishings. Further, low-income homeowners may be more likely to purchase older, less energy-efficient homes.

Also, renters have less consumer demand for such things as furniture and appliances, due to smaller overall living area and the advantage of having such features included within the rental unit. Rent payments also commonly entitle tenants to a variety of household equipment such as a refrigerator, dishwasher, disposal, oven, microwave and the like. Consequently, tenants rarely encounter unexpected needs for the cash to replace major appliances, and may not project a change in this reality after becoming homeowners.

In the U.S., homeownership offers the promise of tax benefits to some. But, for lower-income families this benefit is largely illusory. While homeowner tax deductions do exist, taking advantage of these tax deductions requires foregoing the standard tax deduction. Consequently, lower income families may find that that the net increase in tax deductions is small or even negative after foregoing the standard deduction. This, coupled with the lower marginal tax rates of lower-income families, make the tax deduction of limited benefit for such families. At a time when the U.S. homeownership rate was nearing 70%, fewer than 30% of tax filers actually received benefit from the mortgage interest tax deduction in 2002 (President's Advisory Panel on Federal Tax Reform Panel, 2005). The majority of the tax benefits of the mortgage interest tax deduction go to those with incomes in excess of $100,000 (President's Advisory Panel on Federal Tax Reform Panel, 2005). In 2005, only 5.6% of taxpayers with adjusted gross income below $40,000 actually benefited from the mortgage interest tax deduction; for these 5.6% of taxpayers who did benefit, the average net tax benefit was a mere $310 (Joint Committee on Taxation, 2007).

In order to have a more complete picture, consumers and consumer educators need to have good information on the total costs of homeownership as compared to renting. Information based upon the actual consumer expenditures of homeowners and renters could improve the ability of consumers and consumer educators to make wise choices about homeownership and appropriate levels of mortgage indebtedness. Conversely, to the extent that commonly available information in the form of online "rent v. buy" calculators provides misleading information to low-income consumers, this may heighten the risk of inappropriate purchase decisions.

This paper examines how housing-related expenditures differ between renters and owners, in particular for low-income households and compares this reality with information available to consumers in popular online "rent v. buy" calculators.

Data

Data for this paper come from the Bureau of Labor Statistic's Consumer Expenditure Survey (CE). The CE tracks household expenditures and measures the inflation rate (Consumer Price Index). The CE is a national rotating panel survey. Households participate for five quarters and are then replaced by new households. This study includes households participating in the survey at any point from the second quarter of 1995 through the first quarter of 2005. Consistent with the design of the CE and previous research, the statistical analysis treats each quarterly observation as independent (Passero, 1996; Sharpe & Abdel-Ghany, 1999; U.S. Dept. of Labor, 2006, p. 277). Changes to the CE over the course of ten years add special nuances to the resulting dataset. For the three quarters of data from 1995, the CE truncates certain income and asset subcomponent values at a $100,000 maximum. In subsequent surveys, the CE instead top-codes extreme values with the average of all reported values above the critical level.

All dollar figures are adjusted to constant 2005 dollars using the Consumer Price Index from the quarter in which the interview was taken. The liquid assets variable refers to the sum of all household checking accounts, brokerage accounts, savings accounts, and securities, such as stocks, mutual funds, private bonds, government bonds or Treasury notes. The income variable includes all sources of reported income such as wages, government transfers, interest, capital gains, and the like for the previous twelve months, divided by four to make it comparable with the other quarterly variables. The CE's total housing expenditures variable records all housing expenditures for the previous quarter. It includes rent, mortgage interest, property taxes, maintenance, repairs, insurance, utilities (natural gas, electric, fuel oil, telephone, water), other lodging expenses including vacation homes, cleaning and other domestic services, and house furnishings and equipment (floor coverings, household textiles such as curtains, major appliances, small appliances, miscellaneous housewares and household equipment). Principal payments on the mortgage are not included as a housing expenditure, as they are a form of savings, not consumption expenditure. Indeed, for most borrowers the choice to make principle payments is optional, as interest-only mortgages are commonly available. Because principal payments are not necessary for homeownership or the use of housing services, they are not included in a comparison with the cost of housing services obtained by renting.

Results

Expenditures in Owning and Renting

Table 1 displays descriptive statistics for the current sample. Only unsubsidized renters and homeowners with mortgages are included in the current sample. Subsidized renters, such as those in public housing (council housing) or receiving other forms of rent subsidization, are excluded as these groups pay less than market rent. Homeowners without mortgages are excluded, as this group would unrealistically skew the cost of homeownership in a way that would not be relevant for consumers considering initial housing purchases. Non-homeowners living without payment of rent (for example, because a relative owns the home and is not charging rent) are also excluded from the sample.

As Table 1 indicates, 62,803 unsubsidized renters and 89,479 homeowners with a mortgage remain in the dataset. Simply comparing rent with non-principal mortgage payments reveals only a slight difference between renter and owner expenditures. However, homeowners encounter several additional costs. Property taxes, maintenance, repairs, and property insurance expenses are nearly zero for tenants, but average over $600 per quarter for homeowners – approximately half the cost of mortgage interest payments.

Household furnishings and equipment expenditures are significantly greater for homeowners, averaging more than twice that for renters. These expenses are higher for homeowners in part due to the need to purchase and replace the full range of household appliances. In addition, the typically larger size of owned homes generates greater furnishings need. Homeowners also take on additional expenses in the area of utilities. Many renters pay no or only partial direct utility costs. In this sample, nearly 3/4 of all unsubsidized renters indicated making no payments for water – most likely due to inclusion in the fixed rent. In contrast, homeowners on average pay $84 per quarter for water bills. Even those renters who do pay water bills (where it is not included in the rent) pay significantly less than homeowners do. This may be due to smaller family sizes and potential volume discounts where water is paid on a proportional pass-through basis (i.e., without individual metering).

Homeowners also experience dramatically higher expenses in the area of housing energy costs. Ignoring the 18% of unsubsidized tenants who report no direct costs for gas, electric, or heating oil, homeowners still pay almost twice as much for these utilities than tenants. This is likely driven both by the smaller size of rental units and by the energy advantages of multifamily units. Although residents may own or lease either type of housing, multifamily housing is usually leased, and detached, single-family residences are usually owned (Glaeser & Shapiro, 2002; Linneman & Voith, 1991).

Table 1. Comparison of Quarterly Expenditures for Tenants and Homeowners in the Consumer Expenditure Survey (1995-2005)

Variable	Unsubsidized Renter	Homeowner w/ Mortgage
n	62,803	89,479
Rent / mortgage (non-principal)	$1,236 ($1,040)	$1,239 ($1,302)
Property tax	*n/a*	$358 ($519)
Maintenance, repairs, insurance	$3* ($79)	$249 ($928)
Household furnishings & equipment	$134* ($467)	$336 ($985)
No gas/electric/oil (included in rent)	18%	*n/a*
No water (included in rent)	74%	*n/a*
Gas/Electric/Oil (not included)	$160* ($177)	$326 ($248)
Water (not included)	$22* ($57)	$84 ($102)
Total housing expenditure	$1,826* ($1,560)	$3,103 ($2,849)
Rent or mortgage interest as a % of total housing expenditures	67.7%*	39.9%
Total expenditures	$4,878* ($4,701)	$8,852 ($8,066)
Housing as % of total expenditures	37.4%*	35.1%
Liquid assets	$2,436* (34591)	$10,843 ($99,384)
Married	32.6%*	71.7%
Single male	29.5%*	10.9%
Single female	37.6%*	17.4%
White	78.3%*	86.8%
Age	39.7* (16.6)	45.9 (12.6)
No. of household members	2.3* (1.5)	3.0 (1.5)
Bedrooms	2.0* (1.03)	3.2 (0.86)
Bathrooms	1.2* (0.47)	1.8 (0.70)
Half Bathrooms	0.1* (1.24)	0.4 (0.55)
Other rooms	2.3* (1.05)	3.6 (1.55)
Est. % using mortgage deduction (income <$40k)	0	27%
Est. % using mortgage deduction (income >$40k)	0	79%
Net mortgage deduction benefit (income<$40k)		$21.30
Net mortgage deduction benefit (income>$40k)		$374.44
Net property tax deduction benefit (income<40k)		$6.91
Net property tax deduction benefit (income>40k)		$118.81

* Results from a t-test indicate that the difference in each variable (comparing renters to homeowners with a mortgage) is statistically significant at the >.001 level.

Notes: All dollar figures are constant 2005 inflation-adjusted dollars.

Estimated tax benefit calculated from aggregate statistics in Joint Committee on Taxation (2007) using net tax benefit of mortgage interest deduction of those claiming the deduction reduced by the estimated proportion of those using the standard deduction. Proportion derived by dividing the percentage of households claiming the deduction by the percentage of households with a mortgage for mortgage interest deduction, or divided by the percentage of households owning a home for the property tax deduction.

In contrast with the similarity of average rent and mortgage interest payments, the total housing expenditures of renters and homeowners is dramatically different. This indicates the fundamental problem with the notion of directly comparing rent with mortgage payments. For tenants, rent covers more than two-thirds of total housing costs. For homeowners with mortgages, interest payments cover less than 40% of total housing costs.

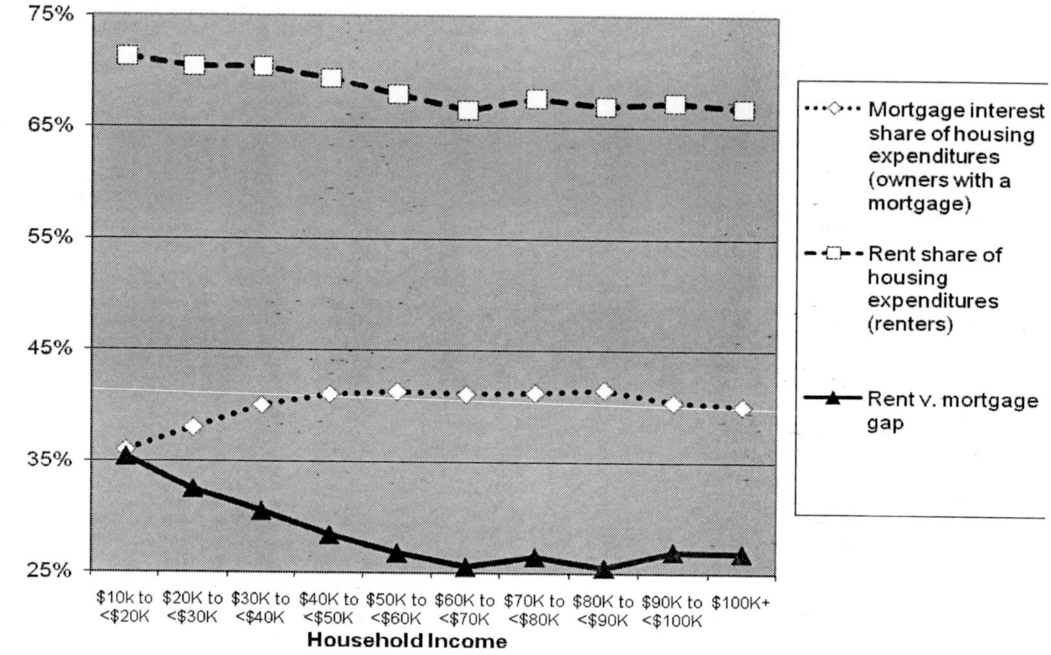

Figure 1. Comparing rent shares with mortgage shares across by income.

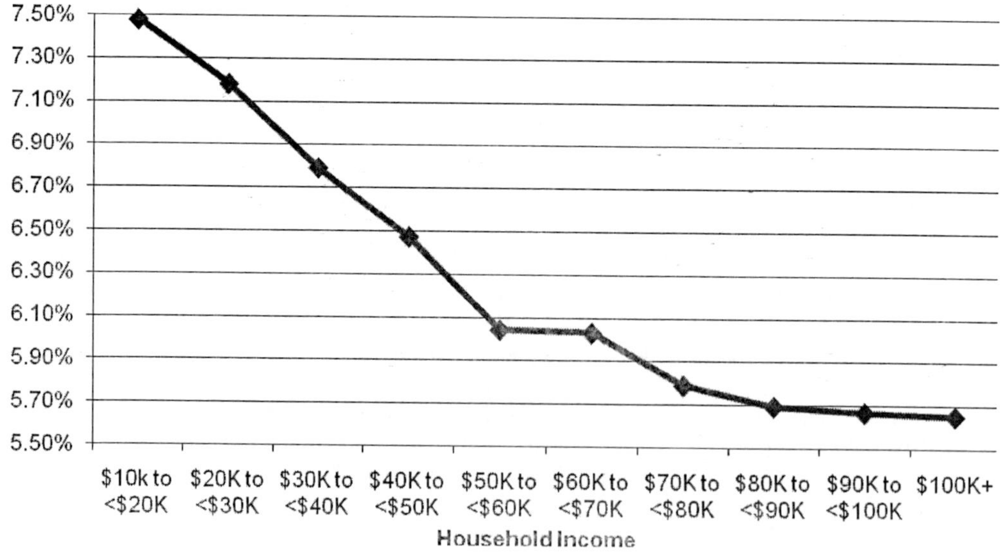

Figure 2. Share of housing expenditures devoted to maintenance among owners with a mortgage in the 1995-2005 Consumer Expenditure Survey.

Table 1 demonstrates the fundamental difficulties with attempting a "rent v. buy" comparison. Although rent and mortgage payments may be easy to compare, the total differences in housing expenditures is more complex. For low-income families comparing current rent with the prospect of homeownership and a mortgage payment, the differences are even greater. Figure 1 compares the share of total housing expenditures represented by the rent payment (for renters) with the share of total housing expenditures represented by the mortgage interest (for homeowners with a mortgage). As demonstrated in Table 1, rent payments constituted a much larger portion of total housing expenditures than do mortgage interest payments. However, this difference grows for lower-income households. For lower-income households, the non-mortgage share of homeownership expenditures was greater, while the non-rent share of housing expenditures was less. Figure 2 shows one example of this increase in non-mortgage homeownership costs as home maintenance costs are a substantially larger proportion of total housing costs for lower-income homeowners.

"Rent v. Buy" Calculators

Table 2. Results from top 10 "rent v. buy" calculators with identical assumptions

Website	Decision	Savings
A	Buy	$5,226.15
B	Rent	$15,021.55
C	Buy	$36,205.00
D	Buy	Not Clear
E	Buy	$26,157.00
F	Buy	$27,518.00
G	Buy	$35,929.00
H	Buy	$61,509.66
I	Rent	$736.00
J	Buy	$40,864.00

Home Purchase Price: $230,000; Property Tax Rate: 1.25%; Property Insurance: $61.33; Interest Rate on the Loan: 7%; Home Appreciation: 4%; Rental Costs: $1,200; Rental Insurance: $30; Rate of Increase on Rental: 2.5%; Possible Interest on Money Saved: 6%; Mortgage Term: 30 years; Time in Home: 5 years; Closing Costs: 3% ($6,210); Amount Down: 5%; Costs to sell the home: 10% of future sales price; Individual Tax Rate: 28%.

"Rent v. buy" calculators are commonplace on the internet today. Typically, companies from industry segments benefiting from home purchases – such as realtors or mortgage companies – create these calculators. (Of the top ten websites generated by a Google search for "rent v. buy calculator," mortgage companies or real estate brokers hosted seven.) However, these calculators can provide an inadequate picture of the true cost trade off between renting and buying. Ultimately, the difficulty in getting appropriate consumer information on such decisions is demonstrated by the results in Table 2. Here, an identical "rent v. buy" scenario was used at the top ten "rent v. buy" calculators based on the Google search engine rating. The recommendations were generally to buy, with estimated savings varying from $736 to $61,509. Even for this identical information, no two calculators gave the same result.

Consistently, such calculators include tax advantages of homeownership, even for those at the lowest incomes and lowest marginal tax rate level. These estimates for tax benefits from homeownership ignore the foregone value of the standard deduction. Commonly, the estimate of tax benefit is simply the amount of the potential deduction multiplied by a reported or marginal tax rate. The cases in which such an estimate is appropriate are quite rare among moderate-income families. Such estimates require both that the renter is already itemizing deductions prior to any homeownership deductions and that the tax benefit from the additional deductions do not alter the resulting marginal tax rate. Given that slightly more than 5% of households with adjusted gross income less than $40,000 benefited from the mortgage interest tax deduction, and that many of those received only slight benefit due to foregoing the standard deduction (Joint Committee on Taxation, 2007) such assumptions are clearly inappropriate.

Universally, there is no recognition in such calculators of the possibility of increased utilities, appliances, or furnishings costs. While a few incorporate maintenance costs of owning, none address this issue of differential home quality for lower-income buyers. These costs are especially critical for moderate-income families as they are more likely to purchase older, affordable homes in need of greater ongoing upkeep and maintenance.

While the lack of consistency in comparing renting and owning could provide a problematic situation for any consumer, the lack of consideration for differences among low-income families suggests that lower-income families are much more likely to receive inappropriate recommendations.

Conclusion

Many nations have targeted increased homeownership as a significant policy goal. This policy environment, combined with the commercial interests of real estate and mortgage agencies, may have created an inappropriate emphasis on homeownership for low-income consumers. Certainly, there are numerous documented potential benefits to consumers from homeownership (McCarthy & Quercia, 2000). Among other things, homeownership provides a pathway for forced savings and leveraged investment.

However, accurately estimating the costs of homeownership is critical for consumers and consumer educators, particularly for lower-income renters transitioning to homeowners. These households may be at risk of foreclosure when unplanned costs of homeownership inevitably arise. As the largest component of consumers' budgets, it is particularly important for consumers to move beyond just a comparison of rent with simply mortgage payments and accurately understand both the obvious and hidden costs of housing choices. Government policies mandating increased lending to low-income households combined with the realities of housing costs differences for these households may have ultimately contributed to the current mortgage default crisis.

References

Brueckner, J. K. (1997). Consumption and investment motives and the portfolio choices of homeowners. *Journal of Real Estate Finance and Economics*, **15**(2), 159-180.

Costa, D. L. (2001). Estimating real income in the United States from 1888 to 1994: Correcting CPI bias using Engel curves. *The Journal of Political Economy,* **109**(6), 1288-1310.

Courchane, M. J., Surette, B., & Zorn, P. (2004). Subprime borrowers: Mortgage transitions and outcomes. *Journal of Real Estate Finance and Economics*, **29**(4), 365-392.

Gieseman, R., & Rogers, J. (1986). Consumer expenditures: Results from the diary and interview surveys. *Monthly Labor Review*, **109**, 14-18.

Glaeser, E. L., & Shapiro, J. M. (2002, October). *The benefits of the home mortgage interest deduction* (working paper 9284). Cambridge, MA: National Bureau of Economic Research.

Goldstein, I. (2004). *Bringing subprime mortgages to market and the effects on lower-income borrowers* (working paper series BABC 04-7). Cambridge, MA: Joint Center for Housing Studies.

Joint Committee on Taxation. (2007). *Selected data related to the federal tax system* (report JCX-11-07). Washington, D.C.: Author. Retrieved February 10, 2007 from http://www.house.gov/jct/x-11-07.pdf

Linneman, P., & Voith, R. (1991). Housing price functions and ownership capitalization rates, *Journal of Urban Economics,* **30**, 100–111.

McCarthy, G. W., & Quercia, R. G. (2000). *Bridging the gap between supply and demand: The evolution of the homeownership education and counseling industry.* Washington, DC: Research Institute for Housing America.

Passero, W. D. (1996). Spending patterns of families receiving public assistance. *Monthly Labor Review,* **119**(4), 21-28.

President's Advisory Panel on Federal Tax Reform Panel. (2005). *Simple, fair,and pro-growth: proposals to fix America's tax system.* Washington, D.C., Author. Retreived July 5, 2007 from http://www.taxreformpanel.gov/final-report/

Rong, F. (2006). *The impact of urban sprawl on U. S. residential energy use*. Doctoral dissertation, University of Maryland, School of Public Policy.

Sharpe, D.L., & Abdel-Ghany, M. (1999). Identifying the poor and their consumption patterns. *Family Economics and Nutrition Review,* **12**(2), 15–25.

U.S. Department of Labor, Bureau of Labor Statistics. (2006). *Consumer expenditure interview survey public use microdata documentation*. Washington, D.C.: Author.

In: Housing, Housing Costs and Mortgages ISBN 978-1-60741-813-9
Editors: Szilrd Kis and Istvan Balogh, pp. 181-242

Chapter 12

MANAGING POWER IN A SMART HOME USING MULTI-AGENT SYSTEMS

***Shadi Abras,** *Stephane Ploix*† *and Sylvie Pesty*‡**
Multi-Agent Systems, Control System, Grenoble, France

Keywords: Multi-Agents Systems, Power Management, Home Automation, Negotiation et Cooperation, Ambient Intelligence.

1. Introduction

A home automation system basically consists of household appliances linked via a communication network allowing interactions for control purposes [Palensky et Posta (1997)]. Thanks to this network, a load management mechanism can be implemented: this is called *distributed control* in [Wacks (1993)]. Load management allows inhabitants to adjust power consumption according to expected comfort, energy price variation and CO_2 equivalent emissions. For instance, during consumption peak periods when power plants emitting higher quantities of CO_2 are used and when the energy price is high, some services can be delayed, heater set-points can be reduced or services run according to the weather forecast or inhabitants' requests. Load management offers further advantages when there are local storage and production means. When combined, all of these possibilities lead to systems offering many degrees of freedom that are very complex for users to manage.

The objective of this study is to design a building electric energy management system able to determine the best energy assignment plan, according to given criteria. A building energy management system can be seen from two points of view: load management and local energy production management. [House et Smith (1995)] and [Zhou et Krarti (2005)] have proposed optimal control strategies for an HVAC (Heating Ventilation and Air Conditioning) system taking into account the natural thermal storage capacity of buildings where the HVAC consumption is shifted from the peak period to the off-peak period. [Zhou et Krarti (2005)] have shown that this control strategy affords savings of up to 10% of the

*E-mail address: Shadi.Abras@gmail.com
†E-mail address: Stephane.Ploix@Grenoble-inp.fr
‡E-mail address: Sylvie.Pesty@imag.fr

electricity cost of a building. However, these approaches do not take into account energy resource requirements, which generally depend on the autonomy needs of off-grid systems [Muselli *et al.* (2000)], or on the total power production limits of suppliers in grid-connected systems.

1.1. Energy Control in a Building

The aim of energy control is to make sure energy resources are allocated to appliances in line with users' needs. Building energy flows must therefore be managed according to three criteria:

- **comfort criteria** relating to the user and which consist in fulfilling a set of energy functions in the building in order to meet the user's needs. The energy flow management system in a building must guarantee the minimum requirement of a secure source of energy or at least enough energy to meet essential needs in terms of comfort (thermal, visual or acoustic).

- **economic and financial criteria** corresponding to the system's investment and operating costs. The criteria to be taken into account may be the return on investment and the running cost. These criteria are highly dependent on the energy purchasing and buy-back cost but also on the investment in appliances.

- **environmental criteria** relating to a lower level of pollution and compliance with environmental requirements. In the current context, there are as yet no environmental requirements relating to greenhouse gas emissions in the residential and service sectors. Sustainable development is considered to be the responsibility of each individual in these sectors.

1.2. Home Automation Systems

Home automation systems are technological systems that aim to automate the various daily tasks in a home such as energy management, alarm management and communication. Building automation systems fulfill the same functions but in buildings (generally in a commercial environment).

The notion of "Home Automation System" and "Building Automation System" emerged in the eighties. To begin with, home automation systems only aimed to offer users greater comfort in terms of leisure and additional services. They did this using a home communication and dialogue system that allowed inter-service communication (automatic shutters, lighting, etc.). They were sometimes more of a gadget than a means of rationalizing energy management.

Energy management is not a new application of home and building automation systems. In ([Wacks (1991)], [Wacks (1993)]), energy demand management in the home was introduced using a home automation system. The notion of building energy management and control system is described in [Stum *et al.* (1997)]. This system consists of a set of appliances fitted with micro-controllers able to communicate via standard protocols, a centralized control and monitoring system and a human-machine interface making it possible to fulfill a certain number of energy consumption optimization, management and monitoring functions. Such systems are generally used in commercial service sector buildings in order to manage heating, air conditioning, sanitary hot water and lighting.

1.3. Ambient Intelligence

The term ambient intelligence [Hellenschmidt et Kirste (2004)] is becoming increasingly widespread. In everybody's minds it corresponds to an important research topic for the development of information and communication technologies. The concept is linked to the development of new interfaces implementing detectors, communication chips, synthesis software, voice recognition, etc.

AmI is located at the point where different research fields converge [Weiser (1995)]. Some of its main characteristics are as follows:

- Ubiquity: the ability of users to interact with a broad array of interconnected appliances, sensors, actuators and, more generally speaking, "embedded" electronic systems and software from wherever they happen to be. This facility is provided thanks to adapted networks and highly distributed computer architecture.

- Attentiveness: the ability of the system to constantly feel the presence of and locate objects, appliances and persons in order to take into account the context of use. All kinds of sensors are required for this: cameras, microphones, radars, biometric sensors, as well as chip technology and radio-frequency identification (RFID) readers.

- Natural interaction: it must be possible to access services in a way that is as natural/intuitive as possible. Unlike traditional interfaces from the computing world (referred to as WIMP:Windows, Icons, Menus and Pointing appliances), the human-machine interface is multi-modal. It is based on voice/movement recognition or on real object handling.

- Intelligence: the ability to analyze contexts and dynamically adapt to situations. The system learns from users' behavior in order to best meet their needs. This requires storage and processing capacities and modeling algorithms.

Of course, access to this ambient intelligence must be as simple as possible and the services offered must be adapted to the user's context and situation. A certain number of obstacles lie in the way of such a prospect becoming a reality: these mainly relate to managing the complexity caused by the multiplicity of users' expectations and their trust in the services offered.

However, in the field of ambient intelligence, research mainly focuses on homes and buildings.

1.3.1. Ambient Intelligence for the Home

Much work in the field of ambient intelligence focuses on the home. For example:

- Crowley (2006) works on medical surveillance in a home referred to as "intelligent". The objective is to help keep patients at home while transmitting alarms to centers dedicated to medical surveillance.

- Gárate *et al.* (2005) have developed a network of connected appliances (refrigerator, television, etc.) managed by a central controller. In this network, users can dialogue with their appliances and ask them in natural language what services and features they offer.

- Le *et al.* (2007) study the recognition of daily activities carried out by an elderly person living alone in a Health Smart House fitted with non-invasive sensors.

- Lashina (2004) describes the prototype concept of an intelligent bathroom. This includes an interactive mirror that plays an essential role in interactions and is able to interact with the appliances regularly used in the bathroom (weight display given by weighing scales, health coach, etc.).

- In the work of Friedewald *et al.* (2005), it is a whole "intelligent house" concept that is defined where the aim is to facilitate inhabitants' living conditions. This house performs tasks automatically, responds to the slightest wishes of the user and is familiar with the user's habits.

However, faced with this increasing complexity in buildings, it is necessary to develop control and monitoring systems able to manage multi-source production and understand the dynamic characteristics of the home in order to anticipate energy needs and dialogue with all the components producing and storing energy. Such control and monitoring systems must also be able to plan ahead for the necessarily changing configuration of buildings. Alongside this approach, it is also necessary to find a solution for lowering the energy consumption of existing buildings.

Towards a Multi-Agent System for Energy Management?

In the home, the energy system is made up of sources, which produce energy, and loads (household appliances), which consume energy. The energy comes from distant producers (national transmission/distribution networks), but may also come from local energy sources (e.g. solar panels, wind turbines and fuel cells).

The system has the following main characteristics:

- distributed:
    - physical distribution of energy sources such as solar panels, generator sets, fuel cells, etc.
    - physical distribution of different types of energy consumers (loads) such as ovens, washing machines, radiators, etc.
- flexible: the energy sources are redundant and some loads can store energy (thermal energy) or meet service demands with a certain delay (deferred washing or cooking).

- open-ended: the number of sources and loads can change without this calling into question the overall running of the system.
- extendible: new types of sources or loads can be added to the system.

Progress in the field of Multi-Agent Systems, designed to solve spatially distributed and open problems, is likely to lead to a "Multi-Agent Home Automation System" made up of agents embedded in different sources and loads all working together in order to solve the problem of energy consumption control in the home. The agents make joint decisions with respect to the operating requirements of the appliances to which they are connected. They can, for example, decide to shed appliances depending on comfort criteria and energy requirements.

The objective of this work is to design an energy management system for the home made up of software agents controlling appliances and sources. Together, all the agents would form a multi-agent home automation system. In other words, they would form an energy management system capable of dynamically setting up a production and consumption policy to suit user criteria and the various load and source requirements.

In what follows, we shall present the service behavior models that characterize the context of the problem. Indeed, in order to solve the energy management problem using Multi-Agent Systems, it is first necessary to model the system components.

Given the broad array of appliances and the fast changes to technology, along with their direct influence on behavior, it is fairly difficult, if not impossible, to define a model suitable for all the appliances belonging to a specific category. This is why we have chosen to introduce the notion of service as the grouped operation of different appliances.

2. Modeling Principles

2.1. Service

A service (i), denoted as SRV_i, transforms energy in order to meet a user's need via one or several appliances.

In housing, the inhabitants are the central stakeholders. Inhabitants are surrounded by three types of services: end-user services, which produce comfort directly for the inhabitants, intermediate services, which manage energy storage, and support services, which produce the electrical power required by intermediate and end-user services. Support services supply electrical power by converting primary energy into electricity. *Fuel cell-based generators, photovoltaic power suppliers, and grid power suppliers*, such as EDF in France, belong to this class. Electrochemical batteries are generally used to meet the needs of intermediate services. End-user services cover common needs such as *washing*, *water heating*, *room heating* and *lighting*.

Let us assume a given time range for anticipating energy needs (typically 24 hours). A service is qualified as *permanent* if its energy consumption/production/storage covers the whole time range of the energy assignment plan, otherwise, the service is referred to as a *temporary service*.

Depending on the way the appliances work, the notion of service can be divided into two categories: temporary service or permanent service. These services differ in terms of their degree of flexibility.

2.1.1. Service Flexibility

The flexibility of a service depends on the operation of each energy service.

Services can be controlled or not. Controlled services may be:

- Interrupted: the service can be temporarily stopped and started again later on. Some services can be interrupted, but only according to a number of requirements relating to the physical capacity of the appliance:
  - Time window requirement: the consumption of a service can be divided up according to requirements but the service must finish within the given time window.
  - The duration of the interruption must not exceed a maximum interruption time.
  - Between two interruptions, there may be a requirement that determines a set minimum waiting time.
- "Shifted": the possibility of shifting some services, such as washing, in order to identify the optimum run time in relation to user comfort criteria and within a given time window.
- Modified: the possibility of changing the energy profile of a service, for example lowering or raising the consumption of a "heating" service at a given moment.

Figure 1 classifies services in relation to their flexibility.

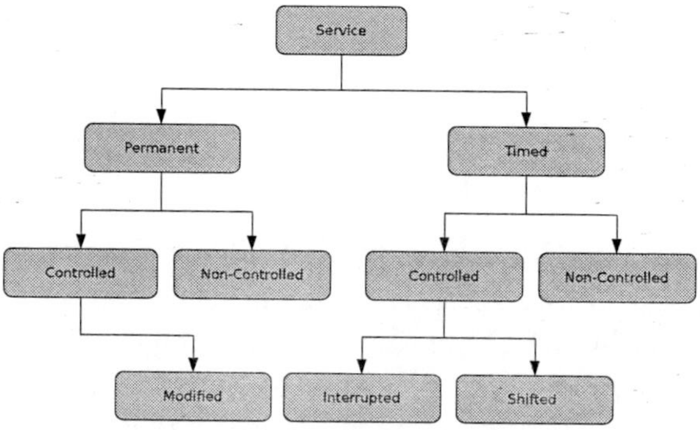

Figure 1. Classification of services.

We have seen the different characteristics of a service. Let us now examine how they can be modeled and validated in order to size energy consumption and production. To manage a home like a system, it is important to structure the behavior of two service categories using models. In what follows, we shall introduce two behavior models for energy services: continuous dynamic models and finite-state machine models.

2.2. Behavior Model for Two Service Categories

By structuring the behavior models of two service categories a home can be managed like a system. We have identified two behavior model groups: the continuous dynamic model group and the finite-state machine model group. Continuous dynamic models describe the ongoing changes in services such as heating. Finite-state machine models describe the temporary changes to services operating in stages such as a "washing" service (pre-washing, washing, rinsing and drying).

2.2.1. Continuous Dynamic Behavior Models

The dynamic behavior model typically corresponds to thermal activities and is used to describe the continuous changes to services such as heating and air conditioning, but also battery charging/discharging. A continuous dynamic behavior model can be described as a system of differential equations.

$$\frac{dX}{dt} = A \times X + B \times P + C \times W \tag{1}$$

- t : time;
- X : vector of state variables.
- P : vector of power assignment.
- W : vector of external disturbance.
- A, B, C: coefficient matrices.

We shall focus especially on modeling heating services because these are essential to the home. Heating is also a topic that has been broadly explored in literature.

Several models modeling temperature changes in a room have been described as a system of differential equations, e.g. the model of energy flow transmissions in a room described by Kampf et Robinson (2006). We shall look at a simplified model modeling temperature changes in a room. We have deliberately chosen the simplified model of [N. Mendes et de Araújo (2001)] as it represents most of the dynamics for our system, i.e. its characteristic behavior. The chosen model can be formulated as follows:

$$\frac{dT}{dt} = -\frac{1}{\tau}T + \frac{K}{\tau}P + \frac{1}{\tau}T_{out}$$

The characteristic variables of this model are:

- K: thermal conductivity relating to the room.
- τ: time constant ($t = 3\tau$ response time).
- T_{out}: outside temperature.
- T: instantaneous temperature under the following conditions:
  $T_{min} \leq T$,$T_{max} \geq T$ where T_{min} and T_{max} are respectively the minimum and maximum temperatures.

- P: average power of this environment under the following conditions: $0 \leq P$,$P_{max}(t) \geq P$ where P_{max} is a function of time.

These are the variables used to implement the thermal model of the heating services in our system.

2.2.2. Finite-State Machine Behavior Model

Continuous dynamic behavior models are not suitable for modeling all services. The finite-state machine model is more appropriate for describing changes to services operating in stages with known periods (e.g. a 4-stage washing service). In literature, a finite-state machine is defined as follows:

- a finite set of states S.
- an initial state $s \in S$.
- a set of final states $F \subseteq S$.
- a set of transitions T: each transition moves from one state to another and is labelled by state change conditions.

Finite-state machine modeling, which determines certain service categories, naturally represents service operation behavior. In our case, service operation is broken down into several stages corresponding to a set of states $\{S\}$, while the state change conditions correspond to the set of state transitions $\{T\}$.

Let us take the example of a washing service operating in 4 stages: pre-washing, washing, rinsing and drying (FIG. 2). Each stage (j) of the washing service is modeled by a quantity P_{i_j} consumed during the period $ET_{i_j} - ST_{i_j}$; ET_{i_j} is the time at the end of stage j and ST_{i_j} is the time at the start of stage j. The finite-state machine of this service is initiated by a run order (given by the user or a system). The stages are run according to a pre-defined order where the transition to the next stage is activated by the end of the previous stage.

2.2.3. Hybrid Dynamic Behavior Models

A hybrid dynamic behavior model can also be defined. Indeed, some services operate in stages, but each stage can be described by a continuous dynamic behavior model.

Let us take the example of the behavior model of a battery. Three stages can be identified: charging, discharging and disconnection from the power grid. In the charging stage, the battery consumes energy and is considered to be an energy consumer. On the other hand, the battery discharging stage is considered as an additional source of energy for the system.

In what follows, we shall present a Multi-Agent System for energy management in buildings. We shall start by modeling the agents and then present the system control mechanism.

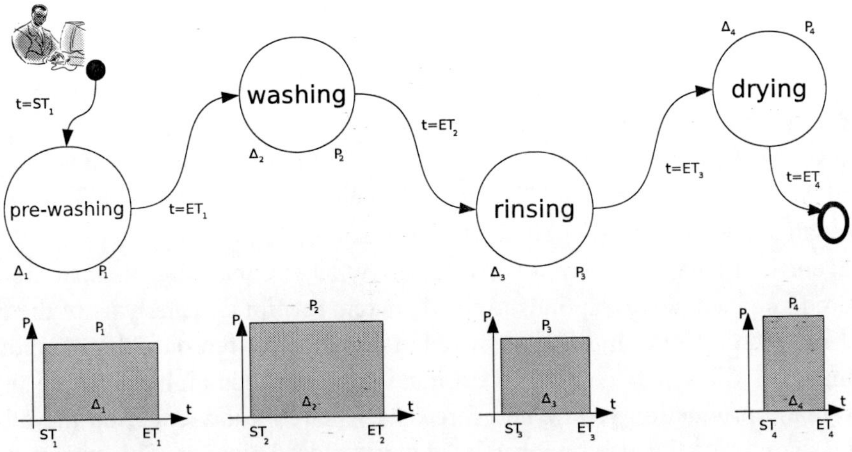

Figure 2. Washing service behavior finite-state machine.

3. Architecture of a MAS for Energy Management

The proposed system is made up of software agents each of which performs a specific task. These agents interact and communicate in order to dynamically establish an energy production and consumption policy meeting different requirements. This system, based on multi-agent system (MAS), is called an MAHAS or "Multi-Agent Home Automation System". Furthermore, in this system, the agents are linked to both the appliances and the energy production sources and are in charge of controlling these. The following diagram (FIG. 3) presents the overall structure of the MAHAS system.

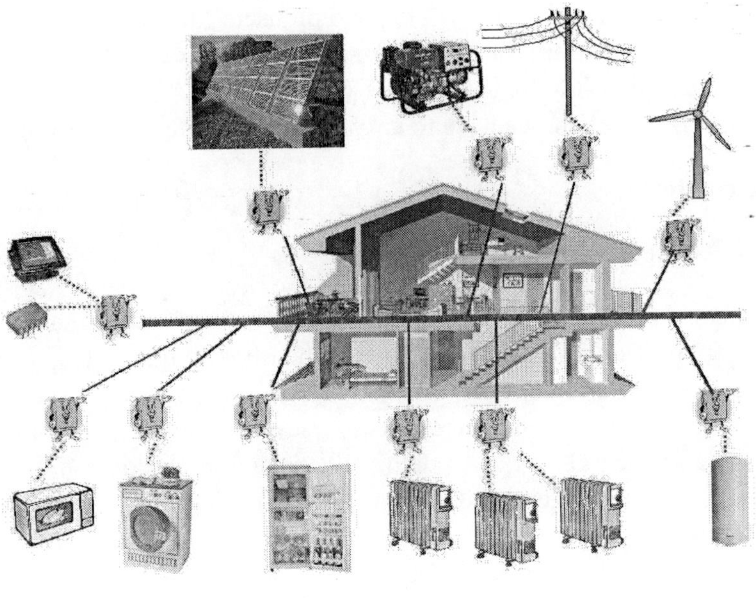

Figure 3. Overall structure of the MAHAS system for energy management.

The components making up the system are energy production sources and household appliances supporting the operation of services. The first idea was to link a software agent to all components. However, we have seen that the notion of service is more generic, allowing us to define two main service categories: temporary services and permanent services. MAHAS system agents are therefore going to be built around this notion of service, i.e. we will refer to "temporary agents" and "permanent agents". In this system, an agent will thus be able to control one or several appliances and/or sources.

Each agent will have its internal (private) knowledge containing its specific behavior model; shared knowledge corresponds to the dispatch, receipt and analysis of the messages exchanged between agents. Internal knowledge contains all the data that cannot be generally formalized. This part is used to estimate energy needs and determine the energy consumption and production profile and forecasts. Shared knowledge, on the other hand, contains the shared data that can be formalized in a standard manner. This means that all the information about the estimated and forecast consumption and production is organized or standardized so that the different system components can communicate. This information is used to build an energy resource assignment plan in line with the services required and aspects relating to user comfort and safety.

3.1. MAHAS System Agent Modeling

In home automation, "user comfort" is one of the most important aspects to take into consideration. The notion of comfort can be directly linked to the concept of satisfaction function [Lucidarme *et al.* (2002)]

3.1.1. Satisfaction Function

Since the notion of comfort is not universal, we shall represent different satisfaction functions for each service-user and these will depend on users' desires. For example, one user will be happy if the temperature in their living room is between 20^oC and 22^oC, while a different user might prefer it to be between 19^oC and 20^oC.

To set up MAHAS system, we have to answer the following two questions:

- What is comfort?
- How can it be represented?

Based on the answer to these questions, the core of each agent can be built.

Since the notion of comfort is too abstract to be directly quantified, we have focused on a notion directly linked to comfort: user satisfaction. From a more mathematical point of view, satisfaction can reflect the perception of a level reached in relation to a previously fixed goal. This approach allows us to define a satisfaction function in each agent and is comparable to the notion of agent satisfaction [Simonin (2001)].

In MAHAS system agents, the satisfaction function characterizes a user's feelings with respect to a service and is fairly close to the notion of personal satisfaction described by [Simonin (2001)]. Satisfaction functions have been defined for appliances (energy consumers) and energy sources (energy suppliers).

The satisfaction relative to a service will be expressed by a function defined over an interval $[0, 100\%]$ where zero is "unacceptable" and 100% "perfect". This can be seen as a degree of belonging to the satisfied whole in blurred logic.

The satisfaction function of a temporary agent can be estimated by a piecewise linear function that depends on the time shift in service offered in relation to the end time desired by the user (FIG. 5). The satisfaction function of a permanent agent can also be estimated by a piecewise linear function that depends on the characteristic service variable. For example, the satisfaction function for a heating service depends on the temperature variable (FIG. 4).

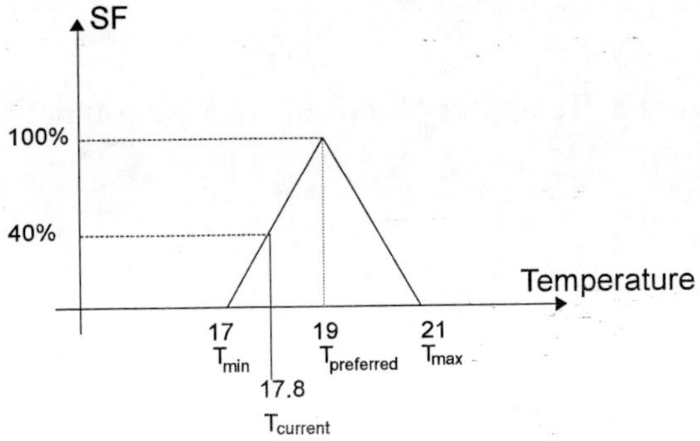

Figure 4. Example of a heating service temperature satisfaction function.

In what follows, we shall present MAHAS system temporary and permanent agent modeling.

3.1.2. Temporary Agent Modeling

A temporary service is characterized by the duration and desired end time of the operation. The flexibility of this service comes from the possibility of shifting its operating time it, i.e. bringing forward or delaying the service. Temporary agent knowledge comprises internal knowledge and some shared knowledge.

Temporary agent internal (private) knowledge can be modeled by:

- a characteristic variable that depends on the service operation end time AET_i where AET_i is the actual service end time.
- a satisfaction function that depends on the difference between the actual end time AET_i and the required end time RET_i but also on the earliest end time EET_i and the latest end time LET_i (FIG. 5).
- a behavior model used to define the energy consumption/production for a service rendered. In this part, a finite-state machine defines the service operation stages. The overall duration of the temporary service is $\Delta_i = n_i \times \Delta$; $n_i \in \mathbb{N}^*$. The durations Δ_{i_j} and energy consumed/produced (negative/positive) $\mp P_{i_j}$ and the operation stages are also known (FIG. 6). The transition time between two stages is zero.

  In this model, interruption of the temporary service can be added: the service can be temporarily stopped and started again later (consumption is zero over a certain time period).

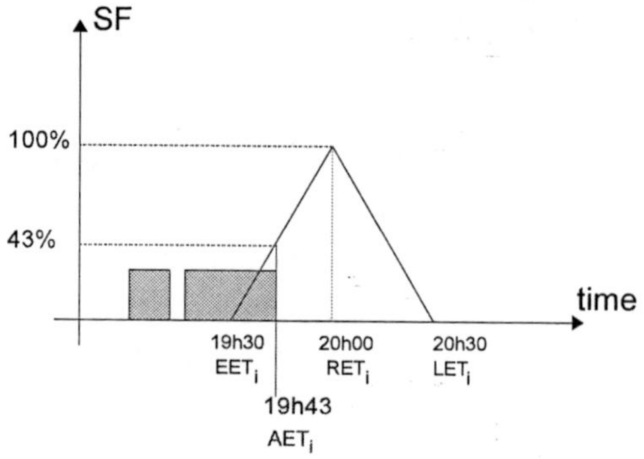

Figure 5. Temporary service satisfaction function.

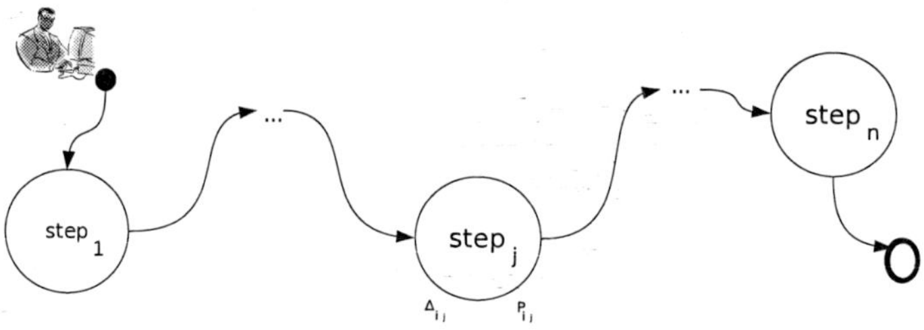

Figure 6. Temporary service behavior finite-state machine

Each stage (j) of the temporary service SRV_i is defined by its duration Δ_{i_j} and its power P_{i_j}. A service stage is said to be interruptible if it can stop consuming power ($P_{i_j} = 0$) for a minimum interruption duration $\Delta_{i_j,int_{min}}$ as long as it is not interrupted for more than a maximum interruption duration $\Delta_{i_j,int_{max}}$ and that the interruption duration total does not exceed $\Delta_{i_j,int_{tot}}$. A temporary service is not interruptible if $\Delta_{i_j,int_{max}} = 0$.

SRV_i, stage j	duration Δ_{i_j}	$\Delta_{i_j,int_{min}}$	$\Delta_{i_j,int_{max}}$	$\Delta_{i_j,int_{tot}}$
uninterruptible	x	0	0	0
interruptible	x	x	x	x

Temporary agent external (shared) knowledge represents the information exchanged between agents. This knowledge can be modeled by a realization:

- a power profile: $\Pi = (P_{i,k}, \ldots, P_{i,k+l})$ where $P_{i,m} \neq 0$ represents the power consumed/produced (negative/positive) by the service throughout the period stretching from k to $k + l$. l represents the time horizon for processing the energy assignment problem. The service duration Δ_i is determined by the length of the profile $length(\Pi)$ where $P_{i,m} \neq 0$.

- a satisfaction function value that depends on the difference between the actual end time of the agent and the required end time of the user for a given service. This value is linked to the power profile put forward by the agent.

A realization therefore corresponds to a power profile denoted as (k, Π, σ) over the time period $[k, k + l]$; σ represents the profile's satisfaction value representing the user's degree of satisfaction compared with the service accomplished by the agent.

3.1.3. Permanent Agent Modeling

A permanent service is characterized by a quantity of energy consumed or produced. The flexibility of this service comes from the possibility of modifying the energy quantities consumed/produced throughout all the periods (decrease or increase in energy consumption or production at a given time).

Permanent agent internal (private) knowledge can be modeled as shown below:

- a characteristic service variable (e.g. the temperature for a heating service).
- a behavior model used to describe the continuous changes in the activity of the service such as heating or air conditioning in relation to the power injected and other contextual magnitudes. As we have already shown, this model can be described as a system of differential equations.
- a satisfaction function that depends on the state variables modeling the service behavior model.

Permanent agent external (shared) knowledge represents the information exchanged between agents. This knowledge can be modeled by a realization:

- a power profile: $\Pi = (P_{i,k}, \ldots, P_{i,k+l})$ where $P_{i,m}$ represents the power consumed/produced (negative/positive) by the service over the period stretching from k to $k + l$. l represents the horizon for processing the energy assignment problem. The service duration Δ_i covers the entire length of the profile: $length(\Pi)$.
- a satisfaction function value that depends on the characteristic variable (e.g. the variable of the energy supplied by an energy source).

A realization therefore corresponds to a power profile denoted as (k, Π, σ) over the time period $[k, k + l]$; σ represents the profile's satisfaction value representing the user's degree of satisfaction with the service accomplished by the agent.

3.2. Multi-level Energy Management System

Now that the agents have been modeled, we must turn attention to the overall operation of the MAHAS system in charge of controlling (controlling and monitoring depending on automation specialist terminology) the home's energy system.

The biggest difficulty when addressing the problem of assigning energy resources in a home is taking into account very different dynamics. Some phenomena require very short response times, such as violation of the maximum resource requirement calling for swift management of conflicting energy demands. The control mechanism offering these properties is called the "reactive mechanism". There are also some physical phenomena that are relatively slow such as inertia in the home, cyclical variations such as the price of energy bought or local energy production capacity such as solar energy. Hence, the system's control architecture must be able to manage the periodic cyclical phenomena occurring in the home. The control mechanism offering these properties is called the "anticipative mechanism".

Consequently, the system architecture must have a reactive mechanism with a short response time as well as an anticipative mechanism with a longer response time. When comfort requirements cannot be met, users can be warned that their requirements cannot be fulfilled. This is followed by negotiation with the users so that they lower their requirements.

The proposed MAHAS system has two main control levels (FIG. 7). These levels can be identified according to the different sampling periods and time horizons. The anticipative mechanism schedules an energy production and consumption plan for events ahead of time (from several hours to a day beforehand). Thus, the information covering a week can be integrated into the anticipative mechanism. The reactive mechanism aims to fulfill the anticipative mechanism's assignment plan. It makes it possible to respond to unscheduled events during the anticipation phase. This mechanism has a short time horizon (roughly one minute) with a shorter response time than that of the anticipative mechanism.

There may also be a third mechanism: a very local regulation mechanism closely linked to the "controllers" of the various appliances or sources (e.g. a radiator thermostat). The response time of this mechanism is generally very short. This mechanism operates in an entirely independent manner until it receives a set-point from its agent (i.e. the agent to which it is directly linked) which then becomes a priority. Conversely, it regularly transmits information about its current state to its agent so that this can be taken into account in its predictions and future negotiations.

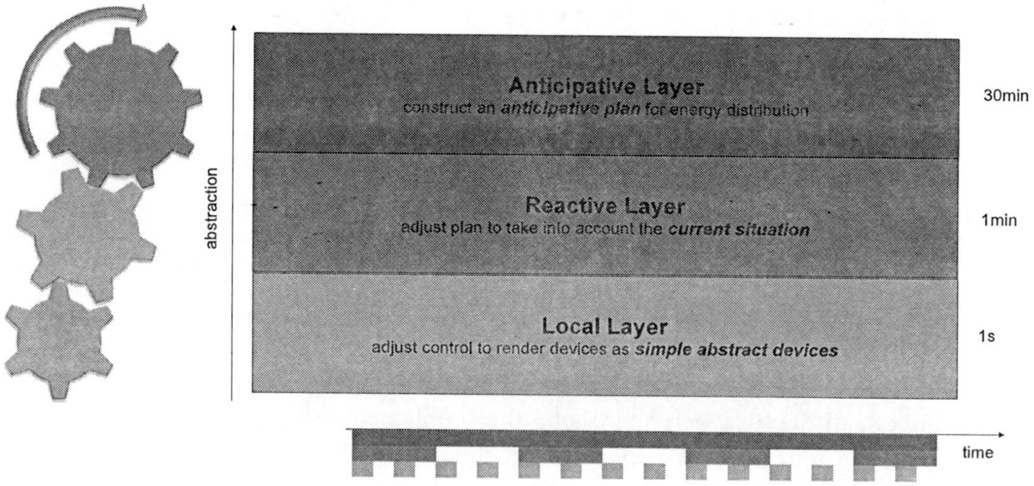

Figure 7. MAHAS system multi-level control system.

4. Reactive Mechanism

Multi-Agent Systems comprising only reactive mechanisms usually have a high number of agents. Each agent is devoid of sophisticated intelligent reasoning (reactive behavior). Intelligent behavior is the result of appropriate exchanges between agents. Imagining a collective therefore involves the problem of organizing the different agent activities so that the collective behaves as a consistent whole and meets the requirements asked of it. All of the agents' behavior converges towards an objective, but there are very few cases where the solution found is the optimum solution. Nevertheless, in complex situations like energy management in the home, a good solution (i.e. an acceptable one) is generally sufficient.

The reactive mechanism is essential to the MAHAS system. It makes it possible to respond to unscheduled events (unexpected lack of power within a time period, unprogrammed consumption, etc.) and to prevent the operation of some predefined appliances from being entirely interrupted (e.g. an oven or a radiator in a room being completely stopped). This makes it possible to deal with urgent situations and maintain a satisfactory level of comfort for the user. This mechanism fulfills what one might call *intelligent load-shedding* since some appliances can be temporarily interrupted. However, unlike conventional load-shedding where the non-priority appliances in an installation are defined, here the agents embedded in the appliances negotiate which ones are to be shed.

This mechanism works on real energy values over a relatively short period (of around one minute) because, on the one hand, its objective is to respond to instantaneous unscheduled events and, on the other hand, a closer level to the equipment is needed in order to take into account the actual energy consumption and production values.

4.1. Principles of the Reactive Mechanism

A Multi-Agent System is said to be *reactive* if its behavior is based on actions triggered according to a stimulus-response process. In the MAHAS system, the reactive mechanism uses the notion of satisfaction to determine its actual state and decide on the actions to be undertaken. This mechanism is triggered when the level of satisfaction of an agent falls below a certain value; an agent will then begin to negotiate with the other agents. Thus, the reactive mechanism makes real-time adjustments to the predicted set-points in relation to the current state of appliance and user requirements and criteria. New set-points are then transmitted to the appliances.

Similarly to the reactive Multi-Agent System, the agents of the reactive mechanism behave according to a stimulus-response process [Vidal *et al.* (2001)] with communication capacity (dispatch/receipt of messages). The role of an agent is as follows:

- it constantly monitors its level of current satisfaction (e.g. the temperature value for the heating service using a physical sensor).
- when its level of satisfaction falls below a given satisfaction level (critical satisfaction), it warns the other agents (help requested in the messages transmitted).
- when it receives requests from other agents, it analyses these and in turn puts forward proposals.

- when it receives responses to its own requests, it opts for the most interesting proposals.

This can be summarized in figure 8.

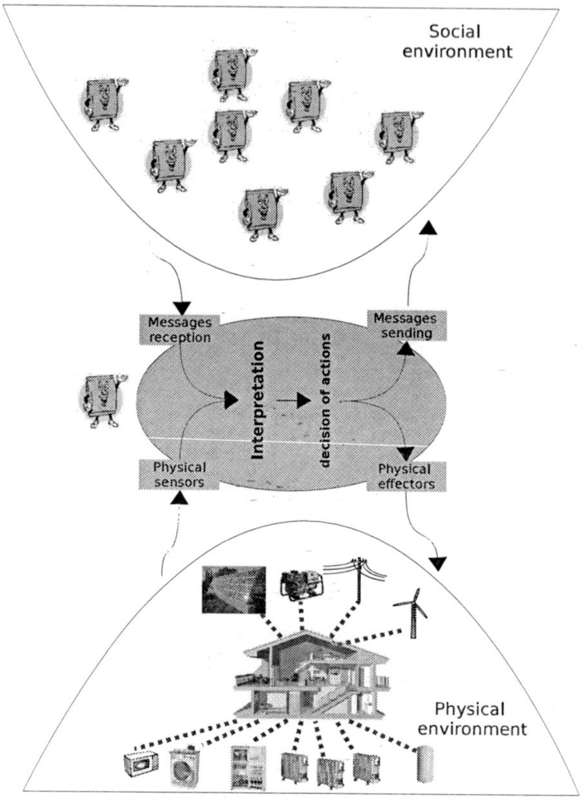

Figure 8. Agent-environment interaction.

In this figure:

- the sensors are the values read indicating current user satisfaction and the behavior of the appliance (e.g. temperatures of a room or end time of a task for an oven).
- the **receive** inputs are either messages from other agents requesting help or informing about a situation, or an event stemming from the physical environment.
- the **send** outputs are messages sent to other agents either asking them for help or submitting proposals to them.
- the effectors are operation set-points for the appliances (temporary interruption of a washing machine, drop in radiator consumption, etc.).
- When an agent perceives inputs (receipt of messages or reading of values), it interprets and responds to these by choosing an appropriate action for the situation from among the predefined rules taking into account both its current and future state.

The main principles of an agent model (i.e. purely reactive) can be found in the agents of the reactive mechanism. On the other hand, these agents have communicating capacity and the reactive agent model is as follows:

- each agent operates according to an infinite loop.
- a perceived event on which it acts.
- its chosen behavior.
- acceptance or refusal of proposals.
- actions are made up of message exchanges.

The agent therefore uses an infinite internal loop (as long as there is one), which ensures the agent is persistent. The agent checks its level of satisfaction during each cycle of its infinite loop. The level of urgency corresponds to the critical satisfaction of the next cycle and determines the reactive period in relation to the satisfaction curve gradient. We shall refer to the infinite loop cycle as the *reactive period*, which is an agent parameter.

The agent monitors its level of satisfaction and, if the critical satisfaction level has been reached, it initializes a message exchange process run. This communication is subject to a protocol that we shall progressively develop in what follows.

One of the essential parameters in the reactive mechanism is the level of critical satisfaction representing the level of urgency for an agent's satisfaction function (i.e. when the satisfaction function drops below this value). It represents the smallest satisfaction of the agents in the system.

4.2. Assessing the Level of Critical Satisfaction

The level of critical satisfaction represents an urgency threshold. This level is the satisfaction threshold of the agents in the system. When an agent's level of satisfaction drops below the critical satisfaction level, the reactive mechanism is triggered. Critical satisfaction is also used to determine how far agents can lower their satisfaction when they submit proposals to another agent in a state of urgency. This threshold can be a set value or a value that is adjusted over time. To adapt this threshold over time, each agent has a function the role of which is to adapt the critical satisfaction level in relation to the frequency of urgent calls.

The critical satisfaction value adapts to urgent calls. Let us assume that there are many urgent calls. The critical satisfaction value drops giving the agents more flexibility in terms of satisfaction and the possibility of submitting more proposals. In the opposite case, when there are not many calls, this value increases thus improving the average level of agent satisfaction.

The agents assess the critical satisfaction value every T_{scan} depending on the urgent call frequency. Let $[f_1, f_2]$ be the urgent call frequency interval and $f = \frac{n}{T_{scan}}$ the urgent call frequency observed during a period $[k * T_{scan}, (k+1) * T_{scan}]$. The critical satisfaction value is assessed at time $k * T_{scan}$ as follows:

- $f < f_1$: there are not many urgent calls, which means that the average satisfaction of agents should be increased while each agent increases the critical satisfaction value as follows:

$$\sigma_{critical,k+1} = (1 - e^{-\frac{T_{scan}}{\tau}})(1 - \sigma_{critical,k}) + \sigma_{critical,k}$$

In this case, only the agents with a satisfaction value that it is higher than the critical satisfaction put forward proposals if urgent action is required:

- $f > f_2$: there are many urgent calls, which means that the critical satisfaction should be lowered so that agents can put forward proposals while each agent lowers the critical satisfaction value as follows:

$$\sigma_{critical,k+1} = e^{-\frac{T_{scan}}{\tau}} \sigma_{critical,k}$$

- $f \in [f_1, f_2]$: the urgent call frequency stabilizes between two values while there is no change to critical satisfaction:

$$\sigma_{critical,k+1} = \sigma_{critical,k}$$

When an agent is unable to quit a state of urgency because it has not received enough interesting proposals upon its first request, this agent asks again for help. This involves lowering the critical satisfaction over the interval $[t - T_{scan}, t]$ as described above ($\sigma_{critical,t} = e^{-\frac{T_{scan}}{\tau}} \sigma_{critical,t-T_{scan}}$).

Dynamically assessing the level of critical satisfaction allows the MAHAS system to adapt to the energy context and homogenize satisfaction levels between agents.

When an agent is connected to the system, it is initialized with the current critical satisfaction value. It should also be remembered that when an agent is connected to the system, it is equipped with a local directory (denoted as D) of agents able to take part in the negotiations: cooperative agents. On the other hand, agents that are unable to take part in the negotiations are not in this directory (e.g. a "heating" service agent cannot lower the temperature in a bedroom where there are children playing).

To explain the agent cooperation mechanisms in the reactive phase, we shall now describe the way a temporary agent and a permanent agent operate.

4.3. Temporary Agent Interaction

As we saw previously, a temporary agent offers a temporary service SRV_i, which is temporally characterized by its duration and its desired operation end time. A finite-state behavior model is usually used to model the operating stages of a service. In what follows, we shall describe how a temporary agent can act and communicate with the other agents by exchanging messages: dispatch of messages, collection and analysis of proposals.

4.3.1. Dispatch of Message: Temporary Agent

Let us assume that a temporary service SRV_i, made up of several stages, is started up and that this service has not been scheduled. Its embedded agent (a_d) asks the agents in its directory D to supply it with energy. It asks them for energy P_{i_1} for a duration Δ_{i_1} corresponding to the first stage of this service over the time interval $[ST_{i1}, ET_{i1}]$; $\Delta_{i_1} = ET_{i1} - ST_{i1}$. Furthermore, it sends a request to the anticipative mechanism to recalculate a new plan taking into account the remaining stages of its service.

Over a pre-defined period, it awaits multiple proposals for energy steps $P_{step} = \frac{P_{i_1}}{n}$, which is the energy required P_{i_1} spread over the number of agents in its directory (n).

When agent a_d receives proposals from other agents, it checks:

- whether there is enough energy and, if so, the service is started.
- otherwise, it calculates the average satisfaction of the agents having responded (m): $\sigma_{average} = \frac{1}{m}\sum_{j=1}^{m} \sigma_j$; it will then ask for more energy when its satisfaction has reached the average satisfaction calculated. This means that homogeneous satisfaction can be achieved for all the active services.

This mechanism can be summarized using algorithm ALG. 1.

```
initial request for energy P_i1 from agents (D) in order to start;
receipt of proposals in response to its start request over a pre-defined period;
If (sufficient energy) then
    start of service;
else
    calculation of σ_average = (1/m) Σ_{j=1}^{m} σ_j ;
    [average satisfaction of agents having responded]
    Wait and request for energy when σ = σ_average;
    receipt of proposals over a pre-defined period;
    If (sufficient energy) then
        start of service;
        [this is used to balance out agent satisfaction]
    else
        wait and request for call when σ_i <= σ_critical ;
    end If
end If
```

Algorithm 1: *Temporary agent energy request mechanism.*

In this case, the message sent by temporary agent a_d to the other agents D may be as follows:

```
request(a_d, D, "reactive", ST_i1, ET_i1, P_i1, P_step)
```

Similarly, let us assume that a service is in process, that there is not enough energy available for one of its stages and that the level of critical satisfaction has almost been reached. The agent adopts the same reasoning as described above (ALG. 1) for the current stage. It asks the other agents for a quantity of energy for a given time interval with the aim of increasing its level of satisfaction to above the critical satisfaction level.

4.3.2. Example of an Energy Request for a Temporary Agent

Let us consider a system that is made up of four appliances: a radiator, a washing machine, an oven and a water heater. Only one $4.6kw$ source of electrical energy is available (such as that provided by the EDF electricity authority).

Let us assume that the temporary "washing" service is made up of 4 stages: pre-washing, washing, rinsing and drying. This service is modeled by a finite-state machine (FIG. 9). Each stage (j) of the washing machine is modeled by a quantity P_{i_j} consumed during the period $ET_{i_j} - ST_{i_j}$; ET_{i_j} is the end time for stage j and ST_{i_j} is the start time for stage j.

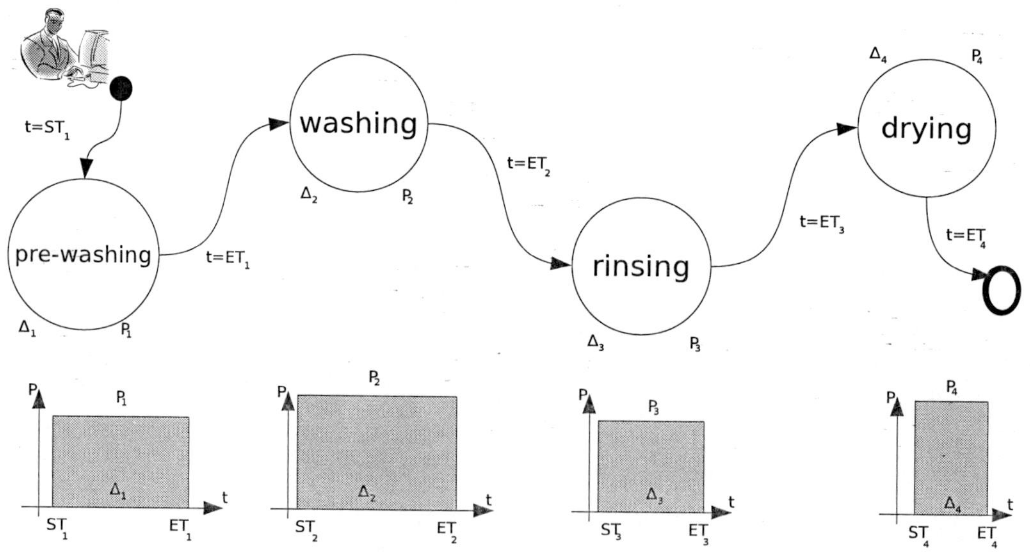

Figure 9. "Washing" service example.

The characteristic parameters of the stages are listed in the table 1.

Table 1. "Washing" service example

Stage	ST_{i_j}	ET_{i_j}	P_{i_j}
Pre-washing	0 min	15 min	$1200W$
Washing	16 min	45 min	$1400W$
Rinsing	46 min	55 min	$1200W$
Drying	56 min	60 min	$1400W$

Let us assume that this service can be shifted by 15 minutes. Figure 10 represents the satisfaction function of this service that depends on the service end time.

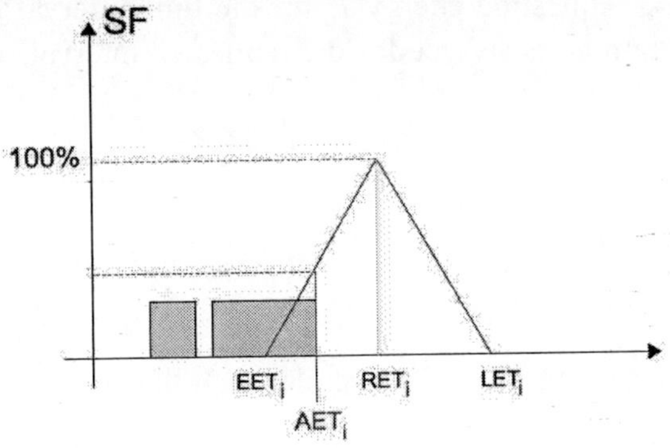

Figure 10. "Washing" service satisfaction function.

Let us assume that the "washing" service has started and that this service has not been scheduled by the anticipative mechanism. The washing machine agent asks the agents in its directory (a radiator, an oven, a water heater and a source of energy) to provide it with energy. It asks them to supply it with energy for its first stage $P_{i_1} = 1200W$ in multiples of $P_{step} = \frac{1200}{4}$ for a duration $\Delta_{i_1} = ET_{i_1} - ST_{i_j} = 15$ corresponding to the first stage interval $[0, 15]$.

The messages sent by the washing machine agent are as follows:

`request(washing machine agent, radiator agent, "reactive", 0, 15, 1200, 300)`

`request(washing machine agent, oven agent, "reactive", 0, 15, 1200, 300)`

`request(washing machine agent, water heater agent, "reactive", 0, 15, 1200, 300)`

`request(washing machine agent, source agent, "reactive", 0, 15, 1200, 300)`

Let us assume that there is not enough energy and that the average satisfaction of the agents having responded $\sigma_{average}$ is equal to 72%. The washing machine agent applies to the other agents again for energy when it has a satisfaction level of $\sigma_{average} = 72\%$: a time difference of 4 minutes.

The messages sent back by the washing machine agent are as follows:

```
request(washing machine agent, radiator agent, "reactive", 4,
19, 1200, 300)
request(washing machine agent, oven agent, "reactive", 4, 19,
1200, 300)
request(washing machine agent, water heater agent, "reactive",
4, 19, 1200, 300)
request(washing machine agent, source agent, "reactive", 4, 19,
1200, 300)
```

4.3.3. Response to a Message: Temporary Agent

In the reactive context, one of the roles of the agents is to respond to actions and notably to respond to requests from other agents. When temporary agent a receives a message from any other agent a_d requesting energy P for the time interval $[t_s, t_f]$, agent a checks the possibility of interrupting its service for the requested interval. It checks the following three conditions:

- whether the requested duration $d = t_f - t_s$ is greater than the minimum interruption duration $\Delta_{i_j,int_{min}}$ (for the current stage j of its service SRV_i).
- whether the requested duration d is smaller than that of the maximum interruption $\Delta_{i_j,int_{max}}$.
- whether the requested duration d is smaller than the accumulated interruption durations $\Delta_{i_j,int_{cum}}$.

If one of the above conditions cannot be satisfied, the agent's service cannot be interrupted for the requested interval and it does not therefore respond to the request of agent a_d.

If all three conditions can be satisfied, its service can be interrupted for the requested duration. It calculates the satisfaction σ, which depends on the temporary service end time (FIG. 10), due to this interruption. It then sends a proposal comprising the satisfaction σ and the power of the current stage P_{i_j}. It also sends a zero proposal of 0 $watt$ (satisfaction of its service without any interruptions σ_0). Sending a proposal of 0 $watt$ enables requesting agent a_d to calculate the average satisfaction for requesting agent a_d to try and reach this satisfaction level. However, any agents unable to be interrupted do not put forward any proposals given that their satisfaction values are not included to calculate the average satisfaction.

This mechanism can be summarized by algorithm ALG. 2.

In this case, the message sent back by temporary agent a to agent a_d having requested energy can be as follows:

propose(a, a_d, "reactive", $proposals$)

where $proposals$ is the set of proposals, each comprising a power and a satisfaction value.

When agent a receives acceptance of its proposal from agent a_d, it modifies the total interruption durations $\Delta_{i_j,int_{cum}}$ and updates the start and end times of all the following stages.

a_d : **Agent**; *[requesting agent]*
a : **Agent**; *[proposing agent]*
$[t_s, t_f]$: **Time interval**; *[requested time interval]*
proposals $\leftarrow \emptyset$: **List of proposals**;
Require : j $\leftarrow$ current stage;
If $((ST_{i_j} \leq t_s)$ & $(t_f \leq ET_{i_j})$ & $(\Delta_{i_j,int_{min}} > 0))$ **then**
  $d \leftarrow t_f - t_s$; *[requested duration]*
  If $((d < \Delta_{i_j,int_{max}})\&(d < \Delta_{i_j,int_{cum}})\&(d > \Delta_{i_j,int_{min}}))$ **then**
    calculation of σ for an interruption lasting d;
    addition of (P_{i_j}, σ) to *proposals*;
  end If
  If (*proposals* $\neq$ zero)) **then**
    calculation of σ_0 for an interruption lasting 0;
    addition of $(0, \sigma_0)$ to *proposals*;
  end If
end If

Algorithm 2: Temporary agent mechanism of response to an energy request

4.3.4. Example of a Temporary Agent's Response to an Energy Request

Let us consider the system described above and assume that all the services have been scheduled by the anticipative mechanism. Let us assume that an agent (the one connected to the radiator) a_d asks for energy $P = 1600W$ for the interval $[19, 29]$. When the agent connected to the washing machine receives the request from the radiator agent, it checks the three interruption conditions listed above. This service can be postponed for 15 minutes assuming that the washing stage can be interrupted. In this case, the washing machine agent calculates the satisfaction for an interruption of $de = 29 - 19$ ($\sigma = 33\%$). It sends two proposals $\{(0, 100), (1400, 33)\}$ where the first proposal represents zero hence specifying "washing" service satisfaction without interruption.

The message sent by the washing machine agent to the radiator agent can be as follows:

```
propose(washing machine agent, radiator agent, "reactive", 0
                        100 1600 33)
```

4.3.5. Analysis of Message: Temporary Agent

Let us assume that agent a_d linked to temporary service SRV_i has already sent an urgent call for energy P_{i_j} for stage (j) corresponding to time interval $\Delta_{i_j} = [ST_{i_j}, ET_{i_j}]$. There is a waiting period for the answers and any answers received outside of this period are ignored.

When this agent a_d receives proposals from other agents in response to its request within the pre-defined time period:

- it sorts the proposals by order of increasing power. This makes it possible to spread out the power requested across all the agents hence preventing their satisfaction level from being decreased.

- it checks whether the proposed power values are sufficient keeping in mind that it only accepts one proposal per agent and which has to be as low as possible. This makes it possible to spread the requirement across all the agents so as not to over penalize another service.
- if the request is satisfied, the agent sends acceptance messages to the agents concerned. Otherwise, it makes a new request for better proposals: assessment of the critical satisfaction of each one.

This mechanism can be summarized by algorithm ALG. 3.

a_d : **Agent**; *[requesting agent]*
a : **Agent**; *[proposing agent]*
P_{i_j} : **Power demand**;
proposal : **Proposal**; *[a proposal (p, σ) sent from a to a_d]*
proposals : **List of proposals received**;
accepted $\leftarrow \emptyset$: **List of accepted proposals**;
agents $\leftarrow \emptyset$: **List of agents**;
[list of proposing agents, some of whose proposals are accepted]
classification of *proposals* in order of increasing power;
$p \leftarrow 0$;
For ((*proposal* $\in$ *proposals*) & ($p < P_{i_j}$)) **do**
  Require : $a \leftarrow$ *proposal.agent*;
  [agent putting forward the proposal]
  $p \leftarrow p + P_{proposal}$;
  addition of *proposal* to *accepted*;
  If ($a \in$ agents) **then**
    proposal $\leftarrow$ former proposal of agent *a* in *accepted*;
    withdrawal of *proposal* from *accepted*;
    $p \leftarrow p - P_{proposal}$;
  else
    addition of *a* to *agents*;
  end If
end For
If ($p \geq P_{i_j}$) **then**
  transmission of acceptance messages to*agents*;
else
  request for new urgent call;
end If

Algorithm 3: Mechanism for analyzing proposals received from a temporary agent.

If the request from agent a_d is satisfied, the message sent back by temporary agent a_d to agent a can be as follows:

accept(a_d, a, "reactive", proposal)

This message tells agent a that one of its proposals has been accepted. If none of the proposals from agent a is selected, no message is sent to agent a.

When an agent is unable to quit the state of urgency because it has not received enough interesting proposals following its first request, this agent applies again for help:

request(a_d, D, "reactive", ST_{i_j}, ET_{i_j}, P_{i_j}, P_{step})

This second request for energy means that each agent has to lower the critical satisfaction level as previously described (§4.2.) so that the agents can put forward more proposals. Receiving more proposals will allow the agent to quit the state of urgency.

Because the aim of the reactive mechanism is to react to unscheduled events occurring in **real time**, if the responses to the second request are still not sufficient, the user is called on to act since the requirements cannot be met.

4.3.6. Example of a Temporary Agent's Analysis of Proposals

Let us consider the previously described system. Let us assume that the agent linked to the washing machine has asked for energy to be supplied to it for its first stage $P_{i_1} = 1200W$ in multiples of $P_{step} = \frac{1200}{4}$ for a duraction of $\Delta_{i_1} = ET_{i_1} - ST_{i_j} = 15$ corresponding to the first stage interval $[0, 15]$.

Let us assume that the agents respond as follows:

propose(radiator agent, washing machine agent, "reactive", 0 90 300 70 600 50 900 20)

The radiator agent sends three proposals for the requested interval $[0, 15]$. It can provide 300W, 600W or 900W but its level of satisfaction will be 70%, 50% and 20% respectively. Otherwise, its satisfaction is 90%.

propose(oven agent, washing machine agent, "reactive", 0 80 1000 40)

The oven agent sends a single proposal for the requested interval $[0, 15]$. It can provide 1000W but its level of satisfaction will be 40%. Otherwise, its satisfaction is 80%.

propose(water heater agent, washing machine agent, "reactive", 0 90 300 80 600 50 900 10)

The water heater agent sends three proposals for the requested interval $[0, 15]$. It can provide 300W, 600W or 900W but its level of satisfaction will be 80%, 50% and 10% respectively. Otherwise, its satisfaction is 100%.

propose(source agent, washing agent, "reactive", 0 100 300 100 600 70 900 50 1200 40)

The agent linked to the electrical energy source sends four proposals for the requested interval $[0, 15]$. It can provide 300W, 600W, 900W or 1200W respectively but its level of satisfaction will be 100%, 70%, 50% or 40% respectively. Otherwise, its satisfaction is 100%.

When the washing machine agent receives the responses, it sorts them by order of increasing power (table 2; E: source agent, H: water heater agent, R: radiator agent and O: oven agent)

By applying the mechanism described above(ALG. 3), the washing machine agent chooses the first proposals from the radiator agent, source agent and water heater agent.

Table 2. Agents' proposals in response to the washing machine agent's request.

Agent	E	H	R	E	R	H	E	R	H	O	E
Power	300	300	300	600	600	600	900	900	900	1000	1200
Satisfaction	100%	80%	70%	70%	50%	50%	50%	20%	10%	40%	40%

When it adds the second proposal of the electrical energy source agent for $600W$, it withdraws the first $300W$. It sends acceptance messages to the agents concerned:

```
accept(washing machine agent, water heater agent, "reactive", 300 80)
accept(washing machine agent, radiator agent, "reactive", 300 70)
accept(washing machine agent, source agent, "reactive", 600 70)
```

We can see that the washing machine agent's request has been shared out between all the agents and that none of the appliances have been penalized.

0W proposals are used when there are not enough interesting proposals. The washing machine agent can thus calculate the average satisfaction of the agents having responded $\sigma_{average} = \frac{90+80+90+100}{4} = 90\%$, and then make a new request for energy once its satisfaction level has been reached 90%.

In the above paragraphs we have seen how a temporary agent can interact with other agents. In the next paragraphs we will present the interaction of a permanent agent with the others.

4.4. Interaction of a Permanent Agent

Taking into account the characteristics of different service categories identified, we have chosen to define the electric radiator located in a room as a *typical* appliance. It is, according to our classification, a "heating" service. This seemed to be the right choice for several reasons: on the one hand, in Europe, the heating service generally represents the service with the highest energy consumption and therefore the service to be worked on the most. On the other hand, the high inertia inherent in this service is intuitively a major part of the solution to an energy management problem. It should also be noted that this type of service is highly representative as all heating services are very similar from a modeling point of view: they can store energy and have a high thermal inertia.

As we saw previously, a permanent agent offers a permanent service SRV_i that is characterized by a quantity of energy consumed or produced over the entire time interval of an energy resource assignment plan. A continuous dynamic behavior model describes the operation of a service. In what follows, we shall describe how a permanent agent can act and communicate with the other agents via messages: dispatch of messages, transmission of proposals and analysis of proposals.

4.4.1. Dispatch of Message: Permanent Agent

Let us assume that a permanent service is started and that this service has not been scheduled by the anticipative mechanism. For the service to start, its agent (a_d) asks the agents in its directory D to supply it with energy. It asks them for power $P_{i_{max}}$ (maximum power) for a duration Δ_i. This duration corresponds to the time interval $[t, t + 3\tau]$; τ being the time constant ($t = 3\tau$ response time). This duration represents the time needed to reach room temperature for users in a room.

Throughout the pre-defined period, it awaits proposals for energy steps $P_{step} = \frac{P_{i_{max}}}{n}$, which is the energy requested shared over the number of agents in its directory n.

In this case, the message sent by permanent agent (a_d) to the other agents (D) can be as follows:

$$\texttt{request}(a_d,\ D,\ \texttt{"reactive"},\ t,\ t+3\tau,\ P_{i_{max}},\ P_{step})$$

Furthermore, this agent sends a request to the anticipative mechanism for it to recalculate a new plan taking into account the presence of this service.

If a service is started and, at a given time, there is not enough energy available and the level of critical satisfaction of the associated agent is going to be reached, the agent applies the same reasoning as that described above. It asks the other agents for a quantity of energy over a time interval with the aim of increasing its level of satisfaction to above the critical satisfaction.

4.4.2. Response to a Message: Permanent Agent

In the reactive context, one of the roles of agents is to respond to requests from other agents. When a permanent agent a receives a message from any other agent a_d requesting power P for a time interval $[t_s, t_f]$, agent a checks the possibility of lowering its consumption or increasing its production for the requested interval.

The permanent agent a tries to change its energy consumption/production for the entire time interval requested $[t_s, t_f]$ by a step of power P_{step}. Then, it calculates the new set-points corresponding to this new power profile [1] $\Pi(p(t)); t \in [t_s, t_f]$ using its continuous dynamic behavior model. It calculates its resulting level of satisfaction, which is equal to the smallest satisfaction value (σ_{min}) for the entire time interval requested $[t_s, t_f]$. If this satisfaction value is greater than the critical satisfaction value, agent a puts forward a proposal to agent a_d: a proposal comprising P_{step} and σ_{min}. It begins again by modifying its consumption/production by a multiple of P_{step} until its satisfaction level is smaller than the critical satisfaction value or until the power proposed is greater than that requested.

This mechanism can be summarized by algorithm ALG. 4.

In this case, the message sent back by permanent agent a to agent a_d, having requested energy, can be as follows:

$$\texttt{propose}(a,\ a_d,\ \texttt{"reactive"},\ proposals)$$

where `proposals` is a set of proposals each one comprising a power value and a satisfaction value.

[1] a power profile: $\Pi = (P_{i,k}, \ldots, P_{i,k+l})$ where $P_{i,m} \neq 0$ represents the power consumed/produced by the service throughout the period stretching from k to $k + l$. l represents the time horizon for processing the energy assignment problem.

a_d : **Agent**; *[requesting agent]*
a : **Agent**; *[proposing agent]*
$[t_s, t_f]$: **Time interval**; *[requested time interval]*
P : **Power**; *[power requested]*
P_{step} : **Power step**;
proposals $\leftarrow \emptyset$: **List of proposals**;
$\Pi(p(t)); t \in [t_s, t_f]$: **Energy profile**;
$x \leftarrow 1$;
While $((x * P_{step} < P))$ **do**
  $\Pi(p(t)) \leftarrow \Pi(p(t) - x * P_{step}); t \in [t_s, t_f]$;
  calculations of new set-points corresponding to $\Pi(p(t))$;
  calculation of σ_{min} for the new set-points;
  If $(\sigma_{min} > \sigma_{critical})$ **then**
    addition of $(x * P_{step}, \sigma_{min})$ to *proposals*;
    $x \leftarrow x + 1$;
  else
    break;
  end If
done
If (*proposals* $\neq$ nil)) **then**
  calculation of σ for a proposal of 0 watt;
  addition of $(0, \sigma)$ to *proposals*; *[current satisfaction]*
end If

Algorithm 4: Permanent agent mechanism of response to a request for energy.

When agent a receives acceptance for one of its proposals from agent a_d, it modifies its power profile.

Sending a proposal of $0\ watts$ allows agent a_d to calculate the average satisfaction in order to try to achieve this satisfaction. On the other hand, agents that cannot be modified do not put forward any proposals. Their satisfaction values are therefore not included for calculating the average satisfaction.

4.4.3. Example of a Permanent Agent's Response to an Energy Request: A Radiator

Let us consider the system described above and assume that all the services have already been scheduled by the anticipative mechanism. Let us assume that an agent (linked to the water heater) a_d asks for energy $P = 1000W$ in multiples of $P_{step} = 250W$ for the interval $[19, 29]$. When the agent linked to the radiator receives the request from the water heater agent, it checks whether it can decrease its consumption. The agent linked to the radiator applies the following reasoning: with each iteration, it decreases its energy profile by a step of power, then it calculates the equivalent temperature profile using the temperature change model. Using this temperature profile, it calculates the smallest satisfaction function value (FIG. 13).

Let us assume that the radiator consumption power profile is illustrated in figure 11.

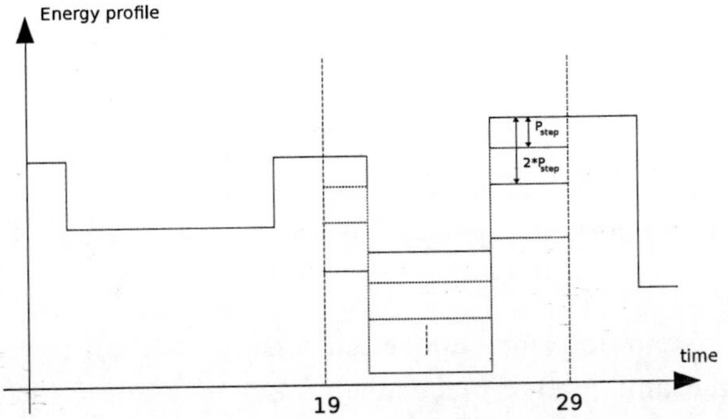

Figure 11. Example of a radiator's power profile.

We can see that when the radiator agent decreases its energy profile, by more than two power steps for the interval [19, 29], the temperature curve is reduced to below the critical temperature (FIG. 12).

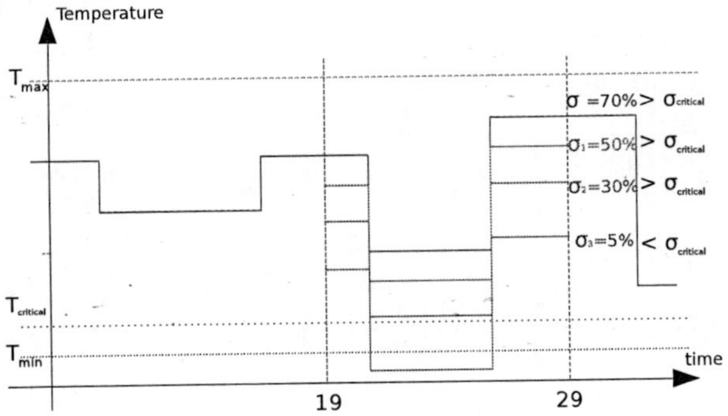

Figure 12. Example of a radiator's temperature curve.

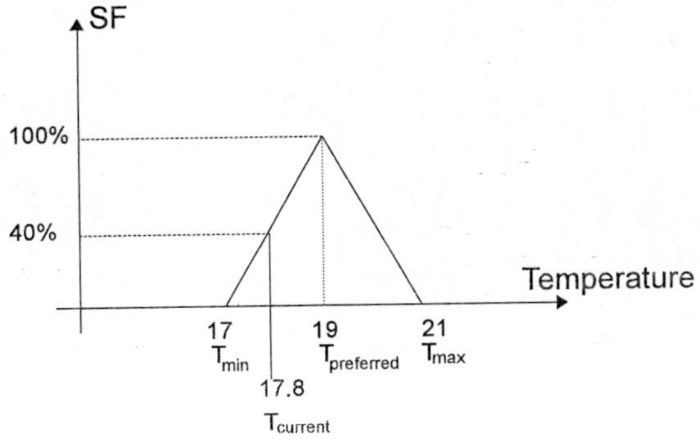

Figure 13. Example of a radiator's temperature satisfaction function.

The permanent agent linked to the radiator only sends three proposals $\{(0, 70), (250, 50), (500, 30)\}$ where the first proposal represents a zero proposal in order to specify the radiator's current satisfaction.

The message sent by the radiator agent to the water heater agent can be as follows:

```
propose(radiator agent, water heater agent, "reactive", 0 70
                    250 50 500 30)
```

4.4.4. Example of a Permanent Agent's Response to an Energy Request: An Electrical Source

Let us consider the system described above and assume that all the services have already been scheduled by the anticipative mechanism. Let us assume that an agent (linked to the water heater) a_d requests energy $P = 1000W$ in multiples of $P_{step} = 250W$ for the interval $[19, 29]$. When the agent linked to the energy source receives the request from the agent linked to the water heater, it checks whether it can increase its production.

Let us assume that the energy profile of the electrical energy source is illustrated in figure 15. We can see that the agent linked to this source increases its energy profile by more than one energy step for the entire interval $[19, 29]$ and that the curve exceeds the electrical energy source's critical production. This means that its level of satisfaction drops below the critical satisfaction value because the satisfaction value is inversely proportional to the power produced by the energy source (FIG. 14). The electrical energy source permanent agent only sends one proposal of $250W$.

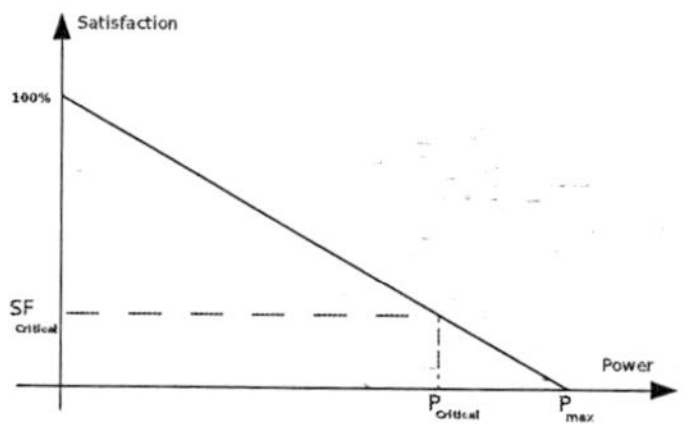

Figure 14. Example of an electrical energy source's satisfaction function.

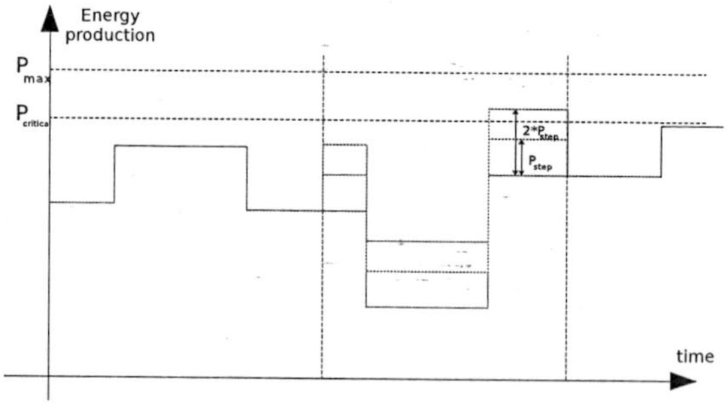

Figure 15. Example of an electrical energy source's power profile.

The message sent by the electrical energy source agent to the water heater agent can be as follows:

```
propose(radiator agent, water heater agent, "reactive", 0 70
                    250 30)
```

4.4.5. Analysis of Message: Permanent Agent

Let us assume that an agent a_d linked to the permanent service SRV_i has already sent an urgent call for energy P_i and for a duration corresponding to the time interval $[t_s, t_f]$. There is a time limit for receiving responses and any responses received after this period are ignored.

When agent a_d receives proposals for its request from other agents within a pre-defined time limit:

- it sorts the proposals by order of increasing power. This makes it possible to share out the power demand across all the agents so that the agents' satisfaction does not have to be reduced.
- it checks whether the power proposed is sufficient by going through the proposals received keeping in mind that it can only accept one per agent. This prevents any one service from being penalized.
- if the agent manages to achieve satisfaction that is greater than the critical satisfaction value, it sends acceptance messages to the agents concerned. Otherwise, it makes a new request for more interesting proposals.

The aim of the permanent agent is to satisfy its need without putting too much stress on the other agents: it does not attempt to achieve 100% satisfaction but instead aims for around average satisfaction.

This mechanism can be summarized by algorithm ALG. 5.

If the request of agent a_d is satisfied, the message sent back by permanent agent a_d to agent a can be as follows:

accept(a_d, a, "reactive", proposal)

This message tells agent a that one of its proposals has been accepted. If none of the proposals of agent a are selected, no message is sent to the agent. Then, permanent agent a_d modifies its energy profile $\Pi(p(t)); t \in [t_s, t_f]$ for the entire time interval $[t_s, t_f]$.

When an agent is unable to quit a state of urgency because it has not received enough interesting proposals upon its first request, this agent asks again for help:

request(a_d, D, "reactive", t_s, t_f, P_i, P_{step})

This second request for energy means that each agent has to lower its critical satisfaction, as previsouly described (§4.2.) so that the agents can put forward other proposals. This enables the agent to receive more proposals in order to quit the state of urgency.

Because the aim of the reactive mechanism is to respond to unscheduled events occurring in **real time**, if the responses received are still not sufficient following the second request, the user is called on to act since the requirements cannot be met.

Only one agent can launch an urgent call at any one time because if several agents did so this would lead to conflicting proposals. Let us assume that agent a_1 and agent a_2 launch an urgent call at the same time:

- if agent a puts forward the same proposals to both agents and if both agents accept them, this leads to a conflict.

a_d : **Agent**; *[requesting agent]*
a : **Agent** ; *[proposing agent]*
proposal : **Proposal**; *[p, σ]*
proposals : **List of proposals received**;
accepted ← ∅ : **List of accepted proposals**;
agents ← ∅ : **List of agents**;
[list of agents, some of whose proposals are accepted]
$\Pi(p(t)); t \in [t_s, t_f]$: **Power profile**;
classification of *proposals* in order of increasing power;
calculation of $\sigma_{average}$ of 0 watt proposals;
$\sigma \leftarrow$ current agent satisfaction a_d;
For *proposal* ∈ *proposals* & $\sigma < \sigma_{average}$ **do**
  Require : *a* ← *proposal.agent* ; *[agent having put forward proposal]*
  $\Pi(p(t)); \leftarrow \Pi(p(t) + p_{pro}); t \in [t_s, t_f]$;
  addition of *proposal* to *accepted*;
  If (*a* ∈ *agents*) **then**
    proposal ← former proposal of agent a in *accepted*;
    withdrawal of *proposal* from list *accepted*;
    $\Pi(p(t)); \leftarrow \Pi(p(t) - p_{proposal}); t \in [t_s, t_f]$;
  end If
  calculation of new set-points corresponding to $\Pi(p(t)); t \in [t_s, t_f]$;
  $\sigma \leftarrow \sigma_{min}$;
end For
If ($\sigma \geq \sigma_{critical}$) **then**
  dispatch of messages to agents ∈ *accepted*;
else
  new urgent call request;
end If

Algorithm 5: Mechanism for analyzing proposals received from a permanent agent.

- if agent a only sends proposals to agent a_1 and if agent a_1 does not accept them, agent a_2 does not receive any proposals from agent a when in fact it could have.

When agent a_d launches an urgent call, a lock is created: a pre-defined time is required for the requesting agent a_d to receive and analyze proposals. This prevents several calls at the same time. This is the drawback of the reactive mechanism, above all because this mechanism is supposed to respond to urgent situations in real time.

There cannot be a problem of deadlock between agents because one of the deadlock conditions has not been checked: the responses have to be given within a pre-defined time limit and any responses received afterwards are ignored.

4.4.6. Example of Analysis of Proposals by a Permanent Agent

Let us consider the system described above and assume that the agent linked to the radiator has asked to be supplied with energy corresponding to a power of $P_{i_1} = 1200W$ in multiples of $P_{step} = \frac{1200}{4}$ for the time interval $[19, 29]$.

Let us assume that the radiator agent has received proposals from the electrical source agent, the water heater agent and the oven agent. The other agents have not responded.

```
propose(source agent, radiator agent, "reactive", 0 80 300 50)
```

The agent linked to the electrical energy source sends a single proposal for the requested interval $[19, 29]$. It can provide 300W but its level of satisfaction will be 50%. Otherwise, its satisfaction is 80%.

```
propose(oven agent, radiator agent, "reactive", 0 90 400 40)
```

The agent linked to the oven also sends a single proposal for the requested interval $[19, 29]$. It can provide 400W but its level of satisfaction will be 40%. Otherwise, its satisfaction is 90%.

```
propose(water heater agent, radiator agent, "reactive", 0 100
300 60)
```

The agent linked to the water heater sends a proposal for the requested interval $[19, 29]$. It can provide 300W but its level of satisfaction will be 60%. Otherwise, its satisfaction is 100%.

When the agent linked to the radiator receives these responses, it sorts them by order of increasing power (table 3; E: source agent, H: water heater agent and O: oven agent)

Table 3. Proposals from agents in response to the radiator agent's request.

Agent	H	E	O
Power	300	300	400
Satisfaction	60%	50%	40%

By applying the previously described mechanism (ALG. 5), the radiator agent opts for the proposals put forward by the agent linked to the electrical energy source, the oven and the water heater. We can see that the power provided in the proposals received ($300W + 300W + 400W$) is below that requested ($1200W$). However, this enables the agent to increase its level of satisfaction (e.g. to 70%) to above the critical satisfaction value.

It sends acceptance messages to the agents concerned:

```
accept(washing machine agent, water heater agent, "reactive", 300 80)
accept(washing machine agent, radiator agent, "reactive", 300 70)
accept(washing machine agent, source agent, "reactive", 600 70)
```

We can see that the proposals were not sufficient to achieve average satisfaction $\sigma_{average} = \frac{80+90+100}{3} = 90\%$ but that they were able to bring the agent out of the state of urgency.

In what follows, we shall introduce the negotiation protocol that characterizes the messages sent between agents.

4.5. Negotiation Protocol

A language for communication between agents makes it possible to coordinate agents with the aim of exchanging information and knowledge. What distinguishes ACLs (*Agent Com-*

munication Languages) from other interaction languages in information technology is the fact they they enable communication between different complex entities (AI entities) in the system and have semantics. ACLs work with proposals, rules and actions instead of simple objects devoid of semantics: an ACL message describes the desired state of an agent in a declarative language. The ACL objective is to develop techniques, methods and software tools in order to share knowledge and reuse it in autonomous information systems.

4.5.1. Communication between Agents

One of the conventional means of agent communication is to send messages. The messages exchanged follow a specific SMA communication protocol. The FIPA (Foundation for Intelligent Physical Agents) has specified the FIPA ACL interaction language([FIPA (2003b)], [FIPA (2003a)]). The FIPA language is a standard agent communication language. Several well-known platforms use the FIPA language such as Jade [jad], The Spyse agent platform [spy] and JACK [jac]. Exchanges occur as "frames" made up of a performative followed by attributes and associated values.

Only a few *meta characters* are required for this:

- "()"to capture groups.
- "."to replace any character.
- "*"to replace a string of 0's, 1's or other characters.

A message frame can be described as follows:

("(.):sender (.*):receiver (.*):content (.*)")*

This frame is made up of four groups:

- group (1), performative.
- group (2), sender's name.
- group (3), receiver's name.
- group (4), content.

The first three groups have been standardized in Multi-Agent Systems (action, sender and receiver). On the other hand, the "content" group is not standard and varies from one system to another depending on the type of system.

Protocols for communication between agents have therefore been created to regulate interactions between artificial agents using KQML and FIPA ACL languages. The FIPA ACL specifications include a description of a set of protocols for interaction between agents such as the very popular *Contract Net Protocol* ([Smith (1980)],[Yang *et al.* (1998)]). Other protocols, such as auctioning or even negotiation protocols complete the specifications [Mathieu et Verrons (2004)].

Concerning the MAHAS system, the negotiation protocol has been defined on the basis of the Contract Net Protocol(CNP) ([Smith (1980)],[Yang *et al.* (1998)]), which is one of the first high level communication protocols for solving distributed problems based on modeling a call for tender, and on contract negotiation work [Mathieu et Verrons (2004)]. Of course, the negotiation is built to accommodate the level of agent satisfaction.

The negotiation protocol (FIG. 16) is divided into three main phases that operate as follows:

- *energy request phase*: during this phase, an agent requests help from the other agents in order to increase its level of satisfaction.
- *decision phase*: the agent, having requested help, analyses the proposals and can either accept or refuse them. If the proposals are insufficient, a new energy request phase can be triggered.
- *proposal phase*: the agents make proposals corresponding to the request of an agent and send these to the agent.

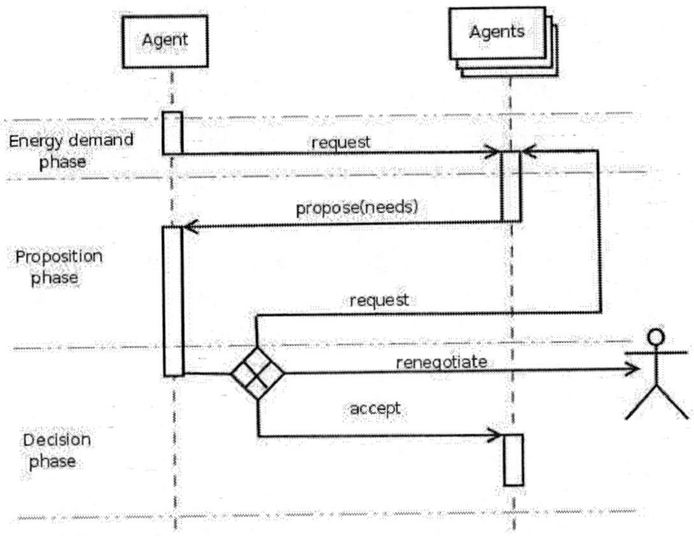

Figure 16. Agent negotiation protocol; reactive mechanism.

A certain number of performatives makes it possible to determine communication acts. The reactive mechanism has three: *request, propose* and *accept.*

Primitives of Negotiation

The reactive mechanism's primitives of negotiation are:

- Request: this message initiates a negotiation and is sent when an urgent situation has been detected. An agent sends this message to other agents when its level of satisfaction falls below the critical level of satisfaction or when it wants to start when this has not been scheduled by the anticipative mechanism. A *request* can be defined as:

```
request(sender, receiver, "reactive", interval,
        asked-energy-value, energy-step).
```

asked-energy-value is the requested energy value in multiples of *energy-steps* for the time interval *interval*.

The frame of a *request* can therefore be:

("(request):sender (a_d):receiver (a):content (["reactive"] [interval] [asked-energy-value] [energy-step])")

- Propose: this message is the response to the*request* message sent by the agent. It contains the set of proposals for the requested interval. This message can be defined as:

```
propose(sender, receiver, "reactive", proposals)
```

where *proposals* is the set of proposals from the proposing agent for the requested interval. These contain power and satisfaction pairs (P, σ).

The frame of a *propose* can therefore be:

("(propose):sender (a):receiver (a_d):content (["reactive"][proposals])")

- Accept: this message tells specific agents that one of their proposals has been accepted. An *Accept* can therefore be defined as:

```
accept(sender, receiver, "reactive", proposal)
```

Such that *proposal* (P, σ) is the value of energy accepted and its proposed satisfaction.

The frame of an *accept* can therefore be:

("(accept):sender (a_d):receiver (a):content (["reactive"][proposal])")

5. Anticipative Mechanism

This section describes a general solving method for the anticipative mechanism that calculates an energy assignment plan taking into account available forecasts. This mechanism determines the average set-points that are adjusted in real time by the reactive mechanism.

The notion of anticipation has also been used in the field of Artificial Intelligence in different contexts. In the field of Multi-Agent Systems, anticipation is used to build complex adaptive behavior and planning in dynamic environments [Fallah-Seghrouchni *et al.* (2004)]. Rosen (1985) introduced a definition that linked up knowledge of the future and decision-making in the present: "an anticipative system is a system that contains a predictive model of itself and/or its environment enabling it to change its state in relation to predictions about future instants". Anticipation can therefore be divided into two main phases: a prediction phase and a prediction interpretation phase.

Anticipation enables an agent to change its current behavior in relation to predictions. For an agent, this consists in checking the state in which it will find itself and adapting its behavior accordingly.

In the field of energy management, several studies have pointed to the advantage of shifting appliance operation from peak periods to off-peak periods in order to reduce energy costs. Ha (2007) suggests a centralized system for managing energy consumption and production in a building. The proposed system makes it possible to manage different energy activities in the home and to control consumption better by using the degrees of freedom offered by the user and those relating to appliance operation.

Adapted to different time scales, this system has two mechanisms: a prediction/predicted scheduling mechanism and a real time scheduling mechanism. The role of the prediction/predicted scheduling mechanism is to look for long-term scheduling (i.e. based on a day) according to appliance consumption forecasts. It helps the prediction mechanism to set up the short-term assignment plan (i.e. based on a minute).

The drawback of this system is the centralization: the energy assignment plans are set up by collecting all the appliance operation models and all the necessary data. To do this, the models have to be transformed into a set of mixed linear constraints comprising continuous and linear variables. It is difficult to automate such an operation and, because of this, it is difficult to take into account any services that have not been planned in the design of the home automation system. This then limits the possibility of upgrading the system. Furthermore, the centralized approach means that all appliance operation models have to be known, keeping in mind that manufacturers do not always want to supply these for competitive reasons. It is therefore difficult to adapt this approach to real home automation system contexts because it is ill-suited to frequent and varied configurations/reconfigurations. The approach does not allow for an open-ended system where appliances can be added or removed without having to reconfigure the system and without calling into question the overall operation of the optimization algorithm that should be potentially capable of taking on any type of constraint.

In the MAHAS system, the anticipative mechanism, described in this section, schedules energy assignment in the long term according to availability of energy sources and predicted use of appliances. For this, the mechanism uses the flexibility of the services, i.e. the possibility of shifting their operating time (moving it forward or delaying it) or the possibility of modifying the quantities of energy consumed/produced. This anticipative mechanism allows an open-ended system where appliances can be added or removed without having to reconfigure the whole system thanks to the distributed global solving approach.

This mechanism relies on the fact that, on the one hand, some appliances are able to store thermal energy and, on the other hand, some services can be run at varying times. Based on these preliminary observations, we can imagine that if the consumption of all appliances can be planned ahead of time, this will improve organization. For example, for a heating service, it is possible to calculate the duration and quantity of "anticipated" overheating so that consumption can be reduced over a period during which energy is unavailable or limited. Similarly, if a service can be delayed or brought forward, here again overall consumption can be better organized.

The building of an overall predicted energy plan is based on the fact that the energy consumption of services must not exceed the energy production of energy sources. This is why the agent embedded in each service generates all the local plan possibilities (power profiles) using the flexibility of its own service.

By adopting an exhaustive approach, the permanent and temporary agents generate all the power profiles that do not violate their constraints. To calculate an overall predicted energy plan, the different combinations of energy profiles have to be examined: this can be represented by developing a research tree. This type of problem requires considerable calculation resources owing to what home automation systems and, above all, energy management involve. Because of the number of power profiles generated by each agent and the energy assignment zone, the research tree explodes when the number of services increases (exponential complexity).

By analyzing the type of tasks to be found in the home, it is possible to break down the overall problem into sub-problems since, in the home, inhabitants never use all of their appliances at the same time.

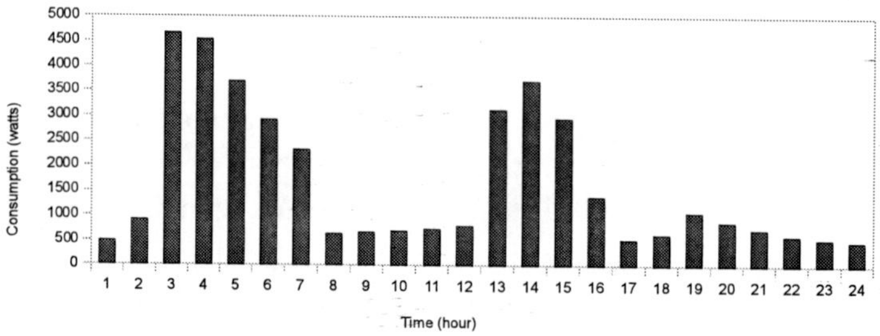

Figure 17. Overall consumption average daily load curve.

The [Sidler (1997-1999)] project involves an experimental study of household electrical appliances with high energy efficiency in a real situation in 98 apartments located in several geographic areas in France. Figure 17 illustrates the overall consumption of the appliances over a complete day for a 140 m^2 apartment in Mercurol [Sidler (1997-1999)]. We can see that the inhabitants of this apartment do not have a permanent stable consumption over the course of the day.

Based on the idea that it is better to "*divide and rule*", the anticipative mechanism solves the problem by dividing it up into independent sub-problems in order to find an acceptable solution to the whole problem.

The main advantage of this method is that the complexity of the overall problem is reduced. The overall solution then depends on the duration of the sub-problems and on the number of services in each sub-problem. When the overall problem is divided up into sub-problems, the complexity of the divided problem is less than that of the overall problem because, on the one hand, each sub-problem does not contain all the services in the home (e.g. use of the vacuum cleaner), and, on the other hand, the duration of a sub-problem is less than or equal to that of the overall problem [Habbas *et al.* (2005)].

In the MAHAS system, we propose to add an agent called the "solving agent" equipped with calculation resources (GLPK has been used). Its role is to facilitate the setting up of an energy consumption and production plan using the local plans produced independently and sent by the agents. This means that it is not necessary to equip all of the agents with substantial calculation resources and, above all, it enables the quantity of information exchanged between agents to be reduced. Unlike the centralized approach, this mixed approach makes it possible to distribute the problem solving: each agent generates its local plans independently based on what it knows while the knowledge embedded in each agent remains confidential. The agents then send their local plans to the solving agent so that it can produce a consumption and production plan using an exact solving method. However, the converging of all of the agents' behavior towards an objective only leads to a good solution and not to an optimal solution like most methods stemming from operational research.

The **main lines** of the overall problem solving, described in what follows, are summarized in the following **procedure**:

```
energy distribution for all services according to the user's wishes;
If (insufficient energy for all periods) then
  | determination of energy requirement violation zones (sub-problems);
  | solving of each sub-problem independently;
  | uniting of sub-problem solutions to obtain an overall solution;
else
  | a satisfactory user solution is found;
end If
```

The problem solving begins with the distribution of energy to the services. This shall be described in the next paragraph.

5.1. Energy Distribution

To identify the overall solution, the energy produced by the sources must first be distributed to all the services (energy consumers) for all the anticipation periods according to the user's wishes.

The temporary agents send a maximum of n power profiles (local plans) to the solving agent. The temporary service end times of these profiles are set according to the user's preferred times. The permanent agents send a maximum of n power profiles to the solving agent. The set-points of these profiles during the permanent service anticipation periods are set according to the user's preferences.

Thus, the energy source agents send the power profiles corresponding to their energy production predictions to the solving agent. They can send zero power profiles corresponding to the user's wish not to spend money.

When the solving agent receives all the agents' profiles, it applies an exact solving method (the Branch and Bound [Lawler et Wood (1966)] has been used) to find a solution to meet all of the system's requirements. If there is enough energy for all the agents and for all periods, the search for a solution is stopped and a solution in line with the user's wishes is obtained. However, if there is not enough energy, sub-problems are identified (§5.2.) then solved (§5.3.). Next, the sub-problem solutions are collected in order to provide an acceptable overall solution to the overall problem.

5.2. Determination of Sub-problem Horizons

The ***time horizon*** of a sub-problem is a set of consecutive periods where the production/consumption constraints are not checked for at least one critical period and during which a certain number of services can change their behavior in order to try to eliminate the critical periods. This time horizon is denoted as $[ib, sb]$ (lower limit, upper limit).

5.2.1. Impact of a Permanent Service

The impact of a permanent service for a given horizon is the time needed by an agent to achieve total satisfaction starting with the critical satisfaction level (the smallest satisfaction value that is acceptable for users).

For example, let us assume that an agent linked to a radiator offers a "heating" service. The impact of this service is the radiator's response time enabling it to reach room temperature starting with the minimum temperature.

5.2.2. Temporary Service Range

The range of a temporary service depends on the end time of the temporary service, its duration and its interruption property (its maximum interruption duration and its minimum interruption duration). The upper limit of the range is equal to the latest service end time: $sb = LET(SRV_i)$ because the service has no more influence after the latest service end time $LET(SRV_i)$. The lower limit of the range is equal to the earliest end time ($EET(SRV_i)$) less the interruption duration ($\Delta_{int_{cum}}$) and the service duration (Δ_i): $ib_{SRV_i} = EET(SRV_i) - \Delta_i - \Delta_{i,int_{cum}}$. The lower limit therefore represents the earliest start time before the service is actually active.

The set of temporary service ranges intersecting a critical period is called the horizon of a temporary service.

In the next paragraph, we shall introduce how to determine a sub-problem's horizon in relation to the temporary service ranges and the impacts of permanent services.

5.2.3. Sub-problem Horizon

To obtain independent sub-problems, the intersection of ranges and service impacts have to be well defined (FIG. 18).

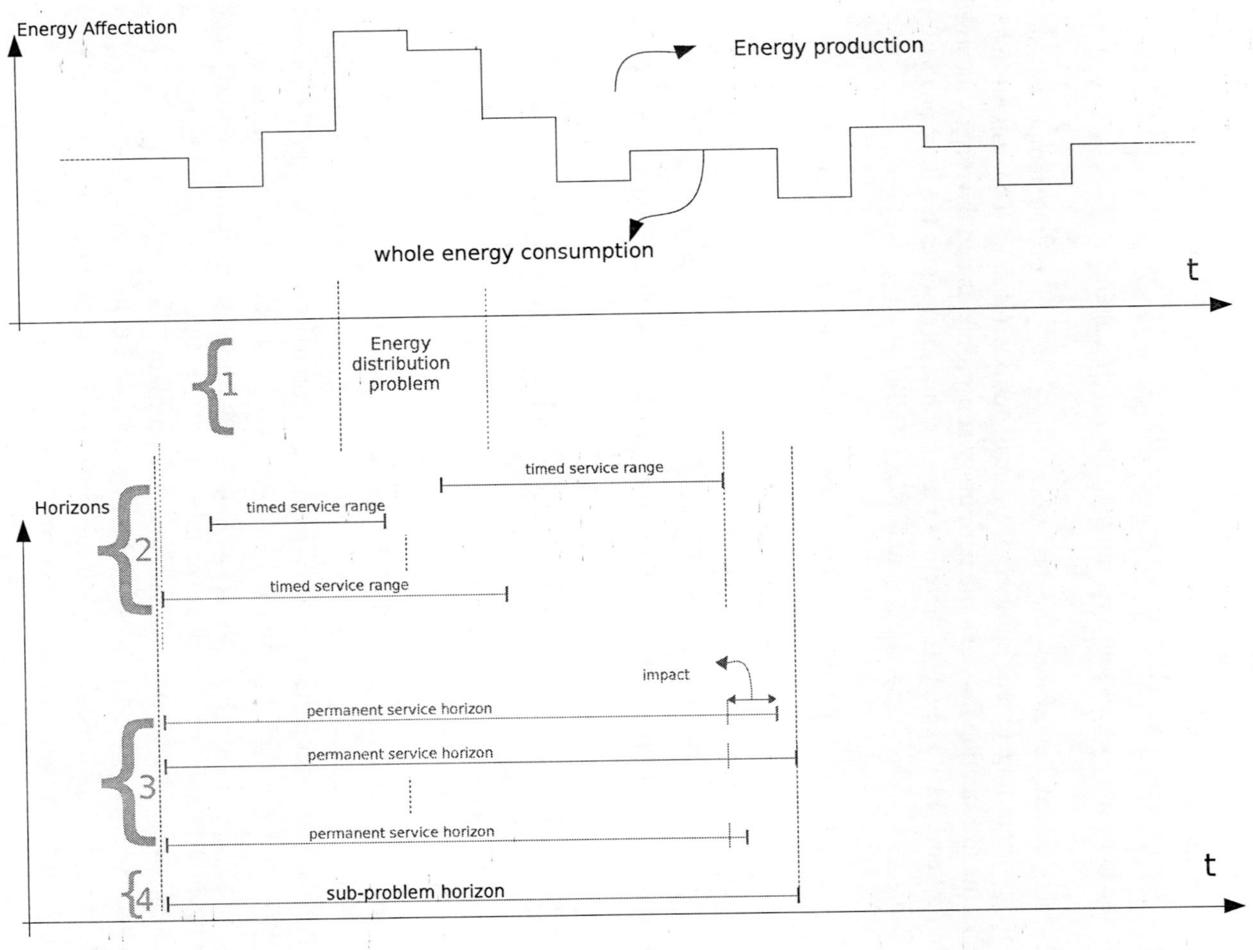

Figure 18. Sub-problem horizon determination.

Sub-problems are determined as follows (FIG. 18):

- calculation of temporary service ranges in relation to the latest service end time and the earliest service start time:
  - a temporary agent creates a range $[ib_{SRV_i} = EET(SRV_i) - \Delta_i - \Delta_{i,int_{cum}}, sb_{SRV_i} = LET(SRV_i)]$ for a service SRV_i.
  - the temporary agent sends its range to the solving agent.
- the solving agent determines the horizons $[ib_{sub_x}, sb_{sub_x}]$ of the temporary sub-problems according to the number of critical periods (§5.1.). The solving agent checks the intersection between the temporary sub-problems and the ranges received from the temporary agents. If there is an intersection, it updates the horizons as follows: $ib_{sub_x} = min(ib_{sub_x}, ib_{SRV_i})$ and $sb_{sub_x} = max(sb_{sub_x}, sb_{SRV_i})$.
- the solving agent sends the updated horizons to the permanent agents in order to calculate their impact:
  - each permanent agent calculates its impact (§5.2.1.) for each sub-problem and sends the horizon ($[ib_{SRV_i}, sb_{SRV_i,imp}]$) to the solving agent.
  - the solving agent updates the horizons as described above: $ib_{sub_x} = min(ib_{sub_x}, ib_{SRV_i})$ and $sb_{sub_x} = max(sb_{sub_x}, sb_{SRV_i,imp})$.
- the solving agent unites two horizons if there is an intersection between them.
- At the end, the solving agent sends the sub-problem horizons to the agents so that they can put forward local plans.

If there are intersections between all the horizons, the overall problem cannot be divided into sub-problems. In this case, it is impossible to reduce the overall problem's complexity.

Adding the impact of a permanent service to a given horizon increases the horizon of a sub-problem. However, this guarantees that there is no more influence on the following periods (quasi-independent sub-problems) as long as the following condition applies: each permanent agent must take into account the set-point at the time of its lower limit when it puts forward proposals for the time horizon of a sub-problem.

Once the overall problem has been broken down into independent sub-problems, an appropriate method is applied to solve each sub-problem. In what follows, we shall propose a solving method for the energy assignment problem.

5.3. Sub-problem Solving

Exact solving methods work on small problems. Large problems, on the other hand, require substantial calculation resources. The current tendency is to combine several solving methods to obtain good results. Bouthilier *et al.* (2005) propose combining a genetic algorithm with tabu search working on the same set of solutions in order to solve a business traveller problem. In [Dahal *et al.* (2006)], a genetic algorithm combined with an exact solving method is put forward to solve the problem of scheduling in an electricity production system. In [Ha (2007)], a combination of a heuristic approach and an exact solving method is suggested for solving the problem of energy consumption scheduling.

Drawing inspiration from these methods, we propose a hybrid approach combining the principles of both: a heuristic approach and an exact solving method. The objective of the heuristic approach is to reduce the complexity of the problem using the specific aspects of the problem in order to divide up the research space into different parts. The exact method then makes it possible to find the best solution for the chosen part. The approach is inspired by **Simulated annealing** [Kirkpatrick *et al.* (1983)].

The heuristic approach proposed uses the notion of neighborhood. In home energy management, the agents cooperate and communicate by sending each other their energy requests in the form of power profiles (part of the shared knowledge). In what follows, we shall present the notion of power profile neighborhood.

Let us first recall the notion of power profile: "A power profile": $\Pi = (P_{i,k}, \ldots, P_{i,k+l})$ where $P_{i,m}$ represents the power consumed/produced (negative/positive) of the service SRV_i over a period stretching from k to $k+l$ where l represents the horizon for solving the energy assignment problem.

5.3.1. Neighborhood of a Temporary Agent Power Profile

The neighborhood of a temporary agent's power profile is linked to temporary service flexibility: the possibility of shifting the operating time of the service. Four neighborhood possibilities can be identified for generating a neighborhood:

- interrupt the service by a single anticipation period if the service so allows.
- reduce the interruption by a single period if the service has already been interrupted.
- bring the service forward by a single anticipation period (specific case where the service is interrupted over the first period).
- delay the service by a single anticipation period (specific case where the service is interrupted over the last period).

Changing a single period makes it possible to gradually guide the solving method towards a solution.

Example: Let the horizon of a sub-problem stretch from period 10 to period 20 where each period is 30 minutes. Let a washing service associated with a washing machine consumes 1500 watts ($P_i = 1500$) over 90 minutes ($\Delta_i = 3 * \Delta_a$). The interruption lasts 30 minutes ($\Delta_{int} = 1 * \Delta_a$) and the user would like the service to end in period 15 ($RET(SRV_i) = 15$). Let us assume that the service can be delayed by 90 minutes ($LET(SRV_i) = 18$) or brought forward by 60 minutes ($RET(SRV_i) = 13$).

The horizon of this service is as follows: $[ib_i, sb_i]$; $sb_i = 18$ and $ib_i = 10$.

The power profile covering instants 13 to 15, without interruption, is as follows (FIG. 19-a): [0,0,0,-1500,-1500,-1500,0,0,0,0,0].

- to bring it forward by one period, periods 13 and 16 are changed with period 13 shifting from -1500 to 0 and period 16 shifting from 0 to -1500: [0, 0, 0, 0, -1500, -1500, -1500, 0, 0, 0, 0] (FIG. 19-b).

- to interrupt the service after its first period, for example, periods 12 and 13 are changed with period 13 shifting from -1500 to 0 and period 12 shifting from 0 to -1500: [0, 0, 0, -1500, 0, -1500, -1500, 0, 0, 0, 0] (FIG. 19-c).

- to delay the service by one period, periods 12 and 15 are changed with period 12 shifting from 0 to -1500 and period 15 shifting from -1500 to 0: [0, 0, -1500, -1500, -1500, 0, 0, 0, 0, 0, 0] (FIG. 19-d).

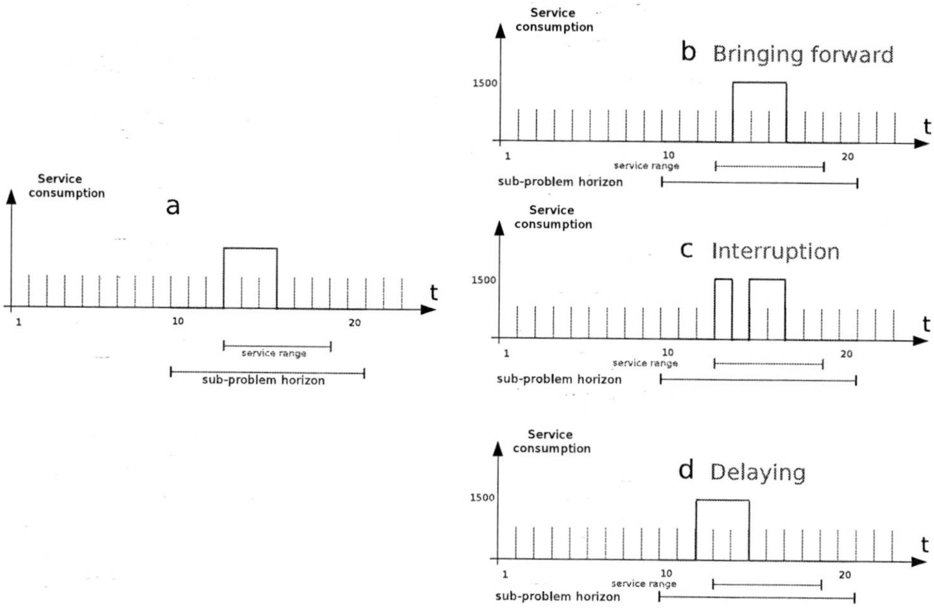

Figure 19. Example of a power profile neighborhoods for a washing service.

Let us take another example, based on the following profile [0, 0, 0, 0, 0, 0, -1500, -1500, -1500, 0, 0], where the service finishes at time 19. The following profile (bringing the service forward by one period) is not acceptable as a neighborhood [0, 0, 0, 0, 0, 0, 0, -1500, -1500, -1500, 0] because the service finishes at time 20 and this is not in line with the service constraints (the end time is at time 19 at the latest)(FIG. 20).

5.3.2. Neighborhood of a Permanent Agent Power Profile

The neighborhood of a power profile for a permanent agent is defined by a modification to the set-point for one of the power profile periods. To begin with, the set-points belong to a discrete value field, but they can belong to a continuous field. The permanent agent can generate a neighborhood as follows:

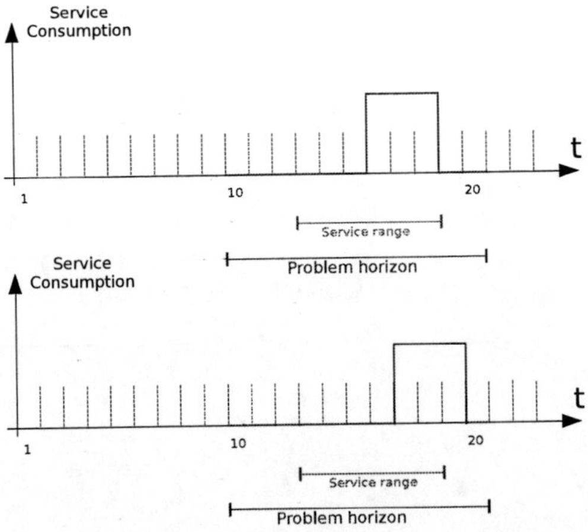

Figure 20. *Example of a power profile neighborhood for a washing service.*

- the permanent agent chooses an anticipation period **at random** from among the periods in its time horizon.
- then, it makes a one step change to this period: either it increases the set-point for the period by one step or it decreases it by one step.

Example: Let us take a radiator in a room where the required temperatures range from 20°C to 23 °C. Let us take a power profile [-400, -400, -500, -550, -350, -400] corresponding to the following set-points: [21°C, 21°C, 22°C, 22.5°C, 20.5°C, 21°C]. By changing the temperature by one step (e.g. from 0.5°C) for the fourth period (FIG. 21), we obtain the following set-points: [21°C, 21°C, 22°C, 22°C, 20.5°C, 21°C]. The radiator agent calculates the corresponding power profile based on the temperature change model(FIG. 21). A power profile neighbor can thus be as follows : [-400, -400, -500, -450, -350, -400].

The following set-point profile [21°C, 21°C, 22°C, 22.5°C, 19.5°C, 21°C] is not acceptable as a neighborhood because the temperature of 19.5°C does not belong to the acceptable temperature field.

We have just described how an agent can generate a neighborhood. This is going to help us to solve a sub-problem

5.3.3. Method for Solving a Sub-problem

A sub-problem is solved by messages (power profiles) being sent between the agents and the solving agent. We suggest an approach based on a combination of two solving methods: an exact solving method (Branch and bound) and a simulated annealing method using the notion of neighborhood. This approach is developed with the aim of adapting it to the management of energy flows in the home.

At the start of the solving operation, all the agents supporting a service generate n power profiles leading to a maximum level of satisfaction. Then, each agent sends its profiles with their satisfaction to the solving agent.

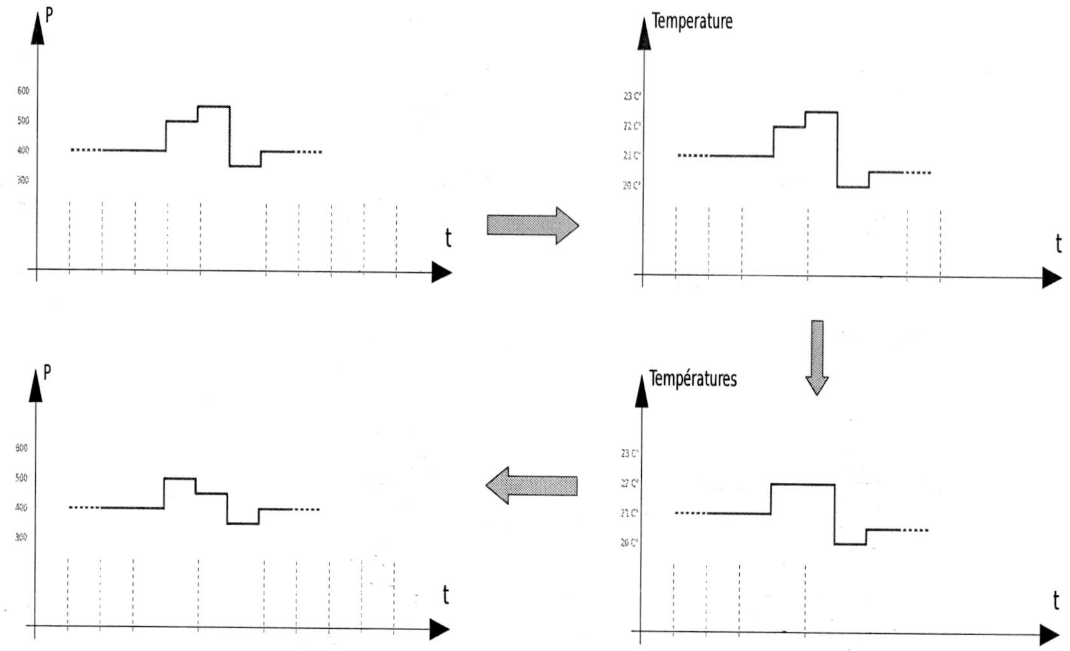

Figure 21. Example of a power profile neighborhood for a heating service.

If no acceptable solution is found during the search phase and after m iterations, the solving agent lowers the overall satisfaction value (initialized at 100%) by one satisfaction step (e.g. 10%). This allows greater flexibility in the generation of power profiles. The search for a solution then starts again for m iterations by generating n power profile neighbors for each agent based on the power profile chosen by the solving agent during the previous iteration and sent to each agent. The search for a solution is then stopped:

- if an acceptable solution is found and the solving agent cannot improve the solution found (during m iterations).
- or if the overall satisfaction is equal to zero: the overall satisfaction does not belong to $[0, 100\%]$, and the local requirements of agents cannot be fulfilled.

Each iteration takes place in two phases:

- **Generation of power profiles**: this solving phase takes place between the service agents and the solving agent where each agent generates n power profile neighbors at random (§5.3.1. and §5.3.2.) based on a power profile sent by the solving agent and selected during the previous iteration for a level of satisfaction greater than or equal to the overall satisfaction.
- **Search for an acceptable solution**: this solving phase takes place in the solving agent. This agent is equipped with a GLPK free solver used to find the best combination of agent profiles (violating energy constraints as little as possible). The solving

agent contains a list that memorizes the best visited combinations of accepted power profiles.

The way the solving agent solving process works is to accept a power profile per agent with each iteration. This is why for each profile and with each iteration the solving agent associates a binary variable $x(\Pi_{i_j})$; $(j \in \{1...n\})$, which is equal to 1 if its profile has been used in the solution. Otherwise, it is equal to 0.

Only one power profile will be selected from among the n profiles for each agent offering a service SRV_i:

$$\forall k \sum_{j=1}^{n} (x(\Pi_{i_j})) = 1$$

where k is the anticipation period number; n is the number of power profiles sent by an agent offering a service SRV_i.

An acceptable solution is found if there is enough energy for the services throughout all the anticipation periods:

$$\forall k \sum_{j=1}^{n} \sum_{i=1}^{I} (\Pi_{i_j})_k \geq 0$$

where $(\Pi_{i_j})_k$ is the consumption or the production during the k^{nth} anticipation period in a profile j sent by the agent offering the service SRV_i. Let us remember that the power profile of agents embedded in energy sources contains a series of positive values while, on the other hand, the agents embedded in appliances (energy consumers) have negative values.

The objective of the solving operation is to maximize agent satisfaction; this means selecting the profile with the highest satisfaction value from among the acceptable profiles:

$$\max \sum_{i=1}^{I} \sum_{j=1}^{n} \sigma_{i,j} * x(\Pi_{i_j})$$

.

The **method** for solving sub-problems is described in ALG. 6 :

Once the sub-problem has been solved, the overall solution is obtained by uniting all the sub-problem solutions. It should be remembered that during anticipation periods that are not part of sub-problems, the service set-points are set according to the user's wishes.

In what follows, we shall present the negotiation protocol organizing the exchange of messages between the agents and the solving agent.

5.4. Negotiation Protocol

Of course, when a sub-problem is being solved, the agents negotiate via messages (FIG. 22). For the anticipative mechanism, the negotiation protocol is broken down into two main phases. The main principles of these are as follows:

- *power profile generation request phase*: during this phase, the solving agent asks the agents to generate power profiles that are neighbors of a profile for a given satisfaction.

```
Π : Profile; [power profile]
S : Solution; [current solution]
S' : Solution; [temporary solution]
OK : Boolean; [solution found?]
σ : Integer; [overall satisfaction]
σ_step : Integer; [satisfaction step]
M : Integer; [number of iterations]
Ł : List; [list of solutions accepted by the solving agent]
OK ← false;
m ← M;
σ ← 1;
While (σ ¿ 0 ) do
    Repeat
        [for agents; J(S')¿J(S)]
        each agent generates n neighbors {Π_i} based on S;
        [for the solving Agent]
          S' ← solvingAgent.PSE(..., Π_i, ...);
        If (∑ Π_S' ≥ 0) then
            OK ← true;
            Ł.add(S');
        end If
        m ← m - 1 ;
        S ← S' ;
    until (m = 0)
    If (OK) then
        break; [acceptable solution is found]
    else
        σ ← σ - σ_step;
        m ← M ;
    end If
done
```

Algorithm 6: *Method for solving a sub-problem*

- *proposal phase*: the agents generate power profiles that are neighbors of the profile received from the solving agent.

5.4.1. Negotiation Primitives

The anticipative mechanism negotiation primitives are:

- Request: the solving agent sends this message to the agents so that they generate power profiles. A *request* can be defined as:

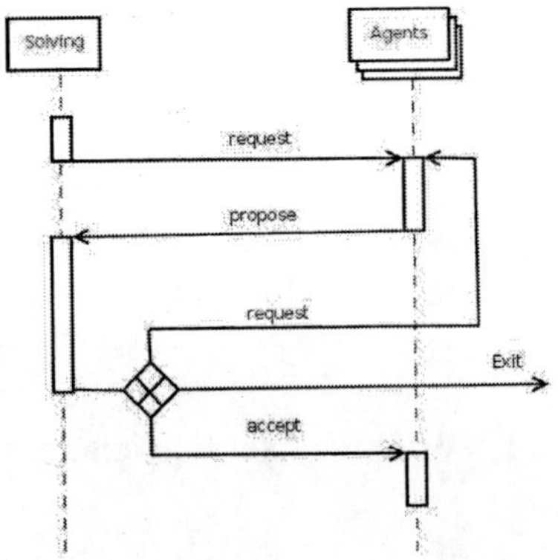

Figure 22. Agent negotiation profile: anticipative mechanism.

```
request(sender, receiver, "anticipative",
sub-problem-horizon, global-satisfaction, profile).
```

The *"receiver"* agents generate neighbors for the *"profile"*. Their satisfaction levels are greater than or equal to *"global-satisfaction"* for the requested sub-problem(*"sub-problem-horizon"*: $[ib_{sub}, sb_{sub}]$) sent by the solving agent *"sender"*.

- Propose: this message is the response to the message *"request"* sent by the solving agent. It contains a single neighbor for the profile and the sub-problem requested. If an agent generates several power profiles, it sends several messages. This message can be defined as:

```
propose(sender, receiver, "anticipative",
sub-problem-horizon, satisfaction, generated-profile).
```

Such that *"generated-profile"* is the generated power profile with the right level of *" satisfaction "* for the requested sub-problem *" sub-problem-horizon "*.

- Accept: this message tells the agents that a solution has been found. The solving agent sends each agent the power profile containing the future set-points for the requested sub-problem. An *"Accept"* can be defined as:

```
accept(sender, receiver, "anticipative",
sub-problem-horizon, accepted-profile).
```

Such that *accepted-profile* is the accepted power profile for the sub-problem *"sub-problem-horizon"*.

5.5. Example

Let us consider a system made up of six appliances and a source of electrical energy (EDF type supply) amounting to $4kW$ for an anticipation period of $\Delta_a = 30$ minutes.

The first appliance, i.e. the "washing machine", will be used twice (FIG. 23):

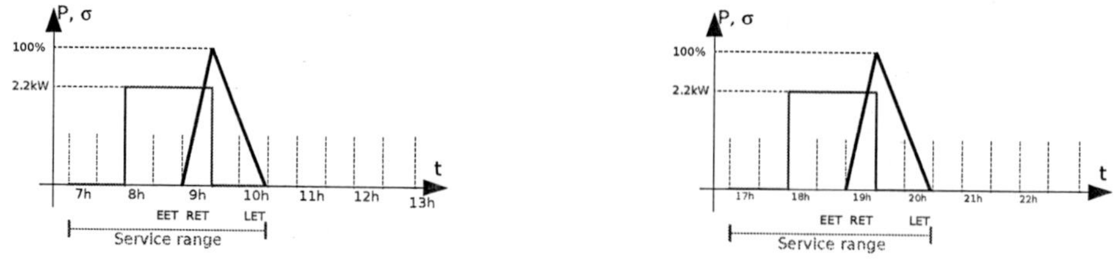

Figure 23. "Washing" service consumption.

- The first *washing* service($SRV_1 = w_1$) offered by the agent linked to the washing machine is characterized by: the requested end time $RET(w_1)$=$9A.M.$, the earliest end time $EET(w_1)$=$8:30AM$ and the latest end time $LET(w_1)$=$10A.M.$, for a power of P_{w_1}=$2.2kW$ during three anticipation periods $\Delta_{w_1} = 3 * \Delta_a$. This service can be interrupted for a single anticipation period $\Delta_{w_1,int_{min}} = 1$, $\Delta_{w_1,int_{max}} = 1$.
- The second washing service ($SRV_2 = w_2$) offered by the agent linked to the washing machine is characterized by: the requested end time $RET(w_2)$=$7P.M.$, the earliest end time $EET(w_2)$=$6:30P.M.$ and the latest end time $LET(w_2)$=$8P.M.$, for a power of P_{w_2}=$2.2kW$ during three anticipation periods $\Delta_{w_2} = 3 * \Delta_a$.

The second appliance, i.e. the "dishwasher", will also be used twice (FIG. 24):

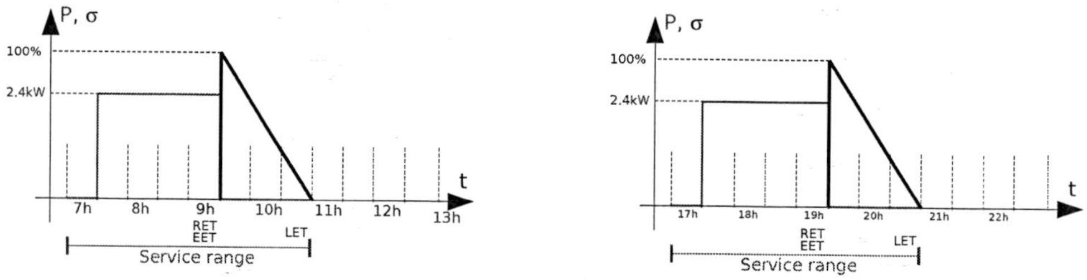

Figure 24. "Dish-washing" service consumption.

- The third *dish-washing* service $SRV_3 = d_1$, offered by the agent linked to the dishwasher is characterized by: the requested end time $RET(d_1)$=$9A.M.$, the earliest end time $EET(d_1)$=$9A.M.$ and the latest end time $LET(d_1)$=$10:30A.M.$, for a power of P_{d_1}=$2.4kW$ during four anticipation periods $\Delta_{d_1} = 4 * \Delta_a$.
- The fourth *dish-washing* service $SRV_4 = d_2$ offered by the agent linked to the dishwasher is characterized by: the requested end time $RET(d_2)$=$7P.M.$, the earliest end time $EET(d_2)$=$7P.M.$ and the latest end time $LET(d_2)$=$8:30P.M$, for a power of P_{d_2}=$2.4kW$ during four anticipation periods $\Delta_{d_2} = 4 * \Delta_a$.

The third appliance, i.e. the "oven", will be used once only (FIG. 25). The *cooking* service $SRV_5 = c$ offered by the agent linked to the oven is characterized by: the requested end time $RET(c)$=11$A.M.$, the earliest end time $EET(c)$=9$A.M.$, and the latest end time $LET(c)$=12h00, for a power of P_c=1.5kW during a single anticipation period $\Delta_w = \Delta_a$.

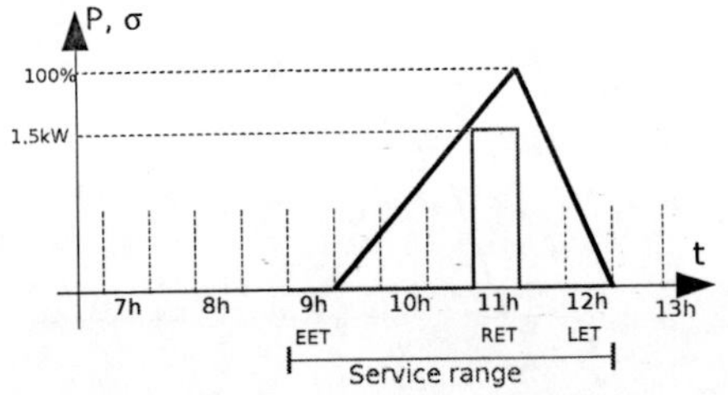

Figure 25. "Cooking" service consumption.

The fourth appliance, i.e. the "vacuum cleaner", will be used once only (FIG. 26). The *cleaning* service $SRV_6 = cl$ offered by the agent linked to the vacuum cleaner is characterized by: the requested end time $RET(cl)$=9$P.M.$, the earliest end time $EET(cl)$=7$P.M.$ and the latest end time $LET(cl)$=22h00, for a power of P_v=1.5kW during a single anticipation period $\Delta_{cl} = \Delta_a$.

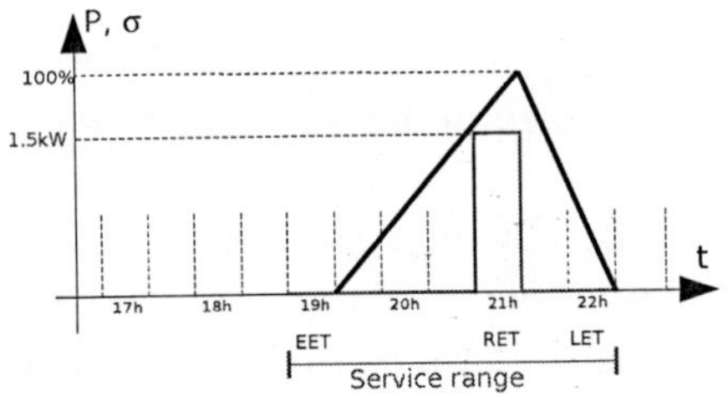

Figure 26. "Cleaning" service consumption.

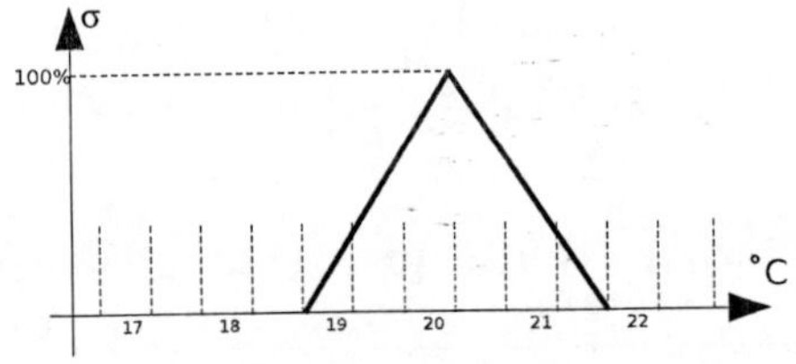

Figure 27. Satisfaction function of the "heating" service $SRV_7 = h$.

The fifth appliance is a radiator in a living room. The *heating* service $SRV_7 = h$ is characterized by: $T_{min,h}$=18.5, $T_{opt,h}$=20.5, $T_{max,h}$=21.5, $P_h = 1.5kW$. The satisfaction function of the *heating* service $SRV_7 = hh$ is illustrated in figure 27. The model for temperature changes in the living room can be characterized by a dynamic behavior model written in the form of differential equations [N. Mendes et de Araújo (2001)]: $T_{h,k+1} = e^{(-1800)} T_{h,k}$ $+40(1 - e^{-1800}) P_{h,k}$ $+(1 - e^{-1800}) \times 10$.

The sixth appliance is a radiator in a bedroom. The *heating* service $SRV_8 = cc$ is characterized by: $T_{min,hh}$=18, $T_{opt,hh}$=19, $T_{max,hh}$=20, $P_{hh} = 1.5kW$. The satisfaction function of the *heating* service $SRV_8 = hh$ is illustrated in figure 28. The model for temperature changes in the bedroom is identical to that of the living room.

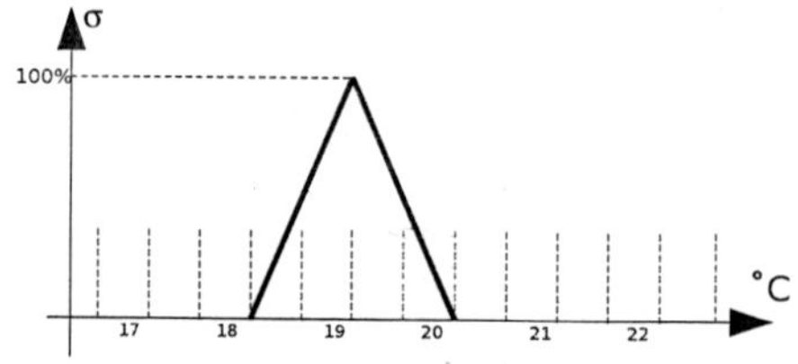

Figure 28. Satisfaction function of the "heating" service service $SRV_8 = cc$.

In this example, the source agent sends its maximum power (FIG. 29).

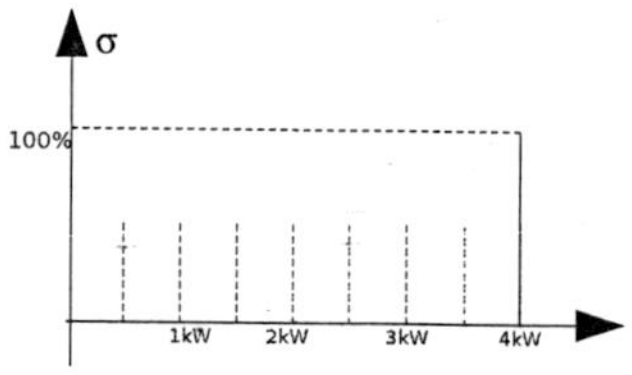

Figure 29. Satisfaction function of power grid source.

As already mentioned, the search for a solution begins with the initialization of the services at their requested end time and at their preferred temperature (§5.1.).

The agent linked to the living room radiator uses the temperature change model, described above, in order to calculate the power profile corresponding to the following set-points $[20.5°C, 20.5°C, \ldots, 20.5°C]$ for the time horizon [7, 23] (table 4).

The agent linked to the bedroom radiator uses the temperature change model, described above, in order to calculate the power profile corresponding to the following set-points $[19°C, 19°C, \ldots, 19°C]$ for the time horizon [7, 23] (table 4).

Table 4 represents the energy profiles requested during energy distribution.

Table 4. Power profiles during energy distribution.

Agent	Service	Service range	Power profile
$agent - w_1$	washing: w_1	[7,10]	[0 0 -2200 -2200 -2200 0 0]
$agent - d_1$	dish-washing : d_1	[7,10.30]	[0 -2400 -2400 -2400 -2400 0 0 0]
$agent - c$	cooking: c	[9,12]	[0 0 0 0 -1500 0 0]
$agent - w_2$	washing: w_2	[17,20]	[0 0 -2200 -2200 -2200 0 0]
$agent - d_2$	dish-washing: d_2	[17,20.30]	[0 -2400 -2400 -2400 -2400 0 0 0]
$agent - cl$	cleaning: cl	[19,22]	[0 0 0 0 -1500 0 0]
$agent - h$	heating: h	[7,23]	[-500 -500 ... -500]
$agent - hh$	heating: hh	[7,23]	[-350 -350 ... -350]
$agent - edf$	production: edf	[0,24]	[4000 4000 ... 4000]

After the energy has been distributed to the services, the solving agent sees that the energy consumption exceeds the energy available over several periods (keeping in mind that the energy source sends its maximum power to the solving agent). The first critical zone appears in the $7:30AM$ - $9A.M.$ periods, followed by the $5:30P.M.$ and $7P.M.$ periods.

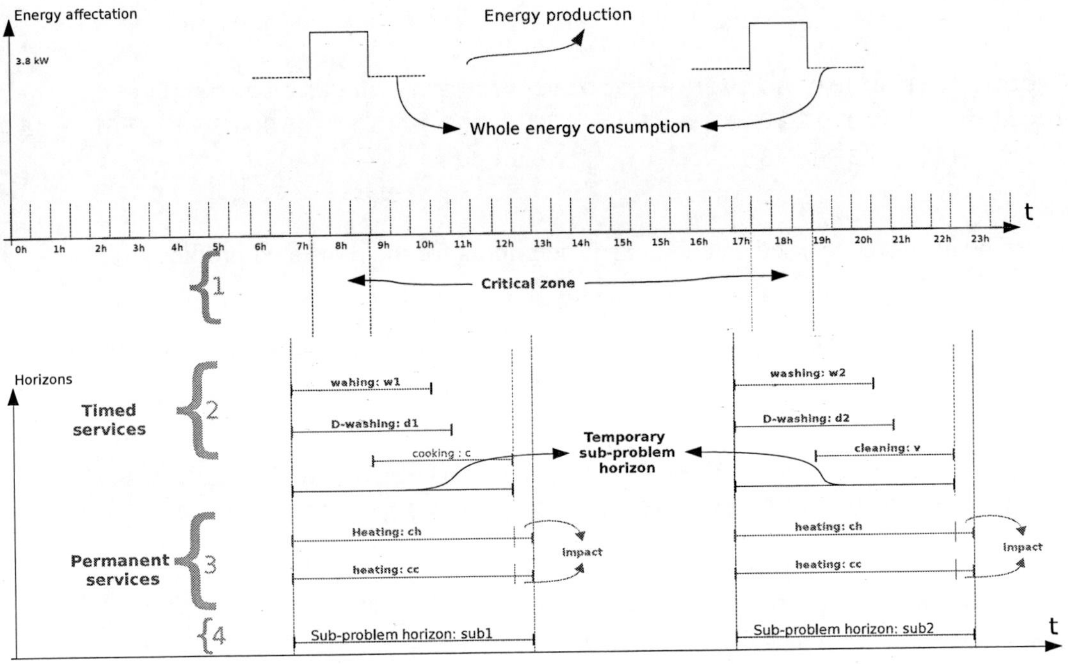

Figure 30. Determination of sub-problem horizons.

Instead of solving the overall problem of 8 services during 48 anticipation periods (a complete day), the problem is broken down into sub-problems. By applying the sub-problem horizon determination method (§5.2.), two sub-problems are obtained (FIG. 30). The first sub-problem involves services w_1, d_1, c, h and hh during 9 anticipation periods for the time horizon $[7A.M., 12:30P.M.]$. The second sub-problem involves services w_2, d_2, cl, h, hh during 9 anticipation periods for the time horizon $[5P.M., 10:P.M.]$.

The solving operation begins with the solving agent dispatching messages to the agents asking them to generate power profile neighbors (in this example $m = 6$: the number of neighbors per agent). To solve the first sub-problem for the $[7A.M., 12:30P.M.]$ horizon, the solving agent begins by sending the following messages to the agents concerned:

```
request:sender solving:receiver agent-w1:anticipative
content 0700 1230 80 0 0 -2200 -2200 -2200 0 0 0 0 0 0 0
```

The solving agent asks agent $-w_1$ to generate energy profiles for the $[7A.M., 12:30P.M.]$ horizon for an overall satisfaction of 80%.

```
request:sender solving:receiver agent-d1:anticipative
content 0700 1230 80 0 -2400 -2400 -2400 -2400 0 0 0 0 0
0 0
```

```
request:sender solving:receiver agent-c:anticipative content
0700 1230 80 0 0 0 0 0 0 0 0 -1500 0 0 0
```

```
request:sender solving:receiver agent-h:anticipative content
0700 1230 80 -500 -500 -500 -500 -500 -500 -500 -500 -500
-500 -500 -500
```

```
request:sender solving:receiver agent-hh:anticipative
content 0700 1230 80 -350 -350 -350 -350 -350 -350 -350 -350
-350 -350 -350 -350
```

The agents concerned calculate their neighbors for the requested profiles.

For example, the agent linked to w_1 can generate six power profiles because the run time of this service can be shifted and it is possible to interrupt it.

```
propose:sender agent-w1:receiver solving:anticipative
content 0700 1230 80 0 0 0 -2200 -2200 -2200 0 0 0 0 0 0
```

```
propose:sender agent-w1:receiver solving:anticipative
content 0700 1230 80 0 -2200 -2200 -2200 0 0 0 0 0 0 0 0
```

```
propose:sender agent-w1:receiver solving:anticipative
content 0700 1230 80 0 -2200 0 -2200 -2200 0 0 0 0 0 0 0
```

```
propose:sender agent-w1:receiver solving:anticipative
content 0700 1230 80 0 0 -2200 0 -2200 -2200 0 0 0 0 0 0
```

```
propose:sender agent-w1:receiver solving:anticipative
content 0700 1230 80 0 -2200 -2200 0 -2200 0 0 0 0 0 0 0
```

```
propose:sender agent-w1:receiver solving:anticipative
content 0700 1230 80 0 0 -2200 -2200 0 -2200 0 0 0 0 0 0
```

Let us take another service, e.g. the agent linked to the h service calculates the temperature profile corresponding to the power profile received from the solving agent. It makes a change of one temperature step for a period chosen at random. Then, it calculates the power profiles corresponding to the temperature profiles using the service change model. The table 5 shows the temperature profiles generated and their corresponding power profiles.

Table 5. Power/temperature profile neighbors for the heating service.

II	σ												
w	100	500	500	500	500	500	500	500	500	500	500	500	500
$°C$	100	20.5	20.5	20.5	20.5	20.5	20.5	20.5	20.5	20.5	20.5	20.5	20.5
$°C_1$	88	20.5	20.5	20.5	20.5	20.5	**21**	20.5	20.5	20.5	20.5	20.5	20.5
w_1	88	500	500	500	500	500	700	400	500	500	500	500	500
$°C_2$	88	20.5	20.5	20.5	20.5	20.5	20.5	**20**	20.5	20.5	20.5	20.5	20.5
w_2	88	500	500	500	500	500	500	400	650	500	500	500	500
$°C_3$	88	20.5	20.5	**20**	20.5	20.5	20.5	20.5	20.5	20.5	20.5	20.5	20.5
w_3	88	500	500	400	650	500	500	500	500	500	500	500	500
$°C_4$	88	20.5	20.5	20.5	20.5	20.5	20.5	20.5	20.5	**20**	20.5	20.5	20.5
w_4	88	500	500	500	500	500	500	500	500	400	650	500	500
$°C_5$	88	20.5	20.5	20.5	20.5	20.5	20.5	20.5	20.5	20.5	20.5	**21**	20.5
w_5	88	500	500	500	500	500	500	500	500	500	500	700	400
$°C_6$	88	20.5	**20**	20.5	20.5	20.5	20.5	20.5	20.5	20.5	20.5	20.5	20.5
w_6	88	500	400	650	500	500	500	500	500	500	500	500	500

The agent linked to the h service sends these power profiles to the solving agent.

When the solving agent receives all the power profiles from the agents, it applies the branch and bound to look for a solution that violates the energy constraints as little as possible. Then, it sends the power profiles for this solution again so that the neighbors can be calculated and so on.

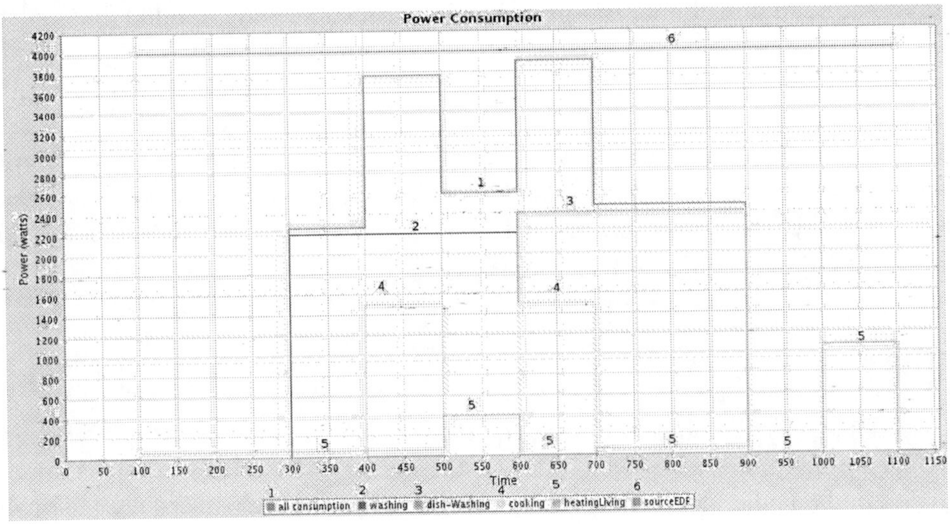

Figure 31. Consumption and production plan.

Figure 31 shows an energy consumption and production plan for the first sub-problem where the energy consumption does not exceed the production. This solution is obtained, via negotiation with the agents, using the flexibility of the services: by bringing forward the operating time of the washing machine by two anticipation periods and by delaying the dishwasher by three anticipation periods.

The temperature maintained in the living room is roughly the temperature requested by the user where the agent linked to the living room radiator tries to increase its temperature with the aim of increasing its satisfaction level, when there is more energy available (the last three periods, FIG. 32).

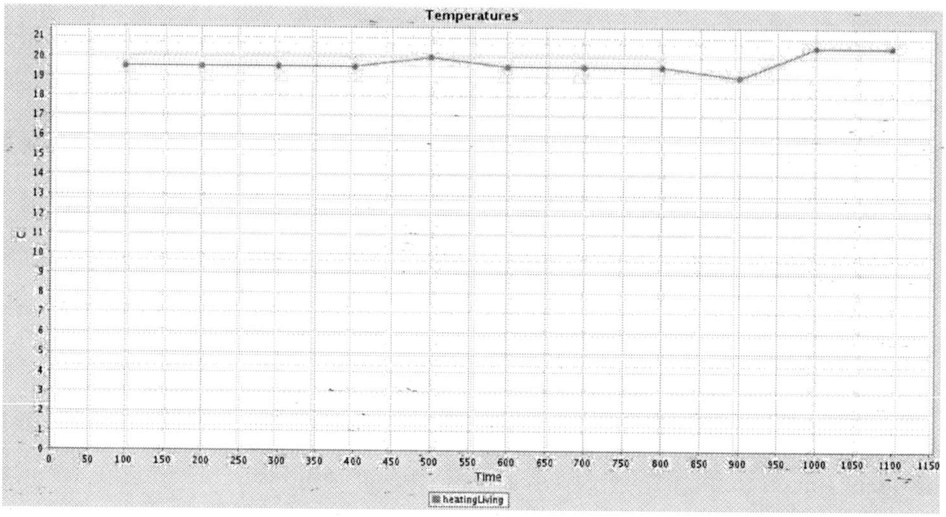

Figure 32. Temperature set-points for the living room radiator.

The second sub-problem can also be solved in the same way. Then, an overall solution containing the solutions of both sub-problems is obtained keeping in mind that, outside of the horizons of the two sub-problems, the service set-points are set to the required values.

Let us now assume that the control system in the apartment is a conventional load-shedding system. When the washing machine and dishwasher are switched on, the load-shedding relay switches off both radiators because the user has defined a higher priority for the two machines compared with the radiators. This causes a drop in temperature, leading to user dissatisfaction. However, a satisfactory solution is found using the anticipative mechanism and the flexibility of the services.

6. Results

In this section, we shall compare the anticipative mechanism with the prediction/predicted scheduling system proposed by Ha (2007) for the management of energy consumption and production in the home. The criteria used to compare these mechanisms are the quality of the solution, linked to the satisfaction function, and the operating time.

Our assessment is based on thirty different examples generated at random for both mechanisms.

We shall begin by comparing the two mechanisms using the first sub-problem in the previous example (5.5.). In figure 33, we can see that the satisfaction of the best solution obtained is 75% for the distributed mechanism proposed and 82% for the centralized system. We can also see that the search for a solution takes more time (35% extra) for the mechanism proposed in relation to the centralized system.

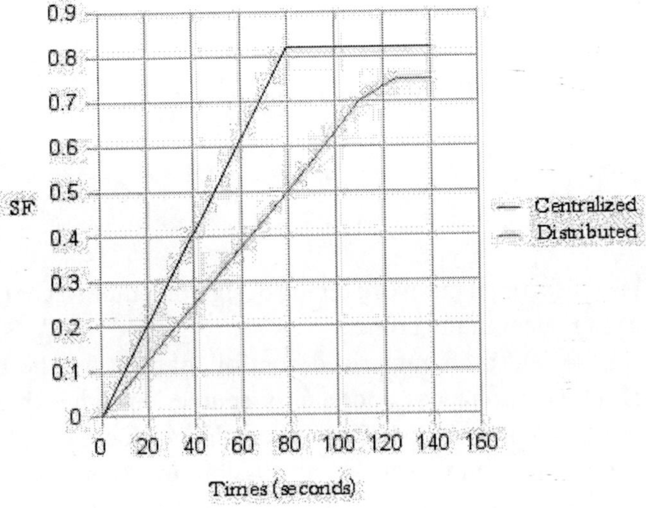

Figure 33. Comparison of the proposed mechanism and the centralized prediction/predicted scheduling mechanism.

Out of the 30 examples, the distributed mechanism produces a 40 s to 120 s greater run time than the centralized mechanism. The quality of the solution obtained is lower by 5% to 20% compared with the centralized mechanism.

Several factors explain these differences:

- satisfaction function: the centralized mechanism looks for the optimum solution unlike the proposed mechanism that aims at an acceptable solution.
- the difference in run time is due to the time needed to send/receive messages so that each agent can analyze and respond to a message.

We can see that the performance of the centralized system is better than that obtained with the proposed distributed system. However, as far as real implementation is concerned, the distributed system based on Multi-Agent System techniques does offer some considerable advantages over the centralized approach:

- it is difficult to adapt the centralized approach to real home automation contexts as this approach is not suitable for frequent and varied configurations/reconfigurations. This means that it is not possible to have an open-ended system unlike with the distributed system where appliances can be added or removed without having to reconfigure the system and without penalizing the overall running of the optimization algorithm that has to be potentially capable of taking on board all kinds of requirements.
- the distributed system based on MAS techniques allows for extendability: new types of appliances can be added to the system without it being necessary to entirely reconfigure it. On the other hand, with the centralized system, the optimization algorithms must be changed to take into account new appliances:

- the distributed system adapts to the type of home automation system via:
  - the physical distribution of different types of energy consumers such as the oven, the washing machine, the radiator, etc.
  - the physical distribution of energy sources such as solar panels, generator sets, fuel cells, etc.

7. Conclusion

In this chapter, we have described our work on the design of a multi-agent home automation system for power management in the home.

The objective was to find a computerized control solution for the home energy system made up of household appliances and energy sources, whether these be remote (via the national electricity transmission/distribution network) or local (e.g. solar panels, wind turbines and fuel cells). This solution makes it possible to dynamically set up an energy production and consumption policy while taking into account user criteria, the various constraints relating to appliances and the availability of energy sources.

Owing to the number and diversity of stakeholders in the home, we have opted for solutions fostering modularity. The need for structural self-adaptation, or more technically the need for plug-and-play appliance, led us to the Multi-Agent paradigm enabling a minimum amount of information to be shared between modules and asynchronous operation to be possible via message exchanges. Indeed, a home automation system must be open-ended and extendible: it must be possible to add or remove appliances (or new types of appliances) at any time without calling into question the overall operation of the system.

Given the broad range of appliances and the swift changes to technology, which have a direct influence on behavior, we defined the notion of ***service*** as the grouped operation of different appliances. A service can be a permanent service or a temporary service. A ***permanent service*** is characterized by a quantity of energy consumed or produced. Its energy activities (consumption and production) impact the entire horizon of an energy resource assignment plan. A ***temporary service*** is temporally characterized by the duration and required run time. Its energy activities are linked to a horizon that is included in the horizon of the energy resource assignment plan of the overall problem. For both types of service, there is a distinction between interruptible, time-changeable and modifiable services. Some services are predictable, either based on weather information or user programming or even via self-adaptation to user habits.

We identified two groups of behavior models corresponding to two types of services: a group of dynamic models and a group of finite-state machine models. Dynamic models can be used to describe continuous changes to appliances such as radiators. Finite-state machine models can be used to describe the temporary changes to appliances operating in stages.

In home automation, "user comfort" is one of the most important aspects to be taken into account. The notion of comfort is too abstract to be directly quantified. This is why we translated it into satisfaction functions. Comfort is a feeling while satisfaction is a state. A satisfaction function characterizes the user's perception as to the quality of a service. We defined satisfaction functions for both appliances and energy sources.

Based on the identification of these two types of services, as well as on the satisfaction functions, we modeled the system agents. These agents control the appliances, but also the energy production sources, while cooperating in order to solve a given problem. Two types of knowledge were identified from these points: private knowledge and shared knowledge. Private knowledge contains all data that cannot be generally formalized. It includes behavior models as well as satisfaction functions because these are not common to all agents. On the other hand, shared knowledge contains the data exchanged between agents that can be formalized in a standard manner.

In this chapter, we have also described the architecture of the multi-agent home automation system; it adapts to different time scales and is made up of a reactive mechanism and an anticipative mechanism. The ***reactive mechanism*** makes it possible to respond to unscheduled events and to prevent services from being entirely interrupted in line with energy requirements and taking into account user wishes. It works with real magnitudes over short periods (of around one minute). We noted that "intelligent" load-shedding via agents guarantees a good level of user satisfaction based on appliance flexibility. The ***anticipative mechanism*** calculates an energy assignment plan taking into account available operating forecasts. This mechanism determines average set-points that are then adjusted in real time by the reactive mechanism. The anticipative mechanism works over long periods (of roughly one hour). A hybrid approach was put forward. This combines both methods: a metaheuristic method and an exact method. The aim of the metaheuristic method is to reduce the complexity of a given problem by breaking down the research space into parts. The exact method is then used to identify the best solution for the chosen part. The proposed architecture makes it possible to tackle the phenomena described using different time scales; a solution integrating all the information available at different levels of abstraction can then be built.

References

`http://jade.tilab.com/`. JADE.

`http://pypi.python.org/pypi/spyse/0.1`. The Spyse agent platform.

`http://www.aosgrp.com/products/jack/index.html`. JACK.

A. L. BOUTHILIER, T. CRAINIC et P. KROPF : A guided cooperative search for the vehicle routing problem with time windows. *IEEE Intelligent Systems*, 20(4):pages 36–42, 2005.

J. L. CROWLEY : Situation models for observing human activity. *ACM Queue Magazine*, 2006.

K. P. DAHAL, C. J. ALDRIDGE et S. J. GALLOWAY : Evolutionary hybrid approaches for generation sceduling in power systems. *European Journal of Operation Research*, InPress, 2006.

A. E. FALLAH-SEGHROUCHNI, I. D. CARTAULT et F. MARC : Modelling, control and validation of multi-agent plans in dynamic context. *In AAMAS '04: Proceedings of the*

Third International Joint Conference on Autonomous Agents and Multiagent Systems, p. 44–51, Washington, DC, USA, 2004. IEEE Computer Society. ISBN 1-58113-864-4.

FIPA : Fipa acl message stucture specification. *In FIPA TC Communication*, Doc n SC00061G, 2003a.

FIPA : Fipa communicative act library specification. *In FIPA TC Communication*, Doc n SC00037J, 2003b.

M. FRIEDEWALD, O. COSTA, Y. PUNIE, P. et S. HEINONEN : Perspectives of ambient intelligence in the home environment. *Telemat. Inf.*, 22(3):221–238, 2005. ISSN 0736-5853.

A. GÁRATE, N. HERRASTI et A. LÓPEZ : Genio: an ambient intelligence application in home automation and entertainment environment. *In Proceedings of the 2005 joint conference on Smart objects and ambient intelligence*, p. 241–245, New York, NY, USA, 2005. ACM Press. ISBN 1595933042.

D. L. HA : *Un systme avanc de gestion d'nergie dans le btiment pour coordonner production et consommation.* Thèse de doctorat, Institut Polytechnique de Grenoble, 19 septembre 2007.

Z. HABBAS, M. KRAJECKI et D. SINGER : Decomposition techniques for parallel resolution of constraint satisfaction problems in shared memory: a comparative study. *International Journal of Computational Science and Engineering (IJCSE)*, 1(2):192–206, 2005.

M. HELLENSCHMIDT et T. KIRSTE : A generic topology for ambient intelligence. *In EUSAI*, p. 112–123, 2004.

J. M. HOUSE et T. F. SMITH : Optimal control of building and hvac systems. *In Proceddings of the American Control Conference, Seattle, Washington*, 1995.

J. KAMPF et D. ROBINSON : A simplified thermal model to support analysis of urban resource flows. *Energy and Building*, InPress, 2006.

S. KIRKPATRICK, C. D. GELATT, JR. et M. P. VECCHI : Optimization by simulated annealing. *Science*, 220:671–680, 1983.

T. LASHINA : Intelligent bathroom. *In* -, Eindhoven, Netherlands, 2004.

E. L. LAWLER et D. E. WOOD : Branch-and-bound methods: A survey. *Operations Research*, 14(4):699–719, 1966.

X. LE, M. D. MASCOLO, A. GOUIN et N. NOURY : Health smart home - towards an assistant tool for automatic assessment of the dependence of elders. *Conf Proc IEEE Eng Med Biol Soc*, 1, 2007.

P. LUCIDARME, O. SIMONIN et A. LIÉGEOIS : Implementation and evaluation of a satisfaction/altruism based architecture for multi-robot systems. *In Proceedings of the 2002 IEEE International Conference on Robotics and Automation*, p. 1007–1012, Washington, USA, 1-5 August 2002.

P. MATHIEU et M. H. VERRONS : Three different kinds of negotiation applications achieved with GeNCA. *In Proceedings of the International Conference on Advances in Intelligent Systems - Theory and Applications (AISTA) In cooperation with the IEEE Computer Society*, Centre de Recherche Public Henri Tudor, Luxembourg-Kirchberg, Luxembourg, 15-18 novembre 2004.

M. MUSELLI, G. NOTTON, P. POGGI et A. LOUCHE : Pv-hybrid power system sizing incorporating battery storage: an analysis via simulation calculations. *Renewable Energy*, 20:1–7, 2000.

G. O. N. MENDES et H. de ARAÚJO : Building thermal performance analysis by using matlab/simulink. *In Seventh International IBPSA Conference*, Rio de Janeiro, Brazil, August 13-15 2001.

P. PALENSKY et R. POSTA : Demand side management in private home using lonworks. *In Proceedings.1997 IEEE International Workshop on Factory Communication Systems*, 1997.

R. ROSEN : Anticipatory systems - philosophical, mathematical and methodological foundations. *In Pergamon Press*, New York, USA, 1985.

O. SIDLER : `http://www.isr.uc.pt/ remodece/database/`. Residential Monitoring to Decrease Energy Use and Carbon Emissions in Europe, 1997-1999.

O. SIMONIN : *Le modèle satisfaction-altruisme : coopération et résolution de conflits entre agent situés réactifs, application à la robotique*. Thèse de doctorat, Université Montpellier II, 2001.

R. G. SMITH : The contract net protocol: High-level communication and control in a distributed problem solver. *IEEE Transaction on Computers*, C-29(12):1104–1113, december 1980.

K. STUM, R. MOSIER et T. HAASL : Energy management systems. Rap. tech., Porland Energy Conservation Inc.(PECI), 1997.

J. M. VIDAL, P. A. BUHLER et M. N. HUHNS : Inside an agent. *IEEE Internet Computing*, 5(1):82–86, jan - feb 2001.

K. WACKS : Utility load management using home automation. *IEEE transaction on Consumer Electronics*, 37:168–174, May 1991.

K. WACKS : The impact of home automation on power electronics. *In Applied Power Electronics Conference and Exposition*, p. 3 – 9, 1993.

M. WEISER : The computer for the 21st century. *In Human-computer interaction: toward the year 2000*, p. 933–940, San Francisco, CA, USA, 1995. Morgan Kaufmann Publishers Inc. ISBN 1-55860-246-1.

J. YANG, R. HAVALDAR, V. HONAVAR, L. MILLER et J. WONG : Coordination of distributed knowledge networks using contract net protocol. *IEEE Information Technology Conference, Syracuse, NY*, -, 1998.

G. ZHOU et M. KRARTI : Parametric analysis of active and passive building thermal storage utilization. *Journal of Solar Energy Engineering*, 127:37–46, 2005.

In: Housing, Housing Costs and Mortgages ISBN 978-1-60741-813-9
Editors: Szilárd Kis and Istvan Balogh, pp. 243-253

Chapter 13

A STRUCTURAL CHANGE IN MORTGAGE PORTFOLIOS

K. Rappl* and T. Nittner†
UBS AG, Firmwide Risk Aggregation, Pelikanstr. 6/8,
P.O. Box, CH–8098 Zurich, Switzerland.

Abstract

During the recent financial crisis default rates in the US mortgage business reached unprecedented levels. Apart from huge write–downs, losses and bankruptcies, this had serious implications, primarily on the assessment and quantification of risks. We consider the Swiss mortgage market with its financial behavior and develop a scenario regarding future default rates. Based on bankruptcy rates at hand, we investigate to what extent increasing default rates affect default correlation and thus, statistical measures of credit portfolio loss distributions. Empirical bankruptcy rate time series are analyzed, translated into default rates and compared to the results arising from our scenario. The impact is analyzed using a simple estimator for default correlation.

1. Introduction

During the recent financial crisis default rates in the US mortgage business reached unprecedented levels. Subsequently mortgage brokers and banks were faced with huge unexpected losses when their clients failed to meet their financial obligations. One of the economic drivers is that the behavior of the market participants has changed considerably. On the supply side for example mortgages were provided under the assumption that expected house price increases would be realized almost for sure. Also the standards for the required affordability have been relaxed. As a consequence for the demand side, many households underestimated or ignored the financial risks when raising a mortgage.

Quantitative risk models are usually calibrated to historical data. These models failed to capture the significant increase of financial risk during the sub prime turmoil. One important lesson is that risk models, in order to represent potential losses in a realistic manner

*E-mail address: karl.rappl@ubs.com
†E-mail address: thomas.nittner@ubs.com

need to consider potential structural breaks in a forward looking way. However historical information remains the most important source to empirically calibrate financial risk models.

We want to demonstrate by means of an example scenario how to amend the historical calibration of default correlation in mortgage markets in order to account for potential future structural breaks. Default correlation is among other inputs like recovery rates and default probabilities one of the major inputs for credit portfolio models.

We have chosen the Swiss market of private mortgages because it represents a risk concentration for all major Swiss banks. Thus, Swiss banks are heavily exposed to Swiss macroeconomic risks and in particular to the Swiss mortgage market. Even though Swiss lending standards are high and an immediate deterioration is not expected problems could arise in the mid to long time horizon. We assume that a mix of demographic development, changes in the financing behavior and a deteriorating economic environment could lead to a dramatic price decline in the Swiss real estate market and subsequently to an increase of default rates in the Swiss economy. Subsequently, we demonstrate an approach to integrate such a scenario in the calibration of default correlation.

2. A Potential Structural Break in the Swiss Real Estate Market

For Swiss banks the Swiss business cycle and the domestic mortgage market represent a huge risk concentration. Mortgages represent 23% of the overall balance sheet of Swiss banks; for Cantonal banks even 59% of their assets are related to mortgages, cf. [SNB], A12, A13. Currently the Swiss real estate market is relatively healthy. There is the risk that the demand declines due to the US sub prime crisis and the subsequent global recession. Expected profits and household income decrease and dampen consumer demand. The demand for owner occupied real estate could decrease and put pressure on real estate prices. Beyond these classic interdependencies there are some economic changes which might impact the development of the Swiss real estate market.

The demand for rental apartments, owner occupied apartments and single family homes has been supported by the immigration from EU countries into Switzerland. These immigrants are highly qualified and therefore have a high affordability of own real estate. Net immigration peaked in 2008. This kind of immigration is new to Switzerland and its development during the crisis is open.

The recession following the US sub prime crisis might dampen the immigration into Switzerland. The majority of immigrants come from EU and EFTA countries. They can draw unemployment subsidies in case they lose their job. Given that also EU is undergoing a recession it is likely that many immigrants will stay in Switzerland throughout the recession and return with a time lag when EU economy recovers.

In the last decade, the financing behavior in the Swiss mortgage market has changed. Pension savings which are mandatory can be drawn to finance the purchase of an owner occupied condominium or single family house. This option together with the favorable development of household income has supported the demand for owner occupied real estate. When people reach retirement they might often want to sell the house or apartment and search for example a smaller apartment instead of a single family home. Within 2 years after the sale the household has the option to keep the drawn amount reserved for a succeeding real estate purchase. After these two years the amount has to be paid back, cf. [EFD]. Obviously there is the risk that the single family house or large apartment can only be sold with a discount and that an appropriate smaller apartment is expensive because real estate prices in urban locations remain high. Consequently prices for single family houses in rural areas would decline and those for small apartments in agglomerations–suitable for senior people–would increase. The household's affordability of real estate might be stressed at the transition from professional life to retirement. If the returns from the sale were not sufficient to cover the pension pay back or the purchase of a new more appropriate home the household would be faced with a financing gap. This might put further pressure on real estate prices and lead to problems in the Swiss market for private mortgages overall. Over the coming years more and more people will retire. According to the population scenarios of the Swiss Federal Statistical Office the ratio between the people of the age 65 years and more versus the working population (of the age between 20 and 64 years) will steadily increase from 25% in 2004 and reach 51% until 2050, [SFSO], p. 6.

Such a scenario develops itself over a longer period of time and is not an immediate stress scenario. Portfolio models which estimate credit portfolio losses use default correlation as input parameters. These can be estimated with historical data, like for example bankruptcy rates. In the subsequent section we show how such a scenario can be factored into the parameter estimation.

3. A Scenario for Increasing Default Rates

One way to assess a macroeconomic stress scenario is by simulating either structural macroeconomic models designed for macroeconomic forecasts and monetary policy analysis, reduced-form VAR models or pure statistical methods that model the multivariate distribution of macro-financial variables using nonlinear dependency structures. In the second stage of the process, macro variables are linked to microeconomic indicators of banks credit risk. Unlike the macroeconomic model, the link model is often estimated on data at individual bank or even individual borrower level.

We follow a different approach. Often such a link model is not in place in banks. However, portfolio models which estimate credit portfolio losses or economic capital are implemented and in use. These models are calibrated to historical data, like for example bankruptcy data. We show how such a stress scenario can impact the calibration of the credit portfolio model. Therefore we demonstrate how the calibration of default correlation increases when we consider the potential increase of default rates which is not present in the historical data set.

3.1. Data Source

As mentioned before, we focus on the swiss economy as well as its financing behavior regarding housing and base our analysis on data from Dun & Bradstreet (DnB)[1]. The sample captures

- the period from January 1997 until December 2008 on a monthly basis

[1] cf. http://dbswitzerland.dnb.com/German/default.htm

- monitoring the number of firms and the number of bankruptcies in Switzerland
- where bankruptcy is defined as the first event of either opening, indication or close of bankruptcy or suspension due to lack of assets;

Using NOGA[2] codes contained in the data at hand, we define the industries services, financials, hotels and restaurants, health, retail and wholesale, construction, real estate and rentals, manufacturing, public authorities, and, others. We observe that the portions are more or less stable over time and find two dominating industries making up about 45–50 %, namely, services and retail and wholesale. The number of firms and the number of bankruptcies is contained in Table 1.

Table 1. # of firms, # of bankruptcies, bankruptcy rate, DnB sample.

Year	# of Firms	# of Bankruptcies	Bankruptcy Rate
1997	420’084	5’755	1.37 %
1998	455’514	5’413	1.19 %
1999	467’579	4’977	1.06 %
2000	478’357	4’520	0.94 %
2001	491’709	4’255	0.87 %
2002	493’080	4’220	0.86 %
2003	499’547	4’829	0.97 %
2004	505’727	5’294	1.05 %
2005	538’872	5’383	1.00 %
2006	549’894	5’048	0.92 %
2007	581’896	4’681	0.80 %
2008	618’478	4’709	0.76 %

We estimate an average bankruptcy rate of 0.98 %[3] within this period which is indicated in Figure 1–where we plot annual bankruptcy rates over time–by a dotted line. Starting with a maximum bankruptcy rate of 1.37 % in 1997 we observe a decrease until 2002 followed by a 2–year increase up to 1.05 % in 2004. Until end 2008 we observe a further decrease down to the minimim of 76 bp. If we were to interprete these data with respect to expectations for 2009 or even some more years by e.g. using weights over the past, the seemingly good years 2006–2008 would have quite an impact on our predictions. That might be dangerous and misleading. This becomes clear when we return to the existing granularity of the data, i.e. focusing on monthly data, cf. Figure 1. In Figure 1 we also plot the annualized monthly bankruptcy rate[4] and indicate the annual values by big dots. There’s quite some fluctuation

[2] Nomenclature Générale des Activités économiques

[3] based on arithmetic mean; similar to geometric mean (0.97 %)

[4] We annualize a monthly default rate DR_m by $\mathrm{DR}_a = 1 - (1 - \mathrm{DR}_m)^{12}$

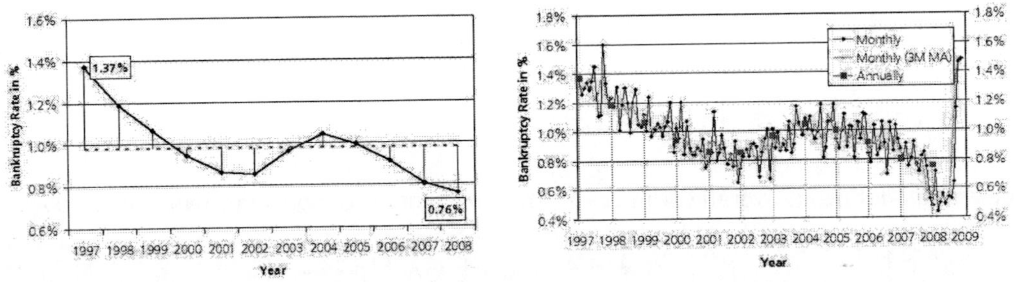

Figure 1. Left graph: Average **annual** bankruptcy rate. Right graph: Average **monthly** bankruptcy rate, 3m moving average, annual rate.

around the annual rate in the course of the years. But what is more striking, is the behavior in the second half of 2008–starting in September 2008 we observe a serious increase in bankruptcy rates, especially for all the months in Q4 2008. This trend is confirmed by two press releases found in April/May 2009,

- CreditReform: bankruptcies in April 2009 increased by more than 18 % compared to March 2009; year–on–year, May 2009 exhibited +34% compared to 2008; 2009 is expected to beat current all–time high records in terms of number of bankruptcies ([CreditReform]);

- DnB: year–on–year, March 2009 exhibited +44 % compared to 2008; an increase of +25 % is expected for the first half of 2009 ([DnB]).

Further calculating statistical measures shows

- maximum bankruptcy rates–with respect to average over time, standard deviation and maximum observed rate for hotels and restaurants as well as construction and real estate;

- maximum correlation of the time series of bankruptcy rates for services, retail and wholesale as well as construction and real estate.

4. A Practical Example

4.1. Bankruptcy Correlation

We consider an empirical estimator for bankruptcy correlation. Further, we link bankruptcy correlation and default correlation. There exist some estimators for default or bankruptcy correlation which are quite similar and differ, among others, in the way consecutive periods enter the calculation, e.g. unweighted or weighted; here we focus on the estimator described in [FreyMcNeil].

Denote marginal and joint probability of bankruptcy by π_1 and π_2. Further, let $Y_{ij} = 1$ indicate bankruptcy for obligor i in period j (and non–bankruptcy by $Y_{ij} = 0$) giving us the number of bankruptcies M_j in a sample of m_j obligors in period $j, j = 1, \ldots, n$, by

$$M_j = \sum_{i=1}^{m_j} Y_{ij} \quad . \tag{1}$$

Now we can define an overall estimator for the marginal probability of bankruptcy by

$$\hat{\pi}_1 = \frac{1}{n} \sum_{j=1}^{n} \hat{\pi}_{1j} = \frac{1}{n} \sum_{j=1}^{n} \frac{M_j}{m_j} \quad . \tag{2}$$

Its bivariate pendant is estimated accordingly, following

$$\begin{aligned} \hat{\pi}_2 &= \frac{1}{n} \sum_{j=1}^{n} \hat{\pi}_{2j} = \frac{1}{n} \sum_{j=1}^{n} \frac{\binom{M_j}{2}}{\binom{m_j}{2}} \\ &= \frac{1}{n} \sum_{j=1}^{n} \frac{M_j \cdot (M_j - 1)}{m_j \cdot (m_j - 1)} \; . \end{aligned} \tag{3}$$

Bankruptcy correlation ρ between any two bankruptcy events for obligors $i_1 \neq i_2$ over all time periods can be estimated via

$$\rho(Y_{i_1}, Y_{i_2}) = \hat{\rho} = \frac{\hat{\pi}_2 - \hat{\pi}_1^2}{\hat{\pi}_1 - \hat{\pi}_1^2} \quad . \tag{4}$$

Now we can estimate bankruptcy correlations in our data at hand–but what about default correlation ?

4.2. Default Correlation

By its definition, the number of defaults exceeds the number of bankruptcies:

- bankruptcy: any opening or indication of bankruptcy;
- default: '90 days past due', i.e. an obligor does not fulfill his financial obligations for at least 90 days.

Obviously, more defaults than bankruptcies happen as an obligor might recover in the sense of paying soon after 90 days. The question arising is, to what extent do defaults occur more often than bankruptcies. This relation clearly depends on the specific economic conditons. We assume for our example that the number of defaults can be approximately halved to get the number of bankruptcies. Applying this rough factor, let's call it r, on the existing formula, we derive for the number of defaults M_j^* and the marginal default probability $\hat{\pi}_1^*$

$$\begin{aligned} M_j^* &= r \cdot M_j \\ \Rightarrow \hat{\pi}_1^* &= \frac{r}{n} \sum_{j=1}^{n} \frac{M_j}{m_j} \\ &= r \cdot \hat{\pi}_1 \, . \end{aligned} \tag{5}$$

To see the impact on the joint probability we focus on the numerator of Equation (3) and prefer to figure out a scaling factor a describing the impact of r on the probability rather than re–calculating all probabilities. Thus,

$$\begin{aligned} M_j & \cdot (M_j - 1) \cdot a = M_j \cdot r \cdot (M_j \cdot r - 1) \\ \Leftrightarrow & \quad a = \frac{r \cdot (M_j \cdot r - 1)}{M_j - 1} \\ \Leftrightarrow & \quad a \approx \frac{r \cdot M_j \cdot r}{M_j} \\ \Leftrightarrow & \quad a \approx r^2 \text{ , and, hence,} \qquad (6) \\ \hat{\pi}_2^* & = r^2 \cdot \hat{\pi}_2 \, . \qquad (7) \end{aligned}$$

As a further, we'd like to conveniently figure out how the correlation changes if $\hat{\pi}_1$ changed to $\hat{\pi}_1^*$. For this reason we derive a relationship describing how the estimated correlation coefficient $\hat{\rho}$ ($\hat{\rho}^{(1)}$) might change. Therefore, we investigate how the correlation coefficient based on the scaled iputs changes relative to the original ones, .i.e

$$\begin{aligned} \frac{\hat{\rho}^{(r)}}{\hat{\rho}^{(1)}} & \approx \frac{r^2 \cdot (\hat{\pi}_2 - \hat{\pi}_1^2)}{r \cdot (\hat{\pi}_1 - r \cdot \hat{\pi}_1^2)} \cdot \frac{\hat{\pi}_1 - \hat{\pi}_1^2}{\hat{\pi}_2 - \hat{\pi}_1^2} \\ & = r \cdot \frac{\hat{\pi}_1 - \hat{\pi}_1^2}{\hat{\pi}_1 - r \cdot \hat{\pi}_1^2} \\ & \Rightarrow \hat{\rho}^* \approx r \cdot \frac{\hat{\pi}_1 - \hat{\pi}_1^2}{\hat{\pi}_1 - r \cdot \hat{\pi}_1^2} \cdot \hat{\rho} \, . \qquad (8) \end{aligned}$$

Equation (8) shows that the (bankruptcy) correlation coefficient can be scaled up by using r and $\hat{\pi}_1$ when we observe a change in the marginal probability of bankruptcy, following our approximation. Hence, we can appriximately estimate

- default correlation ρ^* based on bankruptcy rates by assuming a certain recovery factor $r > 1$, and, additionally,
- we can evaluate the impact of rising bankruptcies and defaults caused by drawbacks in the financing behavior.

In Figure 2 we plot marginal bankruptcy probabilities versus the resulting scaling factor for the base correlation assuming exemplarily $r = 2$ and $r = 3$. Assuming that a main part of a portfolio obeys investment grade, we would have assigned marginal probabilities quite below 5 % and find ourselves in the left part of the graph. In this area, the relationship pictured is almost linear; here doubling bankruptcies to obtain defaults yields an increase in correlation of about 100 %.

The calculations we performed on the DnB sample are summarized in the following table and contain the estimates of marginal probabilities, joint probabilities and bivariate correlations of bankruptcy and default. Under the observed circumstances we estimate a bivariate bankruptcy correlation of about 0.03% which translates into a default correlation using our approximation of roughly 0.05% (values rounded). This value seems to be

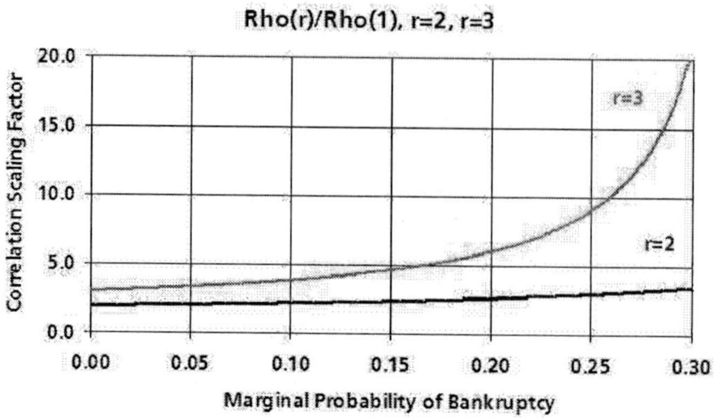

Figure 2. Correlation scaling factor, $r = 2$, $r = 3$, given bankruptcy rates.

Table 2. Bankruptcy / default probabilities and resulting correlation.

	$\hat{\pi}_1$	$\hat{\pi}_2$	$\hat{\pi}_1^*$	$\hat{\pi}_2^*$	ρ	ρ^*
original	0.98	0.01	1.96	0.04	0.03	0.05

low but compared to another study proves some reliability: [Roesch] analyzes bankruptcies of German enterprises from 1980–2001 by using a Merton–style model and estimates asset correlations–depending on the industry categories defined–lying between 0.49% and 3.52% giving a range of default correlation between 0.00% to 1.42%. [ServignyRenault] introduced a similar estimator and applied it to US firms over the period 1981–2001 using default and transition information; they calculate default correlations over all industries between 0.1% and 1.7%.

Assuming the financing behavior to evolve like described in Section 2. and Section 3. we firstly assume a bankruptcy event to evolve from every second default, i.e. double the number of bankruptcies to obtain the number of defaults. Secondly, based on the changing financing behavior and the scenario introduced we assume default rates to be three times of those observed. This seemingly serious scenario is backed by an analysis investigating CreditReform data. It indicates that during the period of real estate stress between 1990 and 1994, bankruptcy rates increased by three times and kept this level for a further 2–3 years. We use these important outcomes to further specify our scenario by assuming additionally to a deemed two–year increase in future years that this level might be kept for a further 2 years. Hence, we might expand the initial table of page 246 by the years 2009–2012 as shown in Table 3. To be precise, we assumed

- the number of firms to increase by 3.6% each year which corresponds to the average increase within the sample,
- the number of bankruptcies in 2009 to increase by 50% as an extension to a 25%

Table 3. # of firms, # of bankruptcies and bankruptcy rate, scenario based.

Year	# of Firms	# of Bankruptcies	Bankruptcy Rate
2008	618'478	4'709	0.76 %
2009	640'613	7'064	1.10 %
2010	663'541	15'129	2.28 %
2011	687'289	15'670	2.28 %
2012	711'887	16'231	2.28 %

increase of what DnB expects for the first half of 2009,

- the number of bankruptcies in 2010–2012 to be triggered by tripling the bankruptcy rate of 2008.

This gives us Figure 3.

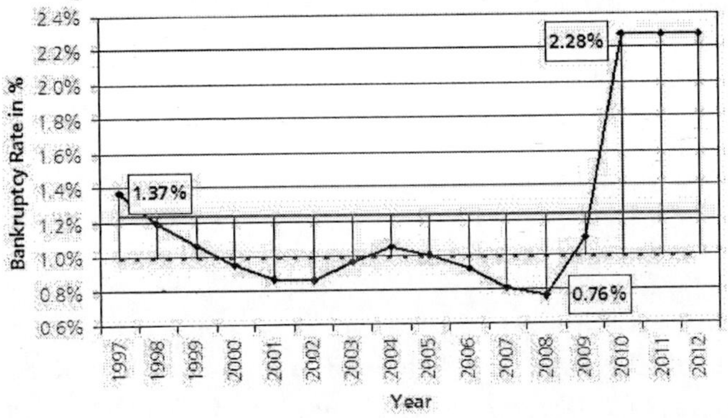

Figure 3. Average **annual** bankruptcy rate, scenario based.

Note that the level of the average annual bankruptcy rates raised to 1.23%. Applying our scenario to marginal and joint probabilities yields the numbers illustrated in Table 4 in an additional line.

The average bankruptcy rate over the whole period increases by 25 % but bankruptcy correlation raised up about its 8–fold. As we've seen by our approximation–which showed an almost linear impact on correlation when marginal PDs change within the lower bands–default correlation is slightly more than doubled compared to bankruptcy correlation.

Table 4. Bankruptcy / default probabilities and resulting correlation.

	$\hat{\pi}_1$	$\hat{\pi}_2$	$\hat{\pi}_1^*$	$\hat{\pi}_2^*$	ρ	ρ^*
original	0.98	0.01	1.96	0.04	0.03	0.05
scenario	1.23	0.02	2.47	0.07	0.23	0.46

5. Conclusions

We have demonstrated one way to incorporate future structural breaks in the calibration of risk models by enhancing the historical data set with scenario paths. This approach is useful when dealing with scenarios which develop over a larger time horizon and thus do not represent immediate stress conditions. It can also be useful when there are doubts whether the available historical data appropriately represent future economic conditions.

Disclaimers

- The opinions expressed in this presentation are our own and do not represent the ones of UBS AG or any affiliates.
- The risk control principles presented are not necessarily used by UBS AG or any of its affiliates.
- This presentation does not provide a comprehensive description of concepts and methods used in risk control at UBS.

References

[Castren] Castrén O., Fitzpatrick T., Sydow M.: Assessing Portfolio Credit Risk Changes in a Sample of EU Large and Complex Banking Groups in Reaction to Macroeconomic Shocks, *ECB Working Paper Series,* Nr. 1002, February 2009.

[CreditReform] `https://secure.creditreform.ch/index.php?id=716`, July 2009.

[CS1] *Swiss Issues Immobilien,* Fakten und Trends, 2008.

[CS2] *Swiss Issues Immobilien,* Fakten und Trends , 2009.

[DnB] `http://dbswitzerland.dnb.com/German/default.htm`, April 2009.

[EFD] Eidgenössisches Finanzdepartement EFD, Eidgenössische Steuerverwaltung ESTV, Hauptabteilung Direkte Bundessteuer, Verrechnungssteuer, *Stempelabgaben: Kreisschreiben* Nr. 17, Wohneigentumsförderung mit Mitteln der beruflichen Vorsorge, Oktober 2007

[FreyMcNeil] Frey R., McNeil A.: *Modeling Dependet Defaults,* 2001, April 2009, http://e-collection.ethbib.ethz.ch/view/eth:26296.

[Jordan] Jordan, Thomas J.: Finanzierung von Hypotheken und die Risiken einer Kreditverknappung in der Schweiz und im Ausland, *Speech* 9. Schweizer Ökonomentag, Universität Zürich, Zürich, 10.09.2008.

[Roesch] Rösch, D.: Correlations and Business Cycles of Credit Risk: Evidence from Bankrupts in Germany, *Financial Markets and Portfolio Management*, 17, 2003, pp. 309–331.

[ServignyRenault] Servigny, A. and Renault, O.: Correlation Evidence. *Technical Paper.* Risk, July 2003.

[SNB] *Schweizerische National Bank: Die Banken in der Schweiz* 2008, Zürich 2009.

[SFSO] Swiss Federal Statistical Office: Szenarien zur Bevölkerungsentwicklung der Schweiz 2005–2050, http://www.bfs.admin.ch/bfs/portal/de/index/themen/01/03/blank/key/index.html

INDEX

C

D

E

F

J

L

M

N

O

P

R

S

T

U

V

W

Y